EU Geopolitical Actorness in a Changing World

"The European Union (EU) has faced massive crises in recent years. Russia's war against Ukraine unleashed a deep shift in the global economy and international politics towards increased geoeconomics and geopolitics. Liridon Lika and Dealan Riga, with their volume, contribute a much-needed scholarly piece on the EU's geopolitical actorness in such a reconfigured world order. The volume provides a nuanced re-assessment of the concept of EU actorness against the background of strategic thinking and a geopolitical turn in the world. Actorness is explored and evaluated in a rich collection of empirical cases, stretching world regions and a breadth of EU foreign policy tools. This book is a pertinent and timely volume—a must-read for scholars and practitioners alike that seek to understand better the EU's positioning and challenges in a reconfigured geopolitical world."

—Professor Katharina Meissner, *University of Vienna (UNIVIE), Austria*

"A necessary and innovative book on the needs of geopolitical leadership for a supranational organization. Actorness and geopolitics are looked through the paradigm of multiplexity to offer insights on the EU's strategic turn in foreign policy, especially after the war in Ukraine. A must read."

—Professor Michela Ceccorulli, *University of Bologna (UNIBO), Italy*

"Liridon Lika and Dealan Riga succeeded in bringing together around fifteen researchers from European and American universities to reflect on the way in which the European Union (EU) is redefining its role(s) in the face of a changing and unpredictable world. These two dynamic researchers and their contributors managed both to deliver innovative understandings on the EU's current engagement in global affairs and reveal nimbly the ongoing shift from a normative actor to a more assertive geopolitical actor. The book provides very useful knowledge for anyone wishing to understand the changes underway in the EU's foreign strategy."

—Professor Sebastian Santander, *University of Liège (ULiège), Belgium*

Liridon Lika · Dealan Riga
Editors

EU Geopolitical Actorness in a Changing World

palgrave
macmillan

Editors
Liridon Lika
Department of Political Science
University of Liège
Liège, Belgium

Dealan Riga
Department of Political Science
University of Liège
Liège, Belgium

ISBN 978-3-031-81159-3   ISBN 978-3-031-81160-9 (eBook)
https://doi.org/10.1007/978-3-031-81160-9

This Palgrave Macmillan imprint is published by the registered company Springer Nature Switzerland AG
The registered company address is: Gewerbestrasse 11, 6330 Cham, Switzerland

Acknowledgments

The achievement of this edited book is the result of rigorous and systematic collective work. The idea of this edited book was born following the preparation by the team of the Center for International Relations Studies (CEFIR) of the Department of Political Science at the University of Liège (ULiège) of a Horizon Europe consortium project composed of 12 partner universities from 11 European countries. The consortium project inspired us to pursue this research. We are grateful to many of you, whom we cannot list exhaustively here, for your thoughtful and engaging conversations, which shaped this edited book.

We are also grateful to the publishing house "Palgrave Macmillan" and the editors of the "The European Union in International Affairs series" Sebastian Oberthür, Knud Erik Jørgensen, and Sandra Lavenex, as well as the executive editor Ambra Finotello, for trusting our project and making the publication of this edited book reality. In addition, we thank the anonymous reviewers for their insightful observations and reviews.

We would like to extend our sincere thanks to all the contributors to this edited book for their cooperation: Adrian Szumowski, Alexandru Balas, Arlind Puka, Elisabeth Johansson-Nogués, Maria Raquel Freire, Nadège Boels, Oana Poiană, Pëllumb Kelmendi, Raluca Moldovan, Robert Dopchie, Valentin Naumescu, and Vincent Bricart. We are especially grateful to Pëllumb Kelmendi, Robert Dopchie, and Vincent Bricart, who not only contributed as authors but also proofread several chapters, significantly enhancing the quality of the volume.

Our host CEFIR of the Department of Political Science at the ULiège deserves special gratitude for its continuous support. A thank you to our colleagues who have encouraged us during conversations, such as Sebastian Santander and Antonios Vlassis.

We are also thankful to professors Katharina Meissner from the University of Vienna (UNIVIE) in Austria, Michela Ceccorulli from the University of Bologna (UNIBO) in Italy, and Sebastian Santander from ULiège in Belgium for their support and endorsements of this book.

Last but not least, we express gratitude to our respective families for their presence and their encouragement which helped us to finish this edited book in all quietude.

Contents

Notes on Contributors

Alexandru Balas, Ph.D., is Full Professor and Coordinator of the International Studies Program, and the Director of the Clark Center for Global Engagement at the State University of New York (SUNY) at Cortland, USA. He received a Ph.D. in Political Science from the University of Illinois, Urbana-Champaign (2011), an M.A. in Conflict Analysis and Resolution from Sabanci University (2006), and a B.A. in Political Science from the University of Bucharest. His books include *Sharing the Burden of Peace* (Peter Lang, 2022), *The Puzzle of Peace* (Oxford University Press, 2016), and *Peace Operations* (Polity Press, 2014). In 2015, he received a European Union (EU) Erasmus+ Jean Monnet Module Grant. In 2017 and 2019 he won EU tenders to develop EU role-play negotiation/mediation simulations and one of these was awarded the best negotiation scenario at E-PARCC (The Program for the Advancement of Research on Conflict and Collaboration) 2018, Syracuse University.

Nadège Boels, Ph.D. Candidate, is Researcher and Teaching Assistant in the Department of Political Science of the Faculty of Social Sciences and Solvay Business School of the Vrije Universiteit Brussel (VUB) in Belgium. She obtained a Master's degree in Political Science: European and International Governance at the VUB. Her research focuses on the European external action in Belarus. She is doing a Ph.D. thesis under the supervision of Professor Vjosa Musliu (VUB), which seeks to assess the extent to which European Union (EU) external action influences and reinforces symbolic geography, Europe/non-Europe, and the

Othering of non-Europe. Her research focuses on a case study of Belarus. Mrs. Boels has presented her findings at various national and international conferences.

Vincent Bricart, Ph.D. student, is a member of the Center for International Relations Studies (CEFIR). He has been working as a research assistant since September 2018 in the Political Science Department at the University of Liège (ULiège). During his work there, he has conducted several seminars and conferences on the theme of the foreign policy of the United States of America (US). He has also been associated with several academic projects such as an online class (MOOC) and insertion programs for new college students. His research area focuses on the foreign policy of the United States, on the US international representation abroad, on the European Union (EU) international identity, and on EU-US bilateral relations. His Ph.D. thesis is entitled "The purpose of transatlantic interregionalism for the construction of the European Union's international identity" under the supervision of Professor Sebastian Santander (ULiège).

Robert Dopchie, Ph.D. candidate, is a researcher at the Center for International Relations Studies (CEFIR) in the Department of Political Science at the University of Liège (ULiège), Belgium. He obtained a Master's (M.A.) degree in International Relations from the same university. He focuses on the European Enlargement Policy (EEP) toward the Western Balkan states. His doctoral research examines the European Union's (EU) efforts to strengthen civil society in (potential) candidate countries, with a particular focus on Bosnia and Herzegovina, through the lens of non-Western international studies, within an increasingly multiplex world. Mr. Dopchie has authored several articles on the subject, including contributions to *Balkanologie* and the *European Foreign Affairs Review*, that he has presented at several national and international conferences.

Maria Raquel Freire, Ph.D. is Researcher at the Centre for Social Studies (CES) and Professor of International Relations at the Faculty of Economics of the University of Coimbra (FEUC). She is also Visiting Professor in the Post-Graduate Program in International Relations at the Federal University of Santa Catarina (UFSC), Brazil. She was Coordinator of the Jean Monnet Centre of Excellence PRONE (Peace Relations, Ontologies and Narratives in Europe: EU and its Eastern Neighbors), and held a Jean Monnet Chair, at the University of Coimbra (UC).

Her research interests focus on peace studies, foreign policy, international security, the European Union (EU), and Eurasia. She has published in journals, such as *Europe-Asia Studies*, *International Politics*, *European Politics and Society*, *East European Politics*, and *International Peacekeeping*.

Elisabeth Johansson-Nogués, Ph.D., is Jean Monnet Chair and Associate Professor at *Institut Barcelona d'Estudis Internacionals*, Spain. Her main area of research is the European Union's (EU) foreign and security policy, with a special focus on relations between the EU and neighboring countries to the east and south. She has also written extensively on state-society relations in Eastern Europe, the Middle East, and North Africa, such as the role of civil society, migration, minorities, gender, (dis)information, and security. She has also worked on analyzing the United Nations (UN) politics from different angles such as, for example, UN group politics, General Assembly voting patterns, and issue-specific topics like the Palestinian Question, human rights, or gender mainstreaming in peacekeeping. Recent publications include an edited volume by *Springer* and articles in *Political Geography, Security Dialogue, Cooperation and Conflict, Democratization, International Peacekeeping, and Mediterranean Politics.*

Pëllumb Kelmendi, Ph.D., is Assistant Professor of Political Science at Auburn University, in the United States. Previously he was Postdoctoral Fellow at the University of Michigan's Weiser Center for Emerging Democracies (WCED) and Predoctoral Fellow at Harvard University's Weatherhead Center for International Affairs (WCFIA). He received a Ph.D. in Political Science from Brown University, an M.Phil. in Development Studies from the University of Cambridge, and a B.A. in Political Science from the University of Chicago. His current research interests focus on civil wars, international intervention, peacebuilding, civic and political participation in post-conflict societies, and the foreign policy of small states. His research has been funded by Auburn University, the United States Institute of Peace (USIP), the Smith Richardson Foundation (SRF), the Open Society Foundations (OSF), and Brown University's Watson Institute for International and Public Affairs. He has published in the *Journal of Conflict Resolution*, *Security Studies*, and *Nationalities Papers*, among others.

Liridon Lika, Ph.D., is Lecturer at the Center for International Relations Studies (CEFIR) of the Department of Political Science of the University of Liège (ULiège) in Belgium. He was Postdoctoral Researcher at the Faculty of Arts and Social Sciences (FASoS) of the Maastricht University in the Netherlands. He holds a Ph.D. in International Relations from ULiège. He obtained a Master's degree in Political Science: International Relations at ULiège, and an advanced Master's degree in Interdisciplinary Analysis of European Integration at the Institute for European Studies (ISE) of the Free University of Brussels (ULB). His research focuses on Western Balkan states, in particular Kosovo and Albania, as well as the EU's external action, the EU's enlargement policy toward the Western Balkans, the foreign policy of rising/emerging powers toward the Western Balkans and theories of International Relations. Dr. Lika is the author of numerous scientific publications and has presented his research at many conferences.

Raluca Moldovan, Ph.D., is Associate Professor of International Relations at Babes-Bolyai University Cluj-Napoca (Romania), where she has been teaching courses at both graduate and undergraduate levels since 2004. She has a Ph.D. in history with a thesis on the representation of the Holocaust on film. Since 2023, Dr. Moldovan has been part of the Horizon project REMIT (Reignite Multilateralism through Technology), funded by the European Union (EU). Her current research interests include the contemporary Middle East and migration studies. She has published extensively in scholarly journals and edited volumes. Among her latest publications is the edited volume *The European Union. Policies, Perspectives and Politics* (New York, Nova Science Publishers, 2020) and the chapter entitled "Beyond the 'Iron Wall': The Strategic Priorities of Israel's Foreign Policy", in Valentin Naumescu (ed.), *Great Powers' Foreign Policy. Approaching the Global Competition and the Russian War against the West* (Leiden and Boston, Brill, 2023).

Valentin Naumescu, Ph.D. is Full Professor of International Relations at Babeş-Bolyai University Cluj, the Faculty of European Studies (Romania). He is Director of the Centre for the Study of the EU's External Relations and the Global Order (EUXGLOB Centre), and founding President of the think tank the Initiative for European Democratic Culture (ICDE). Professor Naumescu was Secretary of State in the Ministry of Foreign Affairs (2005–2007) and Consul General of Romania in Toronto (2008–2012). His most recent books are: *The USA-China War for Supremacy* *and the Five Forces Changing the World* (Polirom, 2022), and *Great Powers' Foreign Policy: Approaching the Global Competition and the Russian War against the West* (Brill, 2023).

Oana Poiană, Ph.D. is Researcher at the Institute of International Relations and Area Studies (IIRAS), the Faculty of European Studies of Babeş-Bolyai University in Cluj-Napoca, Romania. She conducted research at Central European University (Budapest) and Otto von Guericke University (Magdeburg). She is currently involved in the implementation of a Jean Monnet Center of Excellence (Erasmus+) project "Enhancing EU's role in consolidating local democratic resilience in Moldova and Serbia DREMS (2021–2024)" and a "HORIZON-CL2-2022-DEMOCRACY-01-09 project, Reignite Multilateralism via Technology (2023–2027)". Her most recent book is: Regional Cooperation and National Preferences in the Black Sea Region. A zero-sum game perpetuated by energy insecurity (Presa Universitara Clujeana, 2022).

Arlind Puka, Master (M.A.), joined the CEELI Institute (Central and Eastern European Law Initiative) in December 2022 as Program Officer (judicial component). Prior to joining the Institute, he worked as Consultant for the International Organization for Migration (IOM) on the "Engagement of Diaspora to the Social and Economic Development of Albania" program. Previously, he worked for more than 4 years as Administrative Assistant and Policy Adviser for Western Balkans at the European Parliament. In 2015, he was selected by the U.S. Department of State in the training of Young Leaders for Tomorrow's Europe. Arlind holds an LL.M. in Criminal Law and Procedure from the University of Sunderland, United Kingdom, and a Bachelor of Laws from the University of Shkodra "Luigj Gurakuqi", Albania.

Dealan Riga, Ph.D. Candidate, is Teaching Assistant at the Center for International Relations Studies (CEFIR) of the Department of Political Science of the University of Liège (ULiège) in Belgium. He is a junior researcher in the Horizon projects *Reboot* and *Fairmuse.* His research focuses on the European Union's (EU) economic diplomacy, with a particular emphasis on the geopoliticization of its trade policy. His thesis aims to shed light on geopoliticization processes by tracing their genesis through the study of the Comprehensive Agreement on Investment (CAI) negotiations. In addition, he serves on the executive board of Research Committee 03 (*European Unification*) of the International Political Science Association.

Adrian Szumowski, Ph.D., is Researcher in the Department of International Relations at the Faculty of Political Science at the Maria Curie-Skłodowska University in Lublin (Poland). He obtained his Ph.D. in Political Science from the University of Lublin. He has a Master's (M.A.) in International Relations and graduated from the Faculty of Political Science at the Maria Curie-Skłodowska University in Lublin. During his study years, he participated in the Erasmus student exchange program at Salford University, Manchester, the United Kingdom (UK). He was the manager of a scientific project entitled "Dynamics of Power in late-Westphalian International Environment", funded by the National Science Center (NSC), Poland. His main field of study is the evolution of international relations. His main focus of scientific interest is the power in international relations, the theory of international relations, and the methodology of science in international relations.

List of Figures

List of Tables

Introduction: EU Actorness in Transition

Dealan Riga and *Liridon Lika*

Introduction

Events such as Covid-19 pandemic, the wars in Ukraine and in the Middle East, and China's rise, have recently fueled the ongoing dynamic of shifting world order leaving the European Union (EU) to rethink its international actions. Indeed, the idea of being a geopolitical European Commission adapting to current geopolitical turmoil was set from the very beginning of Ursula von der Leyen's administration as the president mentioned in front of the European Parliament during her first speech in 2019: "*My Commission will be a geopolitical Commission committed to sustainable policies. And I want the European Union to be the guardian of multilateralism. Because we know that we are stronger by doing together what we cannot do alone*" (European Commission 2019a). The Russian invasion of Ukraine since 2022 has confirmed this change, as von der Leyen called it a "watershed moment for our Union" (European Commission 2022). Josep Borrell, the High Representative of the Union

D. Riga (✉) · L. Lika
Department of Political Science, University of Liège, Liège, Belgium
e-mail: Dealan.Riga@uliege.be

L. Lika
e-mail: liridon.lika@uliege.be

L. Lika and D. Riga (eds.), *EU Geopolitical Actorness in a Changing World*, https://doi.org/10.1007/978-3-031-81160-9_1

for Foreign Affairs and Security Policy/Vice-President of the European Commission (HR/VP), has boldly proclaimed that the EU's response to the Russian invasion represents "*l'acte de naissance de l'Europe géopolitique*" ("the birth certificate of geopolitical Europe") (EEAS 2022). Yet, this potential shift from the normative actor, very much enshrining the constitutive values of the EU, to highlighting the more geopolitical approach currently pursued by the "geopolitical Commission," still needs to be addressed.

In line with this premise, this book questions the assumption that EU actorness is evolving from a normative to a strategic and geopolitical orientation. The EU is actively pursuing resilience in response to emerging geopolitical upheaval, transnational crises, and economic strains. This situation has opened a strategic window for the EU to reevaluate its global affairs approach. While speeches may suggest a political will for a rapid and adaptive EU in the face of the shifting world order, the book will delve into the as-yet-unexplored capabilities of the EU to effectively address the rapidly changing global reality. Consequently, the central research question of this edited book is: Is the EU's determination to establish a new geopolitical leadership accompanied by the implementation of the practical requirements entailed by these shifts?

To address this research question, the book explores foreign policy through a comprehensive analytical framework that investigates the theoretical approach to EU geopolitical actorness. It employs case study analysis to reveal the specific demands of foreign policy and the requirements of the EU's foreign affairs toolboxes. The objective is to provide a critical perspective on the ongoing shift in the EU's political approach to global affairs, presenting a nuanced understanding of this evolution. The emphasis is on highlighting the necessities of a geopolitical European Commission within the context of complex international relations, while also examining past weaknesses in EU global engagement to discuss the EU's internal reform needs.

This introductory chapter delves into the theoretical foundation that informs the following chapters. It provides the conceptual background of the book by reflecting on the classical challenges of EU actorness and how a shifting world order offers new stimuli for change. In doing so, it draws together theoretical material related to actorness and its challenges, the evolution of EU external policy from its origins to contemporary issues, and the challenges arising from a multiplex world order, which calls for a renewed understanding of actorness. Subsequently, it outlines the research objectives of the book, setting the stage for its structure. This section frames the book's intention around three pillars and introduces each from a conceptual standpoint. Finally, it provides a concise overview of each chapter, illustrating how they contribute to fulfilling the research objectives.

EU Actorness in Transition: Exploring Theoretical Implications of Change

Over the past few decades, the EU has dramatically broadened its scope of action in international relations which allows it to be increasingly involved in most of the major global issues: trade, global warming, human rights, development, and humanitarian issues. To ensure consistent engagement in world affairs, the EU has developed diverse relationships with many countries around the world as well as with international organizations. Academic literature has captured this idea through the concept of actorness (Jupille and Caporaso 1998; Petiteville 2002; Hill and Smith 2005; Bretherton and Vogler 2006; Soderbaum and Van Langenhove 2006). While an academic consensus has emerged on EU actorness in world affairs, its scope, modalities, and effects remain broadly discussed (Manners 2002; Börzel and Risse 2009; Hill et al. 2023).

The EU's external actions have been a focal point of extensive academic research, as scholars have highlighted numerous challenges that the EU encounters in shaping its foreign policy (Niemann and Bretherton 2013; Tocci 2017; Fahey 2020). To begin with, the existence of an international actor like the EU necessitates the convergence of various elements, including authority, autonomy, and coherence (Merle 1988), along with recognition (Jupille and Caporaso 1998). Authority refers to the EU's "legal competence to act on a given subject matter" (Niemann and Bretherton 2013, 265). Autonomy signifies the differentiation of the EU from other actors, encompassing the uniqueness of its geopolitical interests, foreign policy objectives, institutional mechanisms for foreign policy formulation and negotiations, as well as the availability of its own resources required for policy implementation (Jupille and Caporaso 1998; Niemann and Bretherton 2013). Yet, the EU's autonomy remains heavily reliant on the consensus of states and institutions to affect any substantial alterations in its diplomacy (Aggarwal and Fogarty 2004; Puetter 2012; Lika and Weerts 2021, 105). As extensively debated by scholars, this deficiency in EU unity represents one of its most significant challenges to adopt a common and consistent foreign policy (Yakemtchouk 2005; Vanhoonacker 2018). When it comes to addressing its geopolitical positioning, autonomy hinges on the EU's ability to guarantee its own security.

A major drawback of the EU actorness is its susceptibility to inconsistency in foreign policy, primarily stemming from potential disunity. As noted by Viljar Veebel (2019), aside from the evident repercussions of divergence, inconsistency may also emerge due to conflicts between norms and interests. Addressing this issue, Marianne Dony and Lucia Serena (2008) introduce a typology of consistency, which encompasses institutional coherence (both vertically between the Union and its member states and horizontally among the Union's institutions) and substantial coherence (relating to the alignment of various European policies with external dimensions and the Union's actions in line with its internal policies). When examining pre-accession instruments, as emphasized by Anne-Claire Marangoni (2014), while consistency focuses on preventing contradictions between different policies, coherence goes a step further, indicating the presence of synergies between policies. Anne-Claire Marangoni and Sophie Vanhoonacker (2015), for instance, define consistency as the quality of a policy output that is free from contradictions. For instance, a proposal by the European Commission is considered consistent if its content aligns with its primary objective. In her book, Maria Raquel Freire et al. (2022) highlight the EU's lack of coherence exhibited in the context of crisis management. However, as noted by Marangoni (2014) and Simon Duke (2006), the coexistence or interchangeability of these two concepts can complicate their definition.

EU actorness faces a significant challenge arising from the ongoing structural crisis within the EU, which, as numerous scholars have emphasized since the Eurozone crisis, undermines its ability to effectively translate policy objectives into successful crisis management (Stiglitz 2014, 2016). These weaknesses extend beyond financial and macroeconomic aspects, as many scholars highlight structural issues within the EU when dealing with the migration crisis (Menendez 2016; Ceccorulli and Lucarelli 2017; Ceccorulli et al. 2020).

These structural crises have been exacerbated by events such as the wars in Ukraine and Syria, Brexit, as well as the fight against terrorism (Borzël 2016). Notably, Freire et al. (2022) highlight how the EU's lack of responsiveness during the war in Ukraine since 2014 contributed to a shift in the EU's perception of its security. Within the same context, scholars have emphasized the increasing politicization of European integration (De Wilde and Zürn 2012; Börzel and Risse 2018). Politicization is defined as a process characterized by a heightened polarization of opinions, interests, or values and the extent to which they are publicly promoted in EU policy formulation (De Wilde 2011). Given the rise of Euroscepticism inside the EU, analysts of politicization argue that the EU is currently facing a "polycrisis" (Zeitlin and Nicoli 2020; Meissner and Schoeller 2020). A polycrisis is brought about by the current "polycleavage," in which multiple issues are concurrently salient, polarize actors in different ways, and mobilize public opinion on each of the issues at hand (Zeitlin and Nicoli 2020, 966). This polycrisis represents yet another inherent challenge for EU actorness and unity, which are constantly portrayed as hurdles that should be overcome to ensure a consistent geopolitical role.

Yet, despite major pitfalls, numerous authors acknowledge that the EU has been becoming ever more active in various international relations domains (Niemann and Bretherton 2013; Santander and Vlassis 2020; Simão 2022). The focus on a relation to other actors in the international system is also salient in Stephan Klose's recent work (2018, 1144), who conceptualizes actorness as "an entity's capacity to (re)-imagine and realize roles for its 'self' in (specific contexts of) international affairs." EU norms (and its normative aspirations) transcend both the internal and external dimensions of actorness, for instance, the domestic and international role expectations (Klose 2018; Simão 2022). Multiple scholarly works explore EU actorness in various policy contexts (including the European Enlargement Policy (EEP) and the European Neighbourhood Policy (ENP)) (Johansson-Nogués 2007; Dandashly and Kourtelis 2020), the militarization of European integration (Van der Pijl 2021), the debate on contemporary European geopolitics (Bialasiewicz 2016), and its contestation by external actors (Aydin-Düzgit and Noutcheva 2022).

Exploring the complexities that EU actorness encounters, this edited book begins with the foundational notion that the EU exhibits a measure of resilience, guaranteeing the persistence of its external endeavors. Furthermore, as elucidated by Freire et al. (2022), transnational crises and geopolitical upheavals serve as catalysts for the rejuvenation of the EU's foreign engagements, presenting a unique opportunity for transformation. Therefore, this book contributes to the existing literature on actorness by examining the critical aspects of its vulnerabilities while closely analyzing its rejuvenation.

EU Actorness in Action: How to Comprehend EU's Interaction with the World?

Over time, the practical implementation of EU actorness has been described using various concepts that highlight the distinct nature of the EU's global engagements. While this book focuses on actorness, its geopolitical positioning aligns with prior research that characterizes the supranational Union's international actions.

The characteristics of the EU's actions have been understood in the context of civilian power, particularly the utilization of civil tools such as enlargement, multilateralism, socio-economic influence, and inter-regionalism (Duchêne 1972; Maull 1990; Telò 2006; Soderbaum and Van Langenhove 2006). According to civilian power analysis, core values such as women's rights, sustainable development, and respect for minorities shape the European identity and guide EU actorness.

Scholars have also employed the concept of transformative power to comprehend the EU's external actions, particularly in terms of influencing public policy development in Central and Eastern European (CEE) countries during the EU accession process (Grabbe 2006). In this context, the EU utilized membership conditions to assert its influence and promote Europeanization. The promotion of regional good governance is a focal point in EU regional actorness studies and is closely associated with the concept of transformative power (Börzel and Risse 2009). It involves the EU's ability to mold its partners' social, economic, or even cultural behavior through interaction. By promoting its model in neighboring countries, the EU aims to ensure regional stability, with interaction, conditionality, and specific policies serving as mechanisms to exert transformative power.

Others argue that the EU functions as a normative power, rooted in values, standards, and a distinct European identity (Manners 2002). Normative power can be defined as an actor's capacity to shape what is regarded as ideal in international affairs (Manners 2002, 2010; Kavalski 2013). This concept encompasses the notions of civilian and transformative power in various aspects. Over time, it has evolved to become a primary analytical tool for studying the EU's interactions with other countries (Johansson-Noguès 2007; Dandashly and Kourtelis 2020). In this context, EU norms, along with its normative aspirations, extend to both the internal and external dimensions of actorness, including domestic and international role expectations. Additionally, the promotion of what should be considered as ideal plays a role in the ongoing debate on the promotion of alternative models, questioning whether China's ascent counters the EU's normative power (Kavalski 2013).

The concept of normative power, while valuable, has its limitations as it does not fully encompass material, military, and security aspects (Holden 2009). This gap has left European studies ill-equipped to analyze the EU's capabilities in terms of geopolitical and strategic positioning. Traditional geopolitical concepts rooted in Realist theory, such as the balance of power and great power strategy (Mearsheimer 2001; Wu 2018), are centered on nation-states' decision-making models and their pursuit of national interests. However, there has been limited conceptual effort to provide a consistent framework for understanding the geopolitical positioning of a supranational actor like the EU. In other words, the academic literature on EU geopolitical actorness in this changing international context remains underdeveloped. This edited book ambitions to fill that gap, as analyzing the EU behavior and foreign policy is of great significance from a theoretical and empirical standpoint. Therefore, this book seeks to address this academic gap by exploring the theoretical implications of a supranational actor's geopolitical positioning. It is among the pioneering works to tackle this theoretical challenge, aiming to establish a coherent approach to EU actorness that incorporates strategic and geopolitical elements. Addressing this knowledge aspect is essential since existing International Relations (IR) and European integration theories, and current conceptualizations of EU actorness lack the necessary tools to elucidate the existence of an EU's geopolitical role.

EU Actorness in a Changing World: Opportunities and Challenges for Resilience as a Leading Global Player

Since the end of the Cold War at the beginning of 1990s, different theoretical models have been used to understand the dynamics of international relations in terms of polarization, including concepts like unipolarity (Krauthammer 1990/1991), non-polarity (Haass 2008), apolarity (Badie 2013, 2016), and multipolarity (Hansen 2010, Telò 2014; Lieber 2022). While the idea of multipolarity is gaining traction in discussions about the current geopolitical landscape (Smith 2013; Scott 2017), it may not entirely align with the book's primary focus on examining the geopolitical positioning of supranational actors, given its tendency to overly emphasize the state-centric paradigm.

An insightful effort to transcend the limitations of the polarity debate, which often fixates on state actors, is found in the concept of an emerging multiplex order as articulated by Amitav Acharya (2014, 2017). This concept introduces the term "multiplexity" to capture the diversity of actors involved in shaping the global order and the increasing complexity associated with a growing number of transboundary issues, often marked by their multidimensional and unpredictable nature, exemplified by events like the Covid-19 or Ebola outbreaks (Acharya 2019). In Acharya's framework, multiplexity signifies a decentralized, diversified, and multidimensional world influenced by a multitude of actors, encompassing both state and non-state entities, established and rising/emerging powers, global and regional groups, hailing from both the Northern and Southern hemispheres (Acharya 2015, 2019).

Indeed, the concept of multiplexity is of great relevance as it enables researchers to comprehend the evolution as well as the complexification of the global order. It also allows for a contextual understanding of the EU's regional influence and the difficulties posed by illiberal forces within the broader context of global developments. Going beyond the traditional notion of a multipolar world, multiplexity considers the varying distribution of power across different issue areas. The central characteristic of multiplexity is the presence of a multitude of state and non-state actors, contributing to the diffusion of power and actively participating in shaping the international order and addressing transboundary challenges. As articulated by Paulo Esteves and Stephan Klingebiel (2021), analyzing the restructuring of the world order through the lens of multiplexity provides a framework for making sense of the current fragmentation in global decision-making, and the dispersal of global power.

As previously mentioned, the ongoing transformation in the global order and the emergence of multiplexity have compelled the European Commission to assert its geopolitical position. While the Russian invasion of Ukraine since 2022 is often viewed as a pivotal moment, it becomes evident that systemic elements present a more comprehensive and interconnected challenge to the EU's ability to act as a resilient global player. Therefore, the current and anticipated challenges posed by the multiplex world, including the revision of the grand strategies of new powers (Onea 2016), the increasing geopolitical significance of neighboring countries, and the diffusion of power, will serve as the foundational elements of this book's exploration.

The diffusion of power manifests through two main factors: the emergence of alternative models in world politics and the proliferation of transnational actors. Following the claims made by Niall Ferguson and Fareed Zakaria (2017), and Gilford J. Ikenberry (2018) regarding the decline of the international liberal order, extensive research has arisen concerning the ascent of illiberal powers and their strategies for contesting and seeking influence. The EU and its normative foreign policy face significant challenges from illiberal forces, both from within and outside the EU. While numerous illiberal forces are at play in global affairs, the primary challenge to the EU's global role is posed by China and Russia (Taeuber 2020; Casier 2022). Indeed, the framing of China as a systemic rival underscores the growing significance of "alternative model promotion" in EU foreign policy (European Commission 2019b). Similarly, Francis Fukuyama characterizes Russia's invasion of Ukraine as "Putin's war against the liberal order" (Fukuyama 2022). Many scholars have explored how great power's competition contributes to a crisis in the liberal international order, a central concern within the EU's normative agenda (Haass 2017; Colgan and Keohanne 2017; De Graaf and Van Apeldoorn 2018; Duncombe and Dunne 2018).

The confrontation of these contrasting models has tangible and direct consequences as the world concurrently faces a crisis in the functioning of multilateral institutions, a growing resistance to good practices such as human rights compliance, and, most significantly, a global democratic backlash. This democratic decline is encapsulated by the concept of an "autocratization wave" (Lührmann and Lindberg 2019; Cassani and Tomini 2020; Hellmeier et al. 2021). Tomas Ambrosio (2012) observed that the endorsement of the Chinese autocratic model, often referred to as the "Beijing consensus," might play a noteworthy role in undermining democratic principles on a global scale. As a result, the EU's normative commitment to promoting democracy is at risk in the face of the disruptive effect of illiberal challenges.

Moreover, these illiberal challenges may extend to the EU's domestic sphere, undermining its capacity to maintain a consistent global presence. A clear example of this is the connections Russia has established with European far-right parties, seeking to exert influence over both EU internal and foreign policies and erode EU normative standards (Shekhovtsov 2017; Fagerholm 2024). Hence, illiberal challenges are not confined to direct security threats and geopolitical upheavals; they should be understood as a broader phenomenon that impacts the EU and its global role in various ways. These challenges are comprehensively addressed throughout the present edited book to offer a holistic understanding of the factors that EU geopolitical actorness should consider for effective implementation.

Multiplexity also encourages researchers to explore the complexity of world affairs through another dimension of power diffusion stemming from transnational crises, the rise of new stakeholders, and multifaceted issues like global warming. In fact, the capabilities of nation-states to address cross-border and intricate challenges such as the global financial crisis, global pandemics, or terrorism are often inadequate. This has led states to seek new avenues for action, especially through multilateralism. The proliferation of issues that surpass the capacities of individual states has triggered a transformation in the structure of nation-states, a phenomenon described in academic literature as the emergence of a reactive state characterized by internal decentralization (Calder 1988; Slaughter 2004; Cerny 2022).

Interestingly, the rising transnationalization of world affairs over certain issues may actually work to the benefit of the EU (Riga 2024). This book operates on the assumption that transnational crises necessitating a unified response from EU member states create a window of opportunity for increased integration. Indeed, challenges such as the Eurozone crisis, the Covid-19 pandemic, global warming, and the war in Ukraine have all demanded a European response rather than a state-centered one. The edited book thoroughly examines this line of reasoning to analyze whether crisis management can lead to greater integration and consequently result in a renewed political actorness for the EU. While multiplexity poses challenges to the traditional functioning of the EU, it undeniably provides a window of opportunity, making the analysis presented in this book more critical and pertinent than ever.

Exploring Actorness in Times of Crisis and EU Resilience: Bridging Theory, Methodology, and Book Objectives

The imperative of revitalizing EU actorness for the sake of ensuring a resilient leadership in a multiplex global landscape has been extensively examined in contemporary research that explores the EU's evolving global role (Tocci 2017; Vuskane 2019; Lütz et al. 2021; Freire et al. 2022). Academic literature underscores that the emerging multiplex world necessitates a renewed commitment from the EU to maintain a consistent global leadership position (Bialasiewicz 2016). Three principal trends are identified as reshaping the EU's requirements for global engagement: an increase in security demands in a geopolitically volatile world, a need to revise economic approaches in light of challenges to the liberal order, and the necessity of bolstering military capabilities in response to unprecedented security threats (Fahey 2020; van der Pijl 2021; Fahey and Mancini 2022).

The resurgence of great power politics has heightened geopolitical instability, notably by reshaping the international order. While discussions about crises in the liberal international order have been prevalent, it can be argued that the overall approach to conducting international relations is undergoing transformation. Academic literature encapsulates this concept through the notion of the "weaponization of interdependence" in world politics (Hopewell 2022; Farrell and Newman 2019). This concept includes the idea that great power rivalries often involve the weaponization of transboundary issues such as trade, energy, and migration. In this context, "weaponization" refers to the strategic use of these transboundary issues as instruments to enhance one's power on the global stage, with the aim of exerting control over the movement of people, goods, money, and data, and the connections they facilitate (Leonard 2021). Presently, economic statecraft has become a central "battleground" for international actors' competition and influence-seeking. This can be exemplified by Russia's and China's use of various economic coercion tools to influence the EU's external policies (Hackenbroich and Zerka 2021). The weaponization of energy and energy infrastructure has long been a feature of Russia's attempts to exert influence over the EU, especially the largest energy consumers among EU member states (e.g., Germany and Italy) and EU's Eastern neighbors. This trend became particularly pronounced since the Russian invasion of Ukraine (Balmaceda

2021). Additionally, the weaponization of migration and the propagation of anti-immigration discourses by far-right parties within the EU constitute a toolbox used by external illiberal powers (Berzins 2022). This phenomenon underscores the multifaceted and complex challenges that the EU faces in the evolving international landscape.

While it is evident that illiberal powers play a significant role in contributing to the characteristics of multiplexity, the Western actors are also altering their approach to addressing economic interdependency. For instance, academic literature has drawn attention to the "geopoliticization" of the EU trade policy, effectively bridging the gap between politicization and weaponization as research frameworks (Meunier and Nicolaidis 2019). Geopoliticization can be understood as the discursive framing of an issue as a geopolitical problem, where policy instruments are employed to gain allies, counter adversaries, and reshape the global balance of power (Meunier and Nicolaidis 2019, 107). This notion lends support to the book's core assumption that a shift is occurring within the EU's domain as it adapts to the rules of multiplexity.

While academia is gradually recognizing the EU's efforts to incorporate strategic and geopolitical elements into its foreign policy (Dopchie and Lika 2024), this contribution to the academic debate underscores that geopolitical disruptions have reached a new level with 2022 Russia's invasion of Ukraine. Consequently, the imperative for geopolitical actorness goes beyond the requirements of global actorness and emphasizes the need for novel approaches to political alliances and economic interdependencies. Geopolitical actorness can be understood as the integration of strategic thinking into the EU's engagement with global affairs. It goes beyond mere geopoliticization, reflecting an EU strategy that not only addresses economic, energy, and trade interdependencies, but also includes its defense capabilities, the resilience of its democracies, and its ability to uphold and enforce a rules-based international order. This concept embodies the European Commission's pursuit of regional leadership alongside a strategic positioning of the EU in world affairs. It thus encompasses both trade and foreign policy, highlighting the EU's evolving global role in response to external pressures and modern geopolitical challenges.

This book surpasses the current state of the art by recognizing that the shift in actorness extends beyond mere adjustments to practical changes in the way world politics are conducted. EU geopolitical actorness would reflect the result of mounting external pressure that calls for a comprehensive renewal of EU foreign policy, be it in terms of trade, politics, or security issues. By questioning the EU's commitment to establish a new geopolitical leadership and its feasibility, this book underscores the growing imperative for such a transformation. In doing so, it delves into the specific characteristics of EU actorness, scrutinizes its weaknesses and strengths, and offers insights into what EU geopolitical actorness should entail to foster a new approach to European policy. Its objective transcends the prevailing trend of examining EU changes primarily from the perspective of economic interdependence issues, instead focusing on addressing the novel requirements of European geopolitical actorness in the context of multiplexity.

While this reflection is prompted by the aftermath of the war in Ukraine, the book's findings encompass both historical and current issues. EU geopolitical actorness is playing a pivotal role in addressing pressing global challenges, such as climate change, conflicts in the Middle East, democratic backsliding, Indo-Pacific economic integration, and so forth. The aim is to unpack the processes that are driving the reconceptualization of European security and the reshaping of the EU within this evolving global context. The book emphasizes that the EU has shown a political will for such a transformation through the adoption of concepts like strategic autonomy, resilience, bordering and debordering, decoupling, like-minded partners, and the geopolitical European Commission. Yet, the EU's self-definition as a security actor and promoter of norms in the contested international order remains highly relevant and significant. As a result, this book seeks to offer a holistic view of the EU's requirements in the domain of multiplex global politics, the endurance of its actorness, and the development of its geopolitical goals. To investigate the ongoing shift within the EU, this edited book establishes three primary research objectives aimed at avoiding potential pitfalls in the study of EU actorness and ensuring that each analysis contributes to a comprehensive and coherent understanding of the subject under examination.

Firstly, it challenges the idea that speech acts alone are sufficient to define a significant change, and instead, the book aims to assess the practical efforts made by the EU. Consequently, in its first part, drawing on various theoretical perspectives, it endeavors to understand the extent to which the EU possesses the capabilities needed to transition from a normative to a strategic and geopolitical focus. This line of inquiry leads to a critical exploration of how the EU attempts to effectuate this shift, while also evaluating the factors that either impede or enhance this transition. As a result, the book provides a critical overview of the EU's endeavors, fostering reflection that goes beyond the central political assumption from which it derives. This first objective would fuel the research theoretical insights eventually leading to conceptual visions regarding the idea of the geopolitical positioning of a supranational actor.

The second research objective revolves around the examination of the roles played by third-party states in bolstering the EU's capacity to establish itself as a geopolitical actor. While academic literature on EU actorness often focuses on the EU's intentions and capabilities as sufficient indicators of its effectiveness, this research introduces the idea that considering the agency of the rest is an indispensable step in assessing the EU's practical capabilities on the ground. In line with this perspective, the second part relies on case study analyses to evaluate how the EU actorness is perceived in strategic regions, including the Western Balkans, the Eastern neighborhood, the Middle East, and the Indo-Pacific region. Each of these regions presents distinct requirements for EU actorness due to their unique characteristics. By delving into the EU's past actions and scrutinizing previous shortcomings that have hindered its actorness, this part offers a viewpoint on the EU's geopolitical shift, raising questions about its feasibility in terms of local compliance.

The final research objective aims to examine the EU's ability to effectively execute this transformation within the framework of its foreign affairs toolbox. In this third part, the book scrutinizes the concrete steps taken by the EU to promote new strategic thinking using its existing tools. This includes an analysis of sanctions, pre-accession instruments, Overseas Countries and Territories (OCTs), as well as strategic partnerships, such as with the United States and associated mechanisms like the North Atlantic Treaty Organization (NATO). This part conducts a comprehensive examination of these tools from a historical and current perspective, highlighting past shortcomings and inconsistencies within the EU, while also addressing efforts to renew and refine these existing instruments. This final part provides the book with clear empirical evidence of the EU's shift, while offering a critical analysis of the efficiency of these changes.

This edited book constitutes a comprehensive analysis that draws together mainly a group of scholars from Europe and the United States. Each chapter is dedicated to particular issues within EU actorness in a changing world. The book provides a timely, high-quality scholarly account of what could be EU geopolitical actorness. Hence, this edited book incorporates a variety of methodological and disciplinary approaches to encompass the broadest possible understanding of EU geopolitical actorness. The idea for this edited book was born following the preparation of a Horizon Europe consortium project composed of 12 partner universities from 11 European countries. Several contributors to this book had already participated in the writing of this Horizon Europe project, which inspired us to continue this research. Furthermore, to publish this edited book, a call for chapters was also launched in March 2023. Several chapter authors marked their interest in this call. At the same time, some other authors were individually invited to join the book project to contribute to an updated analysis of the EU's global actions. However, in this book, the authors of the chapters write in a personal and individual capacity. Otherwise, the goal was to broaden the geographical focus as much as possible. However, despite many efforts, we have not managed to cover all geographical areas of the world, including Africa and Latin America.

Structure Overview: Navigating from Theoretical Frameworks to Regional Case Studies and Toolbox Analysis

The first part of the edited book explores theoretical considerations that necessitate examining the feasibility of the shift toward EU geopolitical actorness. In her chapter, Maria Raquel Freire explores the EU's role as an actor from a security perspective. She provides a conceptual framework for the EU's security role, particularly in light of the ongoing war in Ukraine since 2014 and the full-scale Russian invasion that occurred on February 24, 2022. Her analysis raises questions about how the EU is adapting to its changing role as a security actor in this evolving context. Furthermore, her work delves into the significance of this geopolitical shift for the EU's understanding of normative and strategic security. This chapter offers valuable insights into how recent geopolitical events have contributed to rethinking security within the EU and the broader European context. In other words, it provides fresh perspectives on the implications for the EU's normative and strategic positioning and the ongoing process of redefining European security.

Vincent Bricart explores the EU's construction of its self-representation on the global stage, with a particular focus on its international identity and global actorness. His chapter delves into the EU's interactions and strategic positioning with other major international players to shape this representation. Specifically, his analysis centers on the EU's socialization processes involving the United States, Russia, and China. This examination highlights the EU's ability to adapt its self-image in response to evolving global dynamics and its engagements with these great international powers. It offers a new avenue to rethink the evolution of actorness in light of external pressures, as well as a conceptual framework to explore the causes of the EU's shift in actorness.

Adrian Szumowski examines the growing ambition expressed at all levels of EU structures, with a particular emphasis on its foreign policy. His chapter revolves around a prospective approach to the potential directions this evolution of the EU power might take. The author outlines three hypotheses proposing: (a) the evolution of EU power from its original normative power, as described by Ian Manners, into a fully fledged state-like power; (b) evolutionary paradoxes where the more successful EU becomes, the more resistance it may encounter; (c) a rise in conflict within EU decision-making although the specifics of this divergence remain to be determined. This chapter assesses the potential trajectory of the EU's shifting actorness while offering key insights into its implications for geopolitical influence.

The second part of this edited book relies on case study analyses to gain insights into how EU actorness is perceived and functions in specific strategic areas of the world. Raluca Moldovan critically examines the EU's endeavors to assume a more assertive role in global politics, with a specific focus on the challenging context of the Middle East. This region has proven to be a persistent arena where the EU's attempts to project its role, influence, and normative authority have yielded limited results. She delves into the resistance exhibited by countries like Turkey, Iran, and Saudi Arabia to the EU's geopolitical influence, raising questions about the viability of liberal democracy as a potential solution for the region. Her analysis aims to determine whether such a shift could enable the EU to establish a more prominent geopolitical presence in the Middle East. Additionally, she explores the role of third-party actors in contributing to the EU's challenges in this region.

Dealan Riga highlights the EU's renewed interest in the Indo-Pacific region and its significance within the ongoing process of geopoliticization. With the Indo-Pacific gaining renewed geopolitical importance, the EU's evolving efforts to enhance its geostrategic influence in the region represent a pivotal aspect of its shifting role. This chapter first assesses the specific requirement for a consistent EU foreign policy toward the region by emphasizing its needs such as multichannel policy, inclusive economic integration, and concrete security cooperation. It then scrutinizes the EU's attempt to be considered as a strategic actor of the Indo-Pacific by delving into the renewal of its economic, political, and security engagement toward the region. Hence, it sheds light on the essential missing elements of the EU's endeavor to establish a geopolitical presence in this newly strategic area.

Pëllumb Kelmendi and Liridon Lika conduct an analysis of Western Balkan countries' public opinion attitude regarding the EU. This research is particularly pertinent due to the fact that the support for EU membership varies from state to state, as well as inside the states between different ethnic groups. Drawing from opinion polls, their chapter reveals that Albania and Kosovo are the two most pro-EU states in the Western Balkans, followed by North Macedonia, Montenegro, and Bosnia and Herzegovina. Regarding Serbia, a traditional ally of Russia, there is significant Euroscepticism and a low support for EU membership. This chapter underscores the paramount role of identity politics, strategic cultures, ethnicity, and broader socio-cultural and historical factors when considering the EU actorness within the Western Balkans.

Elisabeth Johansson-Nogués closely examines the EU's geopolitical stance in Eastern Europe, focusing on the Ukrainian case in particular. While the EU had faced criticism for its perceived hesitancy in engaging with Eastern Europe, the 2022 Russian invasion of Ukraine marked a significant turning point in the EU's approach. This chapter explores the EU's assistance to Ukraine through the lens of actorness. It provides a critical assessment to determine whether the EU's foreign and security policy in this part of the European continent has indeed undergone substantial changes in response to these evolving dynamics. In this chapter, the author looks at a case study of EU economic, humanitarian, and military assistance to Ukraine with the objective of determining whether the EU's response to the 2022 Russo-Ukrainian war actually indicates a shift in EU foreign and security policy toward Ukraine in particular and Eastern Europe in general.

The third part delves into the analysis of specific EU tools for which change is required to ensure a consistent approach to EU geopolitical actorness. Alexandru Balas offers an analysis of the utilization of OCTs and the Outermost Regions (ORs) within the EU's new geopolitical strategy. These territories exist outside the Union but are intricately connected to EU member states, making them the EU's closest partners. This chapter, framed within the context of external governance research, explores a pivotal question: To what extent does the EU employ OCTs and ORs to advance its geopolitical influence across the Atlantic, Caribbean, Indian, and Pacific regions? The hypothesis put forth suggests that the EU leverages its influence in the OCTs and ORs to promote its objectives in these countries, territories, and regions, particularly when they align with the foreign policy and geopolitical interests of the relevant EU member states. This examination sheds light on the complex interplay of territorial dynamics and the EU's broader geopolitical strategy.

Nadège Boels delves into the EU's renewed emphasis on the use of sanctions, focusing on the specific case of Belarus. Sanctions, as defined by the EU, constitute a fundamental tool within the Common Foreign and Security Policy (CFSP) aimed at safeguarding the EU's established norms. She underscores that while sanctions were historically directed primarily at the authorities and individuals responsible for detrimental policies, the rationale behind the EU's approach has shifted, notably since the 2022 Russian invasion of Ukraine. This shift indicates a departure from the EU's traditional normative focus toward a more strategic orientation. In evaluating the strengths and weaknesses of restrictive measures in foreign policy, the chapter emphasizes that, at present, sanctions are prioritizing the economic and security interests of the EU over its normative commitments.

Robert Dopchie provides an in-depth analysis of the role of European soft power and pre-accession assistance (IPA) instruments within the EU external policy framework, with a specific focus on Bosnia and Herzegovina. Against the backdrop of the 2022 Russian invasion of Ukraine, which reignited concerns about potential conflicts in the EU's immediate vicinity, this study investigates the effectiveness of non-military measures in the EU's foreign policy toolkit. The research closely examines the extent to which IPA contributes to the dissemination and adoption of fundamental European values within Bosnia and Herzegovina. Using a mixed-methods approach, it uncovers potential connections between the financial support provided by the EU to Bosnia and Herzegovina and the country's progress in embracing these core European values.

Valentin Naumescu and Oana Poiană explore how the 2022 war in Ukraine has influenced transatlantic ties. The chapter delves into the various regional changes resulting from the war in Ukraine, impacting multiple dimensions, including strategy, geopolitics, security, economy, energy, environment, communication, infrastructure, and technology. The EU, in cooperation with its strategic partners, primarily the United States and NATO, faces the threats, risks, and consequences arising from global order instability. The chapter investigates the geopolitical approach of the EU and the alliance of Western liberal democracies to enhance security in their Eastern periphery. It employs the Advocacy Coalition Framework (ACF) to explain how changing geopolitical processes influence the EU's CFSP and the development of EU–NATO cooperation in the wake of the war in Ukraine.

Arlind Puka reflects on the EU's commitment to achieving strategic autonomy while recognizing the significance of security cooperation. EU member states have collectively agreed to increase their investments in defense capabilities and innovative technologies, marking a significant step toward the reorientation of EU defense policy. The chapter delves into an analysis of the EU's defense policy tools, including the EU Strategic Compass (EUSC), Permanent Structured Cooperation (PESCO), and the European Defence Fund (EDF), to evaluate their effectiveness in promoting defense cooperation among member states. It elaborates on the EU's new strategic approach to defense and security, as well as the potential development of its military capabilities and technological requirements aligned with these objectives. This analysis provides valuable insights into the EU's evolving defense and security policies and their implications for European security and autonomy.

This edited volume brings together contributions from both young and senior researchers, all aiming to present a critical and original analysis of EU actorness. In their chapters, the authors articulate both theoretical and empirical approaches, with the shared objective of enriching academic debates and advancing knowledge about EU geopolitical actorness in a changing world. The specific case studies included in this edited book delve into distinct periods and contexts, collectively demonstrating that the EU has made significant strides in further solidifying its position on the international stage.

References

Acharya, A. 2014. *The End of American World Order*. Cambridge: Polity.

Acharya, A. 2015. The Meanings of 'Multiplex', and the 'Multiplex World Order'. *Multiplexworld*, February 8, available at: https://multiplexworld.com/2015/02/08/the-meaning-of-multiplex-and-the-multiplex-world-order/ (accessed 18 October 2023).

Acharya, A. 2017. After Liberal Hegemony: The Advent of a Multiplex World Order. *Ethics and International Affairs* 31 (3): 271–285.

Acharya, A. 2019. *Understanding the Emerging Multiplex Order*. University College London, July 1, available at: https://www.ucl.ac.uk/global-governance/news/2019/jul/understanding-emerging-multiplex-world-order (accessed 18 October 2023).

Aggarwal, V.K., and E. Fogarty, eds. 2004. *EU Trade Strategies: Regionalism and Globalism*. London: Palgrave Macmillan.

Ambrosio, T. 2012. The Rise of the 'China Model' and 'Beijing Consensus': Evidence of Authoritarian Diffusion? *Contemporary Politics* 18 (4): 381–399.

Aydin-Düzgit, S., and G. Noutcheva. 2022. External Contestations of Europe: Russia and Turkey as Normative Challengers? *Journal of Common Market Studies* 60 (6): 1815–1831.

Badie, B. 2013. *La diplomatie de connivence: Les dérives oligarchiques du système international*. Paris: La Découverte.

Badie, B. 2016. *Nous ne sommes plus seuls au monde. Un autre regard sur 'l'ordre international'*. Paris: La Découverte.

Balmaceda, M. 2021. *Russian Energy Chains: The Remaking of Technopolitics from Siberia to Ukraine to the European Union*. New York: Columbia University Press.

Berzins, V. 2022. Hybrid Warfare: Weaponized Migration on the Eastern Border of the EU? *The Interdisciplinary Journal of International Studies* 12 (1): 1–19.

Bialasiewicz, L., ed. 2016. *Europe in the World: EU Geopolitics and the Making of European Space*. London and New York: Routledge.

Börzel, T.A. 2016. From EU Governance of Crisis to Crisis of EU Governance: Regulatory Failure, Redistributive Conflict and Eurosceptic Publics. *Journal of Common Market Studies* 54 (8): 8–31.

Börzel, T.A., and T. Risse. 2009. The Transformative Power of Europe: The European Union and Diffusion of Ideas. KFG Working Paper, n 1, 1–28.

Börzel, T.A., and T. Risse. 2018. From the Euro to the Schengen Crises: European Integration Theories, Politicization, and Identity Politics. *Journal of European Public Policy* 25 (1): 83–108.

Bretherton, C., and J. Vogler. 2006. *The European Union as a Global Actor*. London and New York: Routledge.

Calder, K.E. 1988. Japanese Foreign Economic Policy Formation: Explaining the Reactive State. *World Politics* 40 (4): 517–541.

Casier, T. 2022. Russia and the Diffusion of Political Norms: The Perfect Rival? *Democratization* 2 (3): 433–450.

Cassani, A., and L. Tomini. 2020. Reversing Regimes and Concepts: From Democratization to Autocratization. *European Political Science* 19: 272–287.

Ceccorulli, M., E. Fassi, and S. Lucarelli, eds. 2020. *The EU Migration System of Governance: Justice on the Move*. Cham: Palgrave Macmillan.

Ceccorulli, M., and S. Lucarelli. 2017. Migration and the EU Global Strategy: Narratives and Dilemmas. *The International Spectator* 52 (3): 83–102.

Cerny, P.G., ed. 2022. *Heterarchy in World Politics*. London: Taylor & Francis.

Colgan, J.D., and R.O. Keohane. 2017. The Liberal Order Is Rigged: Fix It Now or Watch It Wither. *Foreign Affairs* 96 (3): 36–44.

Dandashly, A., and C. Kourtelis. 2020. Classifying the Implementation of the EU's Normative Power in its Southern Neighbourhood: The Role of Local Actors. *Journal of Common Market Studies* 58 (6): 1523–1539.

De Graaff, N., and B. Van Apeldoorn. 2018. US–China Relations and the Liberal World Order: Contending Elites, Colliding Visions? *International Affairs* 94 (1): 113–131.

De Wilde, P. 2011. No Polity for Old Politics? A Framework for Analyzing the Politicization of European Integration. *Journal of European Integration* 33 (5): 559–575.

De Wilde, P., and M. Zürn. 2012. Can the Politicization of European Integration be Reversed? *Journal of Common Market Studies* 50 (1): 137–153.

Dony, M., and L. Serena. 2008. *Démocratie, cohérence et transparence: vers une constitutionnalisation de l'Union européenne?* Bruxelles: Editions de l'Université de Bruxelles.

Dopchie, R., and L. Lika. 2024. The EU Enlargement Strategy in the Western Balkans: Assessing the Implications Amidst the War in Ukraine. *European Foreign Affairs Review* 29 (2): 159–176.

Duchêne, F. 1972. Europe's Role in World Peace. In *Europe Tomorrow: Sixteen Europeans Look Ahead*, ed. R. Mayne, 32–47. London: Fontana/Collins.

Duncombe, C., and T. Dunne. 2018. After Liberal World Order. *International Affairs* 94 (1): 25–42.

Duke, S. 2006. Consistency as an Issue in EU External Activities. Working Paper, European Institue of Public Administration, 1–38.

Esteves, P., and S. Klingebiel. 2021. Diffusion, Fusion, and Confusion: Development Cooperation in a Multiplex World Order. In *The Palgrave Handbook of Development Cooperation for Achieving the 2030 Agenda*, ed. S. Chaturvedi, H. Janus, S. Klingebiel, X. Li, A. de Mello e Souza, E. Sidiropoulos, and D. Wehrmann, 185–215. Cham: Palgrave Macmillan.

European Commission. 2019a. The von der Leyen Commission: For a Union That Strives for More. Press release, 19/5542.

European Commission. 2019b. EU-China a Strategic Outlook, available at: eur-lex.europa.eu/legal-content/EN/TXT/PDF/?uri=CELEX:52019JC0005 (accessed 7 November 2023).

European Commission. 2022. Speech by President von der Leyen at the European Parliament Plenary on the Russian Aggression Against Ukraine. Speech/22/1483.

EEAS. 2022. Russian Aggression Against Ukraine: Speech by High Representative/Vice-President Josep Borrell at the EP Plenary, March 1, available at: https://www.eeas.europa.eu/eeas/russian-aggression-against-ukraine-speech-high-representativevice-president-josep-borrell-ep-plenary-0_en (accessed 26 September 2023).

Fagerholm, A. 2024. Sympathy or Criticism? The European Far Left and Far Right React to Russia's 2022 Invasion of Ukraine. *Europe-Asia Studies* 76 (6): 829–850.

Fahey, E., ed. 2020. *Framing Convergence with the Global Legal Order. The EU and the World*. Oxford: Hart Publishing.

Fahey, E., and I. Mancini, eds. 2022. *Understanding the EU as a Good Global Actor: Ambitions, Values and Metrics*. Cheltenham: Edward Elgar Publishing.

Farrell, H., and A.L. Newman. 2019. Weaponized Interdependence: How Global Economic Networks Shape State Coercion. *International Security* 44 (1): 42–79.

Ferguson, N., and F. Zakaria. 2017. *The End of the Liberal Order?* London: Oneworld Publications.

Freire, M.R. et al. 2022. *EU Global Actorness in a World of Contested Leadership. Policies, Instruments and Perceptions*. Cham: Palgrave Macmillan.

Fukuyama, F. 2022. Putin's War on the Liberal Order, *Financial Times*, available at: https://www.ft.com/content/d0331b51-5d0e-4132-9f97-c3f41c7d75b3 (accessed 7 November 2023).

Grabbe, H. 2006. *EU's Transformative Power: Europeanization Through Conditionality in Central and Eastern Europe*. Houndmills, Basingstoke, Hampshire: Palgrave Macmillan.

Haass, R.N. 2008. The Age of Nonpolarity: What Will Follow U.S. Dominance. *Foreign Affairs* 87 (3): 44–56.

Haass, R. 2017. *A World in Disarray: American Foreign Policy and the Crisis of the Old Order*. New York: Penguin.

Hackenbroich, J., and P. Zerka. 2021. Measured Response: How to Design a European Instrument Against Coercion, *ECFR*, available at: https://ecfr.eu/publication/measured-response-how-to-design-a-european-instrument-against-economic-coercion/ (accessed 20 November 2023).

Hansen, B. 2010. *Unipolarity and World Politics. A Theory and Its Implications*. London: Routledge.

Hellmeier, S., et al. 2021. State of the World 2020: Autocratization Turns Viral. *Democratization* 28 (6): 1053–1074.

Hill, C., and M. Smith. 2005. *International Relations and the European Union*. Oxford: Oxford University Press.

Hill, C., M. Smith, and S. Vanhoonacker, eds. 2023. *International Relations and the European Union*. Oxford: Oxford University Press.

Holden, P. 2009. *In Search of Structural Power: EU Aid Policy as a Global Political Instrument*. Farnham: Ashgate.

Hopewell, K. 2022. Beyond US-China Rivalry: Rule Breaking, Economic Coercion, and the Weaponization of Trade. CUP. Available at: https://S2398772322000034jra58..63 (accessed 20 November 2023).

Ikenberry, G.J. 2018. The End of Liberal International Order? *International Affairs* 94 (1): 7–23.

Johansson-Nogués, E. 2007. The (Non-)Normative Power EU and the European Neighbourhood Policy: An Exceptional Policy for an Exceptional Actor? *European Political Economic Review* 7: 181–194.

Jupille, J., and J. Caporaso. 1998. States, Agency and Rules: The European Union in Global Environmental Politics. In *The European Union in the World Community*, ed. C. Rhodes, 213–229. Boulder: Lynne Rienner Publishers.

Kavalski, E. 2013. The Struggle for Recognition of Normative Powers: Normative Power Europe and Normative Power China in Context. *Cooperation and Conflict* 48 (2): 247–267.

Klose, S. 2018. Theorizing EU Actorness: Towards an Interactionist Role Theory Framework. *Journal of Common Market Studies* 56 (5): 1144–1160.

Krauthammer, C. 1990/1991. The Unipolar Moment. *Foreign Affairs* 70 (1): 23–33.

Leonard, M. 2021. The Power Atlas. Seven Battlegrounds of a Networked World, *ECFR*, available at: https://ecfr.eu/special/power-atlas/ (accessed 20 November 2023).

Lieber, R.J. 2022. Polarity, Non-polarity, and the Risks of A-Polarity. In *Polarity in International Relations. Past, Present, Future*, ed. N. Graeger et al., 171–189. Basingstoke: Palgrave Macmillan.

Lika, L., and A. Weerts. 2021. Jeux et enjeux de l'Union Européenne: quels enseignements peut-on tirer? *Cahiers de Science Politique de l'Université de Liège*, 103–108.

Lührmann, A., and S.I. Lindberg. 2019. A Third Wave of Autocratization Is Here: What Is New About It? *Democratization* 26 (7): 1095–1113.

Lütz, S., T. Leeg, and D. Otto. 2021. *The European Union as a Global Actor: Trade, Finance and Climate Policy* Cham: Springer International Publishing.

Manners, I. 2002. Normative Power Europe: A Contradiction in Terms? *Journal of Common Market Studies* 40 (2): 235–258.

Manners, I. 2010. As You Like It: European Union Normative Power in the European Neighbourhood Policy. In *The European Neighbourhood Policy in Perspective: Context, Implementation and Impact*, ed. R. Whitman and S. Wolff, 29–50. Houndmills Basingstoke: Palgrave Macmillan.

Marangoni, A.-C. 2014. Towards Consistency of EU External Policies? A Case Study on the European Commission, *Doctoral Thesis*, University of Maastricht.

Marangoni, A.-C., and S. Vanhoonacker. 2015. The Consistency of EU External Action Post-Lisbon: Renewing Appropriate Measures Against Zimbabwe in 2012. In Dynamics of institutional cooperation in the European Union: Dimensions and Effects, *European Integration online Papers (EIoP),* Special issue, 19 (1): 1–22.

Maull, H.W. 1990. Germany and Japan: The New Civilian Powers, *Foreign Affairs*, available at: https://www.foreignaffairs.com/articles/asia/1990-12-01/germany-and-japan-new-civilian-powers (accessed 18 October 2023).

Mearsheimer, J. 2001. *The Tragedy of Great Power Politics*. London and New York: Norton.

Meissner, K.L., and M.G. Schoeller. 2020. Rising Despite the Polycrisis? The European Parliament's Strategies of Self-empowerment After Lisbon. In *The European Union Beyond the Polycrisis? Integration and Politicization in an Age of Shifting Cleavages*, ed. J. Zeitlin and F. Nicoli, 113–131. London: Routledge.

Menendez, A.J. 2016. The Refugee Crisis: Between Human Tragedy and Symptom of the Structural Crisis of European Integration. *European Law Journal* 22 (4): 388–416.

Merle, M. 1988. *Sociologie des relations internationales*. Paris: Dalloz.

Meunier, S., and K. Nicolaidis. 2019. The Geopoliticization of European Trade and Investment Policy. *Journal of Common Market Studies* 57 (1): 103–113.

Niemann, A., and C. Bretherton. 2013. EU External Policy at the Crossroads: The Challenge of Actorness and Effectiveness. *International Relations* 27 (3): 261–275.

Onea, T. 2021. *The Grand Strategies of Great Powers*. New York: Routledge.

Petiteville, F. 2002. L'Union européenne, acteur international 'global'? Un Agenda De Recherche. *Revue Internationale Et Stratégique* 47 (3): 145–157.

Puetter, U. 2012. Europe's Deliberative Intergovernmentalism: The Role of the Council and European Council in EU Economic Governance. *Journal of European Public Policy* 19 (2): 161–178.

Riga, D. 2024. Navigating Regionalism in a Heterarchical Global Order: A Comprehensive Analysis of the EU's Empowerment in Global Investment Governance. In *Postinternationalism and the Rise of Heterarchy*, ed. D.M. Ramjit, 165–188. Hershey PA: IGI Global.

Santander, S., and A. Vlassis. 2020. EU in Global Affairs: Constrained Ambition in an Unpredictable World? *European Foreign Affairs Review* 25 (1): 5–22.

Scott, D.A. 2017. Multipolarity, Multilateralism and Beyond...? EU-China Understandings of the International System. *International Relations* 27 (1): 30–51.

Shekhovtsov, A. 2017. *Russia and the Western Far Right. Tango Noir*. London: Routledge.

Simão, L. 2022. Unpacking EU's International Actorness: Debates, Theories and Concepts. In *EU Global Actorness in a World of Contested Leadership. Policies, Instruments and Perceptions*, ed. M.R. Freire et al., 13–32. Cham: Palgrave Macmillan.

Slaughter, A.M. 2004. Disaggregated Sovereignty: Towards the Public Accountability of Global Government Networks. *Government and Opposition* 39 (2): 159–190.

Smith, M.A. 2013. Russia and Multipolarity Since the End of the Cold War. *East European Politics* 29 (1): 36–51.

Soderbaum, F., and L. Van Langenhove. 2006. *The EU as a Global Player: The Politics of Interregionalism*. New York: Routledge.

Stiglitz, J.E. 2014. Crises: Principles and Policies with an Application to the Euro Zone Crisis. In *Life After Debt: The Origins and Resolutions of Debt Crisis*, ed. J.E. Stiglitz and D. Heymann, 43–79. London: Palgrave Macmillan.

Stiglitz, J.E. 2016. The Fundamental Flaws in the Euro Zone Framework. In *The Euro and the Crisis: Perspectives for the Eurozone as a Monetary and Budgetary Union*, ed. N. de Costa Cabral et al., 11–16. New York: Springer.

Taeuber, S. 2020. Reconstructing the Silk Road: Norm Contestation in Sino-European Relations in Times of the Belt and Road Initiative. *Journal of Rising Powers and Global Governance* 1 (1): 31–65.

Telò, M. 2006. *Europe: A Civilian Power? European Union, Global Governance, World Order*. New York: Palgrave Macmillan.

Telò, M., ed. 2014. *Globalisation, Multilateralism, Europe. Towards a Better Global Governance?* New York: Routledge.

Tocci, N. 2017. *Framing the EU Global Strategy. A Stronger Europe in a Fragile World*. Cham: Springer International Publishing.

Van der Pijl, K., ed. 2021. *The Militarization of the European Union*. Cambridge: Cambridge Scholars Publishing.

Vanhoonacker, S. 2018. *The Bush Administration (1989–1993) and the Development of a European Security Identity*. London and New York: Routledge.

Veebel, V. 2019. Why It Would Be Strategically Rational for Russia to Escalate in Kaliningrad and the Suwalki corridor. *Comparative Strategy* 38 (3): 182–197.

Vuskane, L. 2019. *The Role of European Union in World Politics*. München: GRIN Verlag.

Wu, Z. 2018. Classical Geopolitics, Realism and the Balance of Power Theory. *Journal of Strategic Studies* 41 (6): 786–823.

Yakemtchouk, R. 2005. *La politique étrangère de l'Union européenne*. Paris: L'Harmattan.

Zeitlin, J., and F. Nicoli, eds. 2020. *The European Union Beyond the Polycrisis? Integration and Politicization in an Age of Shifting Cleavages*. London: Routledge.

The EU as a Geopolitical Actor: Opening Actorness Theoretical Framework

Reinforcing EU's Actorness? A Look at EU's Reshaping of Security

Maria Raquel Freire

Introduction

European security has been profoundly transformed by the war in Ukraine since 2014 and Russia's full-scale invasion in February 2022. The security order in place after the end of the Cold War and the disaggregation of the Soviet Union, where the North Atlantic Treaty Organization (NATO) reinvented itself, the Organization for Security and Cooperation in Europe (OSCE) reframed its goals, and the European Union (EU) started engaging with security and defense issues in a more structured way, set the stage for the security architecture that Russia soon started contesting. The Warsaw Pact dissolved along with the Soviet Union and 15 new independent republics emerged, with the Baltic States quickly disengaging and the remaining states loosely binding together in the Commonwealth of Independent States (CIS). The low profile of the CIS led Russia to drive forward the creation of the Eurasian Economic Union (EAEU) and the Collective Security Treaty Organization (CSTO), broadly focusing on economic and security issues, respectively, which institutionalized the

M. R. Freire (✉)
CES, FEUC, University of Coimbra, Coimbra, Portugal
e-mail: rfreire@fe.uc.pt

L. Lika and D. Riga (eds.), *EU Geopolitical Actorness in a Changing World*, https://doi.org/10.1007/978-3-031-81160-9_2

differences in objectives for wider Europe dynamics, including in security terms. The EAEU, created with regional economic integration in the agenda just like the European Communities, is a "building block for ideas of regional order" (Lewis 2018, 1614), promoting Russia's vision on this; and the CSTO is a military alliance presenting itself as a regional security provider (Allison 2018).

Russia's criticisms of exclusion from the European security order materialized in some proposals for a reframing of the European security architecture, for example, with a new European Security Treaty (EST) proposal as advanced by Dmitri Medvedev in 2008, or later the "Greater Eurasian" project that Sergueï Karaganov presented at the OSCE, in 2015, in the context of the Panel of Eminent Persons (PEP) on European Security as a Common Project (OSCE 2015; see also Karaganov 2018). These proposals did not find a warm welcome in Western Europe (Lo 2009; De Haas 2010; Averre 2019), which was voiced in Russia as a sign of unwillingness to integrate it in security matters. The many ups and downs in relations between Russia and the Western states created friction but also kept space for political dialogue and cooperation initiatives. However, the latest developments and particularly the full-scale invasion of Ukraine by Russia since 2022 changed the mood, bringing together the West in Russia's condemnation. The declaration made by Josep Borrell, EU High Representative for Foreign Affairs and Security Policy/Vice-President of the European Commission (HR/VP), on behalf of EU member states on the day of the invasion was clear: "[t]he European Union condemns in the strongest possible terms the unprovoked invasion of Ukraine by armed forces of the Russian Federation" (European Council 2022). Russia violated international law and the borders' regime in Europe, with the principle of respect for sovereignty and territorial integrity crushed under its moves in Georgia in 2008, with the annexation of Crimea in 2014, and with the current invasion. The escalation of the war in Ukraine with Russia's full-scale invasion means the attempts at designing an inclusive security architecture definitely crumbled and Russia excluded itself from the process. This was a double exclusion: Russia's self-exclusion by acting against international norms and principles and Western exclusion through, for example, the breakdown in diplomatic relations and the imposition of sanctions that followed.

It is in this framing that this chapter looks at the EU as a security actor in the making in a transformed context, seeking to assess the

EU's responses and positioning toward the contested European security order. How has the EU been repositioning itself as a security actor in this changed context? What does a geopolitical shift mean for the EU's normative and strategic security understandings? At the time of its creation, with the consequences of the two world wars still vivid, the drive to avoid a new war in Europe was very much present in the European Communities project. The objective of attaining a more secure Europe through economic integration and the fostering of collaborative politics underpinned the project. But the security and defense dimension took time to be institutionalized with different understandings among EU member states slowing down the process. The wars in former Yugoslavia in the 1990s contributed to a fair assessment of the need for strategic instruments and some policy coherence. With the Treaty of Amsterdam in 1999, the process of institutionalizing the security and defense dimension within the EU takes off. Progress has been slow, but the policy is shaped and instruments start to be put in place. The events since 2014, but particularly February 24, 2022, were major catalysts in the process of redefining European security and the EU's role in this. The shift from the normative actor, very much embedding the constitutive values of the EU, to include a more geopolitical approach, visible also in the current so-called "geopolitical Commission," needs to be addressed in this context. Strategic considerations have clearly been added to the agenda (Haroche 2023, 970). This shift brings with it concepts such as those of principled pragmatism and resilience, along with bordering and debordering dynamics with clear security implications for what these dynamics mean, whom they are targeting, and how change is envisioned.

Bordering dynamics became particularly clear in EU-Russia relations after 2014. The annexation of Crimea, described by Russia as a historical "reintegration" of territory, activating "geopolitical and historical imaginations of Crimea" (Biersack and O'Lear 2014, 247), clearly violated Ukraine's territorial integrity and state borders. The historical arguments Russia invoked to justify the act of "reintegration" were not convincing. In fact, the ideational dimension of border underlines Russian justifications and impacts on the sovereigntist principle, which Russia has championed. Thus, Crimea's annexation was framed in the identity-driven reading of the post-Soviet area promoted by Russia, while it incarnated geopolitics driven by realpolitik (Freire 2022). The bordering process implied was both material with the construction of border posts and the erection of fences, and symbolic, with the self/other construct underlining differentials and "the other as the enemy" narrative. Russia's borderization strategy points to a dual reading: on the one hand, that symbolic borders are most relevant in identity and national terms, and on the other hand, that territorial borders are still key in international relations and may symbolize power or fragility (Freire 2022). Russia's actions contributed to overriding national and international law principles, incarnated political goals of empowerment, and manipulated symbolic approaches to identity and values-driven narratives. The escalation of war with Russia's full-scale invasion only came to reinforce the violation of the European borders' regime and to reenact the hard borderization process in course. The militarization of the EU's external border is clear with the old dichotomy of self/other, Western/non-Western, gaining new grounds. The EU's external borders and its neighborhood became locus of insecurity as a consequence.

In this context of an unstable and insecure neighborhood where rebordering practices have been feeding insecurity feelings, the EU has refurbished its discourse by including a harder security narrative. The so-called power of attraction of the EU, particularly in its normative potential, has loosened in a contested international order, where other powers have been presenting themselves as attractive alternatives, be it Turkey or China as examples. Russia emerges in this context as a contesting actor critical of what it understands is the Western hegemonic view of order and security. Russia's growing criticisms of Western biased actuation, pursuing double standards and a hegemonic agenda, led to its gradual disentanglement from the Western-led order. The clashing of understandings between Russia and the EU regarding the conceptualization of the European security order meant the return of more insecurity to Europe, accompanied by a more geopolitical narrative (see Casier 2016). From the discourse on contestation to the violation of Ukraine's territorial integrity, the full spectrum of security threats, in their territorial and non-territorial dimensions was ignited. This implied the return of divisive "walls" to Europe, in a rebordering process with territorial claims along with a civilizational and identitarian discourse that seeks to justify Russia's illegal and illegitimate actions. The EU's self-definition as a security actor and norms promoter in this contested international order, along with principled pragmatism in key issues, becomes, therefore, topical to understanding security dynamics. This chapter looks at the EU's security actorness, in the context of the Russian escalation of the war in Ukraine, particularly since February 24, 2022, seeking to understand the dynamics of reconceptualization of security in the EU and the wider European context, and which have been its implications for both the EU's normative and strategic positioning. It does so by framing the argument in the current literature and analyzing major primary source documents, such as the EU security strategies.

EU's Security Actorness: The Narrative and the Practice

EU's security actorness has been evolving hand-in-hand with the perception of threats and challenges the EU faces, as evident, for example, in the rebordering processes of Russia's aggressive policies have been enhancing. This means the objectives, capabilities, and areas of action have been changing both with internal dynamics and developments in the international system, particularly in the geographical areas closer to the EU. The EU's strategic documents on security attest to this reading, positioning the EU as following a comprehensive approach to security, evolving into both a normative and geostrategic actor, and interlinking internal developments and external relations to better address the multilayered crises and contested international system. In this regard, the creation of the European Security and Defence Policy (ESDP, now Common Security and Defense Policy, CSDP) with the Treaty of Amsterdam in 1999 sought to provide the EU with institutional engineering to better respond to security issues. The inability to respond to the challenges coming from the former Yugoslavia, in particular, in the 1990s underlined the need for developing autonomous capacity. The many assets part of its comprehensive approach, combining civilian and military means, and affirming the EU's "civilian power" in crisis management proved useful. But the long-term reliance on NATO showed limits in terms of developing more robust defense capabilities. The United States (US) and NATO's role in European security, as fundamental pillars, have generated intense debates about European strategic autonomy and the dependence dynamics arising from an unbalanced relationship.[1] This unfinished debate is central to the definition of European security, assuring (autonomous) capacity to respond to challenges.

The withdrawal of the United States from European security during the Donald Trump years, and the threats from the former US president to leave NATO (Orenstein 2023, 335), were part of a wake-up call for the reinforcement of means and capacities in security and defense. Despite the "return" of the United States to European security with the current war of aggression by Russia in Ukraine, and of the strengthening of NATO with further commitment from member states and enlargement to Finland and Sweden, the strategic context has changed. Russia's aggressive policy particularly evident from 2014 and the invasion of Ukraine in February 2022 constituted a fundamental turning point in the EU's assessment of its security actorness. This becomes plainly evident in the wording of the 2016 EU Global Strategy (EUGS) and the 2022 Strategic Compass, as further analyzed. The setting up of Permanent Structured Cooperation (PESCO) in security and defense, the Coordinated Annual Review on Defense (CARD), and the European Defense Fund (EDF) established in 2017 are illustrative of the effort to step up cooperation and coordination among member states. Later, the 2021 European Peace Facility (EPF) enabled the EU to "finance operational actions that have military or defence implications under the Common Foreign and Security Policy (CFSP)," aiming at strengthening international security, such as the EU Military Assistance Mission in support of Ukraine (EUMAM Ukraine) launched in November 2022 with the goal of strengthening the capacity of the Ukrainian Armed Forces (UAF). The coordinated action to approve sanctions' packages and the use of the EPF to channel military aid to Ukraine are examples of a change in attitude. Some argue the adoption of concrete instruments has allowed more integrated capacity within the CSDP, overcoming differences among member states and providing for action with more autonomy (Chappell et al. 2020, 583). Whether this will last in face of resurging old cracks, is to be seen, and whether defense structures and means will be seriously reinforced is also to be seen, with assessments not overly optimistic (Howorth 2020; Costa and Barbé 2023). The war in Ukraine pushed for the strengthening of the defense component, but the reality proved limited, according to some. "Despite

[1] For further detail see the chapter by Valentin Naumescu and Oana Poiană in this volume.

the remarkable steps forward over defence (e.g. in the fields of procurement and the provision of military aid), strategic autonomy has been pronounced a 'pipe dream' that has encountered a 'reality check'" (Costa and Barbé 2023, 431).[2] Others argue the EU has been "failing forward" in security and defense mainly due to lack in institutional reforms and policy feedback (Bergmann and Müller 2021). Nevertheless, the realization that security dynamics have profoundly changed and new bordering processes are in course, is clear and visible in the most recent security strategies.

Back in 2003 when the European Security Strategy (ESS) was adopted it conveyed the message that the threats faced were less of a conventional nature, as the September 11, 2001, attacks on the United States clearly reminded. The global challenge terrorism implied called for global action and a coordinated response from the EU. If on the one hand, the dynamics of interdependence allowed more integration and prosperity, on the other hand, transnational organized crime and other non-military threats across borders impended on security. With the war in Ukraine, interdependence will even be equated with vulnerability with the case of energy relations with Russia being illustrative (Costa and Barbé 2023, 432). Moreover, the war in Iraq with the US-led intervention, as a reaction to September 11 and part of the global war on terror, contributed to exposing differences among member states, with different alignments on this issue fragmenting an EU position. The document sought to mend readings of fragmentation and show the collective within the EU, with "effective multilateralism" highlighted as an important mechanism for dealing with international challenges. The call for the "development of a stronger international society, well-functioning international institutions and a rule-based international order" that the ESS makes repositions the EU in what it reads as the basic foundations for the security order. Moreover, the ESS expresses the transformative diplomacy the EU is endorsing, through the promotion of good governance and democratization particularly in its neighborhood (Mälksoo 2016, 379). The document was, thus, "outward looking," but also "reflexive" about the way the EU had to position itself in security matters, building on a comprehensive approach to security (Della Sala 2023, 367).

[2] For further detail on defense issues and the main debates see the chapter in this volume by Arlind Puka.

The EUGS (2016) is a different document. The EU was also different by then, for different reasons, including Brexit, and particularly the 2014 events when the war in Ukraine started and Crimea was annexed by Russia. The threats became closer. This meant the EU response became more about resilience and ownership. It sought to overcome the limitations the transformative diplomacy approach implied, by conferring more agency to the EU's neighbors. This shift to "stability-building resilience" accompanied the shift in discourse within the EU. Resilience is not just directed at the neighborhood, but it also concerns the strengthening of internal security in the face of Russia's aggressive actions against the European security order that the EU promotes (Mälksoo 2016, 381). Through support to projects focusing on issues such as development, fighting poverty, and inequality, the EU sought to capacitate communities, societies, and countries, in order that these become owners of the reforms' processes and capacitated to be responsive to different challenges. This implies also what some call the "geopolitical shift" in the EU (Biscop 2016; Della Sala 2023), in that strategic interest and "principled pragmatism" gain new ground, acknowledging the relevance of military means. This means a bigger emphasis on the EU's "own security, the neighborhood, and hard power" and the document "no longer emphasizing democratization" (Biscop 2016, 2). This is clear in the formulation of the three main pillars of this strategy: Europeans should take more responsibility for their security and defense, new capabilities need to be developed and new financial instruments established for this purpose, and EU-NATO cooperation is to be strengthened (EEAS 2021). Della Sala (2023, 368) argues the EUGS is telling a different story, and this is one where strategic interest becomes central and in the fight against internal and external threats strategic autonomy gains relevance, built over pragmatism in how the world is understood and how the EU acts toward it. This does not mean, however, that the place of the EU as a security provider is well defined, particularly with regard to relations with NATO (Mälksoo 2016, 382). The geopolitical shift, which Ursula von der Leyen's Commission underlines, and which seeks to reaffirm the EU's role in international affairs, has also been understood as a recognition of fragility. "By flying the geopolitical flag, Commission President von der Leyen has exposed the weaknesses of the EU as a whole in playing a decisive role at the high diplomatic table, not to mention the ability of backing up its words with force if needed" (Blockmans 2020). This points to the distancing between the political narrative and the operationalization of policies in response to different challenges, which the most recent strategic document, the Strategic Compass, seeks to overcome.

A Strategic Compass for Security and Defense (2022) is the new document guiding the EU's strategic thinking. It was published after Russia's invasion of Ukraine, reflecting already the new reality. Despite the document being held and revised to consider Russia's aggression, it was criticized by some as already "obsolete" at the time it was made public (Costa and Barbé 2023, 431). But it was also seen as a document that was kept on hold and changed before final publication due to the context, showing the willingness of the EU to be seen as a strong actor in security and defense (Andersson and Cramer 2023, 26). The language is much stronger than the previous documents, which also informs the EU reading about the security context: "Russia's unjustified and unprovoked aggression" needs a collective response, thus "the more hostile security environment requires us to make a quantum leap forward and increase our capacity and willingness to act, strengthen our resilience and ensure solidarity and mutual assistance" (Strategic Compass 2022). The understanding of European security is also clearly lined up: "Sovereignty, territorial integrity and independence within internationally recognized borders should be fully respected," along with the "support for the global rules-based order, with the United Nations at its core. It will also reinforce its strategic partnership with NATO and increase its cooperation with regional partners" (Strategic Compass 2022). The convergence between the normative dimension and the need for a pragmatic response gains shape with the new document.

The EU wants to be a "stronger and more capable security provider. The EU needs to be able to protect its citizens and to contribute to international peace and security" (Strategic Compass 2022). The internal-external nexus is evident in the conceptualization of security and of how the EU wants to be understood as a security actor. In the face of "major geopolitical shifts," the document continues, the objective is to "enhance the EU's strategic autonomy and its ability to work with partners to safeguard its values and interests," bringing in the normative and pragmatic dimensions of EU's actuation in the new geopolitical framing. Borrell titles the foreword to the document "Europe's geopolitical awakening" and under the first title, "the return of power politics in a contested multipolar world" as a sub-title is telling. A comprehensive understanding of security is highlighted as well as a complex geopolitical context where besides the war in Ukraine other regional areas such as the Western Balkans or the Middle East are of relevance, as well as cybercrime, disinformation, and other non-traditional threats, cross-cutting the internal and external nexus. The document seeks to be a guiding model for the development of capacities at the level of crisis management or forces' deployment, but also regarding the combat of disinformation, for example. The EU's integrated approach and strategic autonomy efforts have provided additional tools in the domains of security and defense, but still the EU is better prepared to respond to resilience building than to military threats. "With Ukraine in mind, the odds are in favor of hard power military capabilities, whereas the tools required for the integrated approach, the resilience paradigm, and the instruments to deal with hybrid threats are lower on the priority list" (Dijkstra 2022). This informs the practice of security as perceived and enacted by the EU, within the constraints that inform it.

In a nutshell, in its comprehensive approach to security the EU privileges three combinations: first, the internal-external nexus in security, where EU's external borders gain different meanings and shapes; second, instruments both of a civilian and military nature; and third, the relevance of partnerships, primarily with its wide neighborhood both to the east and south, but also further afield. The civilian dimension of European security and defense has been privileged, as mentioned, with the military component slowly developing and in the last years gaining new momentum. Still, analyses point to the reactive policies of the EU, the inability to find consensus among its members, including over the balancing between the EU and NATO, and the consequent options in terms of reinforcing this component in EU action. The relevance of the neighborhood for EU security has been highlighted for long. Clearly the documents establishing the European Neighborhood Policy (ENP) bring in the security dimension read in a broad sense, including, for example, energy security and societal and political resilience, along with a note on interdependence and how security in the EU cannot be delinked from security in the neighborhood. The Communication from the European Commission on the Wider Europe from 2003 clearly states that "[o]ver the coming decade and beyond, the Union's capacity to provide security, stability and sustainable development to its citizens will no longer be distinguishable from its interest in close cooperation with the neighbours" (European Commission 2003, 3). And one year later, the ENP Strategy Paper reinforced the idea that "[t]he European Neighborhood Policy's vision involves a ring of countries, sharing the EU's fundamental values and objectives, drawn into an increasingly close relationship, going beyond co-operation to involve a significant measure of economic and political integration. This will bring enormous gains to all involved in terms of increased stability, security and well-being" (European Commission 2004, 5).

The core principles of security have been maintained in its comprehensive approach, but the addition of resilience and principled pragmatism show a shift in the EU's approach toward a clearer burden-sharing of responsibilities with the neighbors in the understanding that further capacitation is needed to assure resilient societies. This has resulted in bordering processes that have been in tension, at times. Being socially constructed, borders are continuously adjusting to social practice and discourse. This allows the elasticity of borders to reflect simultaneous movements, at times in different directions, as borders might be open to certain fluxes and closed to others. The "EU fortress" in face of the so-called migrants' successive crises or the openness of the external border to pipeline flows are examples. More than looking at the "what," it is the "how" that matters most, as it leads the EU through bordering processes (Sendhardt 2013, 25; Parker and Vaughan-Williams 2012, 729) and what this entails. If the ENP aimed at debordering dynamics, the insecurity that has developed around the EU's external borders, be it in the form of energy dynamics, migrant flows, or political instability has contributed to rebordering processes that seek to insulate the EU from external threats. These processes are further analyzed in the following section.

Bordering Processes and the Building of European (In)Security: Conflating Views?

The EU follows the principles of comprehensive security, aligns with the cooperative security approach of the OSCE, and keeps close relations with the Atlantic Alliance, sharing the view that security, democracy, and human rights are interrelated concepts. In the conceptualization of security, the EU clearly goes further than its "own space" focusing to a great extent on its enlarged neighborhood, both to the south and east. The ENP (European Commission 2003, 2004), aiming at the development of relations in different areas with the southern and eastern neighbors, illustrates well the dynamic of building good neighborly relations as a way to promote stability at the EU's external borders. The EU relies traditionally on a core set of values on democracy, pluralism, and humanism, as evinced in the ENP model and the emulation it sought regarding neighbors' adaptation to EU norms and principles. The idea was that the approximation of the neighbors to EU ways of dealing would assure more stability and security. This was reinforced again in the Eastern Partnership (EaP), established as part of the ENP, but more tailored to reinforce cooperation with the six Eastern neighbors, as agreed at the Prague Council of the EU in May 2009. Then, it was affirmed that "the Eastern Partnership will seek to support political and socio-economic reforms of the partner countries, facilitating approximation towards the European Union. This serves the shared commitment to stability, security and prosperity of the European Union, the partner countries and indeed the entire European continent" (Council of the EU 2009, 6).

The idea of "approximation" to the EU principles and ways of doing was present from the very start of these frameworks for cooperation, becoming a point of criticism in the way that it conveyed "imposition practices" through mimicking the EU's rules and procedures. Moreover, "the EU's relations with its neighbors are predominantly structured as concentric, as opposed to polycentric patterns" (Makarychev 2018, 4) further implying these uneven relations between the EU, as the dominant partner, and the countries in the EaP as the "recipients" of this collaboration framework. The bi-directional rationale for the Eastern neighborhood policy seems to be clearer on paper than on how relations were developed. Instead of contributing to debordering processes, this unevenness fed rebordering processes that limited both regional dynamics of integration and the EU's political positioning in this area. Neither the neighboring countries were homogenous in the definition of their relations with the EU nor the positive spill-over effect sought was widespread. Local agency and ownership of processes, along with a geopolitical context that created tensions on foreign policy options, in-between the EU and Russia, besides regional cooperation and rivalry dynamics, set the stage for complex dealing with and within the EaP.

The deepening in relations between the EU and countries such as Moldova, Georgia, and Ukraine that led to the signature of Association Agreements and Deep and Comprehensive Free Trade Areas (DCFTAs), and most recently in the accession requests from these three countries, is different from the status of EU relations with Azerbaijan, for example, where the Partnership and Cooperation Agreement (PCA) signed in 1999, which has been under renegotiation for some years, is still in force.

This shows quite a different level of cooperation between these countries and the EU. Relations with Armenia progressed and the signature of the Comprehensive and Enhanced Partnership Agreement (CEPA) in November 2017, attests to the political commitment from both parties to the democratization and reform agenda, along with crisis management support, and to economic and trade cooperation that does not clash with Armenia's membership in the EAEU. Nevertheless, the EU's involvement in crisis management proved rather limited in the Nagorno-Karabakh conflict, with the EU called a "late comer" to the management of differences not only in this specific context in the post-Soviet space (Ghazaryan 2023; Deen et al. 2023; Wolff 2012, 200). Despite diplomatic efforts to bring the parties to the table, the EU did not have sufficient leverage to shift the opposing goals of the authorities in Yerevan and Baku, along with the broader external setting informing the conflict with countries such as Turkey, Iran, and Russia clearly playing strong in the developments on the ground. EU declarations condemning Azerbaijan's military operations against Nagorno-Karabakh and calls in the Autumn of 2023 for "Azerbaijan to reaffirm its unequivocal commitment to the territorial integrity of Armenia, in line with the 1991 Almaty Declaration" (EEAS 2023), positioned the EU but did not change the course of events. As for Belarus, it was always the least involved country in the development of institutionalized mechanisms for furthering cooperation with the EU, and currently given its close partnership with Russia, it is out of the EaP framework.

These differentials in policy options and readings about the EU have to be accounted for in this heterogeneous neighborhood that the Eastern space represents. The often quoted "ring of friends" (European Commission 2003, 4) that the EU sought to establish around its borders and that became a "ring of fire" (The Economist 2014), shows the limits of the EU in promoting transformational diplomacy in the neighboring countries. It became clear that these countries' policy agendas not always drove them closer to the EU, and that the Union's power of attraction was modeled to a great extent by its uneven capacity to further deepen relations with the neighbors. It became clear that without the membership prospect, more than the EU's policies were the neighbor countries' goals toward the EU that most determined their closer or less close relations. Thus, the shift from a framework designed by the EU to promote the narrative and the practices of cooperation and stability-building, through promoting "imitation practices" to a resilience-oriented approach and principled pragmatism comes less as a surprise, and more as a response to events on the ground.

It should, however, also be noted that if the EU's approach toward the Eastern neighborhood followed this rationale, Russia's approach to its neighborhood followed a not so different narrative on stability-building, despite the distinct policy orientation. Almost mirroring themselves, the two approaches in place promoted by the EU and by Russia to deal with the neighbors clashed (Freire 2020). This is even more evident when Russia describes the post-Soviet area as of primary interest and as part of its sphere of influence. Successive foreign policy and security documents in Russia highlight the post-Soviet space as fitting this narrative, and Ukraine becomes a significant illustration of this understanding (Freire and Heller 2018), with the article signed by Vladimir Putin published in the summer of 2021 reiterating the "one people" shared history and the artificial divides that were created with Western support. Putin (2021) writes "the wall that has emerged in recent years between Russia and Ukraine, between the parts of what is essentially the same historical and spiritual space, to my mind is our great common misfortune and tragedy. These are, first and foremost, the consequences of our own mistakes made at different periods of time. But these are also the result of deliberate efforts by those forces that have always sought to undermine our unity."

These distinct views were manipulated into narrative-building leading to a security-based discourse that allowed more insecurity. Russia described itself as excluded from European security, and subject to a policy of encirclement by the West, particularly through NATO enlargements; the EU considered the socialization of Russia in the NATO-Russia Council, the Council of Europe, and the EU-Russia partnership as examples of inclusion and confidence-building. These readings did not match. As much as the divide grows, security and bordering processes go hand-in-hand. The EU's conceptualization of its external borders' neighboring space is based on the Western liberal democratic model which was exported in EU relations with its neighbors, with the aim to influence and shape these countries' policy options. The identity-building component (Kolossov 2005, 614) in bordering processes is central, as the EU's conceptualization of its own external border well illustrates, in close connection with security perceptions.

Borders' performative role is, thus, key to unpack the meanings attributed to rebordering and debordering practices. In fact, "[b]orders not only have a different meaning for different actors but are a manifestation of power relations in society at different scales. In particular, they reflect the normative power of international organizations, including the EU and the power asymmetry between states in different fields" (Kolossov and Scott 2013, 13). This means the way the "other" is interpreted varies, applying both to intra-EU relations and to its external border processes. Relations within the EaP framework are relevant in this regard. A critical approach to bordering quickly unpacks borders' material and symbolic dimensions, meaning these are not simple territorial lines dividing political-administrative entities. Borders are much more complex bringing identity, social, religious, cultural, and other considerations that must be attended. The way Russia talks about the "walls" that emerged between Russia and Ukraine, refers to the "Russian world" or activates the civilizational narrative in its discourse to illustrate these non-material aspects that are so central in the construction of barriers. The extension of the conceptualization of the "Russian world" well beyond Russian physical borders (Suslov 2018, 330) shows how debordering seeks inclusive dynamics along with resistance processes, since not necessarily all actors are aligned. Mikhail Suslov links this concept with the "spheres of influence" approach as this provides ground for justifying the close links between Russia's policies and geographic areas on the basis of shared history, culture, language, and civilizational traits. In the case of countries like Georgia, Moldova, and Ukraine the resistance dynamics that have been developing to the aggressor show the understandings differ sharply across the post-Soviet space. Regarding European security, this is significant in the drawing of the hard and softer border with Russia and its allies. The discussion about "spheres of influence" becomes illustrative here, as this might mean the sovereign space of an actor is diminished, as when Russia talks about the post-Soviet area as its space of primary interest or accuses the EU of seeking to expand its "area of influence" toward this space through processes like the ENP and the EaP. The invasion of Ukraine is one more example of the "spheres of influence" practice (Costa and Barbé 2023, 432), bringing hard rebordering dynamics with both identitarian and territorial dimensions. By applying for EU membership, Moldova, Ukraine, and Georgia put forward a strong statement about their understanding of European security and of bordering practices.

The normative dimension of the border "implies a consideration that borders involve struggles that consist of multiple strategies of resistance against hegemonic discourses and control practices through which they are exercised (what we can call counter-hegemonic borderscapes)" (Brambilla 2014, 20). The bordering processes that accompany the rethinking of European security have this resistance against domination, aggression, and hegemony very much present. If on the one hand, this calls attention to the relevance of debordering processes promoted by the EU toward increasing security, it also highlights, on the other hand, the insecurities associated with these processes, built by contraposition, as the deterioration of relations with Russia show.

Moreover, borders' materiality is not only visible in territorial demarcation, but also in economic power, for example. The way borders become flexible in function of certain fluxes is demonstrative, as in the case of energy flows. Rebordering processes are becoming part of the new security dynamics following Russia's invasion, meaning the return of hard borders, territoriality, and militarization, along with the reshaping of narratives on identity, as visible in the self-other increasingly rigidified dichotomy. In the context of war in Ukraine, and Russia's main role in this, new dynamics emerged catapulting countries such as Moldova, Georgia, and Ukraine to a one-way EU course built against a major threat represented by Russia. This implies debordering dynamics toward the EU, whereas the rebordering of relations with Russia has been taking place, with a strong symbolic dimension. The resistance implied regarding Russia's hegemonic agenda in the post-Soviet space becomes evident. The reconceptualization of borders and security by the opposition became very much present in the narratives of the candidate countries. For example, Moldova's President Maia Sandu, underlined that

> [b]y applying to join the European Union, we want the world to know: we choose democracy over autocracy, liberty over oppression, peace over war, and prosperity over poverty. The EU candidate status gives us hope, a clear sense of direction, a unifying goal, an anchor, and a strong sense of belonging. Belonging to the free world. (Sandu, 2022, 21 September)

And Ukraine's president commented that

> [n]ow, when Ukraine is returning to its native European home, I believe that the Ukrainian language will be spoken here on many occasions from now – while recognizing special contribution to the European unity. Ukrainians will always make Europe stronger! [...] All of us in this room, all who stand with us in defense of freedom and Europe, are more than leaders and politicians, civil society activists and diplomats. We are all

> founders of peace. Exactly the founders of peace. This is our primary duty to our countries, to our Europe, and to our history. (Zelenskyy, 2023, 14 May)

Russia, which sought its inclusion in the European security order, through its actions excluded itself from the Western world, driving these states to seek formal integration in the EU. The balancing and multi-vectorial policies some of these states in the post-Soviet area were developing to manage relations with Russia, the EU, and other actors, have been objectively changed to a one-way course, in the cases of Moldova, Georgia, and Ukraine mostly directed at the EU. The goal of controlling the post-Soviet space developments seems to be eroding, with Moscow not having the capacity to influence the politics of all these states. The resort to military force seems to imply the limits of its political and economic means in keeping these countries close to its policies, even in the context of the imagined historically bound collective. The reborderization exercise here implied is deep, involving both material and symbolic dimensions, as clearly visible in the current violence in Ukraine. Russia's objective of weakening NATO resulted in the strengthening of the Atlantic Alliance's military presence on the Organization's eastern flank, and its enlargement to Finland and Sweden. NATO is clearly reinforced in its mission to provide for European security. The EU took a more expeditious and expressive action of unity in its response, despite the acknowledged differences between its 27 member states, reflected in the various sanctions packages already agreed. It also revamped talks about capacitation in terms of defense and has been using creatively some of its instruments to support Ukraine, such as the EPF. However, the old debate about balancing resources and capacities with the Atlantic Alliance in the provision of security is still high on the agenda. For some (van Hooft 2023; Zandee et al. 2020), this means the EU will fail short of using this opportunity to further deepen capacities in security and defense, for others (Howorth 2020; Tardy and Lindstrom 2019), it means transatlantic cooperation and NATO are strong enough. The United States returned to Europe in response to Russia's war of aggression in Ukraine and transatlantic ties were clearly strengthened. "A geopolitical Europe can be seen as a dual set of institutions with competing logics. When the EU's peace through integration fails, member states turn to NATO's peace through strength approach" (Orenstein 2023, 337).

Russia became a fundamental threat to European security and its pillars, and the EU's support to Ukraine has been very much driven and designed along the threat Russia poses to the rules-based order at the core of the EU's conceptualization of security in a broad sense. In this critical context, Russia has become the biggest threat to European security. It violated the European borders' regime and the territorial sovereignty of Ukraine, contributing to energy and food insecurity, and to political instability. Violating the rules-based order, and acting in an authoritarian way, Russia is questioning the very basic foundations of European security as promoted by the EU. In the Russian narrative, Ukraine appears as a means and an end. An end to the Russian objective of controlling Ukrainian territory by suppressing the exercise of its sovereignty, and a means because it involves a broader reading of European insecurity and the hegemonic international order, which Putin personifies in the United States and its allies, and in the NATO-enemy target. Russia frames the issue as an "existential threat" and in this way seeks to legitimize its aggressive, militarized responses in violation of the sovereignty of the Ukrainian state. But the narrative of protection and liberation also comes up against violence on the ground and the massive destruction of civilian infrastructure, in addition to once again implying the violation of a sovereign border. Putin argues that the "special military operation" that began on February 24, 2022, aims to restore the legitimacy of the Kiev government and force NATO and the United States, in particular, to backtrack on their aggressive policies (Putin 2022). Interestingly, despite Russia defining NATO as a main external threat, Moscow has in the past recognized Ukraine's right to join NATO, commenting that it should not interfere in the country's sovereign decisions; after the September 11 terrorist attacks, it allowed the use of military bases in Kyrgyzstan and Uzbekistan to support NATO actions in Afghanistan (Person and McFaul 2022); within the framework of the NATO-Russia Council, it participated in meetings and had a permanent military mission in Brussels, among other examples. The Russian narrative has become linear and circumscribed in its criticism of the West, highlighting the exercise of blame that has permeated Russian foreign policy and seeking to reverse responsibilities: "[t]hey were the ones who started the war. And we are now using force to finish it" (Putin 2023). The political space for debordering dynamics in wider Europe became minimal. The hard barriers between Western Europe and the countries seeking EU membership, and Russia, are reinforced each day fueled by the ongoing violence.

Conclusion

European security has been hit at its core. Russia's war in Ukraine and the full-scale invasion of the country in February 2022 are clear reminders of the violation of the rules-based order, of Ukraine's territorial integrity, and of the erection of hard walls between Russia's vision for European security and the Western approaches toward it. In this context, the EU has been reinforcing its security actorness, but with limits. The strategic documents that inform the EU's conceptualization of security translate the development of the EU itself, with the EUGS to some extent marking the geopolitical shift in the language and understanding of the place of the EU in the European security order, along with the most recent Strategic Compass making clear the insecurity resulting from Russia's aggressive actions and the need to reinforce EU's security and defense capacities in the changed context. The narrative in the EU clearly shows the relevance of combining the normative actor, with the rule of law, democracy, and human rights components that inform EU's actorness, with a more strategic approach, where principled pragmatism and resilience seek to provide a renewed framework for thinking security. The nexus between the internal and external dimensions of security has been highlighted and translated also in the relevance of the neighborhood and partnerships in the EU's positioning toward security. Bordering dynamics have traveled along the EU's conceptualization of security, materializing the perception of threats and responses to these. Conflicting debordering and rebordering dynamics in EU relations with EaP countries attest to their relevance, and to the need to unpack the material and non-material dimensions of these processes. Identity-building is in this regard central to the EU's security actorness, as analyzed.

European security is in a process of redefinition, where NATO keeps a central role, the OSCE has been relegated once more to inaction by the lack of consensus among member states, and the EU is seeking to reinforce its autonomous capacities in security and defense, in articulation with the Atlantic Alliance. The old debates are on the table, but the course seems to be one where the EU has been adopting new instruments and new language reinforcing its geopolitical and security toolkit, even if in limited ways. Whether these are trends that will be kept and reinforced is nevertheless to be seen, as old cracks are still present, and the debate about which configuration security and defense should have within the EU is still unfinished. The new enlargement driver that has been activated with candidate status granted to Moldova, Ukraine, and Georgia, adds to the agenda. The resistance dynamics that have developed in the post-Soviet area toward Russia have become materialized in these requests for accession. The self/other dynamic became surrounded by hard borders, militarized action, and an irreconcilable narrative. The implications for European security are that this will not be included in the conceptualization of wider Europe. Moreover, the choices implied in joining the Western security architecture or Russia's promoted framing are as clear as they are excluding. European security has changed and the EU's security actorness has also been changing, adapting to the new context and seeking to reposition the Union as a relevant actor in the contested security order in the making.

Acknowledgements The author developed this research work while the Luso-American Development Foundation (FLAD) Visiting Professor at the University of Georgetown, Washington, D.C.

References

Allison, R. 2018. Protective Integration and Security Policy Coordination: Comparing the SCO and CSTO. *The Chinese Journal of International Politics* 11 (3): 297–338, available at: https://doi.org/10.1093/cjip/poy008 (accessed 23 October 2023).

Andersson, J.J., and C.S. Cramer. 2023. The Impact on the European Security Architecture. EUISS Yearbook of European Security, European Union Institute for Security Studies (EUISS).

Averre, D. 2019. Russia Between East and West: Greater Eurasia Reconsidered. In *Five Years After Maidan: Towards a Greater EUrasia?*, ed. E. Korosteleva, Z. Paikin, and S. Paduano, 14–17. LSE IDEAS.

Bergmann, J., and P. Müller. 2021. Failing Forward in the EU's Common Security and Defense Policy: The Integration of EU Crisis Management. *Journal of European Public Policy* 28 (10): 1669–1687, available at: https://doi.org/10.1080/13501763.2021.1954064 (accessed 23 October 2023).

Biersack, J., and S. O'Lear. 2014. The Geopolitics of Russia's Annexation of Crimea: Narratives, Identity, Silences, and Energy. *Eurasian Geography and Economics* 55 (3): 247–269, available at: https://doi.org/10.1080/15387216.2014.985241 (accessed 23 October 2023).

Biscop, S. 2016. The EU Global Strategy: Realpolitik with European Characteristics. Egmont Institute, available at: http://www.jstor.com/stable/resrep06638 (accessed 23 October 2023).

Blockmans, S. 2020. Why the EU Needs a Geopolitical Commission. *CEPS*, September 15, available at: https://www.ceps.eu/why-the-eu-needs-a-geopolitical-commission/ (accessed 23 October 2023).

Brambilla, C. 2014. Exploring the Critical Potential of the Borderscapes Concept. *Geopolitics* 20 (1): 14–34, available at: https://doi.org/10.1080/14650045.2014.884561 (accessed 23 October 2023).

Casier, T. 2016. From Logic of Competition to Conflict: Understanding the Dynamics of EU-Russia Relations. *Contemporary Politics* 22 (3): 376–394, available at: https://doi.org/10.1080/13569775.2016.1201311 (accessed 23 October 2023).

Chappell, L., T. Exadaktylos, and P. Petrov. 2020. A More Capable EU? Assessing the Role of the EU's Institutions in Defence Capability Development. *Journal of European Integration* 42 (4): 583–600, available at: https://doi.org/10.1080/07036337.2019.1666115 (accessed 23 October 2023).

Costa, O., and E. Barbé. 2023. A Moving Target. EU Actorness and the Russian Invasion of Ukraine. *Journal of European Integration* 45 (3): 431–446, available at: https://doi.org/10.1080/07036337.2023.2183394 (accessed 23 October 2023).

Council of the EU. 2009. Joint Declaration of the Prague Eastern Partnership Summit, Brussels, 8435/09 (Presse 78), 7 May, available at: https://www.consilium.europa.eu/media/31797/2009_eap_declaration.pdf (accessed 23 October 2023).

Council of the EU. 2021. European Peace Facility, available at: https://www.consilium.europa.eu/en/policies/european-peace-facility/ (accessed 23 October 2023).

Council of the EU. 2022. Ukraine: Declaration by the High Representative on Behalf of the European Union on the Invasion of Ukraine by Armed Forces of the Russian Federation, February 24, available at: https://www.consilium.europa.eu/en/press/press-releases/2022/02/24/ukraine-declaration-by-the-high-representative-on-behalf-of-the-european-union-on-the-invasion-of-ukraine-by-armed-forces-of-the-russian-federation/ (accessed 23 October 2023).

De Haas, M. 2010. Medvedev's Alternative European Security Architecture. *Security and Human Rights* 1: 45–48, available at: https://www.shrmonitor.org/assets/uploads/2017/09/Haas-de-EOfinal.pdf (accessed 23 October 2023).

Deen, B., W. Zweers, and C. Linder. 2023. The EU in the South Caucasus. Navigating a Geopolitical Labyrinth in Turmoil. *Clingendael Report*, available at: https://www.clingendael.org/sites/default/files/2023-03/the-eu-in-the-south-caucasus.pdf (accessed 23 October 2023).

Della Sala, V. 2023. Ontological Security, Crisis and Political Myth: The Ukraine War and the European Union. *Journal of European Integration* 45 (3):

361–375, available at: https://doi.org/10.1080/07036337.2023.2183396 (accessed 23 October 2023).

Dijkstra, H. 2022. The War in Ukraine and Studying the EU as a Security Actor. *Instituto Affari Internazionali JOINT Brief*, 15, available at: https://www.iai.it/en/pubblicazioni/war-ukraine-and-studying-eu-security-actor (accessed 23 October 2023).

EEAS. 2021. The Shaping of a Common Security and Defence Policy. Strategic Communications. *EEAS*, August 10, available at: https://www.eeas.europa.eu/eeas/shaping-common-security-and-defence-policy_en (accessed 23 October 2023).

EEAS. 2023. Azerbaijan: Statement by the High Representative on Developments in Nagorno-Karabakh. *EEAS*, September 21, available at: https://www.eeas.europa.eu/eeas/azerbaijan-statement-high-representative-developments-nagorno-karabakh_en (accessed 23 October 2023).

EUGS. 2016. European Commission and High Representative of the EU for Foreign Affairs and Security Policy. 'Shared Vision, Common Action: A Stronger Europe. A Global Strategy for the European Union's Foreign and Security Policy'. Brussels.

European Commission. 2003. Communication from the Commission to the Council and the European Parliament, Wider Europe—Neighbourhood: A New Framework for Relations with Our Eastern and Southern Neighbours, Brussels. 11.3.2003 COM(2003) 104 final, available at: https://aei.pitt.edu/38141/1/com_(2003)_104.pdf (accessed 23 October 2023).

European Commission. 2004. Communication from the Commission, European Neighbourhood Policy Strategy Paper, Brussels, 12.5.2004 COM(2004) 373 Final, available at: https://neighbourhood-enlargement.ec.europa.eu/system/files/2019-01/2004_communication_from_the_commission_-_european_neighbourhood_policy_-_strategy_paper.pdf (accessed 23 October 2023).

Freire, M.R. 2020. EU and Russia Competing Projects in the Neighbourhood: An Ontological Security Approach. *Revista Brasileira de Política Internacional* 63 (1): 1–13, available at: https://doi.org/10.1590/0034-7329202000113 (accessed 23 October 2023).

Freire, M.R. 2022. Power and Security in the Mediterranean Global South and at the Eastern EU Borders: Russia in Syria and Ukraine. In *Border Crises and Human Mobility in the Mediterranean Global South*, ed. S. Panebianco, 67–89. Palgrave Macmillan, Cham: Springer International Publishing.

Freire, M.R., and R. Heller. 2018. Russia's Power Politics in Ukraine and Syria: Status-seeking Between Identity, Opportunity and Costs. *Europe-Asia Studies* 70 (8): 1185–1212, available at: https://doi.org/10.1080/09668136.2018.1521914 (accessed 23 October 2023).

Ghazaryan, N. 2023. The EU and the Nagorno-Karabakh Conflict: The Forty-Four-Day War and Its Aftermath. *European Foreign Affairs Review* 28 (1): 53–71, available at: https://doi.org/10.54648/eerr2023004 (accessed 23 October 2023).

Haroche, P. 2023. A 'Geopolitical Commission' Supranationalism Meets Global Power Competition. *Journal of Common Market Studies* 61 (4): 970–987, available at: https://doi.org/10.1111/jcms.13440 (accessed 23 October 2023).

Howorth, J. 2020. EU–NATO Cooperation: The Key to Europe's Security Future. In *EU-NATO Relations. Running on the Fumes of Informed Deconfliction*, ed. S.J. Smith, C. Gebhard, and N. Graeger, 152–157. London: Routledge.

Karaganov, S. 2018. The New Cold War and the Emerging Greater Eurasia. *Journal of Eurasian Studies* 9: 85–93, available at: https://doi.org/10.1016/j.euras.2018.07.002 (accessed 23 October 2023).

Kolossov, V. 2005. Border Studies: Changing Perspectives and Theoretical Approaches. *Geopolitics* 10: 606–632, available at: https://doi.org/10.1080/14650040500318415 (accessed 23 October 2023).

Kolossov, V., and J. Scott. 2013. Selected Conceptual Issues In Border Studies. *Belgeo* [Online] 1, available at: http://journals.openedition.org/belgeo/10532 (accessed 23 October 2023).

Lewis, D.G. 2018. Geopolitical Imaginaries in Russian Foreign Policy: The Evolution of 'Greater Eurasia'. *Europe-Asia Studies* 70 (10): 1612–1637, available at: https://doi.org/10.1080/09668136.2018.1515348 (accessed 23 October 2023).

Lo, B. 2009. Medvedev and the New European Security Architecture. Centre for European Reform Policy Brief, available at: https://www.cer.org.uk/sites/default/files/publications/attachments/pdf/2011/pbrief_medvedev_july09-741.pdf (accessed 23 October 2023).

Makarychev, A. 2018. Normative and Civilisational Regionalisms: The EU, Russia and Their Common Neighbourhoods. *The International Spectator* 53 (3): 1–19, available at: https://doi.org/10.1080/03932729.2018.1483630 (accessed 23 October 2023).

Mälksoo, M. 2016. From the ESS to the EU Global Strategy: External Policy, Internal Purpose. *Contemporary Security Policy* 37 (3): 374–388, available at: https://doi.org/10.1080/13523260.2016.1238245 (accessed 23 October 2023).

Orenstein, M.A. 2023. The European Union's transformation after Russia's attack on Ukraine. *Journal of European Integration* 45 (3): 333–342. https://doi.org/10.1080/07036337.2023.2183393

OSCE. 2015. Panel of Eminent Persons, available at: https://www.osce.org/networks/pep (accessed 23 October 2023).

Parker, N., and N. Vaughan-Williams. 2012. Critical Border Studies: Broadening and Deepening the 'Lines in the Sand' Agenda. *Geopolitics* 17 (4): 727–733, available at: https://doi.org/10.1080/14650045.2012.706111 (accessed 23 October 2023).

Person, R., and M. McFaul. 2022. What Putin Fears Most? *Journal of Democracy* 33 (2): 18–27, available at: https://www.journalofdemocracy.org/articles/what-putin-fears-most/ (accessed 23October 2023).

Putin, V. 2021. On the Historical Unity of Russians and Ukrainians, President of Russia official website, The Kremlin, available at: http://en.kremlin.ru/events/president/news/66181 (accessed 23 October 2023).

Putin, V. 2022. Address by the President of the Russian Federation, President of Russia official website, The Kremlin, available at: http://en.kremlin.ru/events/president/news/67843 (accessed 23 October 2023).

Putin, V. 2023. Presidential Address to Federal Assembly, President of Russia official website, The Kremlin, available at: http://en.kremlin.ru/events/president/news/70565 (accessed 23 October 2023).

Sandu, M. 2022. Statement by H.E. Maia Sandu, President of the Republic of Moldova, delivered at the General Debate of the 77th Session of the UN General Assembly, September 21, available at: https://presedinte.md/eng/discursuri/declaratia-es-maia-sandu-presedinta-republicii-moldova-la-dezbaterea-generala-din-cadrul-celei-de-a-77-a-sesiuni-a-adunarii-generale-a-onu (accessed 23 October 2023).

Sendhardt, B. 2013. Border Types and Bordering Processes. A Theoretical Approach to the EU/Polish-Ukrainian Border as a Multi-dimensional Phenomenon. In *Borders and Border Regions in Europe. Changes, Challenges and Chances*, ed. A. Lechevalier and J. Wielgohs, 21–43. Bielefeld: Transcript Verlag.

Strategic Compass. 2022. A Strategic Compass for Security and Defence. For a European Union that protects its citizens, values and interests and contributes to international peace and security, available at: https://www.eeas.europa.eu/sites/default/files/documents/strategic_compass_en3_web.pdf (accessed 23 October 2023).

Suslov, M. 2018. 'Russian World' Concept: Post-Soviet Geopolitical Ideology and the Logic of 'Spheres of Influence'. *Geopolitics* 23 (2): 330–353, available at: https://doi.org/10.1080/14650045.2017.1407921 (accessed 23 October 2023).

Tardy, T., and G. Lindstrom. 2019. The Scope of EU-NATO Cooperation. In NATO and the EU: The Essential Partners, ed. T. Tardy and G. Lindstrom, 5–14. Rome: NATO Defense College, available at: https://www.jstor.org/stable/resrep19964.6 (accessed 23 October 2023).

The Economist. 2014. Europe's Ring of Fire, September 20, available at: https://www.economist.com/europe/2014/09/20/europes-ring-of-fire?utm_medium=cpc.adword.pd&utm_source=google&ppccampaignID=17210591673&ppcadID=&utm_campaign=a.22brand_pmax&utm_content=conversion.direct-response.anonymous&gclid=CjwKCAjwkNOpBhBEEiwAb3MvvaMJp7HrT15S54SNU79fSV7G9ZszDTBPwTJBaqZyPaYpZFCggtbroRoCJZ0QAvD_BwE&gclsrc=aw.ds (accessed 23 October 2023).

van Hooft, P. 2023. Every Which Way But Loose: The United States, NATO Enlargement, European Strategic Autonomy and Fragmentation. In *Evaluating NATO Enlargement*, ed. J. Goldgeier and J.R.I. Shifrinson, 415–453. Cham: Palgrave Macmillan.

Wolff, S. 2012. The Limits of EU Conflict Management. In *Crisis Management and Conflict Prevention in Eastern Europe and the Balkans: Lessons for Ukraine-EU Cooperation*, ed. T. Malyarenko and S. Wolff, 187–216. Donetsk: Skhidniy Vidavnichiy Dom Publishing House.

Zandee, D., B. Deen, K. Kruijver, and A. Stoetman. 2020. European Strategic Autonomy in Security and Defence. Now the Going Gets Tough, It's Time to Get Going. *Clingendael Report*. The Hague: Netherlands Institute of International Relations 'Clingendael', available at: https://www.clingendael.org/sites/default/files/2020-12/Report_European_Strategic_Autonomy_December_2020.pdf (accessed 23 October 2023).

Zelenskyy, V. 2023. Europe and Other Parts of the World Should Not be a Place Where the Ambitions of Tyrants Destroy the Lives of Nations—Speech by President of Ukraine at the International Charlemagne Prize of Aachen award ceremony, May 14, available at: https://www.president.gov.ua/en/news/yevropa-ta-inshi-chastini-zemli-ne-mayut-buti-miscem-de-ambi-82901 (accessed 23 October 2023).

The Edification of the International Identity and Actorness of the EU: Exploring the Significance of EU's Engagement with Major Powers in Shaping its Global Self-Image

Vincent Bricart

Introduction

When it comes to investigating the way in which the European Union (EU) positions and represents itself on the international stage, academic literature certainly provides an abundance of insightful sources. Among them, two major streams of work emerge: first, studies devoted to the construction of the EU's collective identity within the context of international relations, and second, those focused on the definition of the role it aspires to assume as global actor, considering the capabilities it claims across various fields—in other words, its "actorness." These two themes—the EU's international identity and the narratives surrounding its status as an international actor—are closely intertwined and exert a significant influence on one another. The purpose of this chapter is to address, both conceptually and practically, the following research question: How does

V. Bricart (✉)
Department of Political Science, University of Liège, Liège, Belgium
e-mail: V.bricart@uliege.be

L. Lika and D. Riga (eds.), *EU Geopolitical Actorness in a Changing World*, https://doi.org/10.1007/978-3-031-81160-9_3

the EU's diplomatic engagement with major global powers, such as the United States, China, and Russia, shape its self-representation and identity as a global actor, and how does this engagement influence the EU's perception of its role and influence on the world stage?

To this end, the chapter employs a range of concepts from international relations theories. Within this framework, it argues that the way in which the EU positions itself in relation to other international actors directly impacts its own understanding of its role, nature, and capabilities for action. It is worth noting that these elements are neither static nor consistent, but are rather subject to change, depending on the major powers with whom the EU interacts, as well as on the broader international context in which it evolves. Consequently, the EU's self-representation undergoes continuous adaptation from European authorities in response to external geopolitical and economic developments, particularly in relation to the great powers.

To support this view, this chapter presents discursive analyses of the EU officials' statements regarding its relationship with the United States, China, and Russia. There are several reasons for choosing these three powers. First, they are key international players, economically and politically, representing significant "others" for the EU. Secondly, they offer both similarities and divergences, enabling a relevant comparative analysis. Third, each has or had a significant well-established relationship with the EU. The United States, as a major military and economic power, shares many values with the EU, but is geographically distant. Russia, although geographically close, differs sharply in terms of values and represents a major military power, while having limited economic influence outside the hydrocarbon sector. Finally, China is a leading authoritarian and economic power, although it has not yet reached the level of military power of the United States and Russia. It also stands out for its geographical distance and different values from those of the EU. These factors make it compelling to analyze how the EU has developed its identity in relation to these three powers, in order to better understand how each of them reflects an aspect of the EU's identity.

To do so, a combination of sources, including books, scientific articles, and official documents that offer diverse perspectives, historical context, and critical insights into the discursive strategies employed by the EU, have been analyzed and compiled in this chapter. The purpose is to demonstrate that the EU's international identity and actorness are anything but fixed and are rather undergoing substantial change over time, shaped by the processes of socialization through which the EU rationalizes its relations with external actors. This research promises to shed valuable light on how the EU positions and redefines itself within the global landscape in response to shifting dynamics in international politics and in its engagements with major powers. Furthermore, it underscores the importance of discursive analysis and narratives in understanding the mechanisms that underlie the evolution of the international identity of a political entity like the EU. Thus making it possible to explain how the EU's discursive choices, be they to align itself with or to distance itself from the great powers, affect both its identity and role development, as well as and its relevance as an international actor.

The chapter is structured as follows: the first section delves into the complexities associated with the edification of the EU's self-representation. Following that, the second section scrutinizes the influence of positional theories and narrative construction in the process. Lastly, the third and fourth sections elaborate on the evolution of the EU's narrative regarding its identity and global role by outlooking both the strategic documents and partnerships of the EU from the last two decades.

Three Sides of the Same Coin? EU Self-Representation, International Identity, and Actorness

How does the EU's international identity relate to its self-representation and role on the world stage? In the field of international relations, identities emerge from the complex interactions between actors and are influenced by an actor's own values and norms, as well as by how others perceive this core actor. Thus, an actor's international identity is, therefore, the product of internal and external factors, shaped by relations between states (Reus-Smit 2005). Regarding the EU's international identity, it can be defined as "the images of individuality and distinctiveness ('selfhood') held and projected by an actor and formed (and modified over time), through relations with significant 'others'" (Jepperson et al. 1996, 59). In this context, international identity is of considerable importance for the EU, as it defines its values, characteristics, and actions on the world stage and describes what distinguishes it from others, from its own perspective (Tereszkiewicz 2020). Moreover, it influences the way the EU perceives the other international actors with whom it is engaged (Pishchikova and Piras 2017). In this context, the notion of EU distinctiveness is particularly highlighted in the studies of European integration (Manners and Whitman 2003; Bretherton and Vogler 2005). Indeed, it is often argued that the EU represents a new form of power, implicitly claimed as a superior and more civilized in its approach to traditional power dynamics (Mitzen 2006; Karolewski 2011). It translates into a foreign policy that asserts the EU's special role on the international stage as an actor seeking to promote its norms and ideals without resorting to force (Karolewski 2011; Bengtsson 2021). This has led researchers to successively describe the EU as a civilian power (Duchêne 1972) and a normative power (Manners 2002). This conception of power is closely linked to the edification process of European identity (Manners 2009).

However, over the last two decades (2000–2024), the EU's identity has exhibited signs of fragility. A series of internal crises, shifts in the global landscape, and the gap between the EU's advocated values, its practical capabilities, and the expectations of other actors (Hill 1993) have ultimately led to a scaling back of the EU's ambition for civilian and normative power projection. As a result, the EU has at times adopted a more pragmatic approach in certain areas (Tereszkiewicz 2020; Pishchikova and Piras 2017).

Due to its vulnerabilities, the EU places significant emphasis on its global image, on the recognition of its identity, and on its credibility at the international stage, as these factors are crucial for enhancing the effectiveness of its international policy (Mälksoo 2016). However, this aspiration doesn't guarantee that other international actors will fully acknowledge the role it aims to undertake or that they will perceive it as such, which consequently affects the stability of the EU's identity (Freire et al. 2022). In order for the EU to assert itself in the global arena and develop an effective foreign policy, it needs to establish its credibility as an international player. This involves gaining widespread recognition of both its identity and role narratives by skilfully navigating the delicate equilibrium between the normative aspects of its vision and a pragmatic, reality-based approach firmly grounded in the Union's fundamental principles (Karolewski and Ireneusz 2011; Lindemann and Ringmar 2012; Gustafsson 2016). In practical terms, to enhance its impact on global issues, the EU must align its internal narratives with its objectives, capabilities, and the external expectations of others in the changing international context (Hill 1993; Simão 2022). It is from this desire that the concept of "actorness" emerged.

The concept of "EU actorness" pertains to the study of the EU's capacity to act proactively and intentionally in relation to other international actors (Sjöstedt 1977). This notion can also be defined as a "role conception" that links the dimensions of the EU's identity and foreign policy, in order to better understand what it accomplishes or seeks to accomplish in global politics (Aggestam 2006). The strength and recognition of the EU's actorness vary across sectoral areas. The Union's influence is typically more pronounced in areas where its normative and financial tools are particularly effective, such as in global humanitarian, developmental, and environmental policies. Its trade policy, in particular, stands out as the most prominent field where it can exert its actorness. By contrast, it plays a marginal role in security and defense policies, where hard power (namely military aspects) capabilities predominate (Telò 2009; Hill et al. 2023).

The Edification of EU Global Self-Image

In light of the earlier developments, it appears that the EU's dialogues and social interactions with other global powers on specific issues serve two main objectives. First, from a conceptual perspective, socialization helps to shape and reinforce the EU's distinct international identity. Second, from a pragmatic viewpoint, dialogues are the means through which the EU pursues recognition from other powers concerning its identity and its extensive actorness. The subsequent sections will delve into the theoretical aspects of how interaction and narratives can be used to realize these objectives and explore the practical tools employed by the EU for this purpose.

Tell Me Who the Other Is, and I Will Tell You Who I Am

In this section, positional theories are applied to explain how social discourses contribute to the identity formation of a state or an institution by analyzing how interactions can emphasize either shared attributes or distinctions in relation to other actors (Davies and Harré 1990; Harré and Van Lagenhove 1999). As previously discussed, the identities of international actors are not immune to external influence and are also subject to change over time. Moreover, actors' identities carry international implications, both as transmitters of their own identities or as observers of others. Consequently, identity is partly constructed through relational interaction processes, emphasizing the articulation of the "self," the "other" and the broader context (Rumelili 2004).

The nature of this "other" has profoundly evolved since the inception of the European project. During the Cold War, the otherness establishing the EU's identity was based on a temporal otherness, distinguishing it from its own past. This process thus presented the EU as a postmodern actor engaged in self-criticism by asserting a "self" based on norms, values, and attitudes perceived as superior and more civilized, in opposition to that violent and destructive "other" represented by previous centuries, culminating in both World Wars (Wæver 1996; Pishchikova and Piras 2017).

However, the waves of geographical enlargement in the 1990s and 2000s gradually prompted a redefinition of the concepts underlying the "inclusion" and "exclusion" of the "self" and the "other." As a result, it became necessary for the EU to rest the distinction on more geopolitical and contemporary grounds, in order to highlight otherness (Neumann 1998; Diez 2004). Since then, adherence to or rejection of EU values and norms has become a central criterion in the construction of EU identity. At the core of this approach is the idea that the EU seeks to strengthen its identity as a global actor on the basis of its own values and characteristics by comparing them with those of other actors (Song and Hall 2019).

Consequently, the construction of the "self" entails defining the boundaries of identity, that is, determining which characteristics and values are included and which are excluded (Joenniemi 2009). In the socialization process, this articulation of the "self" is expressed through comparison with the "other," either by association—emphasizing shared values and traits—or by dissociation—highlighting points of divergence that render the "self" as distinct, unique, or even "superior" to the "other" (Rumelili 2004; Karolewski 2011).

Various ways of positioning the "self" in relation to "others" can be observed in the context of the EU's international identity. European identity is often defined in contrast to other actors, with distinctions that may carry connotations of superiority or inferiority regarding certain traits. However, it is important to emphasize that these distinctions do not imply a total rejection of what the "other" represents, nor do they specifically target a single country. For instance, a state geographically close to the

EU might be recognized as European by association, yet factors such as an authoritarian regime, disregard for human rights, or diverging approaches to power may constitute elements of exclusion and reinforce the singularity of the EU identity (Morozov and Rumelili 2012). Furthermore, a high level of adherence to the values of another state does not necessarily mean that distinctive features cannot be put forward. For example, a state that shares a set of common values important to the EU, such as democracy or the upholding of international peace and security, may be presented as similar to the EU, but it may also be dissociated from the EU identity by rejecting singular elements of the "other," such as the use of military force and unilateralism (Bengtsson 2021; Jankovski 2022).

The EU may, on the contrary, seek to associate itself with certain "others" in order to elevate and associate its identity with that of a power of global importance by asserting that it has the same responsibility, willingness, and ability as the "other" to provide leadership in the world (Manners and Whitman 1998). Furthermore, these shared narratives and projects between actors can lead to a mutual identification reinforcing the solidity of their respective identities (Mitzen 2006; Jankovski 2022; Klose 2023). Conversely, by distancing itself from certain powers, the EU signals that its identity and policies are shaped in contrast to those of the "other" (Song and Hall 2019).

Despite the adoption of various strategies by one actor to construct its identity, as mentioned earlier, there are no guarantees that the "other" will accept all the tenants of the defined identity. This is not without consequences. Indeed, the "other" plays a subversive role by accepting, negotiating, or challenging the EU's narrative of its identity and the role of the "self" it has constructed (Morozov and Rumelili 2012). This dynamic can have positive or negative repercussions on the consolidation of the EU's identity, influencing its international policies and self-identity needs. The acknowledgment of the EU's identity and leadership by other powers involves two key aspects: its distinctiveness and its relevance (Blanc 2023). As mentioned earlier, the EU's unique and innovative character is essential in understanding its collective identity. Therefore, when an external actor endorses the way the EU perceives itself and distinguishes itself, these elements are reinforced (Greenhill 2008; Lindemann and Ringmar 2012; Tallberg and Zürn 2019). If, on the contrary, the other challenges this vision, it can pose an existential threat to the EU's identity, weakening its policy, and alienating the actors in question from each other to varying degrees (Gustafsson 2016).

When it comes to recognizing the EU as a significant global actor, despite its ambitions to expand its global presence, as explained earlier, it continues to encounter resistance from other international actors for several reasons. There is often a discrepancy between the roles that the EU seeks to fulfill in addressing global challenges and the roles that other actors expect or believe the EU can or should undertake. Indeed, they may have expectations, whether modest or ambitious, that may diverge from the EU's real capabilities (Hill 1993; Bengtsson and Elgström 2012; Blanc 2023). Furthermore, the "other" must have an interest in recognizing the EU as a relevant international player, and for this, more than mere presence, the perception of the EU's ability to act in specific areas is essential (Gehring et al. 2013). Many international actors still assess the EU based on the nation-state model, affecting their expectations of the EU's actions and approaches (Simão 2022). If one compares the EU's action to that of a state, it is often perceived as insufficient, while if one considers it as that of a multilateral organization, it may be perceived as illegitimate.

The EU's organizational complexity is another factor that negatively impacts how it is perceived. By juggling its quest for autonomy, its declared objectives, its capacity, and the simultaneous presence of its member states with their bilateral policies, the EU makes it difficult for some to understand its identity. This complexity, coupled with concerns about its coherence, reliability, and internal crises, fuels contestation of the EU's presence at various levels (Icaza 2010).

The Union, therefore, faces challenges in terms of recognition and legitimacy as an international actor. Nevertheless, establishing shared narratives and joint projects with other international actors can significantly strengthen its identity and credibility. The process of recognizing one's identity through dialogue passes through three stages: the pursuit of recognition, its attainment through a perceived alignment with self-perception, and its anchoring through visual, discursive, and practical elements (Blanc 2023). Recognition of these elements via diplomatic dialogues, as formalized institutionalized face-to-face interactions, is, therefore, essential to fulfill this need for recognition.

The Significance of Words and Context

Dialogues, whether written or verbal, are central to EU decision-makers, serving as key tools for formulating, structuring, and asserting the EU's identities and roles (Checkel 2006a; Karolewski 2011; Carta and Wodak 2015). These discourses are more than just words, they shape ideas, orchestrate social interactions, and influence reality through language (Carta and Morin 2014; Garnizova 2022; Jankovski 2022). In the context of international relations theories, some focus on foreign policy discourses and their role in constructing the meaning and social reality surrounding the state that emits them (Carta and Morin 2014).

The founding narratives of the EU, based on the emergence of a political order centered on democratic principles and prosperity after the destruction of war, as well as the discourses surrounding the EU's civilian and normative power in the 2000s, have played a significant role in the construction and influence of the EU's international identity (Diez 2005; Karolewski 2011). Today, these narratives remain crucial in shaping the EU's identity and reinforcing its stature as a significant international actor (Della Sala 2018). They not only influence how the EU perceives itself but also affect how it is viewed by other global actors, playing a vital role in fostering a sense of continuity and stability within European identity.

Therefore, highlighting the way in which European policymakers, particularly those at the European Commission and at the EU Council, use discourses and official documents to structure, promote, and transform the EU's identity, with the aim of strengthening its legitimacy and its self-perception in different thematic areas is significant (Della Sala 2018; Garnizova 2022). It should be noted that while the EU does not speak with a single voice on foreign policy, its formulation falling within the remit of the EU Council, the European Commission's initiatives also stand out because of the decisive role it plays in guiding and implementing EU action on an international scale and to conduct international dialogues (Carta and Morin 2014). Furthermore, the European Commission's narratives on relations with the great powers highlight how the EU shapes its identity through the collaboration and the development of shared narratives with its partners, while simultaneously distinguishing from its rivals (Klose 2023). This approach is reflected in the language used in the strategic documents issued by the EU, widely acknowledged as instruments for shaping the EU's identity and role (Wendt 1999; Checkel 2006b). This is also true of the way the EU implements and discusses its strategic partnerships with other major world powers (Blanco 2016; Song and Hall 2019; Ferreira-Pereira and Smith 2021).

Among the various documents issued by the EU relevant to the analysis of identity construction, this chapter can distinguish strategic documents such as the 2003's *European Security Strategy* (ESS) (CEU 2003), the 2016's *European Union Global Strategy* (EUGS) (European External Action Service (EEAS) 2016) and the 2022's *Strategic Compass for Security and Defence* (SCSD) (European External Action Service (EEAS) 2022). Numerous studies have analyzed those documents, their differences, and implications (Mälksoo 2016; Wagner and Anholt 2016; Bengtsson 2021; Müftüler-Bac et al. 2024). Those documents explicitly illustrate the EU's desire to define its presence in coherence with the values and fundamental principles set out in its founding treaties (Bengtsson 2021). Thus, they represent identity-building exercises, setting out the EU's values, interests, and priorities in terms of security and foreign policy at three distinct periods. They reflect the EU's identity as an international actor and highlight the discursive and normative elements that influence its external action, and are, therefore, essential elements of the EU's foreign policy identity discourse. Academic analyses of these texts reveal a growing consideration of external references in European strategies, further emphasizing the relationship between the European "self" with the "others" (Pishchikova and Piras 2017). This highlights processes of self-definition, self-positioning, and relationships with other international actors. Unlike an approach that would emphasize a single "anti-self," this identity is formed in relation to various "others" (Morozov and Rumelili 2012). They establish a connection between the development of the European Union's identity and actorness with the changes in the international system (Bengtsson 2021; Simão 2022).

In addition, strategic partnerships between the EU and other powers are of considerable importance to the EU's identity and role on the world stage. They reflect the constant evolution of geopolitical and economic realities, forcing the EU to skilfully juggle its economic interests with its normative values. The Union thus strives to adjust its strategy in order to remain relevant and effective in an ever-changing world. Whether with established or rising/emerging powers, these partnerships and their evolution through time offer opportunities for the EU to develop and adapt its international profile, while positioning itself as a major player in world affairs and seeking recognition of its role from its partners. They are the product of various dynamics that shape a narrative marked by both cooperation and differentiation (Blanco 2016; Song and Hall 2019; Ferreira-Pereira and Smith 2021; Müftüler-Bac et al. 2024).

In regard to what has been developed, it is clear that the EU's identity-building process is in a state of perpetual transformation. It operates within a set of established reference systems that guide its behavior in known and predictable contexts. However, external threats or internal crises have the potential to disrupt these reference systems if they are found to be inadequate. In such cases, the EU may need to reevaluate and adjust its approach. These reassessments not only influence how it sees itself and its surroundings but also impact its positioning in relation to other entities. As a result, the EU's international identity is not immutable, but rather in constant evolution. Geopolitical changes may prompt it to review its international role and the way it defines the "self" and the "other" as a result of external pressures and internal adjustments initiated by itself (Pishchikova and Piras 2017; Jankovski 2022; Tereszkiewicz 2020).

In recent decades, the EU has grappled with global and regional upheavals, such as Russia's reemergence as a regional security threat, China's ascendancy as a major economic and geopolitical player, the United States diminishing global leadership as it shifts focus to Asia, the emergence of new global powers reshaping geopolitical dynamics, and the erosion of multilateralism. All of these are amid frequent internal crises. The EU has had to adapt to these pressures, striving to maintain its global standing and influence, resulting in notable alterations to its international role (Freire et al. 2022). In the following sections, this chapter will examine how the EU's self-image has evolved in response to global dynamics. It will first explore the changes in the EU's self-perception and identity as expressed in its strategic documents. Then, it will analyze relevant scientific literature to understand the shifts in the EU's social positioning in the context of its strategic partnerships with major global powers.

Self-Perception and Its Implications in Strategic Documents

The central conception of the EU's role, as set out in ESS from 2003, was based on three fundamental elements. First, the EU was seen as a global power, extending its influence beyond the realm of trade to encompass wider spheres of influence. Second, the EU was seeking to cooperate with other players sharing similar values, in particular the North Atlantic Treaty Organization (NATO) and the United States. Third, the EU positions itself as an advocate of security linked to development and human rights, aspiring to a more equitable and secure multilateral system (CEU 2003;

Bengtsson 2021). In the 2016's EUGS, the EU's vision of its role also had three main dimensions. First, the Union was defining itself as a pragmatic, principled actor, reconciling a realistic assessment of its external environment with idealistic aspirations. Second, the EU saw itself as a responsible contributor to global governance, seeking to deliver global public goods and reform the multilateral order. Third, the EU was seen as a key player in regional security, with expanded responsibilities and a crucial role in promoting strategic autonomy and building regional cooperation (EEAS 2016; Bengtsson 2021). In the 2022's SCSD, the EU once again aspires to assert itself as a global player, but it also asses its willingness to defend its interests and values by working with its strategic partners. It thus emphasizes its strategy on defense and security and presents for the first time a shared EU assessment of the threats facing the continent, a first step toward establishing a common strategic culture. Furthermore, it seeks to give the EU an autonomous capacity for action, while complementing NATO. Finally, it positions itself as a defender of its fundamental values (democracy, human rights, rule of law), particularly in response to foreign powers threatening these values (EEAS 2022; Müftüler-Bac et al. 2024; Varma 2024).

Although similarities are evident, it is notable that these strategies and the discourses underpinning them have been adjusted in response to geopolitical and geo-economic developments. While in the context of the writing of the ESS, European soft power and the global liberal order faced little to no significant opposition, in the context of the writing of EUGS, the EU was confronted with a growing global contestation of its influence, internal crisis (Brexit on the top of it), and regional insecurity forcing it to reassess its role and to adapt to external pressures (Bengtsson 2021; Müftüler-Bac et al. 2024). Furthermore, between 2003 and 2016, the EU encountered challenges stemming from the misalignment between its role as a norm-promoting international actor, its core interests, and a lack of clearly defined objectives. These issues, in turn, exerted a detrimental influence on its diplomatic relationships with other actors (Simão 2022). The SCSD, for its part, was drafted (2020–2022) in a context of rising geopolitical tensions and security threats, notably with Russia (cyberattacks, political interference, and the invasion of Ukraine), China (concerns related to its increased ambition and influence), the United States (trade wars, concerns about NATO reliability, rivalry with China). All of that combined with the rise of atypical challenges like the COVID-19 pandemic.

The evolution of the EUGS and of the SCSD, compared to the ESS, also mirrors shifts in European perspectives on the EU's role in global affairs. It shows that the EU is placing increasing emphasis on its ability and the effectiveness of its actions to maintain peace in Europe and to prove its relevance to the people who make it up. It is questioning its role as a security actor, while its concerns persist about its place among the traditional players in global security, while retaining its vision placing importance on norms, values, and multilateralism (Mälksoo 2016; Bengtsson 2021). The EU's ability to rapidly adapt and strengthen its resilience in response to external crises across a broadening range of internal and external issues has become a central theme in its discourse. This has fostered a pragmatic problem-solving approach that recognizes challenges, stays optimistic about solutions, and strategically targets its most sensitive sectors (Wagner and Anholt 2016; Wrange et al. 2024).

In the end, the ESS, established just four years after the launch of the Common Security and Defense Policy (CSDP), primarily had doctrinal significance and was characterized by a bold and confident vision of the EU, reflecting a positive context. Despite its name, it was not designed to be a grand strategy. By contrast, the EUGS presents a more pragmatic and forward-thinking approach, aimed at fostering constructive reflection on the crises and challenges facing the EU. It also outlines how the organization intended to address these issues. Finally, in the SCSD, the EU seeks to deepen the issues already raised in the EUGS while placing greater emphasis on security and defense issues. Russia's full-scale invasion of Ukraine, just two months before the publication of the final draft, further increased this need (Howorth 2016; Wrange et al. 2024). Thus, the self-perception of the EU's role in strategic documents has evolved between 2003 and 2022 to become more pragmatic, adaptable, and mature. This reflects the EU's efforts to better define its role and objectives by learning from its past experiences. Thus demonstrating an internal process of self-reflection, learning, and resilience in response to its identity crises. These have enabled the EU to address increasing external challenges and crises and to strengthen its role on the international stage, all without undergoing major institutional reforms (Bicchi et al. 2024).

The Dynamics of Engagement Processes with Major Powers

The relationship between the EU and the rest of the world has undergone significant change. Against this backdrop, the rest of the chapter will analyze what ESS, UEGS, and SCSD as well as the EU's strategic partnerships with China, the United States, and Russia, reveal about the impact of these association processes on the EU's identity.

The Transatlantic Relation: The Elder Brother I'm Trying to Distinguish Myself from

Since its foundation, the European project has enjoyed a close relationship with the United States. In fact, the United States can be considered as the most significant "other" for the edification of its identity (Joenniemi 2009). While from a historical point of view, this relationship has considerably influenced the process of European integration, on the ideological side the transatlantic relationship represents a pivotal point in the EU's positioning on the international stage. The post-Cold War identity of the EU was largely shaped by its adherence to the liberal international order created by the United States, but also by its contrast with some traits of American power. Taking into account the state of this relationship, its ups and downs, its convergences and divergences, is, therefore, crucial to understand the evolving narratives surrounding the EU's identity and its actorness (Diez 2005; Klose 2023).

The transatlantic relationship is frequently represented by tangible metrics, such as economic data and charts. However, it is also a social construct shaped by narratives surrounding the identities, values, and shared interests of the two parties involved (Joenniemi 2009). The common narrative underpinning this relationship is based on mutual adherence to democratic and neoliberal values, shared concerns for international peace and global stability, an adherence to the institutions of the liberal international order (LIO), and extensive economic, cultural, and political ties (Bricart 2022). Despite these convergences, distinctive elements in EU narratives about its identity have been present for many years. Thus, from a European point of view, the United States tends to project and impose, sometimes by force on the contrary to the EU, its norms and interests without necessarily subscribing to international treaties, whereas the EU favors multilateral dialogue, the promotion of international norms and civilian power (Diez 2005; Joenniemi 2009; Klose 2023). All this is combined with internal societal divergences. As a result, the EU narrative tends to present itself as a distinct and superior alternative model to the United States, because it perceives itself as more civilized and attractive, while also being better adapted to the globalized international society (Karolewski 2011). The transatlantic relationship is thus structured by a subtle balance between convergence and distinctiveness, particularly on the EU side (Joenniemi 2009).

Over the past two decades, the EU's relationship and identity positioning *vis-à-vis* the United States have experienced significant shifts. The George W. Bush administration (2001–2009) was marked by a growing rift between the EU and the United States. The Bush administration made a distinction between what they called the "old" and the "new" Europe, with the aim of (successfully) dividing EU member states over their alignment with American power, ultimately undermining European political cohesion (Zaborowski 2006). Furthermore, Bush's interventionist agenda, which sought to promote democracy through military means, contrasted sharply with the EU's self-image as a "force for good" and a "normative power." This clash highlighted the differences between the United States' unilateral, interventionist tendencies and the EU's preference for multilateralism and diplomacy, emphasizing its role as a more civil and consensus-driven actor on the global stage (Dannreuther and Peterson 2006).

The transatlantic relations during Barack Obama years (2009–2017) have been characterized by a strong emphasis on certain values, particularly in the pursuit of a common multilateral approach to address international crises and efforts to revitalize or reform the international system. In this regard, the Transatlantic Trade and Investment Partnership (TTIP) represented a significant effort by the EU and the United States to align and integrate their mutual norms, values, and standards by establishing common rules and institutions. However, concerns over its potentially intrusive nature and fears about a common uniformity that would not comply with European values and standards sparked major resistance in many EU member states. Paradoxically, this resistance reinforced the emphasis on European specificities (Morin et al. 2016; Alexoaei and Cojanu 2017; Bricart 2021). Thus, in spite of these convergences over values between the executives in charge from both parties, there was no increased cooperation or development of more institutionalized and shared narratives during this period. This can also be attributed to the fact that the EU was in the midst of reform with the implementation of the Lisbon Treaty (2007), which limited external recognition of the EU's role and capabilities beyond trade, as it had not yet proven fully effective in its new functions. In addition, the United States regarded the EU as less relevant in security and defense matters compared to NATO or its member states. Finally, on the economic front, the United States prioritized the Trans-Pacific Partnership (TPP), which slowed down the TTIP negotiations and prevented ultimately its conclusion, due to the reasons mentioned above (Smith 2021).

Throughout Donald Trump's term in office (2017–2021), his administration's doctrine, marked by a mixture of sovereignty, protectionism, and nationalism, created deep concern within the EU due to its incompatibility with European values centered on international rules, multilateral cooperation, and norms. In addition, the Trump administration had adopted a transactional and confrontational approach, regarding the EU as an underperforming ally or an adversary, even questioning its legitimacy in certain areas, that further exacerbated transatlantic tensions. This shift intensified internal EU discussions about dissociating itself from its American counterpart. In fact, the years of the Trump administration have heightened transatlantic tensions and prompted diverging perceptions of the roles of the EU and the United States (Tereszkiewicz 2020; Riddervold and Newsome 2018). The EU was increasingly driven to reconsider its position toward them, weighing whether they were now a challenge rather than a supportive partner. By undermining the reliability of the United States as a close ally and partner, this administration prompted the EU to explore its own strategic autonomy and to strengthen defense cooperation between its member states (Bricart 2022; Bengtsson 2021). The EU has also taken advantage of the United States' protectionism and its criticism of multilateralism to position itself as a staunch defender of the rules-based global multilateral and trade order, while adopting a more proactive stance in other diplomatic and economic areas in light of the United States' actions (Bricart 2022; Garnizova 2022).

In the 2016 UEGS, the absence of any explicit reference to the United States as a key partner in this context is noted compared with the 2003 document, where they were more present (Bengtsson 2021). In the long term, although there are signs that this relationship could evolve toward a more pragmatic and transactional approach, the common value base between the United States and the EU is nonetheless highly resilient in the face of a common external threat (Jankovski 2022; Bricart 2022). This statement is upheld by the Strategic Compass that reaffirms that, consequently to the Russian war in Ukraine, the United States remains, mainly through NATO, a key and indispensable partner for the EU in security matters even though the EU wishes to act independently when required by European interests (EEAS 2022). Over time, the United States has evolved from an irreplaceable partner in the ESS, to a core partner in the EUGS, to finally end up the EU's staunchest and most important partner in the SCSD (Müftüler-Bac et al. 2024).

EU-Russia Process of Association: From Potential Apprentice to Existential Threat

The strategic partnership between the EU and Russia from the late 1990s, initially for the EU a pioneering venture involving a non-Western partner, has since proved to be complex and unsuccessful. This relationship emerged as the EU sought to strengthen its international presence, notably through the construction of the Common Foreign and Security Policy (CFSP) (Haukkula 2021). In the 1990s, the EU and Russia were aiming to establish a strategic partnership based on shared values. The EU's declared aim was to promote Russia's democratization and Europeanization, thereby fostering its economic and political transition with the ultimate aim of strengthening security and stability in Europe (European Council 1999) which mirrors European enlargement and neighborhood policy. At the time, Russia was seen by the EU as a potential apprentice on its path toward democratization and political transition (Deriglazova 2022). However, it is now clear that the EU's goals toward Russia were not met. Over the past two decades, Russia has evolved into a centralized, authoritarian power, now seen as a major threat to security in Europe.

Much of this stems from a lack of common understanding of how to achieve their original cooperation objectives. While the EU emphasized the need for practical implementation of normative convergence, Russia preferred mere declarations of intent and was resistant to the EU's "post-sovereignty" approach (Haukkala 2021). Indeed, Russia's main objective was to be recognized as an equal global player alongside the EU and the United States, while at the same time emphasizing its cultural belonging to Europe and insisting on its political and cultural distinctiveness (Morozov and Rumelili 2012). These divergences included issues such as human rights, as well as authoritarian and anti-democratic turns, with Russia claiming its "moral sovereignty" over the core values the EU sought to see implemented (Della Sala 2018). The EU's inability to enforce its normative demands on Russia through coercion has also damaged its credibility in the latter's eyes (Haukkala 2021).

The EU's association with this significant "other" was also negatively influenced by its discourse and narrative about Russia. The notion of Europeanness has often been defined in opposition to authoritarian Russia (Morozov and Rumelili 2012). This distinction has played a central role in the construction of the EU's identity, as Russia has long been perceived as a remnant of the European past that needed to be overcome (Browning 2017). Ironically, this exclusion of the Russian model, while weakening political cooperation, has helped shape the EU's identity by making Russia a geopolitical "other" to be clearly distinguished from EU values, thereby strengthening the EU's collective identity (Morozov and Rumelili 2012).

Simultaneously, economic priorities frequently overshadowed Russia's political transformation in EU-Russia relations, leading to a transactional approach rather than a values-based one (Jankovski 2022). This deepened the gap in how Russia and the EU perceive one another, emphasizing the dichotomy between Western and Eastern Europe, while weakening the EU's image in Russian eyes as a defender of democratic values, leading them to perceive the EU and European nations as hypocrites (Morozov and Rumelili 2012; Haukkala 2021).

Moreover, attempts to negotiate an institutionalized strategic partnership between the EU and Russia were undermined by several major events, including the color revolutions in Georgia and Ukraine in the early 2000s, the war in Georgia in 2008, Russia's annexation of Crimea in March 2014, and finally the full-scale invasion of Ukraine in 2022 (Freire et al. 2022; Müftüler-Bac et al. 2024). These developments have drastically shifted the EU's stance toward Russia transforming its view of Russia from a "potential partner" in the 2003 ESS to a "disruptive actor" in the 2016 EUGS, and ultimately to a "destabilizing force to be contained and countered" in the 2022 SCSD (EEAS 2022). Since 2014, relations between them have been marked by the end of what remained of the strategic partnership to be replaced by mutual sanctions, illustrating growing divergences in terms of values and objectives (Deriglazova 2022). Russia's evolving assertiveness, unpredictability, and militaristic stances have cemented its perception as a significant threat to security and peace in Europe, thereby reinforcing the unity among EU member states in their opposition to Russia (Kanet 2018; Tereszkiewicz 2020).

Ultimately, the narratives constructed by the EU and Russia have exerted a profound influence on their mutual perception. Over time, these narratives have become sources of ideological and security concerns, as each side was challenging the other's legitimacy, while simultaneously attempting to sway states in their shared neighborhood toward their respective view. This dynamic can be described as an "ontological security dilemma" (Browning 2017; Della Sala 2018).

EU's Association with China: Let's Keep It Professional, Shall We?

Unlike its relationship with the United States or Russia, interaction and cooperation between the EU with China in the 1990s were not necessarily seen at first as obvious, mainly due to major differences in their respective political systems and to the geographical distance separating them. At the outset, the construction of this relationship was strongly influenced by the foreign policy identities that these two players sought to shape. The EU sought in its economic relations with China to establish its status as an international player following the creation of the CFSP in 1992, initially by attempting to promote European values such as democracy, human rights, and the rule of law, as well as Western norms, including support for multilateralism and international trade standards. China meanwhile was aiming to gain recognition as an important rising economic player and a central actor on the global political stage with the goal to achieve World Trade Organization (WTO) membership (Song and Hall 2019; Riga 2022). Although initial interactions date back to the 1970s, EU-China relations became truly institutionalized in the 1990s through a strategic partnership, which was consolidated during the 2000s. This partnership, one of the EU's oldest and best-established, is characterized by numerous sectoral dialogues. Its original goal was mutual recognition and validation of the relevance of each player, thereby reinforcing their own status and identity (Cottey 2021; Chen and Xia 2022). Although this partnership was mutually beneficial, it was not without disagreement. Indeed, the EU has always been concerned about China's human rights record and its lack of ethical consideration in the conduct of its business, while China has always objected to what it perceives as European interference in its domestic affairs (Kinzelbach 2015; Song and Hall 2019).

Economic and political crises, particularly after the 2008 financial crisis, began to test the EU's ability to influence China, prompting the adoption of a pragmatic approach focusing on areas of mutual benefit and deeper institutional cooperation. By 2009, clear divergences emerged in the two sides' approaches: while acknowledging its partner's importance, the EU persisted in promoting its values in China. While China, although accepting some European standards such as multilateralism and sustainable development, gave greater priority to fair trade (Chen and Xia 2022).

Subsequently, China's role in shaping the EU's identity has undergone significant changes over the 2010 decade. This shift can be attributed, on one hand, to its emergence as a major economic power and, on the other, to the launch of large-scale investment initiatives like the Belt and Road Initiative (BRI) and the "Made in China 2025" strategy. These developments heightened the EU's concerns regarding technological competitiveness and control over vital infrastructure. As a result, the economic dynamic between the EU and China has shifted from mutually beneficial cooperation to increasingly pronounced systemic rivalry (Langendonk and Drieskens 2023). China's ascent as a global economic player has introduced new challenges for the EU, forcing it to juggle economic collaboration and competition, while also addressing the human rights situation in China (Song and Hall 2019). Additionally, geopolitical concerns and divergences have increased, partly due to the rise of authoritarian measures in China, Western concerns about human rights abuses in Xinjiang, repression of protests in Hong Kong, and the growing competition between China and the United States. The latter situation has sometimes compelled the EU to make difficult choices between alignment or cooperation (Langendonk and Drieskens 2023). The EU's latest policy papers on China thus reflect the adoption of a more critical and nuanced tone, advocating for a relationship built on reciprocity, particularly on the economic front. Moreover, the aspiration to influence China's values and political system has gradually lost its relevance for Europeans (Cottey 2021; Riga 2022; EEAS 2022).

Moreover, divergences in values have tended to increase, particularly regarding the definition of multilateralism. The EU's identity is firmly rooted in an approach that entails acceptance of certain constraints on the sovereignty of its member states. By contrast, China's approach to multilateralism is characterized by a utilitarian vision, emphasizing non-interference in domestic affairs and the promotion of alternative centers of power worldwide to counter Western and United States hegemony (Kolmas 2016; Cottey 2021). This approach often contrasts with the EU's long-standing alignment with the United States, creating tensions in EU-China relations.

Despite these challenges, some common interests and cooperative efforts persist. For example, EU-China relations have also been influenced in recent years by the Trump administration's opposition to multilateral approaches. This has brought the EU and China closer together on issues such as the defense of multilateralism and international organizations, particularly in the areas of trade, climate change, the Iran nuclear deal, and the World Health Organization (WHO). However, it is difficult to consider that these closer ties and stronger associations were enduring, as the EU's rift with the United States was not permanent (Harris 2020). Furthermore, the COVID-19 crisis hampered these rapprochements, despite the conclusion of the Global Agreement on Investments (AGI) in 2020 which is yet to be ratified by the European Parliament.

To sum up, the relationship between China and the EU has historically played a role in shaping the EU's identity, evolving from an initially idealistic and transformative approach to one that is more pragmatic and transactional, driven by the absence of a sense of common belonging or shared values (Jankovski 2022). The evolution of China's international economic and political status has also spurred the EU's adoption of a geopolitical discourse aimed at reinforcing its own stature as a global player. Ultimately, the EU's need for engagement with China has become more pronounced than the reverse, marking a shift from the earlier phase of an equal need for mutual engagement (Langendonk and Drieskens 2023).

Conclusion

In conclusion, this chapter has offered a nuanced overview of how the EU undertakes to situate and to portray itself within the evolving international landscape. It has highlighted the fundamental importance of discourses, narratives, and interactions with major powers in the shaping of the EU's identity and in defining its role as an international actor. Indeed, it is reasonable to assert that the EU's identity is partly a socially constructed concept, closely tied to the narratives found in its strategic documents, as well as in the narratives surrounding its strategic partnerships. From this perspective, discursive and narrative analysis becomes essential in order to grasp the underlying mechanisms at work.

The chapter has further developed that the EU's self-representation is not static, but rather subject to gradual evolution, adapting in response to changes in international politics particularly those involving great powers. Moreover, the discursive positioning of the EU's identity in relation to actors such as the United States, Russia, or China, emerges as central in establishing its nature as an international actor and in shaping its identity. Over the years, the EU has shifted from an initially ideological orientation to a more pragmatic political discourse, seeking recognition as a relevant actor on the part of these major powers, while at the same time emphasizing its distinct nature and values.

In this respect, the relationship between the EU and the United States has been characterized by a complex process of association and distinction on the part of the EU, marked by adaptations in response to the fluctuations of successive United States administrations. As for Russia, the EU initially sought to align the country with its enlargement and neighborhood policies. However, it was soon confronted with authoritarian and security-related developments, as well as Russia's rejection of the EU's fundamental values. This evolution soon positioned Russia as both a security and ideological threat to the EU's identity, thereby reinforcing its distinctive character. At the same time, the relationship with China has evolved toward a mainly transactional approach, despite the early importance of value-based considerations and recognition of mutual status. Ultimately, even if the EU has not always succeeded in shaping these powers in its own image and in achieving systematic recognition as a legitimate and relevant actor by associating itself with them, it can nonetheless be stated that the narrative of the EU itself has undergone transformations as a result of its contact with those powers. At the same time, these interactions have prompted the EU to acknowledge the limits of both its actorness and influence, triggering a major process of self-introspection and internal reform with the explicit aim of asserting a greater role and relevance as a global player in a wider range of fields. This shift is clearly reflected in the content and the language used in its strategic documents over the years.

This chapter has outlined the conceptual framework surrounding these themes and synthesized key insights from the relevant literature. However, it is clear that these areas of research require further exploration, as numerous factors continue to shape the EU's international identity and its role on the world stage. Future geopolitical developments, as well as interactions with major powers, will continue to play a pivotal role in influencing how the EU is perceived and received by other international actors. In this context, it is imperative to delve deeper into the underlying elements of these themes to gain a more nuanced understanding of the complex dynamics involved in shaping the EU's international identity and its aspirations as a global actor.

References

Aggestam, L. 2006. Role Theory and European Foreign Policy: A Framework of Analysis. In *The European Union's Roles in International Politics: Concepts and Analysis*, ed. O. Elgström and M. Smith, 11–29. New York: Routledge.

Alexoaei, A., and V. Cojanu. 2017. Negotiating the Transatlantic Deal: Focus on the EU's Domestic Constraints. *CES Working Papers* 9 (3): 233–254.

Bengtsson, R. 2021. The European Union's Self-conception of Its Roles in Global Affairs. In *National Role Conceptions in a New Millennium: Defining a Place in a Changing World*, ed. M. Grossman, F. Schortgen, and G.M. Friedrichs, 115–127. New York: Routledge.

Bengtsson, R., and O. Elgström. 2012. Conflicting Role Conceptions? The European Union in Global Politics: Conflicting Role Conceptions? *Foreign Policy Analysis* 8 (1): 93–108.

Bicchi, F., H. Maurer, and K. Raube. 2024. Maturation by Practice: Shaping the EU's International Identity in the Absence of Formal Institutional Change. *European Security* 33 (3): 364–382.

Blanc, E. 2023. Recognition Through Dialogue: How Transatlantic Relations Anchor the EU's Identity. *The British Journal of Politics and International Relations* 25 (1): 102–120.

Blanco, L.F. 2016. The Functions of 'Strategic Partnership' in European Union Foreign Policy Discourse. *Cambridge Review of International Affairs* 29 (1): 36–54.

Bretherton, C., and J. Vogler. 2005. *The European Union as a Global Actor*. London: Routledge.

Bricart, V. 2021. Politique commerciale extérieure: Quel rôle pour les assemblées parlementaires? Le cas des États-Unis et de l'Union Européenne. *Cahiers de Science Politique de l'Université de Liège. Numéro spécial*, available at: https://doi.org/10.25518/1784-6390.1002 (accessed 30 October 2023).

Bricart, V. 2022. L'Amérique a-t-elle dépassé les bornes? L'impact de l'administration Trump sur la relation entre les États-Unis et l'Union européenne. *Revue De La Faculté De Droit De L'université De Liège* 3: 525–551.

Browning, C.S. 2017. Geostrategies, Geopolitics and Ontological Security in the Eastern Neighborhood: The European Union and the 'New Cold War.' *Political Geography* 62: 106–115.

Carta, C., and J.-F. Morin. 2014. Struggling Over Meanings: Discourses on the EU's International Presence. *Cooperation and Conflict* 49 (3): 295–314.

Carta, C., and R. Wodak. 2015. Discourse Analysis, Policy Analysis, and the Borders of EU Identity. *Journal of Language and Politics* 14 (1): 1–17.

Checkel, J. 2006a. Constructivism and EU Politics. In *Handbook of European Union Politics*, 57–76. London: Sage.

Checkel, J. 2006b. Constructivist Approaches to European Integration. *ARENA Working Papers* 6: 1–41.

Chen, D., and Xia, Y. 2022. Chapter 15: China's Considerations and Perceptions About the EU. In *EU Global Actorness in a World of Contested Leadership: Policies, Instruments and Perceptions*. ed. M.R. Freire, P.D. Lopes, D. Nascimento, and L. Simão, 263–278. London: Palgrave Macmillan.

Cottey, A. 2021. The European Union and China: Partnership in Changing Times. In *The European Union's Strategic Partnerships*, ed. L.C. Ferreira-Pereira and M. Smith, 221–244. London: Palgrave Macmillan.

Council of the European Union. 2003. *European Security Strategy: A Secure Europe in a Better World*. Publications Office, available at: https://doi.org/10.2860/1402 (accessed 30 October 2023).

Dannreuther, R., and J. Peterson. 2006. *Security Strategy and Transatlantic Relations*. London: Routledge.

Davies, B., and R. Harré. 1990. Positioning: The Discursive Production of Selves. *Journal for the Theory of Social Behaviour* 20 (1): 43–63.

Della Sala, V. 2018. Narrating Europe: The EU's Ontological Security Dilemma. *European Security* 27 (3): 266–279.

Deriglazova, L. 2022. Chapter 12: Russia vis-à-vis the European Union: Perceptions and Perspectives for Cooperation. In *EU Global Actorness in a World of Contested Leadership: Policies, Instruments and Perceptions*, ed. M.R. Freire, P.D. Lopes, D. Nascimento, and L. Simão, 205–225. London: Palgrave Macmillan.

Diez, T. 2004. Europe's Others and the Return of Geopolitics. *Cambridge Review of International Affairs* 17 (2): 319–335.

Diez, T. 2005. Constructing the Self and Changing Others: Reconsidering 'Normative Power Europe'. *Millennium: Journal of International Studies* 33 (3): 613–636.

Duchêne, F. 1972. Europe's Role in World Peace. In *Europe Tomorrow: Sixteen Europeans Look Ahead*, ed. R. Mayne, 32–47. London: Fontana.

European Council. 1999. *Common Strategy of the European Union on Russia*, available at: https://op.europa.eu/en/publication-detail/-/publication/38943c06-7e5d-4ca3-acc3-c5154bd9c04e/language-en (accessed 30 October 2023).

European External Action Service. (EEAS). 2016. *Shared Vision, Common Action: A Stronger*. Europe, available at: https://www.eeas.europa.eu/sites/default/files/eugs_review_web_0.pdf (accessed 30 October 2023).

European External Action Service. (EEAS). 2022. *Strategic Compass for Security and Defence*, available at: https://www.eeas.europa.eu/eeas/strategic-compass-security-and-defence-0_en (accessed 13 September 2024).

Ferreira-Pereira, L.C., and M. Smith, eds. 2021. *The European Union's Strategic Partnerships: Global Diplomacy in a Contested World*. London: Palgrave Macmillan.

Freire, M.R., P.D. Lopes, D. Nascimento, and L. Simão. 2022. Chapter 1: EU Global Actorness in a World of Contested Leadership: Policies, Instruments and Perceptions. In *EU Global Actorness in a World of Contested Leadership: Policies, Instruments and Perceptions*, 1–13. M.R. Freire, P.D. Lopes, D. Nascimento, and L. Simão. London: Palgrave Macmillan.

Garnizova, E. 2022. Chapter 6: Taking Its Rightful Place? Legitimising Discourse and EU Actorness in the Nexus of Trade and Regulation. In *EU Global Actorness in a World of Contested Leadership: Policies, Instruments and Perceptions*, ed. M.R. Freire, P.D. Lopes, D. Nascimento, and L. Simão, 91–109. London: Palgrave Macmillan.

Gehring, T., S. Oberthür, and M. Mühleck. 2013. European Union Actorness in International Institutions: Why the EU Is Recognized as an Actor in Some International Institutions, But Not in Others. *Journal of Common Market Studies* 51 (5): 849–865.

Greenhill, B. 2008. Recognition and Collective Identity Formation in International Politics. *European Journal of International Relations* 14 (2): 343–368.

Gustafsson, K. 2016. Recognising Recognition Through Thick and Thin: Insights from Sino-Japanese Relations. *Cooperation and Conflict* 51 (3): 255–271.

Harré, R., and L. van Lagenhove, eds. 1999. *Positioning Theory: Moral Contexts of Intentional Action*. Oxford: Blackwell.

Harris, G. 2020. The Unstable Triangular Relationship Between China, EU, and the USA. In *China and the EU in the Era of Regional and Interregional Cooperation*, ed. M. Telò and Y. Feng, 299–316. Brussels: Peter Lang.

Haukkala, H. 2021. The End of Ambiguity: Excavating the Remains of the EU–Russia 'Strategic Partnership'. In *The European Union's Strategic Partnerships*, ed. L.C. Ferreira-Pereira and M. Smith, 177–197. London: Palgrave Macmillan.

Hill, C. 1993. The Capability-Expectations Gap, or Conceptualizing Europe's International Role. *Journal of Common Market Studies* 31 (3): 305–328.

Hill, C., M. Smith, and S. Vanhoonacker, eds. 2023. *International Relations and the European Union*, 4th ed. Oxford: Oxford University Press.

Howorth, J. 2016. EU Global Strategy in a Changing World: Brussels' Approach to the Emerging Powers. *Contemporary Security Policy* 37 (3): 389–401.

Icaza, R. 2010. Global Europe, Guilty! Contesting EU Neoliberal Governance for Latin America and the Caribbean. *Third World Quarterly* 31 (1): 123–139.

Jankovski, A. 2022. Chapter 17: The European Union Actorness: A View from Washington D.C. In *EU Global Actorness in a World of Contested Leadership: Policies, Instruments and Perceptions*, ed. M.R. Freire, P.D. Lopes, D. Nascimento, and L. Simão, 299–327. London: Palgrave Macmillan.

Jepperson, R., A. Wendt, and P.J. Katzenstein. 1996. Norms, Identity and Culture in National Security. In *The Culture of National Security: Norms and Identity in World Politics*, 33–78. P. J. Katzenstein and Social Science Research Council. New York: Columbia University Press.

Joenniemi, P. 2009. Difference Within Similarity: Transatlantic Relations as a 'Community of Neighbors.' *Danish Institute for International Studies* 11: 1–31.

Kanet, R.E. 2018. Russia and Global Governance: The Challenge to the Existing Liberal Order. *International Politics* 55 (2): 177–188.

Karolewski, I. 2011. European Identity Making and Identity Transfer. *Europe-Asia Studies* 63 (6): 935–955.

Kinzelbach, K. 2015. *The EU's Human Rights Dialogue with China: Quiet Diplomacy and Its Limits*. London: Routledge.

Klose, S. 2023. Does the EU Have Friends? *Journal of Common Market Studies* 61 (3): 579–596.

Kolmas, M. 2016. China's Approach to Regional Cooperation. *China Report* 52 (3): 192–210.

Langendonk, S., and E. Drieskens. 2023. The EU's Embrace of Geopolitics: Insights from the EU-China Relationship. In *The EU Political System After the 2019 European Elections*, ed. O. Costa and S. Van Hecke, 479–499. London: Palgrave Macmillan.

Lindemann, T., and E. Ringmar. 2012. *International Politics of Recognition*. London: Routledge.

Mälksoo, M. 2016. From the ESS to the EU Global Strategy: External Policy, Internal Purpose. *Contemporary Security Policy* 37 (3): 374–388.

Manners, I. 2002. Normative Power Europe: A Contradiction in Terms? *Journal of Common Market Studies* 40 (2): 235–258.

Manners, I. 2009. The EU's Normative Power in Changing World Politics. In *Normative Power Europe in a Changing World: A Discussion*, ed. A. Gerrits, 9–24. The Hague: Netherlands Institute of International Relations.

Manners, I.J., and R.G. Whitman. 1998. Towards Identifying the International Identity of the European Union: A Framework for Analysis of the Eu's Network of Relationships. *Journal of European Integration* 21 (3): 231–249.

Manners, I., and R. Whitman. 2003. The 'Difference Engine': Constructing and Representing the International Identity of the European Union. *Journal of European Public Policy* 10 (3): 380–404.

Mitzen, J. 2006. Anchoring Europe's Civilizing Identity: Habits, Capabilities and Ontological Security. *Journal of European Public Policy* 13 (2): 270–285.

Morin, J.-F., T. Novotná, F. Ponjaert, and M. Telò. 2016. *The Politics of Transatlantic Trade Negotiations*. London: Routledge.

Morozov, V., and B. Rumelili. 2012. The External Constitution of European Identity: Russia and Turkey as Europe-makers. *Cooperation and Conflict* 47 (1): 28–48.

Müftüler-Bac, M., S. Aydın-Düzgit, and E. Uzun-Teker. 2024. The EU's Global Strategic Partner(ship): A Tool for the Maturation of European Foreign Policy? *European Security* 33 (3): 426–448.

Neumann, I.B. 1998. European Identity, EU Expansion, and the Integration/Exclusion Nexus. *Alternatives: Global, Local, Political* 23: 397–416.

Pishchikova, K., and E. Piras. 2017. The European Union Global Strategy: What Kind of Foreign Policy Identity? *The International Spectator* 52 (3): 103–120.

Reus-Smit, C. 2005. Constructivism. In *Theories of International Relations*, ed. S. Burchill, 188–212. London: Palgrave Macmillan.

Riddervold, M., and A. Newsome. 2018. Transatlantic Relations in Times of Uncertainty: Crises and EU-US Relations. *Journal of European Integration* 40 (5): 505–521.

Riga, D. 2022. Socialization Through Interregional Relations: EU's Normative Power in Its Dialogue with China. *The Twelfth International Convention of Asia Scholars (ICAS 12)*, 583–593.

Rumelili, B. 2004. Constructing Identity and Relating to Difference: Understanding the EU's Mode of Differentiation. *Review of International Studies* 30 (1): 27–47.

Simão, L. 2022. Chapter 2: Unpacking the EU's International Actorness: Debates, Theories and Concepts. In *EU Global Actorness in a World of Contested Leadership: Policies, Instruments and Perceptions*, ed. M.R. Freire, P.D. Lopes, D. Nascimento, and L. Simão, 13–32. London: Palgrave Macmillan.

Sjöstedt, G. 1977. *The External Role of the European Community*. Farnborough Hampshire: Saxon House.

Smith, M. 2021. The European Union and the United States: Competition, Convergence and Crisis in a Strategic Relationship. In *The European Union's Strategic Partnerships*, ed. L.C. Ferreira-Pereira and M. Smith, 97–120. London: Palgrave Macmillan.

Song, W., and R.B. Hall. 2019. European Union's Construction of International Identity Via Strategic Partnerships: Associating and Social Distancing. *Contemporary Politics* 25 (2): 172–189.

Tallberg, J., and M. Zürn. 2019. The Legitimacy and Legitimation of International Organizations: Introduction and Framework. *The Review of International Organizations* 14 (4): 581–606.

Telò, M., ed. 2009. *The European Union and Global Governance*. London: Routledge.

Tereszkiewicz, F. 2020. The European Union as a Normal International Actor: An Analysis of the EU Global Strategy. *International Politics* 57 (1): 95–114.

Varma, T. 2024. European Strategic Autonomy: The Path to a Geopolitical Europe. *The Washington Quarterly* 47 (1): 65–83.

Wæver, O. 1996. European Security Identities. *Journal of Common Market Studies* 34 (1): 103–132.

Wagner, W., and R. Anholt. 2016. Resilience as the EU Global Strategy's New Leitmotif: Pragmatic, Problematic or Promising? *Contemporary Security Policy* 37 (3): 414–430.

Wrange, J., R. Bengtsson, and D. Brommesson. 2024. Resilience Through Total Defence: Towards a Shared Security Culture in the Nordic–Baltic Region? *European Journal of International Security*, 1–22.

Wendt, A. 1999. *Social Theory of International Politics*. Cambridge: Cambridge University Press.

Zaborowski, M., ed. 2006. *Friends Again? EU-US Relations After the Crisis*. Paris: Institute for Security Studies.

EU Geopolitical Leadership in Late Westphalian International Environment: Evolution of Normative Power Europe

Adrian Szumowski

Introduction

The European Union (EU) is a very peculiar actor in the contemporary international environment despite being very visible and widely commented on (Pietras 2005). However, until today, its existence and source of success and possible fate have been subjected to inconclusive debate. It stretches from classical theories of International Relations (IR) through mid-level theories primed purely on investigating EU (Czaputowicz 2007, 116–128 and 327–371) to constructivist theories (Lombardo 2016, 123–146). Those theories are numerous; nevertheless, they still do not provide a reliable and accepted explanation for the nature of European integration, which could be accepted by academia. First and foremost, EU effectiveness is measured by acquiring the desired objectives and capability to control other international entities and the environment. This feature is particularly widely disputed, mainly because it is deprived of classical tools associated with the notion of power. Scholars

A. Szumowski (✉)
Faculty of Political Science and Journalism, Institute of International Relations, Maria Curie-Skłodowska University, Lublin, Poland
e-mail: adrian.szumowski@mail.umcs.pl

L. Lika and D. Riga (eds.), *EU Geopolitical Actorness in a Changing World*, https://doi.org/10.1007/978-3-031-81160-9_4

like Ian Manners (2002, 235–258) asked questions about EU power, who created and developed the idea of Normative Power Europe (NPE), which attempts to draft a design of its effectiveness and limitations. One of the challenges associated with this feature is the internal composition of the EU, which is distinct from the primary user of power: the nation-state and any other international actor. EU is still an organization under construction, whose eventual shape and capabilities are unknown and disputed among scholars and politicians.

The two main research questions address issues regarding that particular change in the composition of the EU, especially regarding forecasting its future outlooks and performance. What does the evolution of EU power look like, especially when its actorness is at stake? Moreover, if the EU can become a leader in the geopolitical landscape of the contemporary world? The process of change, according to presumptions that serve as a foundation for this chapter, is that the evolution is continuous rather than violent and intermittent. Therefore, the category of evolution will be applied as a theoretical framework. The backbone of these questions is to analyze and construct further details of said process. These considerations were already mentioned in research presented in a monograph published by Adrian Szumowski (2021). However, recent developments like arguments about national plans of recovery and resilience (Bokhorst and Corti 2023), diversified EU response to the war in Ukraine (Anghel and Jones 2023, 766–786), or corruption affair in the European Parliament (Wheaton and Braun 2023), indicates that the evolution of EU power may be directed into unknown territories. Those events seem qualitatively separate from the evolution of the EU's power, but their conjuncture is crucial to its prospect development. NPE is based on three critical features: the success story of a wielder, alternatives for proposed narratives, and cohesion between declarations and actual performance. All three events negatively affect NPE and its future developments. First, it affects the primary perceived success of the EU. Second, it creates alternative discourses for EU narratives even within its framework. Third, it generates a shift between declared values and intentions and actual performance influenced by external powers like Qatar, Mauritania, Morocco, or Russia.

Therefore, determining which direction this evolution should be heading is essential. For some politicians, there should be an answer to whether this evolution should be aborted. This is also the question about EU power, mostly its composition and effectiveness. It is particularly interesting to correlate the evolution of EU power with the acquisition of state components, like armed forces (Weinzierl 2021, 1049–1073), and analyze its effect on EU power, especially when it comes to the growing ambition expressed in every level of EU structures, evident in ambitious foreign policy when one of the more critical issues is the question about its strategic autonomy (Järvenpää et al. 2019, 467–485).

This chapter will have three hypotheses, jointly drafting an answer to the research questions. First, EU power is evolving from a point of origin described as normative power by Manners toward fully fledged state-like power. At least, this is the design created by a group of scholars and politicians labeled as federalists (Fossum and Jachtenfuchs 2017, 467–485), predominantly represented in national and European bureaucratic structures that currently control the process of EU development. Although there are specific arguments regarding the direction and pace of this evolution, in EU member states, the consensus is that this process needs to be supported. Therefore, the structural evolution of the EU will embrace widening its scope of power, which then will steer it closer to the definition of a nation-state (Jellinek 1921, 312).[1] Second, the evolution of the EU is not flawless because it is wrapped around a power paradox, which encompasses the fact that the more EU elites push its evolution forward, the more resistance it is meeting. And this resistance is generated in the most unexpected places, which could be seen during the constitutional referendum failure in France and the Netherlands in 2005 (Qvortrup 2006, 89–97) and Brexit in 2016 (Koller et al. 2019). Therefore, essential for the process of evolution is the consciousness and skill set of elites managing the evolution process, primarily because the transformation of power resources costs a significant portion of said resources. If a specific efficiency level is not met, the process will regress. The third hypothesis, in the process of evolution, is the conflict between EU institutions and member states. The nature and scope of this divergence are to be determined, but this moment in the EU's future need to be addressed. Change always requires confrontation with previous forms of organization, particularly with the Westphalian-style institutions wrapped around nation-states. Therefore, some form of conflict is to be expected. Its analysis should embrace an investigation into the required conditions for

[1] A state is a political entity with three features: territory, population, and sovereign government (Jellinek 1921, 312).

its resolution. Recent indications show that EU institutions have identified the Republic of Poland as a most beneficial and prospective avenue for advancement. However, the surprising resilience toward applied pressure may suggest this could be a false start. Therefore, an assessment of damage needs to be performed.

As a supplementation, the forecast will be based on the scenario method, based on the creation of four possible outcomes of the evolution of EU power and the resulting constructions of its actorness. The produced analysis will be divided into four parts. The first will be dedicated to examining historic and contemporary structures and functions of the EU and its predecessors. The second part will be devoted to providing an analysis of NPE, especially in the context of fuelling the evolution of the EU and posing severe challenges to overcome before the designed objective is fulfilled. The third part will investigate the actual mechanism of change regarding the structural transformation of the EU. It will be labeled as a transnational mechanism and a mirror image of a geopolitical mechanism. It will also be highlighted why this experiment proved so effective that it evolved much faster after the end of communism, the end of the Cold War, and the dissolution of the Union of Soviet Socialist Republics (USSR). The fourth part will be committed to obtaining designed objectives and replacing the nation-state as a central hub for IR, at least in the European regional sub-system.

From European Coal and Steel Community to European Union and Beyond

The most fevered proponents of European integration indicate that the idea stems from events occurring in the Middle Ages, sometimes even during the existence of the Roman Empire. However, it must be stressed that Europe was never genuinely united for at least dozens of centuries, which is derivative of three different factors. First and foremost is sovereignty, which was born and developed in Europe. Since Jean Bodin (1967), this idea was a foundation for the modern state and a number of different entities, such as merchant republics, city-states, or multinational empires, which were extinguished after World War I (WWI). It is still differently defined and varied among scholars (Pietraś 2008, 57–85), but in most cases, the existence of sovereign nations limits or completely excludes the existence of overarching authority. The second issue is the mutual cultural similarities regarding the background of European nations, even when waves of migrations and conflicts disrupted and fractured the political structure of the continent. The universality of the triad of European culture (Koneczny quoted in Bokia 2000): Christian morality, Roman law, and Greek art connected nations despite their differences. This was supplemented by transnational institutions such as the Roman Catholic Church and Roman Empire, which sparked frequent attempts to reconstruct lost political unity, which always faltered. This was due to a third reason, pointed out by Paul Kennedy (1995), who stated that there was no singular source of power in Europe, especially in its most pristine form of military power, neither in quality nor quantity. European history is filled with instances where the expected victory on the battlefield was turned to sorrowful defeat and reversed (Weigly 2004, 192–193). Therefore, despite scoring significant victories and conquering swaths of land outside of the continent, European nations were usually unsuccessful within Europe itself.

In the twentieth century, there could be observed change in European composition, especially with the advent of European integration, after the end of World War II (WWII). Three significant factors caused it. First of all, there could be observed a rise of non-European powers, primarily the United States and Russia (later the Soviet Union), which surpassed European nation-states in terms of power. The second issue is the deepening state of European economies' social and economic decline, coupled with the effects of decolonization, which gravely impacted growth capabilities (Kesternich et al. 2014, 103–118). Third, Europe suffered greatly from the three greatest geopolitical disasters of the twentieth century: WWI, WWII, and the rise of communism.

European integration gained momentum by exploiting development opportunities after WWII, like the Marshall Plan (Geremek 2008, 43–50), where one political condition was creating political institutions of conflict prevention, especially in the late 1940s. Many works and essays were written (*inter alia* Urwin 2014) about history, procedures, legal documents, and diplomacy events, which were part of the whole process. When it comes to European power, its nature, and scope, three intertwined factors need to be taken into consideration: range of power (how many issues could be managed through it), scope of the power (if the European institutions can apply disciplinary tools for nation-states) and national state resistance toward integration. The first period, labeled as the European Coal and Steel Community (ECSC), was the narrowest when it comes to scope, the firmest when it comes to reach, and the most robust when it comes to national resistance. The second period, the European Economic Community (EEC), is characterized by a widening range due to the success story of the former iteration of European integration, with minimal scope and limited national resistance. Third, it could be labeled as a Single European Act (SEA) when the range and scope of power grew, and resistance faded further away. Fourth, which will be analyzed in the following section, is connected with the European Union (EU), accompanied by the growing duality of its nature.

On the one hand, it is an intergovernmental organization whose power could be described as the broadest range, limited scope, and dwindling national resistance; on the other, as a supranational entity with the power of even more comprehensive range, advancing scope, and the lowest level on national resistance. However, it still needs to be determined which direction of EU actorness evolution will be embraced, primarily due to recent setbacks, such as the rejection of the European Constitution in France and the Netherlands in a popular referendum (Philippopoulos-Mihalopoulos 2009, 309–323) and Brexit (Arnorsson and Gylfi 2018, 301–323). Both issues may have crippling effects on NPE.

NPE Revisited Once More

The three factors mentioned above create and shape the evolution of EU's power. Their conjuncture produces tools and strategies for organizations on which they rely today. Their contemporary interactions coin the direction of its evolution toward a qualitative breakthrough. However, before analyzing the potential directions of its evolution, there is a need to answer the question about the nature of EU power.

The critical element of actorness is power, which could be understood as an ability to control other actors and the environment up to the point of completely nullifying the impact of external factors on one's actions. The contemporary debate in the IR community is about the investigation, and some scholars have tied it to new forms of power, more complex and sophisticated, because of deprivation from pristine military power. Therefore, the idea of civilian power (Orbie 2006, 123–128) was raised quite often, especially when underlining differences between the EU and nation-state, oriented toward violence and war. This idea stems from the post-war situation of Germany and Japan, where military capabilities were strictly limited and subjected to severe legal and international restrictions up to the point of banishing even the name of "armed forces" from legal vocabulary (Japan). The definition of civilian power encompasses three significant features: reinforced inclination toward international cooperation, a severely limited pool of military capabilities, even with substantial technological potential, and overreliance on supranational structures when dealing with significant international challenges (Maull 1990, 92–93). However, as a drawback, defining this power or how it should be efficiently applied to other entities in international relations is tough. What could be labeled in its entirety in the hands of the EU or even member states, for instance, cultural tools such as religion? Therefore, describing the EU as a master of civilian power could be misleading, suggesting that the EU possesses tools that the EU does not control as an actor.

The same could be said about terms market (Damro 2012, 682–699), trade (Meunier and Kalypso 2006, 906–925), and financial (Posner and Veron 2010, 400–415) power. Although the primary nature of EU power stems from its association with the economic success of the continent, represented by thriving national economies, effective post-war reconstruction, and the rise of a welfare state, there is a need to signify that the EU does not have control over those processes and assets produced by them. In most cases, national governments are deciding how much influence of European institutions they are willing to accept. This could be seen primarily in the correlation between EU income and the size of the European economy. It is much lower than, for instance, in the United States and other major players.[2] A deeper analysis would point out that despite the EU's development of the capacity to influence financial flows inside and outside of the Single European Market (SEM), it is not the exclusive influencer or generator of those money torrents.

Despite criticism (Hyde-Price 2006, 217–234) and some flaws, one of the most accurate theories was created by Manners (2002) in the form of the conception of NPE. It was supplemented by research conducted by Anu Bradford (2020), which was presented in a monograph entitled *The Brussels Effect: How the European Union Rules the World*, especially

[2] The EU budget for 2022 was 170,6 bln EUR compared to the EU GDP (2022), which was 16.613,06 bln USD, which means 1,03%. Comparison: The US budget was US 8.371,00 bln USD compared to the US GDP (2022): 26.854,599 bln USD, representing 31,17% (OJEU 2022; IMF 2022).

investigating relations between the EU and non-European nations and companies and why in most cases, those entities comply with demands of EU institutions expressed during trade negotiations. Another book was written by Klaus Bachmann (2013) and his cooperatives, which was given a poetic title: *Kiedy związane ręce zapewniają przewagę* (English: *When tied hands provide advantageous*), which investigates issues between the EU and abroad partners. The most important feature of trade negotiations is that the most effective trade negotiations in which the EU participated were successful only when the non-decision or unfavorable decision was the most effective strategy. Actually, the less the EU did, the more successful it became. Therefore, all three authors point in the same direction: the EU's most potent regulation is norm-creating strategy. It may be seen as an undermining of an actorness concept highlighted with broader concerns of different issues (Bertherton and Vogler 2006; Hill et al. 2017), but what this manuscript provides is an interesting model for performance based on accessibility of a particular and valuable space. Both scholars agree that this regulation of access to EU space is the most effective means to project power by the EU as a separate actor in international relations.

Although normative power was coined by Manners in 2002, this type of interaction could be added to Joseph Nye's soft power. Soft power was defined as the capability of an actor to influence other actors with attraction rather than coercion. Usually, soft power is non-military, which generally relies on an actor's ideology, culture, values, and past performance (Nye 2007, 34). What makes it extremely specific are two features. First and foremost, it is used very subtly, without the participation of the consciousness of the actor targeted with it. According to Kenneth Boulding (1989), the classification it belongs to is the third face of power, which corresponds to soft power. However, it is passive and applied without conscious awareness of the actor targeted with it. In essence, normative power is a set of tools and strategies aimed primarily at creating and applying norms, which regulate behavior and manage the perception of a targeted entity into what could be considered a normal situation or necessity to achieve certain results. The best example is fashion, which could be understood as a manner in which certain things have to look to be desired.

In many cases, those qualities promoted by fashion (Nye 2011, 13) are superficial and sometimes completely irrelevant. Nonetheless, influence through tools promoting fashion, such as influences, commercials and advertisements, and product placements, convinces customers that a complete outlook is not only worthwhile but also inevitable. A similar process occurs in global politics, where primary and minor power centers are primed to shape each other perceptions through various means, stretching from advertisements, scholarship programs, training and conferences, epistemic networks, and many more, to shape and direct perception of others, especially in the form of what is necessary and what is imminent. Undoubtedly, scholars mentioned above that the EU is exceptionally skilled in projecting this power. However, this does not mean it does not have access to other forms of power or that other actors do not use it. The EU relies mainly on controlling other entities and their surroundings.

Normative power is an extraordinarily effective and costless power projection, at least when used skillfully. Therefore, most actors willingly pursue this kind of resources to improve their performance in the international environment. However, it takes work to use those resources properly. In most cases, they need to be applied in very particular conditions. Among these, three qualities stem to be of utmost importance.

First and foremost, it is the distance. It could be measured in at least three axes. Firstly, it is geographical distance: the closer entities function in terms of distance, the more links between them are created and maintained. Therefore, delivering quant of power at the designated point of gravity of targeted actors is easier. In the case of the EU, there is a geographical limit to the effectiveness of its performance based on the geographical and cultural boundaries of European confines. Therefore, the Western Balkan states, Belarus and Ukraine, are particularly susceptible to NPE. Beyond that, its effectiveness dramatically declines (Kavalski 2013, 252). Second, the mutual cultural background enables the delivery of more complicated and sophisticated messages that could be easily decoded and absorbed. This is why the EU model is adopted mainly in Latin America. Existing differences also cause severe mutations in existing patterns (Lenz 2013, 211–228). Third comes the level of mutual hostilities. The more hostility between actors, the higher the level of awareness, and the more normative power is recognized and transformed into other forms.

The second issue concerning the effectiveness of normative power is the question of alternatives. The purpose and condition of success is that the message lacks alternatives. Therefore, the proposed solution seems to be the only available option. Anecdotally, one of the African leaders asked why Africa pursued the European integration model and replied that it was the only one that worked (Babarinde 2007, 8). This condition is among the first to be achieved when applying normative power. Sense of historical inevitability or necessity, even if it is not based on a reasonable foundation. That is why Brexit, as proof of the mere existence of an alternative for European integration, was so damaging to the EU in terms of its power, and its results must be constantly dealt with more or less success. It does not matter whether that alternative is more effective or not. Its mere existence is a constant drain of resources for the actor, which will last till this alternative is terminated. This concept is derived from the idea of the *fleet in being* from strategic studies, where inferior naval forces are a constant burden for a larger navy, even when anchored in the harbor.[3]

Third quality, is a success. It is connected with the issue of credibility, labeled as the scarcest resource of international relations by Nye (2012), which is, in fact, one of the foundations of normative power efficiency. Success in global policy, no matter how achieved, always draws followers and copycats. It has been widely spread throughout the history of international relations, for instance, when it comes to developing and popularizing the Westphalian nation-state, usually due to its successful deployment of armed forces. In this aspect, two issues need to be underlined. Firstly, those resources are of external origin. Therefore, it is beyond actors' control when, where, how, and in what quantities it will provide, in other words, how important it will be for targeted entities. The same applies to losing credibility, which may be ignited by factors unrelated to the designated issue. For instance, the migration crisis that the EU has faced since 2015 could be seen as a reason for diminishing positive feedback on the achievements in public security and welfare (Szumski 2023). Secondly, it is tough to recover or recreate once credibility is lost. Once an actor is labeled as not credible, any action undertaken will be met with doubt, disbelief, and counteractions, sometimes undertaken at first glance at odds.

Applying normative power may seem to be a perfect solution for international relations. However, the application of it is a burden with two

[3] It was first used in 1690 by Lord Torrington, commanding officer of the British fleet in the English Channel (Maltby 1994, 160).

serious drawbacks. First and foremost, the actor cannot direct that application. In other words, the final results depend on the reaction of the object of power application. By design, the actor applying this kind of power should not be proactive. Primarily, this could be visible in the case of the EU, when a lack of decisions is more beneficial for its external activities than anything else. It is the thesis of monographs by Bachmann (2013) and Bradford (2020) when both scientists individually underline that the crucial element for normative power is the perception of external actors. This is connected with success, but not as the EU wants to be perceived but as external actors usually perceive it: as an oasis of welfare and security rather than a force of change on a global scale. Therefore, although many external entities desire to comply with the EU perception of the world expressed in norms and values, in most cases, it is done according to their individual beliefs. That is why most transplants of EU institutions outside are tainted with regional conditions so much that they are barely recognizable (Lenz 2013).

The second vulnerability of actors relying on normative power is susceptibility to hypocrisy. In essence, hypocrisy is a distance between vocalized values and the level of their actual application into reality. Therefore, the more values are preached rather than exemplified by one's actions, the more normative power effectiveness is limited. The hypocrisy of the Western nations is one of the reasons why China has overcome EU, especially when it comes to developing nations of Africa, Asia, and Latin America during the two decades of the twenty-first century (Kavalski 2013, 254). However, according to John Rothgeb (1993), power needs to be only in situations when actors have at least a partially contradictory hierarchy of preferences; therefore, the Chinese model of normative power, which relies on limiting mutual interventions, is reflected by the model "do as I do, not as I say" resemble a situation in which power is not used at all.

In summary, normative power is an element of power potential for nearly all existing state and non-state actors. Within international actors, the EU stands as an NPE whose effectiveness relies mainly on normative power, partially because it was deprived of other tools for power projection but primarily due to its internal composition and experiences of the latter part of the twentieth century. However, EU norms also affect those areas of state activity, but the final decision about applying those assets rests with national governments. Therefore, despite being highly effective, there is no need to break resistance not directed as outcomes depend on targeted actors' decisions. For instance, the application of EU-based institutions in Latin America or Africa is tainted with local conditions, which distort the final outcome (Lenz 2013). The solution—it is still unclear whether by accident or by design—is to continue developing institutions to improve and advance the EU project.

Transnational Mechanism for EU Transformation

Within the creation of the EU, there is an underlying objective of deepening integration extending beyond the current state. It is not a linear or steady process but is driven by circumstances and opportunities. The main aim of this drive is to supplement NPE with remaining pools of power capabilities, to bolster and improve its capabilities to influence other actors and the environment with more direct and efficient means, not relying purely on the receptiveness of an actor subjected to its influence. Therefore, some aspects of its structure must take form and function similarly to those of nation-states. Still, since the circumstances of this change and the point of origin will differ, the most likely outcome will be similar by design principles to nation-states. Still, in the details of the application, there will be various categories of international entities.

Since the process is far from completion, it is tough to forecast the final form of the EU. Three factors contribute to this NPE erosion. First and foremost, this is internal fatigue of EU nations and societies, which could be seen in the form of rise to prominence parties and entities openly skeptical, if not outright hostile, to the idea of European integration; in the form of shallowing public support for the EU; and in the form of quarrels about the validity of democratic formalities like elections and referenda, mainly when they are not producing desired results. Second, the deterioration of the international situation is too steep, which could be summarized by stating that the golden age for global affairs is gone. The EU and its member states are facing severe and diversified challenges for their security, stretching from war, migration flow, economic and financial issues, and global pandemic issues. Usually, first and foremost, response and accountability for precaution and counteractions were expected and provided by nation-state governments. This damaged the EU success story. Thirdly, what links directly to the previous point is the growing resistance of the national government, stemming from proposed changes in decision-making procedures, which could be summarized in a statement: "less unanimity, more majority voting." This means European integration will produce losers for the first time in history. This, coupled with electoral accountability of government, is stirring resentment for control or stopping the evolution of the EU.

The power transformation process from NPE to EU with nation-state functionalities became even more difficult. The greatest challenge of the whole process is that it limits and disperses available power resources for three reasons. First and foremost, it is a cost of said transformation. Scholars and politicians do not recognize this, but the transformation of this sort is a process that could be described as "endothermic."[4] Every quantity of produced power on desired fields usually requires the consumption of at least two quants of normative power already in possession of the EU. That means the evolution of the EU is not sustainable from a strategic perspective. Therefore, it requires coupling with external sources of power to supplement dwindling assets, either from within (nation-state level) or without. It could be observed with overreliance of EU institutions on the Federal Republic of Germany (FRG), even if this means alienating other member states. Paradoxically, it may further deplete NPE assets wildly when the process spirals into irrationality (The Economist 2023).

Secondly, frequent and repeated crises exist within the European international relations sub-system. This is wearing down international conviction that only European integration guarantees economic, political, and cultural success. Even though those crises faded in public opinion's memory, it left suspicion that the European model of regional integration was not as effective as it was assumed a few years ago. What is more important, those crises, since the 2008 financial crisis, through the 2015 migration crisis, the 2020 COVID-19 pandemic, and the recent 2022 fuel crisis and war in Ukraine, are constantly switching between active and dormant phases and were never honestly dealt with by EU institutions.

The new conception arose to bolster the fledgling capabilities of the EU with new capabilities in two fields. First is the issue of adding tools

[4] A process in which a closed system usually absorbs thermal energy from its surroundings, which is heat transfer into the system. Thus, an endothermic reaction generally leads to an increase in the temperature of the system and a decrease in that of the surroundings. It may be a chemical process, such as dissolving ammonium nitrate ($NH4NO_3$) in water (H_2O), or a physical process, such as the melting of ice cubes (for more details, see Oxtoby et al. 2015).

usually associated with hard power, which emphasizes the so-called European army (Kucharski quoted in Małczyński 2022). Hard power is a concept created by Nye and could be defined as a means to influence other actors through coercion. It is usually associated with military power and, to some extent, economic (Nye 2007, 34). The second is to modernize and reform transnational institutions of the EU, with attempts to introduce majority voting mechanisms, which means that there will be a category of losers in the process of European integration and a spillover of competencies within the transnational institutions and primacy of European common law over national constitutions. Those were the main objectives of the European Constitution, which was downgraded toward the Treaty of Lisbon (2007).

However, the main task was obtaining those ambitious goals with current capabilities. Within the EU, there was an unofficial mechanism labeled as a transnational mechanism for this chapter. In this form, it was, to some extent, a reversal of the classical mechanism labeled as geopolitical, where the legitimacy of an entity was coined through kinetic conquest of geopolitical space and controlling it long enough to transform it into legitimacy to mere existence as well as the capacity to wield more advanced and sophisticated forms of power.

By contrast, the EU needs to reverse this logic. With the application of current legitimacy to work and function, it needs to acquire primacy over the sovereignty of nation-states and simultaneously manage to achieve some level of control over "harder" tools for power classically associated with nation-states. Tomasz Grosse (2020, 233–288) characterized a process based on defense politics in the EU. However, it must be stressed that cycles must be continuously repeated, especially in small, insignificant cases, to produce desired and significant progress. The main point is to establish precedence as a point of reference, which will change the social perception of the value and effectiveness of the EU. The analyzed mechanism is created through the conjunction of four steps, the main focus of which is to change the perception of NPE without triggering a violent response at the nation-state level. In essence, the whole operation will be conjured in legal and social terms, which means that without geopolitical changes, social legitimacy for using power assets within the EU possession and member states directly by EU institutions. Therefore, without bloodshed, the center of gravity of European activities will be moved from the nation-state level to the supranational level.

First, when the problem is identified, usually it is the issue not put into treaties or mentioned briefly. One of the recent, although extremely visible, is the issue labeled as a "rule of law," which, albeit present in the treaties, is not adequately designed by them.[5] The document usually originates from a low level in the EU's internal order of laws and, in most cases, requires the engagement of one of the supranational EU institutions.

The second phase is conducting casual everyday activities based on said documents, which clarify, extend, and sometimes distort the content of major treaties. To the utmost, this phase relies on the normative power of the EU because, in most cases, member states and other institutions of the international environment, due to the underlying assumption of a lack of alternatives and guarantee of success, rely on the latter. However, in this phase, transformation is vulnerable to challenges posed by resistance from others and less vulnerable to NPE actors. In the case of the "rule of law," this kind of opposition stemming from awareness is in the case of Poland and Hungary, which both are conscious about exerting influence which is outside of treaty limits. Therefore, normative power is reduced to the soft power legal dimension. When it comes to the perception of the governments of Poland and Hungary, it may even be considered hostile and coercive.

The third part of this is how to deal with resentment and opposition. However, this phase was constructed when NPE remained a significant factor for the whole process. In this part, the European Court of Justice (ECJ) validates the adopted course of action (Blauberger and Schmidt 2017, 907–918). The main task of this EU institution is to solve this particular conflict situation. Furthermore, it is dedicated to interpreting treaty provisions. This means that ECJ is a crucial element in applying NPE. The European Commission and the ECJ must reach a consensus to advance the evolution. European Commission documents will become officially legitimized and bound to treaties if this happens. However, if NPE is undermined, this situation may be protracted or ignored by the subjected actor. Therefore, the present phase may further limit the normative power.

The fourth element is that the change will be tested, verified, and treated as an ordinary practice of EU institutions. The primary purpose

[5] This term was barely mentioned, without a proper definition and criteria to define it.

of applying normative power is to determine and impose the norm on the remaining actors. However, in this case, the procedure will create two levels of legal documents: officially accepted treaties and the daily function of the EU institutions, which may be contradictory. In classical situations, the NPE model will enact sufficient influence to outweigh this perceived hypocrisy, with the promise of wealth and power, but only to a certain extent. When reached, this will not be compensated and may undermine the successive cycles of evolution or even abort the whole process. Therefore, sometimes, there is a strong sense that a fifth phase is required, where the EU practice would be legitimized in the form of a new treaty, which took place in 1990. However, with the failure of the Constitution for the EU, this practice was largely abandoned.

In summary, the transnational mechanism of the evolution of non-state actors in an international environment seems effective but slow and insignificant, even unnoticed by IR academics, because it is drawn into repeated and countless processes. Even eventual changes will produce a new category of actor: state-like entities in function and power, but not structured and named. The result will be barely visible but felt when power shifts within the European international sub-system, with the EU equipped with attributes of sovereignty and member states, reduced purely to supportive roles. This implies the complete reversal of contemporary relations between those structures today. Despite that, the assumption is that there still needs to be more data to forecast the shape and form of the EU after the completion of this process. The EU will be equipped with more power tools, including military capabilities.

The main challenge with completing the transformation is that those changes stem from NPE. Therefore, evolution requires consuming a quantity of that power with every cycle. The question remains: how many cycles need to be completed before the awareness level of the national government rises to a point when normative power starts to be identified as harder and hostile, which will trigger a hostile response from the nation-state as a collective category? Even now, academics can observe that states with various levels of awareness and vulnerability may initiate counterreaction to the advancement of the evolution of the EU, which means further dispersal of scarce normative power resources. This disadvantage may be particularly challenging, especially when a mindset similar to the notion of "too big to fail" is present within the decision-making circles of the EU and supporters of deepening and widening integration in different nation-states, often disregarding challenges for EU: the existence of alternative, in the form of the United Kingdom (UK) of Great Britain and Northern Ireland after 2016 and stains on the European success story, which limit the effectiveness of NPE. It will not wholly nullify the process but certainly protract it and raise uncertainty for its result. The process is mainly caused by breaking the prerequisite assumption that the proposed solution is the only one available to achieve the desired objectives. It was completed by creating an extensive network of institutions within the EU and for closest European neighbors, like Switzerland, Norway, the Western Balkan countries, and Ukraine. Therefore, it is not possible to disconnect their performance from the EU's influence.

Contrary to this, the withdrawal of the UK from EU structures, combined with the severing of most of the ties between the EU and the UK, created situations where whatever happens with the UK means that the role of the EU is insignificant. Therefore, since 2016 there could be observed serious consequences for NPE. First, the fate of the UK became a role model and alternative to those dissatisfied with EU performance. Second, the UK became the focal point, and the diversion of assets for NPE became less effective. The EU and its supporters tend to fervently discard the UK as a loser of Brexit, which may produce contrary results, primarily when the EU cannot deliver success.

Outcome of NPE Transformation: Scenarios for the Future

Ultimately, one more issue needs to be addressed. It is the assessment of the possibility of potential outcomes for EU evolution. As with every forecast, it needs to be stressed that the future can only be predicted partially due to events that are not predictable by design but also due to the limitations of forecasting scientists. The last feature is harrowing because people like to consider themselves flawless. Despite those flaws, forecasts are essential because they allow politicians and scholars to prepare themselves for upcoming events, especially when they pose serious challenges for direct participants and neighboring communities and individuals.

The best method for forecasting political events will be the method of scenario. In this case, alternative future versions will be drafted and described. They will have one aspect in common: they will be derivative of a single variable. In this case, it will be seen that the effectiveness of the transnational mechanism of evolution of non-state actors will be a complete success or failure or partial of both things. This success will be measured by obtaining the desired capacities and creating new quality actors in international relations. The scenario method is particularly challenging when assessing the probability of scenario occurrence, which is not directly present in contemporary but is created instead by extrapolations and subjective assumptions. They must be constantly revised and reexamined to correct and develop scenarios. What will be presented should be considered a draft rather than an actual scientific analysis. The following scenarios will be drafted: hyperpower EU, normative power EU 2.0, international organization EU, and European confederacy.

The first scenario, hyperpower EU, embraces the concept of success despite the challenges and setbacks of the process. In this scenario, the EU will manage to nullify the negative impact of its actions and efficiently drive it to a conclusion, which means that the EU will produce much more quants of power than it will consume. Therefore, an accumulation of power potential will be observed, bolstering NPE even more. The success story will appease national governments so that the subsequent transfer of power and sovereignty will be perceived as beneficial and justified. This appeasement will lead to establishing a federation and complete the creation of a new quality international actor, inspiring similar processes in other regions of the globe. When it comes to the concert of powers, the merging of 27 states will create the potential for strategic autonomy of the EU. It will empower it to seek national interest and areas of influence, which may lead to conflict with other powers: Russia mainly fighting for primacy over Ukraine and Belarus; the United States, China, and India, more indirectly and concerning trade issues rather than political ones. The probability of this scenario happening is low. This assessment is based on three significant factors, which, all combined, will limit the possibility of this development.

First and foremost is the change in the international environment, which has become more turbulent and challenging. Wars, pandemics, and financial crises merge in a continuous and unified struggle that may eventually overcome the EU's capabilities. This challenge will undermine the EU's success story, thus limiting the drive to equip supranational institutions with hard power capabilities. Second is the existence of an alternative in the form of the UK outside of the EU, which is and continues to divert assets toward tackling this challenge, thus raising the awareness of NPE activity, which downplays its effectiveness. The third factor concerns the hardening of the nation-states' resistance, primarily due to a shift in the European political landscape toward the right, which is usually unwilling to bolster EU competencies. There is a possibility that those challenges will be overcome, but it is implausible. This scenario will become a starting point for replacing a geopolitical leader of the contemporary world. The remaining scenario's basic assumption is that the EU will remain constrained to the geopolitical space it is currently occupying.

The second scenario, namely NPE 2.0, is a scenario of the partial success of the process mentioned above of evolution. It means that despite significant progress, the eventual objective of federalization will not be achieved. Mark 2.0 signifies that the EU will manage to at least partially regain the momentum of the 1990s. Even resentful states, like Poland and Hungary, will perceive that participation and deepening integration will benefit and support their national interests. Therefore, the result will be similar to the contemporary shape of the EU, with few corrections on behalf of transnational elements of its structure at the expense of intergovernmental ones. This result, however, will demand a shift in the internal narratives of the EU, at least partially lessening the pressure on Poland and Hungary over ideological issues and addressing their shifting national interests, primarily when each government represents ideologies different from those the EU embraces. This change will affect the creation of a community of interest, where the success and, to some extent, development of those institutions will be perceived as beneficial to all member states. Although they will be reluctant to allow access to other power resources, this positive feedback bolsters normative power assets to the extent that the EU will become much more respected and, thus, an influential international player. Admittedly, the qualitative shift will not occur, and the EU will be reduced only to its intergovernmental organization aspect. The probability of this scenario happening is high. Once again, this assessment is based on three significant factors, which, all combined, will bolster the possibility of this development. First, what was presented in this chapter is an endemical statement about European integration for over 70 years now. Usually, ambitious projects tend to fail due to the reluctance of nation-states to give up their competencies and sovereignty, satisfied with fulfilling only unanimously accepted interests. Therefore, improving EU mechanisms is likely, but without severe design transformation. Second, the international turmoil and the need to dedicate assets, such as weapons and munition production, will limit resources available to fuel and improve European integration. There will be no resources left to construct improved EU structures. Third, it will be correlated to public opinion attitude, which is still profoundly delved into enlargement fatigue and igniting a slide toward the right in the European political landscape. All in all, this scenario is the most rational extrapolation of the contemporary international situation.

The third scenario is that the EU will embrace partial failure. It may be seen as a twin to the second scenario but is significantly different. That difference is visible in the social reception of the situation. Because in this situation, nothing will change. The situation will not improve in the following years, as both transnational and national institutions will not see a reason for that.

Consequently, the EU will look inward, focusing on managing internal dynamics and power struggles. The external context will be swept aside, especially challenges for frontier states, further complicating the situation. The biggest threat will come from different avenues. The EU will disregard the challenge of Brexit (the creation of the alternative), and its success story will remain the same. That means its attractiveness will start deteriorating, highly detrimental to normative power assets. Sooner or later, they will be depleted, which will result in the decline of the attractiveness of the EU. Its importance will remain intact, but transnational institutions will be subjected to strengthened national control. The probability of this scenario happening is medium. This assessment is based on three combined significant factors, which will modify the possibility of this development.

First and foremost, the lack of success produced by the EU will eventually undermine the social legitimacy of its continuous existence. Crisis coupled with an inability to manage them efficiently will deprive the EU of its legitimacy, and thus, changes will be introduced to limit the scope of EU mechanisms. Second, this development assumes the complete reversal of the long-standing tendency of step-by-step development of European institutions. This development is unlikely to happen because the EU has become an essential part of the European landscape, especially in terms of the political and social perception of the continent. External pressure is the third factor against this scenario, which provides the EU additional stimulus for its development, especially concerning Ukraine's pro-EU and pro-Western aspirations. This stimulus is the leverage that could increase the legitimacy of European institutions, thus improving chances for survival and development.

The fourth and final scenario is a scenario for a European confederacy. A confederacy is the opposition of a federation, which means that national governments will get the upper hand in relations to transnational institutions, allowing them to cherry-pick whatever they find interesting and beneficial from European integration and reject everything else. Effectively, the EU will be back in 1980s to the times of the EEC, primarily because the attractiveness of the EU will be depleted. How this will happen is hard to determine. However, some unprecedented events need to happen to produce that significant effect. The EU would become an empty husk of what it is today, with only those elements that benefit every member state. Due to a lost conflict with member states, the EU will be reduced to its intergovernmental organization form. The probability of achieving this outcome is unlikely. The EU has become a valuable element of the international community and too much revered to be discarded so easily. A widespread consensus states that the EU is to be maintained, mainly because it is usually connected with success, even for relatively small states. It may change, but it will take time and effort. The probability of this scenario happening is low. This assessment is based on three combined significant factors which will impede the possibility of this development.

First and foremost, this development assumes a complete reversal of the long-standing tendency of step-by-step development of European institutions. Second, this scenario implies the massive breakdown of EU legitimacy, probably connected with unpredictable and destructive events. This event occurrence is probable but unlikely and unpredictable. The third factor is the fact that the EU is helpful to nation-states in terms of managing international communication between European nation-states. This facilitation is so convenient that the EU's continuous existence will continue despite possible costs and limitations superimposed on nation-states.

Conclusion

In this chapter, the evolution of the EU was derived from the evolution of EU power, which was identified as NPE by Manners. When adopted in an international environment, this category embraces specific features and vulnerabilities for actors. Usually, it is the most cost-effective as it relies primarily on the reception of said actor by its pars, especially those targeted by power applications. However, it is not controllable, and in most cases, the final effect is different from the original intent, as may be seen in attempts to replicate the European model for integration in other regions. Thus, one of the tenets of EU evolution is to bolster the NPE with more state-like mechanisms, which depend on more straightforward, visible, and punitive forms of power.

However, those changes, which could be seen as hardening the EU, come with a price, usually expressing widespread dissatisfaction with EU performance, displayed on societal and governmental levels. In short, this transformation of NPE consumes resources, not quantitative like money, but qualitative like approval, credibility, and reliability. The question that is crucial for the future form and shape of the EU is whether it can generate new power resources faster than it consumes them. There could be observed evidence indicating both possible answers, meaning this fate is not decided.

The crucial element of future scenarios is effectiveness in managing conflict with nation-states, which is critical for the evolution of every non-state entity. The nature of this conflict and its parameters will differ. However, conflict with the state system to complete the transformation process is inevitable. Because the struggle is currently waged and both parties achieve certain successes, therefore further and more detailed evaluation of which scenario will be realized should be conducted. And the EU and its actorness will be on the scientific agenda for at least the next decade. This inquiry means that achieving geopolitical leadership is subjected to even longer processes, comparable in length to historical processes. It requires more than the simple development of hard power capabilities with a punitive function. There needs to be a corresponding development of institutional competence to run strategic operations on a global scale. According to the scenario labeled hyperpower EU, the first step toward its success is the transformation of NPE.

References

Anghel, V., and E. Jones. 2023. Is Europe Really Forged Through Crisis? Pandemic EU and the Russia-Ukraine War. *Journal of European Public Policy* 30 (4): 766–786.

Arnorsson, A., and Z. Gylfi. 2018. On the Causes of Brexit. *European Journal of Political Economy* 55: 301–323.

Babarinde, O. 2007. *The EU as a Model for the African Union: The Limits of Imitation*. Jean Monnet/Robert Schuman Paper Series. Miami: Florida European Union Center.

Bachmann, K. 2013. *Kiedy związane ręce zapewniają przewagę. Siła przetargowa Unii Europejskiej w negocjacjach międzynarodowych* (English: *When Tied Hands Give Advantage. Bargaining Power of EU in International Negotiations*). Warszawa: Scholar.

Bertherton, J., and C. Vogler. 2006. The European Union as a Protagonist to the United States on Climate Change. *International Studies Perspectives* 7 (1): 1–17.

Blauberger, M., and S.K. Schmidt. 2017. The European Court of Justice and Its Political Impact. *West European Politics* 40 (4): 907–918.

Bodin, J. 1967. *The Six Books of the Commonwealth*, trans. M.J. Tooley. Oxford: Alden Press.

Bokhorst, D., and F. Corti. 2023. Governing Europe's Recovery and Resilience Facility: Between Discipline and Discretion. *Government and Opposition*, 1–17, available at: https://doi.org/10.1017/gov.2023.14 (accessed 6 November 2023).

Bokia, A. 2000. *Cywilizacja łacińska. Studium na podstawie dorobku historiozoficznego Feliksa Konecznego* (English: *Latin Civilization: Study Based of Historiozofic Work of Feliks Koneczny*). Legnica: Wyższe Seminarium Duchowne Diecezji Legnickiej.

Boulding, K. 1989. *The Three Faces of Power*. London: Sage.

Bradford, A. 2020. *Brussels Effect: How the European Union Rules the World*. Oxford: Oxford University Press.

Czaputowicz, J. 2007. *Teorie stosunków międzynarodowych. Krytyka i systematyzacja* (English: *International Relations Theories: Critique and Systematization*). Warszawa: Wydawnictwa Naukowe PWN.

Damro, C. 2012. Market Power Europe. *Journal of European Public Policy* 19 (5): 682–699.

Fossum, J.E., and M. Jachtenfuchs. 2017. Federal Challenges and Challenges to Federalism. Insights from the EU and Federal States. *Journal of European Public Policy* 24 (4): 467–485.

Geremek, B. 2008. The Marshall Plan and European Integration. In *The Marshall Plan: Lessons Learned for 21st Century*, ed. E. Sorel and P.C. Padoan, 43–50. Paris: OECD Publications.

Grosse, T.G. 2020. Rozwój polityki obrony i przemysłu zbrojeniowego w Unii Europejskiej (English: Development of Defence Politics and Military Industry in European Union). In *Paliwo dla dominacji. O ekonomicznych podstawach supremacji geopolitycznej* (English: *Fuel for dominance. Economic foundations of geopolitics supremacy*), ed. T.G. Grosse, 233–288. Warszawa: Instytut Studiów Politycznych Polskiej Akademii Nauk.

Hill, C., M. Smith, and S. Vanhoonacker. 2017. *International Relations and the European Union*. Oxford: Oxford University Press.

Hyde-Price, A. 2006. "Normative" Power Europe: A Realist Critique. *Journal of European Public Policy* 13 (2): 217–234.

International Monetary Fund (IMF). 2022. World Economic Outlook Database, October 2022, available at: https://www.imf.org/en/Publications/WEO/weo-database/2022/October/weo-report?a=1&c=998,&s=NGDPD,PPPGDP,PPPPC,&sy=2021&ey=2022&ssm=0&scsm=0&scc=0&ssd=1&ssc=0&sic=0&sort=country&ds=.&br=1 (accessed 30 September 2023).

Järvenpää, P., C. Major, and S. Sakkov. 2019. *Report: European Strategic Autonomy: Operationalising a Buzzword*. Tallinn: International Center for Defence and Security.

Jellinek, G. 1921. *Ogólna nauka o państwie* (English: *General Science on the State*). Warszawa: F. Hoesicka.

Kavalski, E. 2013. The Struggle for Recognition of Normative Powers: Normative Power Europe and Normative Power China in Context. *Cooperation and Conflict* 48 (2): 247–267.

Kennedy, P.M. 1995. *Mocarstwa świata. Narodziny, rozkwit, upadek* (tłum. M. Kluźniak) (English: *The Rise and Fall of the Great Powers*). Warszawa: Książka i Wiedza.

Kesternich, I., B. Siflinger, J.P. Smith, and J.K. Winter. 2014. The Effects of World War II on Economic and Health Outcomes Across Europe. *The Review of Economics and Statistics* 96 (1): 103–118.

Koller, V., S. Kopf, and M. Miglbauer. 2019. Introduction: Context, History and Previous research. In *Discourse of Brexit*, ed. V. Koller, S. Kopf, and M. Miglbauer, 1–14. London and New York: Routledge.

Lenz, T. 2013. European Union Normative Power and Regionalism: Ideational Diffusion and Its Limits. *Cooperation and Conflict* 48 (2): 211–228.

Lombardo, E. 2016. Social Constructivism in European Integration Theories: Gender and Intersectionality Perspectives, Gendering European integration theory: Engaging New Dialogues. In *Gendering European Integration Theory: Engaging New Dialogues*, ed. G. Abels and H. MacRae, 123–146. Opladen, Berlin, Toronto: Columbia University Press.

Maltby, W.S. 1994. The Origins of a Global Strategy: England from 1558 to 1713. In *The Making of Strategy: Rulers, States and War*, ed. W. Murray, M. Knox, and A. Berstein, 151–177. Cambridge: Cambridge University Press.

Małczyński, B. 2022. Powstanie armii UE trudne ze względu na różnice wśród państw członkowskich [Wywiad z Bartłomiejem Kucharskim] (English: Creation of EU Army Difficult Due to Differences Among Member States [Interview with Bartłomiej Kucharski]), *Euractiv.pl*, May 31, available at: https://www.euractiv.pl/section/polityka-wewnetrzna-ue/interview/armia-ue-cofoe-przyszlosc-ue-unia-europejska-europa/ (accessed 30 September 2023).

Manners, I. 2002. Normative Power Europe: A Contradiction in Terms? *Journal of Common Market Studies* 40 (2): 235–258.

Maull, H. 1990. Germany and Japan: The New Civilian Powers. *Foreign Affairs* 69 (5): 91–106.

Meunier, S., and N. Kalypso. 2006. The European Union Was a Conflicted Trade Power. *Journal of European Public Policy* 13 (6): 906–925.

Nye, J.S. 2007. *Soft Power: The Means to Success in World Politics*, trans. J. Zaborowski. Warszawa: Wydawnictwo Akademickie i Profesjonalne.

Nye, J.S. 2011. *The Future of Power*. New York: Public Affairs.

Nye, J.S. 2012. China's Soft Power Deficit, The Wall Street Journal, May 8, available at: https://www.wsj.com/articles/SB10001424052702304451104577389923098678842 (accessed 30 September 2023.

Official Journal of the European Union (OJEU). 2022. Definitive Adoption (EU, Euratom) 2022/182 of the European Union's General Budget for the Financial Year 2022, February 24, available at: https://eur-lex.europa.eu/legal-content/EN/TXT/?uri=uriserv%3AOJ.L_.2022.045.01.0001.01.ENG&toc=OJ%3AL%3A2022%3A045%3ATOC (accessed 30 September 2023).

Orbie, J. 2006. Civilian Power Europe: Review of the Original and Current Debates. *Cooperation and Conflict* 41 (1): 123–128.

Oxtoby, D.W., H.P. Gillis, and L.J. Butler. 2015. *Principle of Modern Chemistry*. Boston: Brooks/Cole.

Philippopoulos-Mihalopoulos, A. 2009. Moment of Stasis: The Successful Failure of a Constitution for Europe. *European Law Journal* 15 (3): 309–323.

Pietraś, M. 2008. *Hybrydowość późnowestfalskiego ładu międzynarodowego* (English: *Hybrid late-Westphalian International Order)*. In *Późnowestfalski ład międzynarodowy* (English: *Late-Westphalian International Order*), ed. M. Pietraś and K. Marzęda, 57–74. Lublin: Wydawnictwo Uniwersytetu Marii Curie-Skłodowskiej.

Pietraś, Z.J. 2005. *Prawo wspólnotowe i integracja europejska* (English: *Acquis Communitaire and European integration*). Lublin: Wydawnictwo Uniwersytetu Marii Curie-Skłodowskiej.

Posner, E., and N. Veron. 2010. The EU and Financial Regulation: Power Without Purpose? *Journal of European Public Policy* 17 (3): 400–415.

Qvortrup, M. 2006. The Three Referendums on the European Constitution Treaty in 2005. *The Political Quarterly* 77 (1): 89–97.

Rothgeb, J.M. 1993. *Defining Power: Influence and Force in the Contemporary International System*. New York: St. Martin Press.

Szumski, C. 2023. *Szwecja: Wojsko na ulicach? Była premier mówi „tak"* (tłum. S. Otfinowska), (English: *Sweden: Army on the Streets? Former PM Says "Yes"*), *Euractiv.pl*, September 29, available at: https://www.euractiv.pl/section/bezpieczenstwo-i-obrona/news/szwecja-wojsko-na-ulicach-byla-premier-mowi-tak/ (accessed 30 November 2023).

Szumowski, A. 2021. *Ewolucja zbieżna niepaństwowych uczestników stosunków międzynarodowych* (English: *Convergent Evolution of Non-State Actors in International Relations*). Lublin: Wydawnictwo Uniwersytetu Marii Curie-Skłodowskiej.

The Economist. 2023. Poland's Rule-of-Law Conflict with the EU Is Coming to a Head, February 23, available at: https://www.economist.com/europe/2023/02/16/polands-rule-of-law-conflict-with-the-eu-is-coming-to-a-head (accessed 30 November 2023).

Treaty of Lisbon amending the Treaty on European Union and the Treaty establishing the European Community, signed at Lisbon, 13 December 2007, OJ C 306, 17.12.2007.

Urwin, D.W. 2014. *The Community of Europe: A History of European Integration Since 1945*. London: Routledge.

Weigly, R.F. 2004. *The Age of Battles. The Quest of Decisive Battles from Bretenfeld to Waterloo*. Bloomington, Indianapolis: Indiana University Press.

Weinzierl, J. 2021. An Army of Peoples? A Democratic Perspective on a Future European Army. *European Papers—A Journal on Law and Integration* 6 (2): 1049–1073.

Wheaton, S., and E. Braun. 2023. *Sentencing of ex-OLAF Chief Threatens More Tensions over EU Justice System*, *Politico*, September 17, available at: https://www.politico.eu/article/giovanni-kessler-ruling-threatens-more-tensions-over-eu-justice-system/ (accessed 30 November 2023).

The EU in Actions: Assessing EU Geopolitical Actorness Through Its Foreign Policy

EU Actorness in the Middle East: An Enterprise Doomed to Fail?

Raluca Moldovan

Introduction

In recent years (especially since Brexit, the COVID-19 pandemic, Russia's 2022 invasion of Ukraine and, most recently, the 2023 Gaza war between Hamas and Israel), the capacity of the European Union (EU) to act as a genuine global power on the international stage, has come under ever closer scrutiny. While it is true that Brussels has always aspired to a heightened status in international affairs (something attested by the numerous attempts to revamp the EU's foreign policy in subsequent treaties), in practice this has rather rarely been the case, hence the general perception of the Union as an economic giant, but a military and political dwarf. But what does EU actorness really mean, and why has it consistently failed (with the exception of some successful trade agreements) to turn meaningful results into account in a more geopolitical sense, specifically with regard to the Middle East? Could this failure be a sign that the EU's foreign policy approach towards the region, long based on the principles of normativity and liberal institutionalism, should be reconsidered and replaced by a more pragmatic, "less-carrots-more-sticks," outlook? The

R. Moldovan (✉)
Babes-Bolyai University Cluj-Napoca, Cluj-Napoca, Romania
e-mail: raluca.moldovan@ubbcluj.ro

L. Lika and D. Riga (eds.), *EU Geopolitical Actorness in a Changing World*, https://doi.org/10.1007/978-3-031-81160-9_5

present chapter attempts to answer this two-fold question in relation to a turbulent region whose importance and influence on the world stage has been amplified by recent and troubling international developments, notably the ongoing war in Ukraine.[1] Specifically, the chapter will look into the recent history of relations between the EU and Turkey, Iran and, respectively, Saudi Arabia, using a qualitative research methodology, in order to see why these countries have been less than enthusiastic about dealing with the EU as a whole and recognising its global actorness capabilities, preferring instead to maintain bilateral relations with individual EU members and to forge (more or less) interest-based partnerships with authoritarian states such as Russia and China. The study is based on various sources, many of them books, chapters and scholarly articles on the topic, as well as some official documents outlining the EU's foreign policy outlook.

The EU has consistently failed to derive any meaningful political benefits (in terms of recognition, leverage and influence), on a par with its economic investment in the Middle East (Bretherton and Vogler 1999, 43). The first section of the chapter focuses on the meanings and implications of EU actorness. The second, third and fourth sections are organised in the form of mini-case studies investigating EU actorness *vis-à-vis* Turkey, Iran and Saudi Arabia. After examining the relations between the EU and the three above-mentioned Middle Eastern states in the past decade or so, the concluding section will attempt to formulate an answer to this thorny question.

The Meanings and Implications of EU Actorness

Actorness, much like beauty, is, to a large extent, in the eye of the beholder: in other words, it results from one's perception by others, as well as from a set of internal features, which in the case of the EU, make it, as has often been argued, a *sui generis* actor in international relations (Bretherton and Vogler 1999, 1; Peters 2016a, 38; Müller 2012,

[1] As Natalie Tocci (2022, xxii) rightfully argues, "[a]ll major global and regional cleavages in fact are now tragically on display in the region: from the Russia-West and Israel-Iran confrontation in Syria to the Turkish-EU tensions in the Eastern Mediterranean, from the Turkey-[United Arab Emirates] UAE/Egypt struggle over political Islam in Libya to the Iran-Saudi conflict in Yemen, or the Gulf and Israeli scepticism of the Iran nuclear deal."

63).[2] This perception is influenced by several important factors, among which one could count presence (i.e., the capacity to exert influence and to shape the views and expectations of other actors), opportunities (i.e., developments in the external environment that facilitate or impede actorness) and capability (i.e., how one can respond effectively to these various developments and behave in consequential, autonomous ways that cannot be entirely predicted by reference to other actors) (Bretherton and Vogler 1999, 5, 2006, 30; Hopkins and Mansbach 1973, 36; Cosgrove and Twitchett 1970, 12; Sjöstedt 1977, 13).[3] According to Charlotte Bretherton and John Vogler (1999, 9), there are five basic requirements for actorness in international politics: "commitment to shared values and principles,[4] the ability to formulate coherent policies,[5] the capacity to undertake international negotiations, access to policy instruments and the legitimacy of decision processes," all of which influence an actor's (in this case, the EU's) presence on the international stage and its ability to exert influence. Upon closer examination, one can see that the EU's internal coherence, its ability to "speak with one voice," has, in recent years,

[2] In a strictly legal sense, from the perspective of international public law, states are the primordial international actors, since they are able to sign treaties, join international organisations, or be held responsible by other actors (Bretherton and Vogler 1999, 16 and 18). Seen from this perspective, also shared by the school of Realism (see Bull 1983, 151) and, to a smaller extent, Neo-realism (see Dessler 1989, who argues that this is a positional model in that the options available to any given state depend on its position within the power structure), there is little correlation between the possession of legal personality and actorness in behavioural terms, since small or weak states do have full legal status but are insignificant as actors, while the EU can play important roles without having legal personality.

[3] Gunnar Sjöstedt (1977, 16) defines actorness as "the measure of a unit's capacity to behave actively and deliberately towards other actors in the international system". This capacity is retained even though an actor's actions are not effective. Joseph Jupille and James A. Caporaso (1998, 214) identify four components of actorness in global politics: recognition (the *sine qua non* condition), authority (seen as legal competence to act), autonomy (independence from other actors) and cohesion (the ability to formulate and carry out internally consistent policy choices). For more details, see also Labinot Greiçevci (2011, 286–287).

[4] These are very clearly stated in the EU's treaties, most recently in the 2007 Treaty of Lisbon.

[5] Of course, in principle, this ability is not questioned, but rather, the extent to which it is realised in practice. Similarly, it is not the EU's ability to negotiate that is questioned, but rather, its effectiveness as a negotiator, as will be discussed below in the sections on Turkey and especially Iran.

been affected on several of these counts by events such as Brexit, the rise of populism and illiberalism in various member states, the cumbersome decision-making processes and the lack of more decisive leverage beyond mere economic instruments. Consequently, the EU's presence (which is a function of being rather than action, although it does play an important role in promoting actorness [Bretherton and Vogler 1999, 33]) and its ability to produce tangible impacts in its relations with various other global actors has been affected as well, especially considering that the EU as a whole cannot rely on traditional and widespread instruments of foreign policy such as national interest (Kratochvil et al. 2011, 391–392) and can sometimes play a rather limited role as a framing actor in the internal debates about the foreign policy choices of its member states.[6]

This leads to something of a contradiction, since two main features of actorness (external recognition and internal legitimacy) are rarely questioned in relation to EU member states, but are sometimes disputed when it comes to the perception of the EU as the legitimate representative of its citizens or its recognition by external powers as a coherent actor (Kratochvil et al. 2011, 392). Moreover, one also needs to question the attractiveness of the EU model (or, as Ian Manners puts it, its "normative power" [2002], i.e., the ability to change the norms, standards and prescriptions of world politics by inspiring other states and actors to follow its example), and its capacity to inspire emulation in outsiders, a third feature directly derived from the other two. So, while very few would dispute the fact the EU does possess the basic requirements for actorness in principle, there seems to be a visible gap between principle and practice (often referred to as "the capabilities-expectations gap" [Hill 1998; Ginsberg 1999; Lonardo 2023, 7; Thomas 2012]), in the sense that, more often than not, Brussels has difficulty projecting its foreign policy clout onto the global stage and persuading other actors to align to its views and principles. This study argues that, in the case of the Middle Eastern countries discussed below, this gap stems less from their perception of the EU's internal legitimacy and coherence (they appear

[6] The European Commission can usually exert this framing influence either by a preemptive action (by publicly presenting its position towards a major issue in documents such as the White Papers) or by persuading the public and media in individual member states that a policy would be best handled at the Union level (Kratochvil et al. 2011, 397). When this framing power is diminished, the EU is unable to persuade its member states to react similarly to external events, which partially explains the sometimes-dissenting positions of various EU states towards Russia's 2022 invasion of Ukraine.

rather unconcerned by this since they prefer to maintain bilateral ties with specific EU member states anyway) and more from their disinclination to recognise the Union's actorness as a whole, to emulate its model[7] or to put norms and principles above their own national interest.[8]

In the case of the Middle East, the image of the EU as a normative power should not be taken for granted, considering that Brussels often prioritised stability over democratisation and human rights (even in the aftermath of the Arab Spring), in true realist fashion (Teti et al. 2020, 44; Bouris et al. 2022, 2). For both Turkey and Iran, to give but two examples, conditionality and incentives have failed to bring about meaningful change, which has undermined the EU's credibility as a genuine normative power and diminished its attractiveness and influence. In other words, in addition to the capabilities-expectations gap mentioned earlier, there is also a gap between the value-driven normative actor the EU rhetorically envisages itself to be and the self-interested policies it is seen to pursue in practice (Teti et al. 2020, 83, 2022, 217 and 225), or between the liberal-institutional norms it professes to uphold and the neorealist actions it carries out, which would all the more justify the need for a genuine change of foreign policy paradigm.[9] The European Union Global Strategy (EUGS), designed to redefine the Union's external role, released in June 2016 (shortly after Brexit) hints at this transformation, since it emphasises resilience (i.e., the ability of states and

[7] Since this model is based on voluntarily incorporating EU norms by non-member states, not on the use of force (Kratochvíl et al. 2011, 394), the fact this has limited attractiveness should unfortunately come as no surprise, given the current international milieu.

[8] Even when Middle Eastern states did manifest their willingness to emulate the EU model (during the Arab Spring, for example, when calls for democratisation rang across the region), the EU official discourse appeared to emphasise a more narrow, procedural understanding of democracy focused on civil and political rights rather than on the social rights and justice the protesters demanded (Teti et al. 2020, 41 and 54). After the uprisings, the EU announced that "negative conditionality" (sanctions for not meeting human rights and democratisation standards) would be supplemented by a "more-for-more" approach, i.e., countries meeting those standards would be rewarded (Teti et al. 2022, 218).

[9] There is yet another view on this issue: Raffaella Del Sarto (2016) argues that the EU is a genuine normative power when it comes to its transfer of rules and practices to outsiders, but does so to serve its own interests. The EU's human rights and democratisation foreign policy paradigms have failed to live up to their rhetorical heights in the case of the 2015–2016migration crisis and deal with Turkey, the murder of Jamal Khashoggi or the failure of the JCPOA, to give but a few examples (Bouris et al. 2022, 6).

societies to reform, thus recovering from domestic and external crises) as the solution for eradicating the causes behind various states' weakness and fragility, and does not highlight the diffusion of EU norms, principles and values which underpins the European Neighbourhood Policy (ENP) (Giusti 2019, 23).[10] The document also puts forward a new approach in the EU's foreign policy, i.e. principled pragmatism, which indicates a scaling down of the Union's external relations ambitions[11] and a transition to a post-normative phase in its foreign policy. This new approach is supposed to replace the "effective multilateralism" that the EU relied upon since the 2003 European Security Strategy (ESS), itself a reaction to the 2003 US invasion of Iraq (Cronberg 2017, 34–35).[12] It is perhaps in the name of this principled pragmatism that the EU, while continuing to represent itself as a force for good (Kaya 2013, 32), persists in referring to the Middle East primarily in terms of securitising speech acts (Cebeci 2022, 73). Brussels' preferred method of dealing with conflict and instability in the region takes the form of multilateral, institutionalised engagement and cooperation with both state and non-state actors and partnerships with various regional organisations, which may explain why its success has been sporadic and limited to specific missions (such as the EU Advisory Mission to Iraq (EUAM Iraq) (Tuncel 2022, 88). Therefore, it is doubtful whether the EU will be, for now and the foreseeable future, in a position to shape the regional order and to have a meaningful contribution to solving the Middle East's many troubling issues. Since the Middle East is a region that naturally conforms to realpolitik, which means that the pursuit of power and security systematically frustrates normative engagements (Halliday 2005, 25), it would normally follow that realism/neorealism would be the relevant position from which

[10] The EUGS calls for a less ideological and more pragmatic external approach (liberalism and democracy are not mentioned as explicit goals), better equipped to shape the risks of state fragility in the EU's neighbourhoods on a case-by-case basis (Giusti 2019, 27 and 36). The adoption of EU norms only works when there is the reward of membership at the end of the tunnel, something that is not the case for Middle Eastern states—not even for Turkey, anymore.

[11] Principled pragmatism, as it is presented in the document, is both a cognitive (assessing a situation realistically) and behavioural (finding pragmatic solutions) tool and is the consequence of the EU's failure to efficiently deal with various crises, from the 2014 invasion of Crimea to Brexit (Giusti 2019, 33).

[12] The EU's effective multilateralism was also seen as a counterweight to the US's assertive multilateralism (Cronberg 2017, 42).

to examine the EU's relations with this part of the world (Dionigi 2022, 94). This shift would surely fall in line with the desire of the European Commission to undertake a more active and assertive geopolitical role, as can be seen from the EUGS and from the positioning adopted by Brussels with regard to the conflicts in Ukraine and the Middle East, the latter reignited in early October 2023 after the Hamas attack on Israel. However, it might be too early to tell whether this pursuit of assertiveness will yield tangible results—but it is an encouraging sign that the EU means to leave a stronger, more visible foreign policy footprint.

EU Actorness *vis-à-vis* Turkey

Turkey represents an excellent case study for testing the clout of EU actorness in the Middle East, given the country's long relationship with what used to be the European Community (EC) and its interest in becoming a full member state of the EU (having applied to join as early as 1987), which has now all but completely waned. One could rightfully argue that the development of the EU's (and its predecessors) relations with Turkey has always been a fairly accurate mirror of the times, from a rapprochement spawned by Cold War strategic priorities to the hope that Turkey would be a reliable partner and stability factor in Central Asia and the Middle East as a whole (Bretherton and Vogler 1999, 163). Throughout this time, starting with the 1964 Ankara Association Agreement (AAA), Turkey became a member of "all the right clubs" North Atlantic Treaty Organisation (NATO), Commission on Security and Cooperation in Europe (CSCE), Organisation for Economic Co-operation and Development (OECD), Council of Europe (CoE), a customs union with the EU (Baracani and Calimli 2019, 90), but full-fledged membership in the EU seems to no longer be in the cards.[13] The image that Turkey projected at the time, as a Western-oriented, secular, quasi-democratic country, no longer matches Turkey's realities today, when none of these features are all that manifest anymore: under Recep Tayyip Erdogan's twenty-year strongman rule, Turkey has shifted from Ataturk's secularism and turn

[13] Considerable progress was made in those early years: between 2002 and 2004, Turkey amended 200 law articles covering a wide range of political reforms, passing eight harmonisation packages, which demonstrates the success of the EU's leverage as a "gatekeeper" to push through a democratic norm transfer to Turkey (Zihnioglu 2020, 2).

towards the West into a state driven by regional ambitions of power politics where democratic values often exist only on paper. So one could justifiably wonder why the influence of and ties with the EU, given the two entities' long history (for more details on this, see Moldovan 2020) have proven so ineffective in stopping Ankara's slide into authoritarianism and in improving its own growing credibility deficit in Turkey.[14]

This was not always the case: after the 1980 military takeover in Turkey, the EC was able to exert considerable economic and diplomatic pressure to ensure a return to civilian rule and the adoption of a number of civil and political reforms (Bretherton and Vogler 1999, 167). However, this pressure may have also led to some deep-seated resentment against the influence of Brussels in Turkey's domestic politics, which would resurface decades later in various ways. The rise of the Justice and Development Party (JDP or AKP in Turkish) in Turkish politics (starting with 2002) roughly coincided with a new phase in the relations between the EU and Turkey, one which seemed—at least in 2005, when the accession negotiations officially started—to lead to the ultimate prize, full membership.[15] It was through this conditionality and the promise of incentives that the EU was able to call for the adoption of a number of significant reforms, many of which were aimed at improving the status and rights of the Kurdish minority in Turkey. The level of support for EU membership, as well as an overall positive image of Brussels among ordinary Turks were reasons to believe, at the time, that the accession process, despite its slow pace, would ultimately be successful.

However, in the following ten years or so, the lengthy and difficult negotiation process, in which the rewards were quite few and far between (Zihnioglu 2020, 11) the events of the Arab Spring—which led to a shift in the Middle Eastern balance of power, Erdogan's growing authoritarianism and increasingly aggressive regional ambitions (despite the often-invoked "zero problems with neighbours policy") (Baracani and Calimli 2019, 87 and 89), the Syrian crisis and the accompanying refugee problems it created and the emergence of new terrorist threats in the

[14] This credibility deficit has a lot to do with the fact that the EU would like to transfer to Turkey some values and norms that are under attack at home, within the EU itself (Zihnioglu 2020, 3).

[15] However, Brussels made it clear in this case that negotiations were an open-ended process, whose outcome cannot be guaranteed beforehand, which—in retrospect—could not have helped Turkey's accession aspirations (Baracani and Calimli 2019, 93).

region meant that Ankara and Brussels started drifting apart, especially considering that the former began cultivating closer ties with Moscow in an attempt to draw advantages without having to comply with any obligations concerning human rights or rule of law.[16] Gradually, Turkey started relishing its position as a regional power player and its pursuit of past hegemony, while Erdogan started to understand that his country can still enjoy the economic benefits that come with the customs union and economic ties with the EU without having to jump through all the democratic hoops that full membership entails. The aftermath of the failed 2016 coup against Erdogan and the unconvincing messages of support he received from Brussels and Washington further cemented his idea that the advantages of continuing to pursue the EU membership path did not outweigh the drawbacks (Aydintasbas and Shapiro 2023; Zihnioglu 2020, 41).[17]

Especially since the start of the 2022 war in Ukraine, as has been explained at length elsewhere (Moldovan 2023), Erdogan has positioned himself as an indispensable international player, a vital mediator that can help bring about an end to the conflict (since he has maintained rather cordial relations with both sides), or–barring that–at least broker important deals such as the 2022 grain deal. Turkey does not see Vladimir Putin's war against the West in moral or ideological terms (Aydintasbas and Shapiro 2023) and is guided solely by pragmatism and self-interest. Under these circumstances in which Turkey is no longer interested in being just "one of 28," it should come as no surprise to anyone that the influence the EU was once able to exert on Turkish politics through its conditionality and (more or less firm) promise of membership has now all but vanished (Zihnioglu 2020, 13). Brussels, as well as Washington, would be best served by understanding that transactionalism may now be the best policy in dealing with what some authors call a "post-Western Turkey" (Aydintasbas and Shapiro 2023). Simply put, Turkey's

[16] In 2013, during a joint press conference with Russian president Putin, Erdogan called on the latter to "save us from the trouble" or trying to become an EU member (Zihnioglu 2020, 38).

[17] As early as 2013, Erdogan did not mince words when discussing Turkey's membership bid: "The EU wants to forget us, but it holds back, it cannot forget us. However, if they make public [that they do not want us], we will be relieved. Instead of wasting our time, make it public, so that we get on" (Erdogan quoted in Zihnioglu 2020, 38). Apparently, Brussels heard him, since no new accession negotiation chapters have been opened since June 2016.

EU membership no longer holds the same attractiveness it once did, as Ankara's ambitions extend far beyond being a part of an entity that presupposes adhering to a set of norms and values that do not have much appeal anymore. Since both parties understand this to be the current state of facts, Brussels has no instruments at its disposal to force a course correction similar to the one it was able to impose in 1980. Erdogan (and, by extension, Turkey) now operates according to the premise that the West (primarily embodied by Brussels and Washington) is in decline and that the emerging multipolar world is the country's best chance to rise once more to great-power status (Aydintasbas and Shapiro 2023), all the while carefully carrying out a delicate balancing act as the "ultimate fence-sitter" to maximise benefits and reduce risks.[18]

Certainly, the EU and Turkey still have a number of relevant common interests (Middle Eastern regional stability, a peaceful resolution of the Syrian crisis and the safe return of refugees to their homeland, curbing Iran's nuclear ambitions and the terrorist threat [Müftüler-Bac and Cihangir-Tetik 2022, 191]), which means that collaboration between them is both still possible and necessary and that Turkey still remains a significant EU strategic partner (Baracani and Calimli 2019, 95). But neither side should harbour illusions about the relationship: at least as long as Erdogan holds the reins of power (given that he has made it clear he is not interested in domestic political reforms and has little patience for being lectured on human rights), this "cold peace" will persist and the EU should give up the illusion it can project its influence onto Ankara's decision-making process, since the leverage it possesses with Turkey has not led to a change in the status quo of the relationship in the last decade or so. Revitalising EU actorness *vis-à-vis* Turkey would probably require either a dramatic regional change that would affect Turkey's standing, thus making it more likely to gravitate closer to Brussels or a more forceful

[18] This state of facts could also be an opportunity for the EU: by accepting that Turkey's membership bid cannot be resurrected and that appeals to shared values will fall on deaf ears, Brussels now has the chance to appeal to a newly-re-elected Erdogan's pragmatism and ambitions to make a productive relationship possible. The recent concessions Turkey obtained in exchange for not opposing Sweden's NATO bid could serve as a blueprint for this (Aydintasbas and Shapiro 2023). Another relevant instance of maximising benefits is the recent rapprochement between Turkey and Saudi Arabia, exemplified by Erdogan's July 2023 high profile visit to Saudi Arabia, which resulted in tens of billions of dollars in investments in Turkey's struggling economy (Hiltermann 2023).

EU approach to show Turkey how much it would have to lose by moving further away from a liberal democratic system.

EU Actorness *vis-à-vis* Iran

The case of Iran presents one important similarity with Turkey, in that EU actorness mattered in influencing the country's policy choices up to a point, after which Brussels' influence waned to the point of now being close to zero. Of course, the two cases are significantly different in that Iran was never an EU candidate state and thus, EU conditionality was always going to play a very marginal role here in that respect. Even so, in the lead-up to the signing of the Joint Comprehensive Plan of Action (JCPOA), also known as the Iran nuclear deal, the contribution of the EU to the negotiation process was anything but negligible (Cronberg 2017, 25; Adebahr and Alcaro 2022, 380). The involvement of the EU in the signing of the deal was a relevant example of its commitment to effective multilateralism and the rules-based international order (Dessi and Ntousas 2022, 187).

Given the space constraints of the present chapter, this section will primarily focus on the particular case of the nuclear deal and how it exemplifies the varying influence of EU actorness concerning Iran. The JCPOA was hailed as a prominent foreign policy achievement for the EU, so much so that the then High Representative of the Union for Foreign Affairs and Security Policy and Vice-President of the European Commission (HR/VP), Federica Mogherini, stated in 2015 that "the international community has made an historical step towards peace. With pride, I can say the European Union made it possible" (Mogherini quoted in Akbarzedeh 2023, 245). This statement was no gratuitous self-congratulation, since the EU, which had traditionally had much closer ties with Iran than the United States after the 1979 Iranian Revolution, indeed began nuclear talk with Tehran long before Washington took over the initiative. Throughout the 1990s, the EU-Iran relations were mostly conducted through the Critical Dialogue Forum (CDF) by which Brussels, betting on engagement rather than isolation to moderate the Ayatollahs' regime (Perteghella 2019, 149), tried to address issues such as Iran's abysmal human rights record and involvement in terrorism and get the country to adopt some reforms with a view to improving bilateral relations, especially in economic terms (Adebahr and Alcaro 2022, 378).

This also enabled the EU to act as a mediator between Washington and Tehran (Akbarzedeh 2023, 246).

Evidence first emerged in 2002 that Iran was developing a secret nuclear proliferation programme, at which point the E3 group (Germany, France and the United Kingdom (UK), all of which were EU members at the time) started a dialogue with Iran to prevent the matter from turning into an international crisis, a very likely scenario if, for instance, other regional states (Saudi Arabia, Turkey, perhaps Egypt) had started nuclear programmes of their own (Adebahr and Alcaro 2022, 379). The talks started in 2003, soon after the US invasion of Iraq, as the EU feared that escalating tensions between the United States and Iran could lead to another regional war, a fear compounded by Washington's calls for regime change in Tehran (Cronberg 2017, 44 and 326).[19] Given the divisions that the US invasion caused among EU member states, for Brussels, solving the Iran nuclear file would prove that it still was a significant global actor that could solve pressing issues through effective multilateral cooperation (Adebahr 2017, 3). The EU thus aimed to upheld the principles of the Non-Proliferation Treaty (NPT) (which entered into force in March 1970; today, it has 191 state parties)[20] and to safeguard its economic interests in Iran, threatened by the mounting US sanctions regime that affected the trade relations between the two. In October 2003, the E3 foreign ministers meeting resulted in the Tehran Declaration which spelled out Iran's commitment to nuclear non-proliferation and cooperation with the International Atomic Energy Agency (IAEA). A year later, following the Paris Agreement, Iran agreed to suspend its uranium enrichment activities (Perteghella 2019, 150; Bayramov and Sezal 2023, 229). From then on, both the E3 and the EU as a whole played a key role in all direct nuclear talks with Iran, despite criticism from the United States, as Washington feared these would legitimise the Tehran regime. The main principles of EU foreign policy during these negotiations were effective multilateralism, support for international institutions

[19] Although Tehran would have preferred, at the time, to negotiate directly with Washington, during president Mohammad Khatami's term, the Americans refused, so the E3 emerged as the best alternative, the Iranians hoping that the EU could also deliver US support for a deal (Cronberg 2017, 152 and 154).

[20] The treaty's main pillars are nuclear disarmament, non-proliferation and peaceful uses of nuclear technology (Cronberg 2017, 53).

and the legitimacy of international treaties and agreements (Cronberg 2017, 48).

These fears proved somewhat justified in 2006, when Iran, following the election of hardliner president Mahmoud Ahmadinejad, resumed its uranium enrichment programme and refused to cooperate with the IAEA, which forced the E3/EU to refer the nuclear file to the United Nations Security Council (UNSC), thus marking the start of the P5 + 1 (namely China, France, Russia, the UK and the United States, plus Germany) negotiation framework and the emergence of the United States as the main force behind the talks, with the EU missing the chance to maintain its autonomous position and perhaps secure a deal by itself (Cronberg 2017, 82 and 336). From this point forward, the EU and its HR/VP Mogherini took on the role of facilitator between Iran and the P5 + 1 (Akbarzedeh 2023, 247). Negotiations proceeded slowly and with little result and, in 2010, the EU started sanctioning Iran and imposing an oil embargo against Tehran in 2012 (Adebahr and Alcaro 2022, 380).[21] The combined pressure of international sanctions and their crippling effect on the Iranian economy forced Tehran to return to the negotiating table in 2013, thus paving the way for the signing of the JCPOA in 2015, despite very vocal concerns from Israel and Saudi Arabia. Both countries feared that the economic boost from the removal of sanctions would help Iran expand its regional influence and secretly pursue its nuclear enrichment programme despite the terms of the deal.

Given the EU's instrumental role in bringing about the Iran deal, how can one explain its inability to prevent its failure and its very limited capacity to exert a moderating influence on Tehran now, amidst renewed repressive measures of the regime against its opponents? Much of the answer has to do with former US president Donald Trump's unilateral decision to withdraw the United States from the JCPOA in May 2018, despite vocal protests from the other parties to the deal that Iran was indeed meeting its obligations under the terms of the agreement. This proves that the future and transformative potential of the nuclear deal was always tied to the general trajectory of US-Iranian relations, a lesson that the EU had to learn the hard way (Adebahr and Alcaro 2022, 381), since it is never easy realising that one's own importance and influence is not

[21] The EU reluctantly agreed to impose sanctions, despite in principle doubting their efficiency, in order to deter a very likely Israeli military action against Iran, which could have easily escalated (Cronberg 2017, 327).

quite as great as one envisaged. Moreover, the EU was not able to stop Washington from imposing secondary sanctions on European companies that conducted business with Iran, thus becoming caught in the crossfire between the Trump administration and Tehran (Akbarzedeh 2023, 253). In response, in January 2019 the EU created an Instrument in Support of Trade Exchanges (INSTEX) to circumvent US sanctions and facilitate legitimate trade with Iran (Bayramov and Sezal 2023, 233; Suchkov and Vasilenko 2022, 207), since the EU reiterates its belief that Iran still adhered to the terms of the nuclear deal. However, under mounting US pressure, the efficiency of INSTEX was very limited, as the volume of EU-Iran trade continued to collapse (Adebahr and Alcaro 2022, 383).

Donald Trump's defeat in the 2020 presidential race reignited hopes that the deal would be resumed, especially since president-elect Joe Biden made renegotiating the nuclear deal one of his foreign policy priorities, but—at the time of writing in September 2023—despite eight rounds of indirect negotiations in which the EU took part from the very beginning, no progress has been made either in revisiting the 2015 agreement or in securing a new one. Meanwhile, the sanctions regime continues, to the disillusionment of the Iranian population, whose high expectations about the 2015 deal's benefits were never met in the first place (Perteghella 2019, 137), and the Tehran regime no longer makes any attempt to pretend it has not resumed its nuclear enrichment programme. Moreover, Iran has drifted ever closer into Moscow's and Beijing's orbits, since both countries share a common view of international affairs and aspire to be leaders in a multipolar, non-US-led order.

Under these circumstances, it is highly improbable for the EU to find any instruments that would enable it to exert some influence or pressure on Iran and determine the regime to reconsider its position on nuclear proliferation, human rights, support for terrorist organisations or pretty much anything else, since Brussels has proven that it cannot act as an autonomous actor and stand up to Washington to preserve the deal without US support, despite multiple vocal official statements affirming its commitment to it.[22] The same credibility deficit that has affected the

[22] Some American commentators (among them, Robert Kagan), argued that the brand of effective multilateralism that the EU employed to bring about the JCPOA was a "weapon of the weak," meaning that states that seek multilateral arrangements lack the power to impose solutions to international problems that serve their own interests (Kagan quoted in Cronberg 2017, 43).

EU's clout in Turkey is also manifest in Tehran: the leaders of the Iranian state do not believe that the EU can act independently and offer anything valuable in exchange for their moderation or compliance. Moreover, they know that such offers inevitably come with strings attached, in the form of compliance with human rights and liberal norms: in other words, the sweetness of the carrots is not worth the pain of the sticks. That is why Tehran prefers to deal with Moscow or Beijing, both of which provide benefits and financial incentives without asking too many uncomfortable questions—something that also explains why Beijing was able to mediate the recent 2023 historical rapprochement between Iran and Saudi Arabia, which has the potential to considerably alter the regional power balance in the Middle East.

EU Actorness *vis-à-vis* Saudi Arabia

Of the three cases analysed, Saudi Arabia is the state that has probably had the least deep relationship with the EU in the past few decades, since the Kingdom was never in the position of a candidate state, like Turkey, or the object of significant foreign policy interest, like Iran. For a long time, Riyadh gravitated in Washington's shadow, depending on its US partner for security guarantees against its arch nemesis, Iran—although it should be pointed out that the rivalry between the two actors had less to do with the Shia–Sunni divide (as it is commonly assumed) and more to do with geopolitics and regional influence. But, especially since the ambitious Crown Prince Mohammed bin Salman became the de facto leader of the Kingdom soon after his father's 2015 accession to the throne, Saudi Arabia has started to manifest its global ambitions and to position itself as an influential and, perhaps, indispensable mid-level power akin to, for instance, Brazil (Hiltermann 2023), which means that Brussels might seek, if possible, to draw the Kingdom closer in its orbit.

As in the case of Iran, the EU has hoped to exert a moderating influence on Saudi Arabia, particularly considering the country's rather appalling human rights record, laid bare for the entire world to see in the aftermath of Saudi journalist Jamal Khashoggi's assassination in 2018—with very little discernible success so far. The fact the EU maintained a conspicuous silence on the Khashoggi murder during its regular EU-Gulf Cooperation Council (GCC) meetings certainly did not help boost its clout with the Saudi Kingdom (Schumacher 2022, 162).[23] The EU-Saudi relations have mostly been limited to the economic sphere, with the EU being the Kingdom's second trading partner, after China, while Saudi Arabia is only the EU's 17th trading partner in goods, with only 1.1% of the EU market share. Brussels and Riyadh signed a 2021 cooperation agreement providing the framework for their economic and political relations,[24] but Saudi Arabia has consistently resisted any EU attempts to influence its domestic politics through negative conditionality (which in this case provides weak leverage anyway), denouncing them as interference in the country's internal affairs and pointing out to the "different systems of values" governing the two entities (Schumacher 2022, 161).

The US's recent disengagement from the Middle East and a significant cooling of the relationship with Saudi Arabia (Constantini and Santini 2019, 119–120) have forced the Kingdom to look elsewhere for partners to serve its interests and it was in this vacuum that Beijing has eagerly stepped in, becoming Riyadh's prominent business partner. Additionally, Saudi Arabia still enjoys cordial relations with Moscow, even after the start of the 2022 war in Ukraine, and has recently been invited to become a member of the BRICS (Brazil, Russia, India, China, South Africa) bloc, further cementing its rising/emerging powerhouse status. Its quest for security, particularly in the aftermath of the Arab Spring, which threatened to upend the long-established status quo by calling for regime change, has

[23] In this case, Brussels' position contrasts sharply with that of the United States: soon after the Biden administration took over in 2021, the Central Intelligence Agency (CIA) published the results of its investigation into the Khashoggi murder and sanctioned several Saudi nationals involved in the incident. The report also named Mohammed bin Salman as having ordered the assassination, yet the Crown Prince suffered no consequences as a result. It took two weeks after the murder for the HR/VP Mogherini to state that the EU "expected" the Saudi regime to carry out a "full investigation" to reveal "proper clarity on the circumstances". At no point did the EU or any member state officially demand that Mohammed bin Salman be personally held accountable, despite overwhelming evidence. The British, German and French foreign ministers issued a joint statement in October 2018, declaring that they would "ultimately make our judgement based on the credibility of the further explanation we receive about what happened", but no subsequent evidence made them jeopardise their bilateral ties with the Kingdom (Schumacher 2022, 163–164).

[24] The EU delegation in Riyadh, which opened as recently as 2004, helps oversee a series of projects involving the GCC as a whole, based on the existing 1988 EU-GCC Cooperation Agreement.

driven Saudi Arabia to pursue a more assertive regional foreign policy,[25] whose rewards it is now reaping in the form of massive oil revenues (Constantini and Santini 2019, 114), significant foreign investments and a path to regional hegemony after normalising its fraught ties with Iran in an historic agreement brokered by China in March 2023.

Certainly, Saudi Arabia understands the advantages that a large market such as the EU provides, especially considering Mohammed bin Salman's ambitious agenda, known as Vision 2030, to diversify the country's economy and reduce its dependence on oil revenues and his willingness to engage economically with the EU, as long as this provides significant benefits, but not to the point where it will agree to adopt domestic reforms in exchange for financial advantages, because it can easily find the same rewards elsewhere. Simply put, the EU is not that attractive a partner for Saudi Arabia, as it does not have all that much to offer: the United States continues to be the Kingdom's main security partner and sophisticated weaponry provider, China has already injected billions in the Saudi economy and has helped broker the agreement with Iran, Russia remains a source of cheap oil that the Kingdom buys below market price and then resells at a significant profit, considering that the price per crude oil, at the time of writing, is above $90 per barrel. And none of these partners exert pressure on Saudi Arabia to correct its human rights record and implement liberal domestic reforms—not even the United States, despite occasional rhetorical condemnations against the treatment of women, political prisoners or religious minorities. The EU cannot even act as a mediator in facilitating a possible Saudi-Israeli treaty (something that both Mohammed bin Salman and Israeli Prime Minister Benjamin Netanyahu have envisaged for some time), similar to the Abraham Accords, i.e. the normalisation agreements that Israel has signed with the United Arab Emirates (UAE), Qatar, Morocco and Sudan: despite enjoying a close and relatively cordial relationship with Israel, Brussels is in no position to act as a go-between, as it lacks the kind of credibility that only the United States can offer in this case.[26]

[25] A few examples in this respect include crushing the 2011 Arab Spring uprising in neighbouring Bahrain to help the al-Khalifa ruling family keep their throne, starting the 2015 military campaign in Yemen and launching a blockade against Qatar in 2017 (Constantini and Santini 2019, 118).

[26] According to Israeli sources, the three main demands that Saudi Arabia has presented to the United States in order to start negotiating a treaty with Israel are: a NATO-style

What is certain, at least for the foreseeable future, is that Saudi Arabia, driven by Mohammed bin Salman's quest to fulfil his global ambitions, will continue to act in its own self-interest and engage in whatever partnerships will help further its aspirations. Therefore, relations with the EU will continue to be subordinated to this agenda, being based on a kind of ad-hoc transactionalism that will allow Brussels to exert only a minimal influence in the Gulf Kingdom.

Conclusion

The present chapter has attempted to answer the question of why the EU, despite being recognised as a legitimate actor in global politics, has failed to project a significant influence in the Middle East (specifically, in the three instances discussed above) in order to obtain meaningful results. The answer to this question appears quite straightforward at this point: in all three cases analysed, the carrot-and-stick approach often employed by Brussels to a more or less visible extent did not lead to a noteworthy change in the states' behaviour in the direction desired or envisaged by the EU.

The negative conditionality and the "rewards system" the EU used in Turkey's case failed when the country's leaders (specifically, President Erdogan) decided that pursuing full membership in the Union was no longer an attractive option, since the country would not be free to fulfil its regional and global aspirations as a "Brussels vassal" and that enjoying the economic benefits of access to the common market without conforming to the Copenhagen criteria (the well-known broad set of rules concerning democracy, rule of law, human rights, market economy and implementation of the EU acquis adopted in 1993) would be more advantageous. As far as Iran is concerned, the EU's inability to act independently of the United States in the case of the JCPOA and prevent the reinstatement of economic sanctions meant that Brussels was not reliable and credible enough to warrant even considering adopting the domestic reforms that a closer partnership with the EU would have entailed; thus, Tehran chose the path of least resistance and resumed its nuclear programme, showing little willingness to renegotiate the kind of deal towards which the EU spent years working. And Saudi Arabia sees itself as too important an

defence pact, access to advanced American weapons and US support for a civilian nuclear project (Tibon and Harel 2023).

actor, and views the EU as perhaps not important or attractive enough, to pursue a closer relationship, despite the current economic benefits—so in this case, neither carrots nor sticks would make a difference, since Riyadh's ambitions can only be fulfilled by partnerships with those actors it perceives to be the true leaders of the current international order.

In other words, none of the many attributes ascribed to the EU as an international actor (such as a transformative power, a mediating power, a global conflict manager, a Kantian power, a civilising power, a quiet superpower or a normative power (Tuncel 2022, 83) appear to have made any substantial difference in its attempt to exert more influence in the Middle East. The fact that the EU does not enjoy a great reputation among populations in the region, due to a mismatch between its own self-perception and how its actions and consequences are viewed (Teti et al. 2022, 217) also contributes to its lack of credibility as a genuinely influential actor. Certainly, the EU is not the only Western actor suffering from a lack of credibility in the Middle East, but the United States, often affected by the same issue, has a longer history of involvement in the region and of trying to impose some kind or order by trying to supplant the various empires that dominated the Middle East for countless centuries (Kaplan 2023).

The EU remains, ultimately, a regional organisation that can only take on the capabilities that the member states agreed to bestow upon it, which has often severely limited its participation in multilateral initiatives where it is required to speak with one voice (Gaenssmantel et al. 2023, 270) or in matters that require the imposition of restrictive measures (Lonardo 2023, 8). This fact has been quite evident since the start of the Israel-Hamas war in October 2023. The principled pragmatism announced in the EUGS might signal, as this study has already argued, a paradigm shift in the Union's foreign policy towards a more neorealist matter-of-fact approach that acknowledges that, in Robert D. Kaplan's words (2023), the world (and the Middle East in particular) cannot be neatly divided into "evil dictatorships and exemplary democracies" but rather includes "many shades of grey" in between.[27] This new pragmatic view should also lead to the understanding that neither democracy nor respect for

[27] Kaplan (2023) is right in observing that in Saudi Arabia and other Gulf monarchies there is not real social contract between the rulers and the people: "the rulers provide predictable governance and smooth transitions of power, allowing for an enviable quality of life; in return, the populations do not challenge their hold on power. [...] They

human rights can be either persuasively or forcefully imposed on actors whose positions are based on deviating (normative or interest-based) rationales (Peters 2016b, 837). While trying to persuade others that these are worthy ideas, it is equally important for the EU to keep in mind that engaging in such endeavours might not lead to success despite every best intention there is—and the three case studies discussed above have proven this point. Being able to see the many shades of grey that the Middle East can take on and being prepared to address them pragmatically and firmly, in keeping with its envisaged geopolitical turn, will probably benefit the EU in the medium and long term more than the tried and often failed strategies it adopted in the past. Sadly, as political realities have often demonstrated, one cannot continue to remain an idealist committed to principles in a sea of pragmatists who pursue their own self-interest and expect to make a genuine difference.

Acknowledgements This research has been funded by the **Re**ignite **M**ultilateralism via **T**echnology (REMIT) project, funded from the European Union's Horizon Europe research and innovation programme under grant agreement No 101094228.

References

Adebahr, C. 2017. *Europe and Iran: The Nuclear Deal and Beyond*. London: Routledge.

Adebahr, C., and, R. Alcaro. 2022. The EU and Iran: How a Critical Relationship Became a Troubled One. In *Routledge Handbook of EU-Middle East Relations*, ed. D. Bouris, D. Huber, and M. Pace, 377–387. London and New York: Routledge Taylor & Francis Group.

Akbarzedeh, S. 2023. *Middle East Politics and International Relations. Crisis Zone*, 2nd ed. London and New York: Routledge Taylor & Francis Group.

Aydintasbas, A., and J. Shapiro. 2023. Erdogan's Post-western Turkey. *Foreign Affairs*, available at https://www.foreignaffairs.com/turkey/aydintasbasshapiro (accessed 19 September 2023).

Baracani, E., and M. Calimli. 2019. Shifting Dynamics in Turkish Foreign Policy in the Trans-European Space. In *The EU in a Trans-European Space. External*

considered the anarchy unleashed by the many attempts at democracy during the Arab Spring to be proof that the West has no useful lessons to teach them."

Relations Across Europe, Asia and the Middle East, ed. S. Giusti and I. Mirkina, 87–112. New York: Palgrave Macmillan.

Bayramov, A., and M.A. Sezal. 2023. Failing Forward: US Withdrawal and the Increasing Role of the EU and China vis-à-vis the Iran Nuclear Deal. In *Multilateralism in Peril: The Uneasy Triangle of the US, China and the EU*, ed. C.-H. Wu, F. Gaenssmantel, and F. Giumelli, 227–242. London and New York: Routledge Taylor & Francis Group.

Bouris, D., D. Huber, and M. Pace. 2022. Introduction: Entanglements in EU-Middle East Relations. In *Routledge Handbook of EU-Middle East Relations*, ed. D. Bouris, D. Huber, and M. Pace, 1–12. London and New York: Routledge Taylor & Francis Group.

Bretherton, C., and J. Vogler. 1999. *The European Union as a Global Actor*. New York: Routledge Taylor & Francis Group.

Bretherton, C., and J. Vogler. 2006. *The European Union as a Global Actor*, 2nd ed. New York: Routledge Taylor & Francis Group.

Bull, H. 1983. Civilian Power Europe: A Contradiction in Terms? In *The European Community: Past, Present and Future*, ed. R. Tsoukalis, 149–170. Oxford: Blackwell.

Cebeci, M. 2022. The EU's Constructions of the Middle East. In *Routledge Handbook of EU-Middle East Relations*, ed. D. Bouris, D. Huber, and M. Pace, 70–80. London and New York: Routledge Taylor & Francis Group.

Constantini, I., and R.H. Santini. 2019. Saudi Arabia's Regional Space Shifting: Making or Unmaking a Region? In *The EU in a Trans-European Space*. In *External Relations Across Europe, Asia and the Middle East*, ed. S. Giusti and I. Mirkina, 113–132. New York: Palgrave Macmillan.

Cosgrove, C.A., and K.J. Twitchett, eds. 1970. *The New International Actors: The United Nations and the European Economic Community*. London: Macmillan.

Cronberg, T. 2017. *Nuclear multilateralism and Iran: Inside EU Negotiations*. New York: Routledge.

Del Sarto, R. 2016. Normative Empire Europe: The European Union, Its Borderlands, and the Arab Spring. *Journal of Common Market Studies* 54 (2): 215–232. https://doi.org/10.1111/jcms.12282 (accessed 19 September 2023).

Dessi, A., and V. Ntousas. 2022. The Transatlantic Relationship and the Middle East: Converging Interested, Diverging Praxis. In *Routledge Handbook of EU-Middle East Relations*, ed. D. Bouris, D. Huber, and M. Pace, 181–190. London and New York: Routledge Taylor & Francis Group.

Dessler, D. 1989. What's at Stake in the Agency-Structure Debate? *International Organization* 43 (3): 441–473. https://doi.org/10.1017/S0020818300032999 (accessed 19 September 2023).

Dionigi, F. 2022. International Relations Theory and EU-Middle East relations. In *Routledge Handbook of EU-Middle East Relations*, ed. D. Bouris, D. Huber and M. Pace, 92–101. London and New York: Routledge Taylor & Francis Group.

Gaenssmantel, F., F. Giumelli, and C.-H. Wu. 2023. Conclusion: Multilaterialism in Peril? In *Multilateralism in Peril: The Uneasy Triangle of the US, China and the EU*, ed. C.-H. Wu, F. Gaenssmantel, and F. Giumelli, 262–274. London and New York: Routledge Taylor & Francis Group.

Ginsberg, R. 1999. Conceptualizing the European Union as an International Actor: Narrowing the Theoretical Capability-Expectations Gap. *Journal of Common Market Studies* 37 (3): 429–454. https://doi.org/10.1111/1468-5965.00172 (accessed 19 September 2023).

Giusti, S. 2019. From a Regional to a Global Power, in Potency: The EU's Global Strategy. In *The EU in a Trans-European Space: External Relations Across Europe, Asia and the Middle East*, ed. S. Giusti and I. Mirkina, 21–42. New York: Palgrave Macmillan.

Greiçevci, L. 2011. EU Actorness in International Affairs: The Case of EULEX Mission in Kosovo. *Perspectives on European Politics and Society* 12 (3): 283–303. https://doi.org/10.1080/15705854.2011.596307 (accessed 19 September 2023).

Halliday, F. 2005. *The Middle East in International Relations. Power, Politics and Ideology*. New York: Cambridge University Press.

Hill, C. 1998. Closing the Capabilities-Expectations Gap? In *A Common Foreign Policy for Europe? Competing Visions of the CFSP*, ed. J. Peterson and H. Sjursen, 18–36. New York: Routledge.

Hiltermann, J. 2023. Is the Middle East's Makeover a Mirage? Why a Spate of Diplomatic Deals Won't End Conflict. *Foreign Affairs*, available at: https://www.foreignaffairs.com/middle-east/middle-easts-makeover-mirage (accessed 19 September 2023).

Hopkins, R.E., and R.W. Mansbach. 1973. *Structure and Process in International Politics*. London: Harper & Row.

Jupille, J., and J. Caporaso. 1998. States, Agency and Rules: The European Union in Global Environmental Politics. In *The European Union in the World Community*, ed. C. Rhodes, 213–230. Boulder: Lynne Rienner.

Kaplan, R.D. 2023. Order After Empire: The Roots of Instability in the Middle East. *Foreign Affairs*, available at: https://www.foreignaffairs.com/middle-east/order-after-empire (accessed 19 September 2023).

Kaya, T.O. 2013. *The Middle East Peace Process and the EU: Foreign Policy and International Strategy in International Politics*. London: I.B. Tauris.

Kratochvil, P., P. Cibulkova, and M. Benik. 2011. The EU as a 'Framing Actor': Reflections on Media Debates About EU Foreign Policy. *Journal of*

Common Market Studies 49 (2): 391–412. https://doi.org/10.1111/j.1468-5965.2010.02122.x (accessed 19 September 2023).

Lonardo, L. 2023. *EU Common and Security Policy After Lisbon: Between Law and Geopolitics*. Cham: Springer.

Manners, I. 2002. Normative Power Europe: A Contradiction in Terms? *Journal of Common Market Studies* 40 (2): 235–258. https://doi.org/10.1111/1468-5965.00353 (accessed 19 September 2023).

Moldovan, R. 2020. The European Union and Turkey: The End of a Dream? In *The New European Union and Its Global Strategy: From Brexit to PESCO*, ed. V. Naumescu, 195–222. Newcastle upon Tyne: Cambridge Scholars Publishing.

Moldovan, R. 2023. Republica Turcă între Est şi Vest. Balans geopolitic şi securitate energetică în contextul Războiului din Ucraina (Turkey Between East and West: Geopolitical Balancing and Energy Security in the Context of the War in Ukraine). In *Războiul. Consecinţele invaziei ruseşti în Ucraina la nivel global, european şi românesc* (The War: The Consequences of Russia's Invasion of Ukraine for the World, Europe and Romania), ed. V. Naumescu and R. Moldovan, 173–200. Cluj Napoca: Presa Universitară Clujeană.

Müftüler-Bac, M., and D. Cihangir-Tetik. 2022. Turkey and the European Union in the Middle East: Potential for Cooperation or Continuing Discord? In *Routledge Handbook of EU-Middle East Relations*, ed. D. Bouris, D. Huber, and M. Pace, 191–203. London and New York: Routledge Taylor & Francis Group.

Müller, P. 2012. *EU Foreign Policy Making and the Middle East Conflict: The Europeanization of National Foreign Policy*. New York: Routledge Taylor & Francis Group.

Perteghella, A. 2019. Iran: An Unrecognised Regional Power. In *The EU in a Trans-European Space. External Relations Across Europe, Asia and the Middle East*, ed. S. Giusti and I. Mirkina, 133–156. New York: Palgrave Macmillan.

Peters, I. 2016a. Introduction: The European Union's Foreign Policy "Actorness and Power": Foundations of and Challenges for a Comparative Research Design. In *The European Union's Foreign Policy in Comparative Perspective: Beyond the "Actorness and Power" Debate*, ed. I. Peters, 33–141. London and New York: Routledge Taylor & Francis Group.

Peters, I. 2016b. Conclusions: The European Union's Foreign Policy "Actorness and Power" in Comparative Perspective. In *The European Union's Foreign Policy in Comparative Perspective: Beyond the "Actorness and Power" Debate*, ed. I. Peters, 801–862. London and New York: Routledge Taylor & Francis Group.

Schumacher, T. 2022. The EU and the Gulf Cooperation Council: A Troubled Relationship. In *Routledge Handbook of EU-Middle East Relations*, ed. D.

Bouris, D. Huber, and M. Pace, 157–168. London and New York: Routledge Taylor & Francis Group.

Sjöstedt, G. 1977. *The External Role of the European Community*. London: Saxon House.

Suchov, M.A., and P. Vasilenko. 2022. Russia and the EU in the Middle East: From Mutual Distrust to Forced Cooperation? In *Routledge Handbook of EU-Middle East Relations*, ed. D. Bouris, D. Huber, and M. Pace, 204–214. London and New York: Routledge Taylor & Francis Group.

Teti, A., P. Abbott, V. Talbot, and P. Maggiolini. 2020. *Democratisation Against Democracy: How EU Foreign Policy Fails the Middle East*. New York: Palgrave Macmillan.

Teti, A., G. Gervasio, and P. Abbott. 2022. Perceptions of the EU: Activists and Public Opinion in the Middle East. In *Routledge Handbook of EU-Middle East Relations*, ed. D. Bouris, D. Huber, and M. Pace, 217–230. London and New York: Routledge Taylor & Francis Group.

Thomas, D. 2012. Still Punching Below Its Weight? Coherence and Effectiveness in European Union Foreign Policy. *Journal of Common Market Studies* 50 (3): 457–474. https://doi.org/10.1111/j.1468-5965.2011.02244.x (accessed 19 September 2023).

Tibon, A., and A. Harel. 2023. There's No Economic Reason for Saudi Enrichment: The Real Question Is: What Does MBS Want? *Haaretz*, available at https://www.haaretz.com/israel-news/2023-08-25/ty-article/.pre...estion-what-does-mbs-want/0000018a-27b6-da97-a7cb-67b678ba0000 (accessed 19 September 2023).

Tocci, N. 2022. Foreword. In *Routledge Handbook of EU-Middle East Relations*, ed. D. Bouris, D. Huber, and M. Pace, xxii–xxiii. London and New York: Routledge Taylor & Francis Group.

Tuncel, Z.A. 2022. Security Within and Beyond the Borders of Europe: Locating the European Union as a Security Actor. In *Routledge Handbook of EU-Middle East Relations*, ed. D. Bouris, D. Huber, and M. Pace, 81–91. London and New York: Routledge Taylor & Francis Group.

Zihnioglu, O. 2020. *EU-Turkey Relations: Civil Society and Depoliticization*. London and New York: Routledge Taylor & Francis Group.

The EU as a Geopolitical Player: A Distant Ambition? Exploring EU Strategy for Cooperation in the Indo-Pacific Strategy

Dealan Riga

Introduction

In 2019, Ursula Von der Leyen, President of the European Commission, declared her Commission's commitment to becoming a geopolitical entity dedicated to sustainable policies and a defender of multilateralism (European Commission 2019). Since then, the European Union's (EU) global trade activities have attracted significant attention, driven by the growing importance of strategic factors in economic exchanges. Key terms such as "like-minded partner," "systemic rival," and "level playing field" have become integral to the EU's discussions on foreign trade. The war in Ukraine since 2022 has further intensified these ongoing dynamics, with the European Commission publicly stating its intention to transform itself into a geopolitical player. This move amplifies the economic and political shifts and transformations associated with such aspirations.

Within the academic realm, the ongoing weaponization of interdependence has been examined in the context of the resurgence of great power politics (Hopewell 2021; Mearsheimer 2003). However, in the specific

D. Riga (✉)
Department of Political Science, University of Liège, Liège, Belgium
e-mail: Dealan.Riga@uliege.be

L. Lika and D. Riga (eds.), *EU Geopolitical Actorness in a Changing World*, https://doi.org/10.1007/978-3-031-81160-9_6

context of the EU, strategic considerations often revolve around trade policy, encapsulated by the concept of geopoliticization of the EU's trade policy (Meunier and Nicolaidis 2019). While recent EU strategies, such as the Global Gateway, New Indo-Pacific strategy, and EU-China Strategic Outlook, affirm the growing inclination towards strategically leveraging trade; other concerns closely tied to security issues are also coming to the forefront. This leads this research to a central question for this chapter: Can the EU's strategic objectives surpass mere trade policy assertiveness to align with the demands of the shifting world order?

In line with this, the chapter leans on a case study analysis: the EU's endeavour to establish strategic positioning in the Indo-Pacific. With the involvement of major players such as China, the United States (US), and regional powers like Japan, Australia, and India, the Indo-Pacific has evolved into a highly strategic arena marked by contested leadership. While the EU's traditional positioning often relies on trade deals, the existing trade agreements within the region render trade alone an insufficient variable for attaining leadership. In other words, spearheading a free trade agreement under the EU's guidance won't be enough to establish a robust presence in the region, given the intricate network of intertwined trade agreements involving regional leaders and even China. As a result, the research delves into how the EU's diplomatic efforts align with the strategic needs of the Indo-Pacific region.

This chapter argues that, despite the emphasis on "geopolitical inspiration," the EU still struggles to reinvent its foreign policy beyond trade policy assertiveness and to actively promote normative concerns. While it highlights the consistent adoption of an ad-hoc multichannel framework by the European Commission to ensure geopolitical positioning, it also exposes weaknesses and underscores further requirements. Despite economic and security proposals, the EU has failed to put forward any inclusive framework that could be positioned as an alternative to Chinese or American regional alignments. Drawing from an extensive literature review that encompasses academic, official documents, and grey literature, the chapter emphasizes that, despite the geopolitical narrative, the EU's normative concerns remain a fundamental aspect of its external engagement. This calls for a reassessment of the integration of a strategic focus as a multifaceted approach to global affairs rather than a substantial shift. While the EU demonstrates intentions to act as a geostrategic actor in the region, the political will necessitates substantial internal reforms before there is a viable chance of implementation.

This chapter is divided in two sections. Section "Unravelling Indo–Pacific Complexity: Assessing EU's Geopolitical Actorness Requirements in a Region of Contested Leadership" starts with an exploration of the challenges presented by the Indo-Pacific, identifying the prerequisites for the EU to establish itself as a global actor in this particular region. It evaluates how the Indo-Pacific constitutes a distinct region with unique economic integration and security needs, crucial for ensuring an effective geopolitical positioning by the EU. Section "The New EU's Indo-Pacific Strategy: Assessing Policy Objectives Adequation to Regional Needs" delves into an examination of both existing and novel cooperation mechanisms employed by the EU. It scrutinizes the renewed multichannel approach and questions its effectiveness in addressing the economic and security challenges highlighted in the previous section. This section offers a critical assessment of the EU's foreign policy to the region by probing into its overall consistency and success. Ultimately, the conclusion engages with the notion of a perceived transition from strategic to normative concerns, initiating a discussion on the EU's requirements in this regard.

Unravelling Indo-Pacific Complexity: Assessing EU's Geopolitical Actorness Requirements in a Region of Contested Leadership

The Indo-Pacific region is entrenched in a complex scenario, witnessing the resurgence of major power politics. This section is dedicated to dissecting the regional landscape to pinpoint key players crucial to EU foreign policy. Its goal is to provide an outline of consistent focal points for the EU's foreign policy within this region. Subsequently, it delves into examining the economic and security hurdles, seeking to comprehend the region's requirements in relation to EU engagement. The present analysis enables this chapter to contemplate how the EU can establish a consistent and unwavering foreign policy.

Understanding the Complex Strategic Landscape of the Indo-Pacific Region: Identifying Key Stakeholder

The notion of an Indo-Pacific region is a construct that encompasses India and the Indian Ocean within the ongoing discourse of the Asia-Pacific (Beeson and Wilson 2018). Initially advocated by the former Japanese

Prime Minister Shinzo Abe (Kitaoka 2019), it was further developed by the US Donald Trump administration through the concept of a "free and open Indo-Pacific" (US Department of State 2019). The idea has gained popularity among United States allies like Japan, South Korea, Australia, and India, becoming a pivotal element in US strategy towards Asia (Scott 2018; He and Feng 2020). Scholars concur in characterizing the region as a fusion of security and economic concerns amid the Sino-American rivalry (Kwon 2023; Saeed 2017; Auslin 2020; Liu and He 2023; Cannon and Rossiter 2018). In the words of Ash Rossiter and Brendon J. Cannon, "[a]n intensification of economic activity and the heightening of geopolitical competition within the vast maritime area are thought to provide the *raison d'être* for conceptualizing the Indo-Pacific as a distinct (albeit yet-to-be delineated) region" (Rossiter and Cannon 2020, 15). Consequently, the Indo-Pacific emerges as a region inherently integrated with interconnected economic and security challenges.

The Indo-Pacific concept traces its origins to major power rivalries, with several regional stakeholders emerging as key contenders for leadership. Academic literature underscores the pivotal role of middle powers—India, Australia, Japan, and South Korea—in prioritizing Indo-Pacific leadership (Abbondanza 2022; Kang 2020; Taylor 2020; Rajagopalan 2020). Each of these countries has devised specific strategies to solidify their presence in the region amidst the US-China rivalry. India's "Act East" strategy aims to address China's increasing presence in its vicinity, encapsulated in the notion of the "string of pearls" (Khalid and Gul 2017). Its Act East policy focuses on transforming the country's North East into a gateway to the Indo-Pacific while fostering stronger ties within India's extended neighbourhood (Wadhwa 2019). The Australian government, in its 2017 foreign policy white paper, emphasizes the establishment of "A Stable and Prosperous Indo-Pacific" as a primary goal. Consequently, the document stresses the necessity of improved cooperation with Indo-Pacific allies like India, Japan, and South Korea (Australian Government 2017). Seoul, more recently, has joined in formulating an Indo-Pacific strategy, following a similar path to Australia, centring on regional alliances with India and Australia to foster a free, peaceful, and prosperous Indo-Pacific (South Korea Government 2022). As mentioned earlier, Abe played a pioneering role in the Indo-Pacific concept, and Japanese foreign policy continues to steer this concept. In this context, Fumio Kushida, Prime Minister of Japan, stated during his visit to India in 2023:

> Even at this turning point [after mentioning the war in Ukraine], the fundamental concept of Free and Open Indo-Pacific (FOIP) remains the same. It is simple. We will enhance the connectivity of the Indo-Pacific region, foster the region into a place that values freedom, the rule of law, free from force or coercion, and make it prosperous. With this backdrop, we should reaffirm and share the understanding that at the root of the concept of FOIP is defending "freedom" and the "rule of law". (Kishida 2023)

Hence, the middle powers in the region closely align themselves with US strategic objectives by advocating for an Indo-Pacific founded on Western values. However, they all seem to prioritize a regional alliance supported by the United States rather than relying strictly on Washington as their sole security provider. Moreover, each of these nations manages its own policy initiatives with various actors in the region, including China. South Korea and Japan engage in trilateral dialogues with China (Hahn-Kyu 2017; Zhang 2018); India and China collaborate within the BRICS (Brazil, Russia, India, China, and South Africa) framework (Xing 2016). Australia, while highly concerned about Chinese influence, is reluctant to engage in collaboration with Beijing across various fields. It stood out as the only partner that exhibited mixed feelings regarding the Belt and Road Initiative (BRI), exemplified by the Victoria government's signing of a Memorandum of Understanding in 2018, which was later dismissed by the federal government in 2020 (Varano 2021). Although these countries' preference for a US partnership stance is clear, the Trump administration and the threat of potential United States withdrawal have reinforced their resolve to diversify their strategic collaborations in order to balance the great power rivalry within the region (Akaha and Hirata 2021; Job 2022; Pempel 2019; Narine 2018).

Finally, within the Association of Southeast Asian Nations (ASEAN), a collective of 10 regional players comes together to pursue their distinct approach to the Indo-Pacific (Anwar 2020; Yoshimatsu 2023; ASEAN 2019). The ASEAN outlook on the Indo-Pacific, unveiled in 2019, was designed with the following objectives:

- Providing a roadmap for collaborative efforts in the region;
- Fostering an environment that supports peace, stability, and prosperity by addressing shared challenges, upholding a rule-based

regional framework, fostering closer economic ties, and thereby bolstering confidence and trust;
- Strengthening ASEAN's community-building process and reinforcing existing ASEAN-led mechanisms like the East Asia Summit (EAS);
- Executing ongoing initiatives while exploring additional areas of priority cooperation within ASEAN, including maritime collaboration, connectivity, Sustainable Development Goals (SDGs), and potential economic partnerships (ASEAN 2019, 2).

Since its inception, one of the fundamental principles of the institution has been to safeguard the Asia-Pacific region from foreign influence (Narine 1998; Nischalke 2000; Beeson and Stubbs 2012). To ensure a consistent implementation of its foreign policy agenda, it has established various multilateral frameworks to engage effective cooperation with its surrounding partners. The more prolific of those is the ASEAN Plus Three (APT), a forum integrating Japan, South Korea, and China into the ASEAN structure after the 1997 Asian debt crisis. While it has been particularly instrumental in advancing deeper economic integration, the APT is broad collaboration framework encompassing security and political issues. The APT operates through the conducting of annual summits and high-level dialogues across various sectors (ASEAN 2023a). To foster cooperation, specific work plans are adopted every five years, with the 2023–2027 plan setting ambitious goals in both security and economic domains (ASEAN 2023b).

Additionally, ASEAN launched the EAS, which brought together APT, India, Russia, the United States, Australia, and New Zealand into a multilateral framework, along with the ASEAN Regional Forum (ARF) that encompasses 27 countries. While those forum scopes are encompassing with specific focus on both security, economic, and political issues, the achievements of these summits are not on par with the APT framework. Another forum more prolific, albeit constrained to economic issues, is the Asia-Pacific Economic Cooperation (APEC). Yet, this economic institution couldn't be considered as being under ASEAN leadership and therefore hardly contributes to the development of its Indo-Pacific strategy; Asia-Europe Meetings (ASEM) holds for the same logic. The extensive network of these multilateral initiatives has been extensively explored in academic literature. While some authors have discussed ASEAN's efforts to shape a "security community" or foster a new regional identity (Acharya 1997; Katzenstein 2000; Gilson 2006; Acharya 2021), others highlight the limitations of ASEAN's multilateral approach in consistently monitoring the Sino-American rivalry within the region (Goh 2014; Bisley 2019; He 2019; Beeson 2016). Thus, this chapter embraces a nuanced perspective on ASEAN leadership in the region. While recognizing its pivotal role in advancing a multilateral agenda, it acknowledges that the dynamics of middle and great powers rivalry continue to be crucial factors shaping the region's geo-economic structure.

Ultimately, the region's political structure is highly intricate, stemming from intense power rivalries. The Indo-Pacific concept forms the backbone of foreign policies for both middle powers and multilateral organizations in the region. Despite each entity pursuing its distinct political goals, collaboration occurs within diverse political frameworks. Therefore, for the EU to effectively execute an Indo-Pacific strategy, a holistic approach merging the objectives of middle powers and ASEAN is necessary, respecting the strategic interests of each. As a result, it's likely that the EU will need to adopt a multichannel strategy tailored to meet the specific trade and security needs of its partners.

Growing Economic Integration in a Conflictual Arena: Challenges to EU's Positioning in the Indo-Pacific

The concept of a geopolitical Commission strategically placing the EU's interests in the Indo-Pacific confronts two significant challenges within the region: the simultaneous existence of numerous economic integration frameworks, diminishing its influence *vis-à-vis* China, and an intricate security landscape that demands tailored military responsiveness, presently entrenched in the alliance with the United States.

EU's foreign policy engagement traditionally relies on trade policy, a main feature of its actorness and normative power (Aggarwal and Fogarty 2004; Manners 2009; Börzel and Risse 2017). However, the Indo-Pacific is already deeply intertwined in economic integration with various stakeholders in the region. While the United States was initially the more advanced partner in this sense with the Trans-Pacific Partnership (TPP), the Trump administration's withdrawal from the agreement leaves them ill-equipped to be considered the greatest promoter of deeper economic integration within the region.

Against this background, the recent US Joe Biden administration proposal of an Indo-Pacific Economic Framework for Prosperity

(IPEF) is symptomatic of the US's commitment to pursuing previous economic efforts in the region (United States of America, Department of Commerce 2023). Although it is too early to assess the potential of the IPEF, its focus on trade, supply chains, clean economy, and fair economy clearly demonstrates the US's intention to ensure deeper economic integration with the region (Forough 2022). The involvement of all ASEAN members and middle powers in the region might indicate the Indo-Pacific's openness to new US-led economic projects (United States of America, Department of Commerce 2023).

Yet, since Trans-Pacific Partnership (TPP) negotiations, China has actively fostered economic integration in the region through robust bilateral economic diplomacy (Economy 2005; Yahuda 2020). Indeed, the Chinese-led BRI has been a widely discussed subject in Southeast Asia, anticipating three corridors to cross the region: the China-Indochina Peninsula Economic Corridor (CICPEC), the Bangladesh-China-India-Myanmar corridor (BCIM), and the "maritime silk road," even though these have lost salience (Rana and Ji 2020; Albana and Fiori 2021; Li 2020). All ASEAN member states are collaborating with China within this framework, with Laos and Cambodia closely following specific action plans for economic cooperation (FMRPC 2023). Vietnam, the Philippines, and Thailand engage in a less structured collaboration, evaluating BRI bids on a case-by-case basis (Gong 2022). The recent Belt and Road Forum (BRF) featured a joint statement between China and Indonesia on deepening comprehensive strategic cooperation (BRF 2023), underscoring the ongoing commitment of major ASEAN countries to participate in the BRI. Supporting this trend, data reveals a doubling of China's Foreign Direct Investment (FDI) flow into Southeast Asia within the BRI framework (Gong 2022).

Furthermore, China's multilateral initiatives, such as the Asian Infrastructure Investment Bank (AIIB), have been welcomed by all ASEAN states (AIIB 2023). The collaboration of India, South Korea, and even Australia in this context may be seen as indicative of the region's strategic ambivalence and middle power receptiveness to Chinese finance. Consequently, China has established itself as a key stakeholder in the region for economic and financial integration through both bilateral and multilateral channels. Japan, as an exception, has not completely ruled out a future contribution to the AIIB but rather chooses to prioritize financial commitments to the Asian Development Bank (ADB), an institution led by Japan (Reuters 2015).

Nevertheless, China is not the sole advocate for regional economic integration. Following the United States' withdrawal from the TPP, Japan took the lead in launching an initiative based on a similar framework, resulting in the Comprehensive and Progressive Agreement for Trans-Pacific Partnership (CPTPP). The addition of "comprehensive" is described by former Japanese Prime Minister Abe as an effort to make the agreement more extensive than its economic predecessor, the TPP (Huong 2018). However, the CPTPP could hardly be considered as comprehensive as initiatives like the BRI or the Regional Comprehensive Economic Partnership (RCEP—*see below*) in promoting Indo-Pacific economic integration, as it only incorporates three ASEAN members: Brunei, Vietnam, and Malaysia (Wu 2020). Therefore, it might be perceived as an attempt to diversify trade relations among member states or to fulfil specific trade objectives (Wu 2020). It is noteworthy that Australia, another middle power in the region, is contributing to the CPTPP, once again indicating its openness to a Pacific-oriented economic framework and its willingness to participate in economic initiatives that do not involve Chinese partnerships.

ASEAN has instituted its own framework to promote regional economic integration through the initiation of a multilateral agreement known as the Regional Comprehensive Economic Partnership (RCEP). Launched in 2011 during the 19th ASEAN summit (ASEAN 2012), this economic initiative extended invitations to India, Australia, China, Japan, South Korea, and New Zealand to engage in negotiations for the most extensive free trade agreement in the region (ASEAN 2019). In 2019, India opted to withdraw from the negotiation process, making it the sole actor in the region that failed to join the economic agreement (Iqbal Dar 2023). Signed in 2020, the RCEP has evolved into the most comprehensive proposal for the region, establishing a privileged framework for all regional partners. Nevertheless, academic literature remains divided on its potential implications (Gong 2022). Some highlight its capacity to strengthen Chinese economic leadership within the region (Gao and Shaffer 2021), while others view the ASEAN-led agreement as part of an alternative to great power rivalry (Yoshimatsu 2023).

Thus, when advocating for a strategic trade policy, the EU must recognize the economic dominance China wields in the region. China not only stands as the primary economic partner for almost all the countries under study but has also interwoven its economic influence into various multilateral agreements for cooperation throughout the entire region. Moreover, the RCEP stands out as the most comprehensive trade deal in the Indo-Pacific. While its practical implications can only be forecasted at the moment, it might be prudent to consider that any economic proposal from the EU to the region should be at least as comprehensive as the RCEP. Crucially, the EU's proposal for economic integration must account for the ongoing norms embedded in the RCEP, BRI, and CPTPP, potentially complicating the negotiation process. Furthermore, this intricate economic interdependence is entangled with specific political ties that hold important strategic implications for regional security. Consequently, the EU should exercise caution to avoid pressuring its partners into dismantling existing agreements in the region, acknowledging the complex power distribution.

In the Indo-Pacific region, a myriad of complex security challenges spans from North Korea to the Malacca Straits, encompassing the South China Sea, and Taiwan. Numerous territorial disputes have prompted a renewed military build-up and strategic realignment in the area. Behind ostensibly peaceful rhetoric, China, leveraging economic growth, has fortified the People's Liberation Army (PLA) and adopted an assertive stance on Taiwan while concurrently managing territorial disputes peacefully with neighbouring countries (Slaughter 2020; Scott 2019; European Commission 2021a). Conversely, the United States has bolstered its military presence in the region, a trend observed through both the Trump and Biden administrations Indo-Pacific strategies (Pempel 2019; United States of America, Department of State 2019; The White House 2022). This security dilemma has engendered growing strategic concerns among several states in the region, prompting them to seek strategic alignment in response to security challenges (Pan 2014).

Regarding strategic alliances, Chinese endeavours in the region appear somewhat hesitant. Despite entering strategic cooperation agreements with numerous partners, China's primary focus remains on the economy and regional economic integration. Scholars encounter challenges in defining the BRI's aspirations beyond economic integration, with no academic consensus emerging on the strategic impact of this Chinese mega-project (Shambaugh 2018; Gong 2019; Zhou and Esteban 2020). While Chinese investments and economic exchanges are generally welcomed, many states harbour concerns about Beijing's potential strategic use of these interactions (Albana and Fiori 2021; Economy 2005; Scott 2019). This uncertainty prompts partner states to collaborate with China while actively exploring other strategic alternatives.

In this context, the United States appears to be regarded as a viable alternative, aiming to enhance its strategic presence in the region through regional and multilateral alliances. Within its Indo-Pacific strategy, the United States has highlighted the Quadrilateral Security Dialogue (QUAD), the trilateral security partnership for the Indo-Pacific region between Australia, the United Kingdom (UK), and the United States (AUKUS), and the North Atlantic Treaty Organization (NATO) as key frameworks to ensure a prosperous Indo-Pacific. In essence, the US Indo-Pacific security strategy revolves around the following principle:

> We will continue to modernize our treaty alliances with Australia, Japan, the Republic of Korea, the Philippines, and Thailand; steadily advance our Major Defense Partnership with India and support its role as a net security provider; and build the defense capacity of partners in South and Southeast Asia and the Pacific Islands. (The White House 2022, 12–13)

To enhance its effectiveness, the United States relies on two security multilateral frameworks, QUAD and AUKUS, aligning the security objectives of India, Japan, the UK, the United States, and Australia in the region. The QUAD was initially launched in 2007 but remained inactive for several years due to Australia's decision to withdraw from the forum (Gale and Shearer 2018). However, during the East Asia Forum (EAF) in 2017, the United States, India, Australia, and Japan reached an agreement to revive the proposal. In 2021, the QUAD held its first summit, during which the summit leaders issued a joint statement stating that:

> Together, we commit to promoting a free, open rules-based order, rooted in international law to advance security and prosperity and counter threats to both in the Indo-Pacific and beyond. We support the rule of law, freedom of navigation and overflight, peaceful resolution of disputes, democratic values, and territorial integrity. We reaffirm our strong support for ASEAN's unity and centrality as well as the ASEAN Outlook on the Indo-Pacific. (The White House 2021, 1)

In contrast, AUKUS represents a recent collaboration between the United States, the UK, and Australia focused on military cooperation, technological exchange, and arms sales. Unveiled in 2021, AUKUS's initial notable move involved Australia opting out of a deal for the procurement of French submarines, turning instead to its new partners as the primary weapons supplier. Despite actively promoting Western values, AUKUS has faced substantial criticism from France and the EU as it generates the "submarine crisis" (Guillemard 2022; Herszenhorn 2021). The alliance appears to embody a strategic vision where the EU has limited involvement, leaving some sceptical about the United States' will to integrate European partners into its Indo-Pacific security strategy.

The EU's geopolitical influence in the region also demands a distinct strategic alternative for regional partners. While middle power alignment with the United States is secured through multilateral alternatives, ASEAN countries continue to navigate a delicate balance between the United States and China by shaping their own ASEAN Political Security Community (APSC), remaining unaligned with either major power. Considering this, the EU may contemplate adopting a security focus akin to NATO. However, recent events, such as AUKUS, have exposed vulnerabilities in the EU's image as a security provider for the region. Therefore, for the EU to assert itself as a geopolitical actor in the region, there is a need for a revamped foreign security toolbox to ensure efficient implementation acknowledging ongoing security dilemmas.

This section has underscored the complexity of the region in terms of intricate power relations and complex interdependence. Additionally, it has highlighted specific challenges for the EU's geopolitical positioning within the region. The next section will delve into the EU's Indo-Pacific engagements and the policy objectives set within the Indo-Pacific strategy to assess its geopolitical potential.

The New EU's Indo-Pacific Strategy: Assessing Policy Objectives Adequation to Regional Needs

A well-organized geopolitical Commission should engage with the Indo-Pacific by taking into account three key characteristics of the region. Firstly, the intricate power structure calls for a multichannel approach that considers diverse actors, encompassing great powers, middle powers, and regional organizations. Secondly, based on the afore analysis EU foreign trade policy should acknowledge existing regional agreements and be flexible enough to accommodate China's economic dominance in the area. Lastly, a foreign security policy should be in harmony with the strategic priorities of regional states without intensifying existing security dilemmas.

The EU has a long-standing alliance with the United States, encompassing security, economic, and political dimensions. In the context of the Indo-Pacific, both allies collaborate through a dedicated framework established in 2021 (EEAS 2021a). The United States-EU high-level consultations on the Indo-Pacific where: "The United States and the European Union share a strategic interest in strengthening cooperation with partners in the Indo-Pacific on the basis of shared values and interests, and in support of multilateral rules-based frameworks. Both sides reaffirmed the importance of ASEAN centrality and supporting a strong and independent ASEAN" (United States of America, Department of State 2021, 2).

However, the EU's engagement with China appears to be less straightforward. In its most recent EU-China strategic outlook, the Indo-Pacific region remains unaddressed (European Commission 2019). This trend is evident even in EU-China summits where, despite discussions on global issues such as North Korea, COVID-19, global warming, or the war in Ukraine, the Indo-Pacific is not designated as a topic for dialogue, at least according to official press releases. However, recent security and defence consultations between the EU and China may suggest a shift, as they exchanged views on Indo-Pacific strategy (EEAS 2023a).

Nevertheless, concerning great power rivalry, the EU logically aligns with the United States. Unfortunately, the lack of dialogue with China on this topic might indicate that the EU's approach fails to encompass key stakeholders in the region. While both actors contribute to the transnational forum of ASEM, it remains an informal platform for dialogue and cooperation, and its scope makes clear Indo-Pacific coordination challenging and, in some cases, unaddressed (Camroux and Lechervy 1996; Council of the EU 2021a). Regarding middle powers, the EU appears to recognize the necessity of adopting a comprehensive framework, evident in the establishment of various frameworks. In this context, the EU entered into a strategic partnership with Japan in 2019, revitalizing its relations with a state considered one of its "closest like-minded partners" (Council of the EU 2021b). During their latest summit, both partners elaborated on the Indo-Pacific, affirming "the importance of a free and open Indo-Pacific, which is inclusive, prosperous, and secure, and that protects shared principles including sovereignty, territorial integrity, peaceful resolution of disputes, rule of law, human rights, and fundamental freedoms" (Council of the EU 2023a, 6). The EU has long-standing bilateral relations with India, marked by an ongoing strategic partnership since 2004. However, the EU has been pin-pout as having low strategic output from this bilateral approach as both actors failed to reach strong achievement on international affairs (Kavalski 2016). This is confirmed in their latest framework for cooperation, titled "A Roadmap for 2025," wherein the Indo-Pacific only emerges as a priority for connectivity (EEAS 2020; Carteny and Di Stefano 2023). Additionally, the perception of India as a strategic partner in the Indo-Pacific may have been undermined due to its strategic ambivalence in the wake of the war in Ukraine (Tellis 2022). In 2020, the EU and South Korea elevated their cooperation framework to launch a strategic partnership. While trade and the Korean peninsula remain on top of the EU's priorities in the area (Chung and Lee 2019), both partners underscored their cooperation framework in the Indo-Pacific as a main priority to ensure a "free, open, and rules-based Indo-Pacific" (Council of the EU 2023b, 5). Last but not least, the EU and Australia have been cooperating through a Framework Agreement since 2015 (Council of the EU 2016). The latest leader summit concluded with a joint statement establishing the Indo-Pacific as a top priority for both partners, covering various topics from energy cooperation to placing specific emphasis on Taiwan (Council of the EU 2022).

Therefore, in the past years, the EU has established new frameworks to strengthen cooperation with Japan and South Korea, building upon existing ones with Australia and India to ensure a multichannel diplomacy in the Indo-Pacific. These partners are considered key stakeholders for the EU's positioning in the region, aligning with both the EU Global Gateway and Indo-Pacific perspectives (Mohan 2020; Borrell quoted in EEAS 2021b; European Commission 2021a). In summary, the EU's engagement aims to: "at maintaining a free and open Indo-Pacific for all, while building strong and lasting partnerships to cooperate on matters from the green transition, ocean governance or the digital agenda to security and defence" (Borrell quoted in European Commission 2021b, 1).

Finally, the EU has long-standing bilateral relations with ASEAN and actively advocates for its centrality, emphasizing the need to empower the institution as a central actor in the region when engaging with other partners (EEAS 2021a; Council of the EU 2023a, 2023b). Academic literature has long emphasized that the EU privileges interregional actions to deal with partners in a specific region, effectively empowering them and supporting regional integration (Gilson 2013; Hettne et al. 1999; Söderbaum 2016). However, EU-ASEAN relations have often been criticized for failing to adopt a comprehensive approach, limiting their scope to trade and normative focus (Robles 2006; Mattheis and Wunderlich 2017). Meanwhile, the challenges in the Indo-Pacific present a window of opportunity for pragmatic interregionalism between both stakeholders (Gilson 2020). In this context, both regional actors have "reaffirmed their commitment to strengthening ASEAN-EU cooperation and upholding ASEAN centrality based on the shared relevant fundamental principles of their respective Indo-Pacific approaches" (EEAS 2023b). Therefore, interregional ties may be adapting to the new realities of the Indo-Pacific, and it is anticipated that EU-ASEAN interregional relations will yield crucial outcomes in addressing the challenges of the region.

As a result, the EU has aptly adopted a multichannel approach, incorporating engagement with great powers, middle powers, and ASEAN. This marks a positive stride towards establishing a consistent geopolitical positioning within the region. Nevertheless, coordination between the EU and China, as well as between the EU and India, regarding the region appears to be insufficient to yield efficient results. Although negotiation channels are open, the EU should ensure their effective utilization, which may require some adjustments to existing frameworks.

Regarding trade diplomacy in the region, the EU strategically engages through specific trade agreements facilitated by its strategic partnerships. Noteworthy in this context is the renewed EU effort in various bilateral economic frameworks. Since 2019, the EU has entered into free trade agreements with Singapore, Vietnam, and Japan, while strengthening its existing framework with South Korea (Carteny and Di Stefano 2023; European Commission 2023). Additionally, the EU has also officially initiated negotiations for free trade agreements with India, Indonesia, Australia, and ASEAN (European Commission 2023). In light of these efforts, it can be observed that EU economic diplomacy aligns with the objective of securing its geopolitical positioning within the region. However, as highlighted in the previous section, free trade agreements alone may not be sufficient, given that many states in the region already have alternative agreements in place. This prompts a reflection in this chapter on how the EU recognizes the interconnected economic integration of the region and the influence exerted by China.

EU's Indo-Pacific strategy puts the emphasis on a mix of ruled-based system promotion and defence industrial strategy as key to comprehend EU's trade policy within the region by establishing that: "It is essential for the EU to reinforce cooperation with Indo-Pacific partners, including in bilateral, regional, and multilateral contexts, and to promote the rules-based international order and access to open markets and ensure a stable trading environment. This engagement should contribute to strengthening Europe's strategic reach and security and to securing the resilience of its supply chains" (European Commission 2019, 3).

The initial standpoint might pose challenges, as the defence of a "rules-based international order" or an "open market" has been employed in opposition to "Chinese unfair trade practices" (European Commission 2019). Interestingly, similar concerns form the foundation of EU-Japan, EU-South Korea, and EU-ASEAN coordination mechanisms (European Commission 2023; EEAS 2023b). However, these states all contribute to the RCEP, prompting a consideration in this chapter that their perspectives on these principles may not entirely oppose China's integration in the region. Moreover, in their joint statement announcing RCEP, participants affirm: "RCEP Agreement demonstrates our strong commitment to supporting economic recovery, inclusive development, job creation, and strengthening regional supply chains as well as our support for an open, inclusive, rules-based trade and investment arrangement" (Ministry of Foreign Affairs (MOFA) of Japan 2020). This double standard might indicate an ambivalence among states in the region concerning the EU's trade policy. Although many of them appear to share a similar approach with the EU, certain elements indicate their reluctance to pursue a strategic economic alignment with it. Despite the EU maintaining its trading attractiveness, it appears that key actors in the Indo-Pacific view it as part of a strategy to diversify their supply chains rather than a crucial geo-economic alliance.

In a similar vein, despite the EU's intention to breathe new life into the EU-ASEAN Free Trade Agreement (FTA), it remains to be determined how previous hurdles encountered might be overcome. The first attempt to negotiate the agreement dates back to 2007, facing strong backlash due to what academic literature emphasizes as the EU's lack of consideration for ASEAN's heterogeneity (Meissner 2016; Robles 2008; Wu 2019). Part of this heterogeneity was the EU's concern with Myanmar's human rights record, which, despite many changes, still remained hardly compliant with human rights standards. Aligning with strategic shifts and a quest for its geopolitical position in the region, the EU has renewed its approach, moving from multilateral negotiations to bilateral agreements, as exemplified by the latest agreements with Singapore, Vietnam, and ongoing negotiations with Indonesia (Meissner 2018). The results of this approach are twofold. On the one hand, it demonstrates the EU's pragmatic adaptation to regional realities, which could be considered a part of the EU's shift to strategic interests. On the other hand, it emphasizes the EU's incapacity to deal with the region's "unlike-minded partners," resulting in a failure to offer a comprehensive economic framework. The EU's weaknesses in addressing countries such as Myanmar, Cambodia, or Laos contrast with Chinese abilities to ensure economic ties with the entire region. Furthermore, these bilateral preferences raise deep concerns about the chances of EU-ASEAN cooperation, either in terms of trade or policy, similar to what is observed in APT or RCEP.

In summary, the EU has failed to promote a comprehensive trade policy towards the region, limiting its scope of action to like-minded partners. While its economic presence in the region is growing, the preference for bilateral engagements contrasts with China's all-encompassing approach. In terms of economic output, the EU has been more successful in promoting normative concerns such as sustainable governance and adherence to World Trade Organization (WTO) rulings throughout the region than in establishing a viable and inclusive trading alternative that considers the diversity of the Indo-Pacific. Despite numerous efforts, the EU is still hindered by the divergence of approaches among its member states in ensuring consistent economic integration in the region. Indeed, the Indo-Pacific strategies of France, Germany, and the Netherlands propose different guidelines when it comes to engaging with China's economic dominance in the region (Carteny and Di Stefano 2023; Wacker 2021). In other words, the EU's inability to promote a comprehensive trade policy towards the region is evident as its scope of action only includes like-minded partners. While its ongoing economic presence in the region continues to expand, the preference for bilateral engagements contrasts with China's all-encompassing approach. Moreover, considering the Indo-Pacific strategies of France, Germany, and the Netherlands, it could be hypothesized that the EU's approach to address China's economic dominance in the region lacks consensus across member states (Carteny and Di Stefano 2023; Wacker 2021).

When it comes to EU's positioning as a security provider, academic literature emphasize it hasn't been considered a such in the region as demonstrated by AUKUS submarines crisis (Wu 2019; Barnes and Makinda 2022). Yet, some emphasize the growing security considerations advanced as new positive sign towards European military presence within the regions (Wong 2019; Mohan 2020; Pugliese 2023). Indeed, in its new framework settings the guidelines for Indo-Pacific engagement the EU clearly mentioned: "The EU will intensify its dialogues with partners on security and defence, including counterterrorism, cybersecurity, non-proliferation and disarmament, space and maritime security dialogues" (EEAS 2021b, 15). This document is among the first to address security concern and EU's military objectives as a top priority for an engagement towards the region.

However, the EU's Indo-Pacific security policy tends to be presented in broad terms, concealing past weaknesses in military engagement through specific discursive strategies. Firstly, it underscores the EU's geographical presence in the region, aligning with French intentions to utilize Overseas Countries and Territories (OCTs) as key strategic actors for regional military build-up (*see* the chapter of Alexandu Balas in this book). Secondly, to obscure its limited previous military presence in critical regions, it expands the definition of the Indo-Pacific to include the west coast of Africa. By doing so, it highlights the success of EU Naval Force Somalia (EU NAVFOR), especially Operation Atalanta, and the European Training Mission in Mozambique (EUTM) (EEAS 2021b, 14). However, these efforts can hardly be equated with missions that would be required in the Strait of Malacca, Strait of Taiwan, or the South China Sea. Lastly, it advocates for a greater security dialogue with partners in the region as a key element of its strategic positioning (EEAS 2021b, 14). However, except for its contribution to the ASEAN Defense Ministers Meeting Plus (ADMM+), limited progress can be noted in this regard. Furthermore, this forum already includes China and the United States, suggesting that it may not be the best platform for the EU to ensure any strategic alignment with ASEAN partners (ASEAN 2023c).

Therefore, the EU's strategic approach would require a new framework to ensure a comprehensive security strategy for the region. In this context, the EU is rapidly progressing with the establishment of specific projects such as Enhancing Security Cooperation In and With Asia (ESIWA). However, ESIWA is still in the early stages and has not yet yielded significant achievements. The expansion of the Critical Maritime Routes in the Indian Ocean (CRIMARIO) project to encompass the Indo-Pacific (CRIMARIO II) is indicative of the EU's willingness to adapt to regional needs. Yet, these cooperation frameworks do not entirely overlap with existing ones such as AUKUS or QUAD. Regarding the latter, the EU officially claims it will engage with the forum (EEAS 2021b, 14). While this alignment may be logical given the similarities in their Indo-Pacific agendas it might result in inconsistencies in the EU's strategic alignment with its security policy, potentially undermining the EU's pursuit of strategic autonomy (*see* the chapter of Arlind Puka in this book). Furthermore, the consistency of EU-China policy might also be undermined, as the EU's stance towards the regional power differs from the confrontational strategy adopted by the United States.

In conclusion, the EU's security strategy in the region is still in its early stages, requiring strong interinstitutional and member state cohesion to achieve consistency. Presently, the EU's strategy towards the region relies heavily on its normative commitments. The EU has been more successful in advocating for the respect of international law, such as the United Nations Convention on the Law of the Sea (UNCLOS), than in establishing a clear military presence in the South China Sea. Overall, the most prominent proposal for the EU's geopolitical positioning in the region, especially in terms of security, suggests aligning with the QUAD under US leadership. Once again, the role of the EU as a security provider appears to be entangled in the significance of transatlantic ties rather than emphasizing strategic autonomy (*see* the chapter of Valentin Naumescu and Oana Poiană in this book).

Conclusion

This chapter highlights the growing strategic importance of the Indo-Pacific in world affairs and underscores the inherent complexity of the region. The Indo-Pacific is characterized by an intricate web of interdependence, aligning great powers, middle powers, and regional organizations in diverse economic and security collaborations. This complexity poses a significant challenge for the implementation of a geopolitical Commission and serves as an insightful case study to assess: Can the EU's strategic objectives surpass mere trade policy assertiveness to align with the demands of the shifting world order?

The EU's geopolitical aspirations are accompanied by the adoption of an ad-hoc approach to the Indo-Pacific. While the EU establishes clear guidelines, it consistently adopts new instruments to ensure that its capabilities are recognized as those of a geopolitical actor within the region. The EU has established a multichannel diplomacy involving all regional stakeholders, developing new trade agreements and revitalizing existing frameworks such as strategic partnerships. Beyond the economic sphere, the EU acknowledges the need to be considered a security provider in the region through its contributions to regional mechanisms and the launch of its own programs. In summary, this chapter strongly indicates that the EU's intentions to geopolitical positioning are complemented by efforts to become such an actor across all relevant indicators.

However, the EU's attempts at geopolitical positioning are still in their early stages, representing nascent political endeavours that leave the EU ill-equipped to follow a learning curve rather than implement a successful foreign policy. Despite the multichannel approach, the EU has failed to provide the region with a clear alternative to the Chinese economic stranglehold. While it has successfully advanced trade integration with like-minded partners, it falls short of proposing an inclusive and open economic framework that meets the region's requirements. In terms of security, the AUKUS agreement has demonstrated the region's inclination to view the EU as a security provider. In response, the EU has made fresh attempts to change this state of play; however, the more promising frameworks still rely on alignment with US military build-up rather than EU-led alternatives.

In conclusion, the EU's new multichannel approach to the region has been more successful in fostering normative claims, such as green governance, compliance with specific WTO rules, and adherence to international law regarding maritime security. However, when it comes to ensuring a strategic alignment, the primary explanatory force in the region continues to be great power rivalry. China is pursuing regional economic and political cooperation through APT and RCEP, while the United States remains a key security provider by forming new alliances such as QUAD and AUKUS. In this context, the EU has failed to propose any alternative to existing models and remains ill-equipped to establish something similar in the coming years.

This chapter leads to the conclusion that the EU's strategic objectives are still confined to trade policy assertiveness, advocating for the respect of the rule-based world order but lacking the necessary toolbox to align with the demands of the shifting world order. However, this negative assessment must be nuanced by highlighting the efforts of the European Commission to secure a geopolitical positioning. The EU's attempts are evident, and further academic research on the evolution of its Indo-Pacific policy will be necessary to understand how new trends are unfolding. While the EU has not yet achieved a shift from normative to strategic focus, it is clearly making attempts to do so.

References

Abbondanza, G. 2022. Whither the Indo-Pacific? Middle Power Strategies from Australia, South Korea and Indonesia. *International Affairs* 98 (2): 403–421.

Acharya, A. 1997. Ideas, Identity, and Institution-building: From the 'ASEAN Way to the 'Asia-Pacific Way'? *The Pacific Review* 10 (3): 319–346.

Acharya, A. 2021. *ASEAN and Regional Order: Revisiting Security Community in Southeast Asia*. Abingdon, Oxon: Routledge.

Aggarwal, V.K., and E. Fogarty, eds. 2004. *EU Trade Strategies: Regionalism and Globalism*. London: Palgrave Macmillan.

AIIB. 2023. Members, available at: https://www.aiib.org/en/about-aiib/governance/members-of-bank/index.html (accessed 15 November 2023).

Akaha, T., and K. Hirata. 2021. US Bilateralism Under Trump, Power Shift in East Asia, and Implications for Regional Security and Prosperity: A Theoretical Analysis of Japan's Strategic Adjustment. In *Trump's America and International Relations in the Indo-Pacific: Theoretical Analysis of Changes and Continuities*, ed. T. Akaha, J. Yuan, and W. Liang, 19–52. Cham: Springer.

Albana, A., and A. Fiori 2021. China and the BRI: Challenges and Opportunities for Southeast Asia. In *Rebalancing Asia: The Belt and Road Initiative and Indo-Pacific Strategy*, ed. P. Jaiswal and D Prakash Bhatt, 149–159. Cham: Springer.

Anwar, D.F. 2020. Indonesia and the ASEAN Outlook on the Indo-Pacific. *International Affairs* 96 (1): 111–129.

ASEAN. 2012. ASEAN Framework for Regional Comprehensive Economic Partnership, available at: https://asean.org/asean-framework-for-regional-comprehensive-economic-partnership/ (accessed 15 November 2023).

ASEAN. 2019. ASEAN Outlook on the Indo-Pacific, available at: https://asean.org/asean2020/wp-content/uploads/2021/01/ASEAN-Outlook-on-the-IndoPacific_FINAL_22062019.pdf (accessed 13 November 2023).

ASEAN. 2023a. ASEAN Plus Three—Area of Cooperation, available at: https://aseanplusthree.asean.org/about-apt/areas-of-cooperation/ (accessed 13 November 2023).

ASEAN. 2023b. ASEAN Plus Three Cooperation Work Plan, available at: https://asean.org/wp-content/uploads/2022/08/APT-Cooperation-Work-Plan-2023-2027.pdf (accessed 13 November 2023).

ASEAN. 2023c. About the ASEAN Defence Ministers' Meeting Plus, available at: https://admm.asean.org/index.php/about-admm/about-admm-plus.html (accessed 13 November 2023).

Auslin, M.R. 2020. *Asia's New Geopolitics: Essays on Reshaping the Indo-Pacific*. Stanford: Hoover Institution Press.

Australian Government. 2017. *2017 Foreign Policy White Paper*, available at: https://www.dfat.gov.au/publications/minisite/2017-foreign-policy-white-paper/fpwhitepaper/pdf/2017-foreign-policy-white-paper.pdf (accessed 10 November 2023).

Barnes, J., and S.M. Makinda. 2022. Testing the Limits of International Society? Trust, AUKUS and Indo-Pacific Security. *International Affairs* 98 (4): 1307–1325.

Beeson, M. 2016. Multilateralism in East Asia: Less Than the Sum of Its Parts? *Global Summitry* 2 (1): 54–70.

Beeson, M., and R. Stubbs, eds. 2012. *Routledge Handbook of Asian Regionalism*. New York: Routledge.

Beeson, M., and J. Wilson. 2018. The Indo-Pacific: Reconceptualizing the Asian Regional Space. *East Asia* 35: 79–84.

Belt and Road Forum (BRF). 2023. Joint Statement on Deepening Comprehensive Strategic Cooperation Between the People's Republic of China and the Republic of Indonesia, available at: http://www.beltandroadforum.org/english/n101/2023/1019/c127-1229.html (accessed 14 November 2023).

Bisley, N. 2019. Contested Asia's 'New' Multilateralism and Regional Order. *The Pacific Review* 32 (2): 221–231.

Börzel, T.A., and T. Risse. 2017. From Europeanization to Diffusion. In *Domestic Politics and Norm Diffusion in International Relations*, ed. T. Risse, 290–307. London and New York: Routledge.

Camroux, D., and C. Lechervy. 1996. 'Close Encounter of a Third Kind?' The Inaugural Asia-Europe Meeting of March 1996. *The Pacific Review* 9 (3): 442–453.

Cannon, B.J., and A. Rossiter. 2018. The 'Indo-Pacific': Regional Dynamics in the 21st Century's New Geopolitical Center of Gravity. *Rising Powers Quarterly* 3 (2): 7–17.

Carteny, A., and E.T. Di Stefano. 2023. The EU and the Indo-Pacific. In *Handbook of Indo-Pacific Studies*, ed. B. Kratuik, J.J.J. Van Den Bosch, A. Jaskolska, and Y. Sato, 405–428. New York: Routledge.

Chung, S.W., and J.S. Lee. 2019. Building the Pillars of the EU-South Korea Strategic Partnership. *Asia Europe Journal* 17 (3): 327–340.

Council of the EU. 2016. Council Decision (EU) 2017/1546, available at: https://eur-lex.europa.eu/legal-content/EN/TXT/?uri=celex%3A32017D1546 (accessed 18 November 2023).

Council of the EU. 2021a. 13th ASEM Summit "Strengthening Multilateralism for Shared Growth," Chair's Statemen, available at: https://www.consilium.europa.eu/media/53136/asem13-chair-s-statement.pdf (accessed 16 November 2023).

Council of the EU. 2021b. EU-Japan Strategic Partnership, available at: https://www.consilium.europa.eu/media/49921/eu-japan-2021-05-final.pdf (accessed 16 November 2023).

Council of the EU. 2022. Australia-EU Leaders' Meeting 2022: Joint Press Release, available at: https://www.consilium.europa.eu/en/press/press-releases/2022/11/16/australia-eu-leaders-meeting-2022-joint-press-release-by-australian-prime-minister-anthony-albanese-european-council-president-charles-michel-and-european-commission-president-ursula-von-der-leyen/ (accessed 16 November 2023).

Council of the EU. 2023a. EU–Japan Summit 2023: Joint Statement, available at: https://www.consilium.europa.eu/en/press/press-releases/2023/07/13/eu-japan-summit-2023-joint-statement/ (accessed 16 November 2023).

Council of the EU. 2023b. Joint Statement European Union—Republic of Korea Summit 2023, available at: https://www.consilium.europa.eu/media/64522/st09590-en23.pdf (accessed 17 November 2023).

Economy, E. 2005. China's Rise in Southeast Asia: Implications for the United States. *Journal of Contemporary China* 14 (44): 409–425.

EEAS. 2020. EU-India Strategic Partnership: A Roadmap to 2025, available at: https://www.eeas.europa.eu/sites/default/files/euindia_strategic_partnership_a_roadmap_to_2025_0.pdf (accessed 16 November 2023).

EEAS. 2021a. EU-U.S.: Joint Press Release by the EEAS and Department of State on the High-Level Consultations on the Indo-Pacific, available at: https://www.eeas.europa.eu/eeas/eu-us-joint-press-release-eeas-and-department-state-high-level-consultations-indo-pacific_en (accessed 16 November 2023).

EEAS. 2021b. The EU Needs a Strategic Approach for the Indo-Pacific, available at: https://www.eeas.europa.eu/eeas/eu-needs-strategic-approach-indo-pacific_en (accessed 18 November 2023).

EEAS. 2023a. Security and Defence: The European Union and China Hold Their 13th Consultations, available at: https://www.eeas.europa.eu/eeas/security-and-defence-european-union-and-china-hold-their-13th-consultations_en (accessed 16 November 2023).

EEAS. 2023b. ASEAN: 30th Joint Cooperation Committee Meeting with the European Union convenes in Jakarta. Available at: https://www.eeas.europa.eu/eeas/asean-30th-joint-cooperation-committee-meeting-european-union-convenes-jakarta_en (accessed 8 November 2023).

European Commission. 2019. EU-China a Strategic Outlook, available at: https://commission.europa.eu/system/files/2019-03/communication-eu-china-a-strategic-outlook.pdf (accessed 16 November 2023).

European Commission. 2021a. The EU Strategy for Cooperation in the Indo-Pacific, available at: https://www.eeas.europa.eu/sites/default/files/jointcommunication_2021_24_1_en.pdf (accessed 7 November 2023).

European Commission. 2021b. EU and Indo-Pacific: Natural Partner, available at: https://ec.europa.eu/commission/presscorner/detail/en/IP_21_4704 (accessed 9 November 2023).

European Commission. 2023. Negotiations and Agreements, available at: https://policy.trade.ec.europa.eu/eu-trade-relationships-country-and-region/negotiations-and-agreements_en (accessed 10 November 2023).

Forough, M. 2022. America's Pivot to Asia 2.0: The Indo-Pacific Economic Framework. *The Diplomat*, May 26, available at: https://thediplomat.com/2022/05/americas-pivot-to-asia-2-0-the-indo-pacific-economic-framework/ (accessed 19 November 2023).

Gale, J.B., and A. Shearer. 2018. The Quadrilateral Security Dialogue and the Maritime Silk Road Initiative. Center for Strategic and International Studies (CSIS), available at: https://www.csis.org/analysis/quadrilateral-security-dialogue-and-maritime-silk-road-initiative (accessed 15 November 2023).

Gao, H.S., and G. Shaffer. 2021. The RCEP: Great Power Competition and Cooperation Over Trade. *UC Irvine School of Law Research Paper*, n 2021-09, 1–5.

Gilson, J. 2006. Region Building in East Asia: ASEAN Plus Three and Beyond. In *Integration in Asia and Europe: Historical Dynamics, Political Issues, and Economic Perspectives*, ed. P.J.J. Welfens, F. Knipping, S. Chirathivat, and C. Ryan, 217–234. Berlin: Springer.

Gilson, J. 2013. New Interregionalism? The EU and East Asia. In *The EU as a Global Player*, ed. F. Sodermaum and L. van Langenhove, 59–78. London: Routledge.

Gilson, J. 2020. EU-ASEAN Relations in the 2020s: Pragmatic Inter-Regionalism? *International Economics and Economic Policy* 17 (3): 727–745.

Goh, E. 2014. East Asia as Regional International Society: The Problem of Great Power Management. In *Contesting International Society in East Asia*, ed. B. Buzan and Y. Zhang, 167–187. Cambridge: Cambridge University Press.

Gong, X. 2019. The Belt and Road Initiative and China's Influence in Southeast Asia. *The Pacific Review* 32 (4): 635–665.

Gong, X. 2022. Weathering the Storm? RCEP, Chinese Regionalism, and Great Power Competition. In *Chinese Regionalism in Asia*, ed. T. Boon Hoo and J. Morgan Mckinney, 44–56. London: Routledge.

Guillemard, V. 2022. Crise des sous-marins: huit mois après le choc, l'Australie et la France veulent aller de l''avant. *Le Figaro*, available at: https://www.lefigaro.fr/societes/crise-des-sous-marins-huit-mois-apres-le-choc-l-australie-et-la-france-veulent-aller-de-l-avant-20220611 (accessed 15 November 2023).

Hahn-Kyu, P. 2017. The China–Japan–South Korea Trilateral Summit: Realpolitik or Liberal Peace? In *China-Japan Relations in the 21st Century: Antagonism Despite Interdependency*, ed. L. Peng Er, 291–317. Singapore: Palgrave Macmillan.

He, K. 2019. Contested multilateralism 2.0 and Regional Order Transition: Causes and Implications. *The Pacific Review* 32 (2): 210–220.

He, K., and H. Feng. 2020. The Institutionalization of the Indo-Pacific: Problems and prospects. *International Affairs* 96 (1): 149–168.

Herszenhorn, D.M. 2021. EU Leaders Accuse Biden of Disloyalty to Allies, available at: https://www.politico.eu/article/eu-charles-michel-biden-disloyalty-allies-aukus/ (accessed 11 November 2023).

Hettne, B., O. Sunkel, and A. Inotai, eds. 1999. *Globalism and the New Regionalism*. Basingstoke: Palgrave Macmillan.

Hopewell, K. 2021. When the Hegemon Goes Rogue: Leadership Amid the US Assault on the Liberal Trading Order. *International Affairs* 97 (4): 1025–1043.

Huong, N. 2018. Key Differences Between CPTPP and TPP. Vietnam Investment Review, available at: https://vir.com.vn/apicenter@/print_article&i=56904 (accessed 15 November 2023).

Iqbal Dar, A. 2023. Understanding India's Exit from the RCEP: A "Two-Level Game" Conundrum. *Asian Survey* 1: 1–26.

Job, B.L. 2022. Between a Rock and a Hard Place: The Dilemmas of Middle Powers. In *The Strategic Options of Middle Powers in the Asia-Pacific*, ed. C.-K. Kou, C.-C. Huang, and B. Job, 34–56. London and New York: Routledge.

Kang, S. 2020. Geoeconomics of the Indo-Pacific: Competing Economic Architectures and South Korea. In *The Korean Peninsula and Indo-Pacific Power Politics*, ed. J.P. Panda, 225–241. London and New York: Routledge.

Katzenstein, P.J. 2000. Regionalism and Asia. *New Political Economy* 5 (3): 353–368.

Kavalski, E. 2016. The EU–India Strategic Partnership: Neither Very Strategic, Nor Much of a Partnership. *Cambridge Review of International Affairs* 29 (1): 192–208.

Khalid, I., and A. Gul. 2017. Indian Response to Chinese String of Pearls Doctrine. *Global Political Review* 2 (1): 27–35.

Kishida, F. 2023. New Plan for a "Free and Open Indo-Pacific": Policy Speech by PM Kishida. Government of Japan, available at: https://www.japan.go.jp/kizuna/2023/05/new_plan_for_free_and_open_indo-pacific.html (accessed 10 November 2023).

Kitaoka, S. 2019. Vision for a Free and Open Indo-Pacific. *Asia-Pacific Review* 26 (1): 7–17.

Kwon, M. 2023. The Emergence of the Indo-Pacific: Geopolitical Turn or Continuity? *E-international relations*, available at: https://www.e-ir.info/2023/04/11/the-emergence-of-the-indo-pacific-geopolitical-turn-or-continuity/ (accessed 9 November 2023).

Li, M. 2020. The Belt and Road Initiative: Geo-economics and Indo-Pacific Security Competition. *International Affairs* 96 (1): 169–187.

Liu, F., and K. He. 2023. China's Bilateral Relations, Order Transition, and the Indo-Pacific Dynamics. *China Review* 23 (1): 11–43.

Manners, I. 2009. The Social Dimension of EU Trade Policies: Reflections from a Normative Power Perspective. *European Foreign Affairs Review* 14 (5): 785–802.

Mearsheimer, J. J. 2003. *The Tragedy of Great Power Politics (Updated Edition)*. WW Norton & Company.

Meunier, S., and Nicolaidis, K. 2019. The Geopoliticization of European Trade and Investment Policy. *Journal of Common Market Studies* 57: 103.

Mattheis, F., and U. Wunderlich. 2017. Regional Actorness and Interregional Relations: ASEAN, the EU and Mercosur. *Journal of European Integration* 39 (6): 723–738.

Meissner, K.L. 2016. A Case of Failed Interregionalism? Analyzing the EU-ASEAN Free Trade Agreement Negotiations. *Asia Europe Journal* 14: 319–336.

Meissner, K.L. 2018. *Commercial Realism and EU Trade Policy: Competing for Economic Power in Asia and the Americas*. London: Routledge.

Ministry of Foreign Affairs (MOFA) of Japan. 2020. Joint Leaders' Statement on the Regional Comprehensive Economic Partnership (RCEP), available at: https://www.mofa.go.jp/mofaj/files/100114930.pdf (accessed 20 November 2023).

Mohan, G. 2020. A European Strategy for the Indo-Pacific. *The Washington Quarterly* 43 (4): 171–185.

Narine, S. 1998. ASEAN and the Management of Regional Security. *Pacific Affairs*, 195–214.

Narine, S. 2018. US Domestic Politics and America's Withdrawal from the Trans-Pacific Partnership: Implications for Southeast Asia. *Contemporary Southeast Asia* 40 (1): 50–76.

Nischalke, T.I. 2000. Insights from ASEAN's Foreign Policy Co-operation: The "ASEAN Way", a Real Spirit or a Phantom? *Contemporary Southeast Asia* 22 (1): 89–112.

Pan, C. 2014. The 'Indo-Pacific' and Geopolitical Anxieties About China's Rise in the Asian Regional Order. *Australian Journal of International Affairs* 68 (4): 453–469.

Pempel, T.J. 2019. Right Target; Wrong Tactics: The Trump Administration Upends East Asian Order. *The Pacific Review* 32 (6): 996–1018.

Pugliese, G. 2023. The European Union's Security Intervention in the Indo-Pacific: Between Multilateralism and Mercantile Interests. *Journal of Intervention and Statebuilding* 17 (1): 76–98.

Rajagopalan, R. 2020. Evasive Balancing: India's Unviable Indo-Pacific strategy. *International Affairs* 96 (1): 75–93.

Rana, P.B., and X. Ji. 2020. BRI and Southeast Asia. In *China's Belt and Road Initiative: Impacts on Asia and Policy Agenda*, ed. P.B. Rana and X. Ji, 93–111. London: Palgrave Macmillan.

Reuters. 2015. Japan Abe's Ruling Party Calls for Cautious Approach to AIIB, available at: https://www.reuters.com/article/japan-economy-aiib/japan-abes-ruling-party-calls-for-cautious-approach-to-aiib-idUKL3N0YP3O020150603 (accessed 15 November 2023).

Robles, Jr. A.C. 2006. The Association of Southeast Asia Nations (ASEAN) and the European Union: Limited Interregionalism. In *Interregionalism and International Relations*, ed. H. Hänggi, R. Roloff, and J. Rüland, 97–112. New York: Routledge.

Robles, A.C., Jr. 2008. An EU–ASEAN FTA: The EU's Failures as an International Actor. *European Foreign Affairs Review* 13 (4): 541–560.

Rossiter, A., and B.J. Cannon, eds. 2020. *Conflict and Cooperation in the Indo-Pacific: New Geopolitical Realities*. London and New York: Routledge.

Saeed, M. 2017. From the Asia-Pacific to the Indo-Pacific: Expanding Sino-US Strategic Competition. *China Quarterly of International Strategic Studies* 3 (4): 499–512.

Scott, D. 2018. The Indo-Pacific in US Strategy: Responding to Power Shifts. *Rising Powers Quarterly* 2 (2): 19–43.

Scott, D. 2019. China's Indo-Pacific Strategy. *The Journal of Territorial and Maritime Studies* 6 (2): 94–113.

Shambaugh, D. 2018. U.S.-China Rivalry in Southeast Asia: Power Shift or Competitive Coexistence? *International Security* 42 (4): 85–127.

Slaughter, P.C. 2020. China's Global Military-Security Interactions. In *China and the World*, ed. D. Shambaugh, 181–207. Oxford: Oxford University Press.

Söderbaum, F. 2016. *Rethinking Regionalism*. London: Palgrave Macmillan.

South Korea Government. 2022. Strategy for a Free, Peaceful and Prosperous Indo-Pacific Region, available at: https://overseas.mofa.go.kr/eng/brd/m_5676/view.do?seq=322133 (accessed 20 November 2023).

Taylor, B. 2020. Is Australia's Indo-Pacific Strategy an Illusion? *International Affairs* 96 (1): 95–109.

Tellis, A. J. 2022. "What Is in Our Interest": India and the Ukraine War. Carnegie Endowment for International Peace, available at: https://carnegieendowment.org/2022/04/25/what-is-in-our-interest-india-and-ukraine-war-pub-86961 (accessed 16 November 2023).

The White House. 2021. Quad Leaders' Joint Statement: "The Spirit of the Quad", available at: https://www.whitehouse.gov/briefing-room/statements-releases/2021/03/12/quad-leaders-joint-statement-the-spirit-of-the-quad/ (accessed 15 November 2023).

The White House. 2022. Indo-Pacific Strategy of the Unites States, available at: https://www.whitehouse.gov/wp-content/uploads/2022/02/U.S.-Indo-Pacific-Strategy.pdf (accessed 15 November 2023).

United States of America, Department of Commerce. 2023. Indo-Pacific Economic Framework, available at: https://www.commerce.gov/ipef (accessed 13 November 2023).

United States of America, Department of State. 2019. A Free and Open Indo-Pacific: Advancing a Shared Vision, available at: https://www.state.gov/wp-content/uploads/2019/11/Free-and-Open-Indo-Pacific-4Nov2019.pdf (accessed 9 November 2023).

United States of America, Department of State. 2021. EU-U.S.: Joint Press Release by the EEAS and Department of State on the High-Level Consultations on the Indo-Pacific, available at: https://www.state.gov/eu-u-s-joint-press-release-by-the-eeas-and-department-of-state-on-the-high-level-consultations-on-the-indo-pacific/ (accessed 16 November 2023).

US Department of State. 2019. A Free and Open Indo-Pacific: Advancing a Shared Vision. Available at: https://www.Free-and-Open-Indo-Pacific-4Nov2019.pdf (accessed 16 November 2023).

Varano, J. 2021. Tearing up the Belt and Road Initiative: Australia's Rejection of China's New Silk Road in Victoria. *International Affairs (Australian Outlook, Australian Institute of International Affairs)*, May 6, available at: https://www.internationalaffairs.org.au/australianoutlook/tearing-up-the-belt-and-road-initiative-australias-rejection-of-chinas-new-silk-road-in-victoria/ (accessed 19 November 2023).

Wacker, G. 2021. Europe and the Indo-Pacific: Comparing France, Germany and the Netherlands, available at: https://media.realinstitutoelcano.org/wp-content/uploads/2021/10/ari29-2021-wacker-europe-and-the-indo-pacific-comparing-france-germany-and-the-netherlands.pdf (accessed 16 November 2023).

Wadhwa, A.A. 2019. India's Act East Policy. Indian Ministry of Foreign Affairs, available at: https://www.mea.gov.in/distinguished-lectures-detail.htm?840 (accessed 10 November 2023).

Wong, R. 2019. The European Union's Security Strategy in the ASEAN Region. In *The European Union in the Asia-Pacific*, ed. W. Song and W. Wang, 184–199. Manchester: Manchester University Press.

Wu, C.H. 2019. The EU's Engagements with the Asia Pacific. In *Research Handbook on the European Union's Engagement with International Organisations*, ed. R.A. Wessel and J. Odermatt, 1–16. Northampton: Edward Elgar Publishing.

Wu, C.H. 2020. ASEAN at the Crossroads: Trap and Track Between CPTPP and RCEP. *Journal of International Economic Law* 23 (1): 97–117.

Xing, L. 2016. *The BRICS and Beyond: The International Political Economy of the Emergence of a New World Order*. London: Routledge.

Yahuda, M. 2020. China's Relations with Asia. In *China and the World*, ed. D. Shambaugh, 270–290. Oxford: Oxford University Press.

Yoshimatsu, H. 2023. ASEAN and Great Power Rivalry in Regionalism: From East Asia to the Indo-Pacific. *Journal of Current Southeast Asian Affairs* 42 (1): 25–44.

Zhang, M. 2018. Proceeding in Hardship: The Trilateralism–Bilateralism Nexus and the Institutional Evolution of China–Japan–South Korea trilateralism. *The Pacific Review* 31 (1): 57–75.

Zhou, W., and M. Esteban. 2020. Beyond Balancing: China's Approach Towards the Belt and Road Initiative. In *China's New Global Strategy*, ed. S. Zhao, 36–50. London and New York: Routledge.

Public Attitudes Towards the EU in the Western Balkans

Pëllumb Kelmendi and Liridon Lika

Introduction

Since 2000, European officials and institutions have regularly stated that the future of the Western Balkans (Albania, Bosnia and Herzegovina, Kosovo, Montenegro, North Macedonia, Serbia) is in the European Union (EU).[1] The European perspective of the region was especially emphasized at the Thessaloniki Summit in 2003. The EU promised a case-by-case, merit enlargement process (European Commission 2003). This vision intended for the Western Balkans to achieve peace, stability, and economic prosperity, and full membership in the EU. In this context, the EU aimed to first stabilize the region and subsequently accept these states into the common European project. Through its mechanisms and declarations, the EU engendered great hopes for change in the Western

[1] The concept "Western Balkans" is a political, geopolitical and social construct first used by the EU in 1998 (Lika 2024).

P. Kelmendi (✉)
Department of Political Science, Auburn University, Auburn, AL, USA
e-mail: kelmendi@auburn.edu

L. Lika
Department of Political Science, University of Liège, Liège, Belgium
e-mail: liridon.lika@uliege.be

L. Lika and D. Riga (eds.), *EU Geopolitical Actorness in a Changing World*, https://doi.org/10.1007/978-3-031-81160-9_7

Balkans, fueled also by its prior enlargement toward Central and Eastern Europe (CEE) (Elbasani 2008, 306). Since the opening of the European perspective in Thessaloniki, moreover, the governments of the Western Balkan states have listed EU membership as a strategic priority.

However, more than 20 years have passed, and EU enlargement into the Western Balkans has not taken place. The last country from the region to join the EU, Croatia, did so in 2013, and the prospects for others to follow seem distant at best, despite continuous EU statements that the future of the region is in the EU. Throughout this time, moreover, overall public support for EU membership in the Western Balkans has begun to wane. Some scholars have argued that the "very length of the process contributes to intensifying public frustration, and to raising suspicions about Brussels' ultimate intentions" (Belloni 2016, 538). It is important to note, however, that although public support for the EU was generally high across the region in the early 2000s, it nevertheless varied across Western Balkan countries. For example, public sentiment in Serbia was lukewarm towards the EU even in the early 2000s. Moreover, the recent trend towards Euroskepticism in the region has also been markedly uneven. Opinion poll data show that while the publics in Bosnia and Herzegovina, Montenegro, North Macedonia, and especially Serbia have turned significantly more Euroskeptic over time, public opinion in Albania and Kosovo has been consistently pro-EU.

What explains variation in public support for EU integration in the Western Balkans? Public support for EU membership varies from state to state in the Western Balkans and even across different ethnic groups within these countries. In other words, there have been and still exist important differences in support for EU membership across the Western Balkan countries. These differences extend beyond the level of countries, moreover. While polls show rising Euroskepticism among Orthodox Slavic citizens in the Western Balkans, particularly in Serbia, the perception is completely different among ethnic Albanians, not only in Albania and Kosovo, but also elsewhere where Albanians live in the Western Balkans, such as in North Macedonia, Serbia, and Montenegro. This chapter aims to analyze these trends in support of EU membership. The objective of this chapter, therefore, is to examine public opinion in the Western Balkan states which are seeking European integration in order to better understand the effectiveness of EU actorness in the region.

While the existing literature has emphasized different factors, such as Europeanization and the state-building process, the timing and impact of the integration process, economic cost-benefit calculus, and trust in national institutions, this chapter highlights the importance of national identity-based factors. The chapter employs various public opinion data sources, including Balkan Barometer data, to investigate variations in public opinion towards EU membership across different countries and ethnic groups. It is also supported by other sources including books, social science articles, official statements, reports, and press articles. This chapter begins with an overview of the process of EU integration in the Western Balkans and public attitudes towards this process. The subsequent section summarizes the existing literature on attitudes towards the EU in the region. The last three sections explain the observed variation in public support for the EU, explaining high support in Albania and Kosovo, moderate support in Bosnia and Herzegovina, Montenegro, and North Macedonia, and the consistently low support for EU membership in Serbia.

Perceptions of EU Membership in the Western Balkans

The Western Balkans, home to around 18 million inhabitants, is a diverse region of various states, nations, languages, and cultures. Some of the countries in the region have interstate rivalries, bilateral political disputes, divergent foreign policies, as well as economic and social challenges. As already noted, despite its repeated promises, the EU has delayed the region's accession process for a long time. The Western Balkans has thus undergone a slow process of Europeanization (Noutcheva 2009). In particular, the EU has focused primarily on stabilitocracy (BiEPAG 2017), which has been associated with increased authoritarianism, especially in Serbia (Bieber 2020). At the same time, the Western Balkans faces global security threats and the rising influence of powers such as Russia, China, and Turkey (Lika 2021; Bieber and Tzifakis 2020; Rrustemi et al. 2019). The 2022 Russian invasion of Ukraine seems to have changed the EU's approach to the Western Balkans. As the security of the European continent has become more tenuous, the EU has begun to act—or is encouraged to act—as a geopolitical actor (Dopchie and Lika 2024; Anghel and Dzankic 2023; Keil 2023). In this context, in August 2023, Charles Michel, European Council President, stressed that the EU must be ready for a new enlargement by 2030 (Michel quoted in Bayer 2023).

After the promises of the Thessaloniki Summit in 2003, the Western Balkan states had great hopes and expectations to join the European project as soon as possible. However, for more than 20 years, the EU enlargement strategy towards the Western Balkans has produced mixed results. With the exception of Croatia, which was initially part of the Western Balkans until 2013, when Zagreb joined the EU, the rest of the Western Balkan states are still in the waiting room. The EU granted candidate status to five countries: North Macedonia (2005), Montenegro (2010), Serbia (2012), Albania (2014), and Bosnia and Herzegovina (2022). These five states are therefore more advanced in the accession process. However, there are disparities between them. Montenegro (since 2012), Serbia (since 2014), Albania, and North Macedonia (since 2022) have opened accession negotiations. Montenegro is the most advanced country in the accession process with all negotiation chapters open and three already closed. It is followed by Serbia with 22 open chapters and two closed.

However, based on the current dynamics, the negotiations for accession could last for years. The Republic of Kosovo is a potential candidate country for EU membership, having applied for candidate status in December 2022, which means that it is currently the furthest away in the accession process. Thus, the Western Balkan states have not progressed at the same pace because they are conditioned by the merit principle. This conditionality is criticized by some scholars, who argue for a collective regional policy that promotes EU membership en bloc for these six countries (Marciacq 2017, 17).

Public opinion surveys, such as those organized by Balkan Barometer, provide quantitative data on the perceptions and expectations of public opinion in the Western Balkan countries regarding European integration. Table 1 shows the percentage of survey respondents in each Western Balkan state who declared that their country's membership in the EU would be a good thing.

The public support trends for EU membership show that Albania and Kosovo are by far the most pro-EU states in the Western Balkans, followed by North Macedonia, Montenegro, and Bosnia and Herzegovina. The results reveal a very favorable opinion among the citizens of Albania and Kosovo. As for North Macedonia, Montenegro, and Bosnia and Herzegovina, public opinion is generally moderately favorable. It is worth emphasizing that when it comes to Bosnia and Herzegovina's accession to the EU, the country's inhabitants are divided along

Table 1 Share of respondents who declare that EU membership would be a good thing

	2006	*2008*	*2009*	*2010*	*2016*	*2017*	*2018*	*2019*	*2020*	*2021*	*2022*
Albania	84	83	88	81	31	81	83	86	87	84	89
BiH	70	59	77	75	33	31	45	47	56	50	50
Kosovo	87	89	88	87	83	90	84	69	75	91	73
Montenegro	64	57	67	73	38	44	53	52	54	51	57
N. Macedonia	76	66	62	60	47	54	59	51	57	53	56
Serbia	61	58	50	44	21	26	29	32	26	42	38

Source Compilation of data by the authors based on surveys conducted by Gallup Balkan Monitor (2010) and the Balkan Barometer (RCC 2019; RCC 2023)

ethnic lines: Bosniaks and Croats are generally in favor, while Serbs are largely unfavorable. The same is true for the multiethnic state of Montenegro, where the Serb community is less favorable to EU membership. Regarding Serbia, a traditional ally of Russia, the responses in favor of the EU are the lowest. In this country, fewer than half of the survey respondents believe that EU membership would be a good thing for Serbia, and this number is as low as 21% in 2016 and 26% in 2017. What explains this variation in public support for EU membership?

Explanations of Variation in Public Support for EU

Relying on the literature on attitudes towards the EU in general, and Euroskepticism in particular, this chapter identifies four sets of explanations for public attitudes towards the EU in the Western Balkans. Utilitarian factors focus on economic cost-benefit calculations. According to this school of thought, support for the EU is stronger when and where economic gains from EU integration are most visible (see Damjanovski et al. 2020, 331). At the macro-level, scholars have noted that the eurozone crisis highlighted the economic vulnerabilities associated with EU integration, particularly in countries that were the most advanced in the EU integration process, leading in turn to a decline in support for the EU (Belloni 2016, 537). At the micro-level, scholars have posited that some segments of the population in Western Balkan countries—such as those scoring higher in income, education, and socio-economic status—may be more likely to support EU integration because they expect to gain more from market liberalization and increased competitiveness (Damjanovski et al. 2020, 331–332).

Public opinion data does not support this explanation, however. First, if this explanation were correct, empirical analysis would reveal a decline in support for the EU across all Western Balkan countries, especially after 2007—namely following the global financial crisis and subsequently the European debt crisis. In four out of the six countries, however, support for EU membership either stays the same or increases somewhat during this period. Balkan Barometer data also indicates that the percentage of the population that associates EU membership with economic prosperity is not necessarily higher in countries where support for the EU is higher. This suggests that the drivers of variation in support (or lack thereof) for EU membership in the Western Balkans are not related to concerns about the economic benefits of EU membership. Moreover, existing individual-level analyses do not reveal an association between utilitarian variables (such as occupational status and income levels) and support for the EU (or lack thereof) (Damjanovski et al. 2020, 341). This suggests that other factors are at play.

Another group of explanations centers on public trust in national institutions and governments, suggesting that citizens base their judgments about the EU on their attitudes towards national institutions, about which they are better informed. According to this line of thought, the public is not well-informed about the EU and therefore uses its assessment of national institutions to extrapolate (see Damjanovski et al. 2020, 332–333). The literature is divided on the hypothesized direction of the effect of trust in national institutions, however. Some scholars hold that positive views of national institutions and effective governance can foster a favorable attitude towards the EU, as citizens may see European integration as a complementary and beneficial process (Ehin 2001). Conversely, negative perceptions of national institutions, corruption, or ineffective governance may lead the public to view the EU with skepticism, associating it with similar concerns and contributing to a more critical stance on European integration (Vetik 2003). Other scholars, however, have argued that people who distrust their domestic institutions are more inclined to support EU integration, seeing it as a key generator of reforms (Sanchez-Cuenca 2000).

This explanation, however, is not borne out by the data from the Western Balkans either. Using Balkan Barometer data, Table 2 presents

Table 2 Share of respondents who tend to trust or totally trust the country's government

	2017	*2018*	*2019*	*2020*	*2021*	*2022*
Albania	27	43	28	39	41	45
Bosnia and Herzegovina	15	21	35	20	26	25
Kosovo	30	25	34	27	26	68
Montenegro	42	47	58	50	46	28
North Macedonia	36	41	48	27	30	25
Serbia	31	30	27	38	58	49

Source Compilation of data by the authors based on surveys conducted by the Balkan Barometer (RCC 2023)

the percentage of survey respondents in each Western Balkan country who stated that they either tend to trust or totally trust their government (Table 2).

As can be seen from Table 2, trust in government across all Western Balkan countries tends to be relatively low. To the extent that there is variation, however, it does not correspond with attitudes towards the EU. Between 2017 and 2022, trust in government, on average, tended to be the lowest in Bosnia and Herzegovina and the highest in Montenegro. In Serbia it varied from as low as 30% in 2018 to as high as 58% in 2021. But these inter-temporal variations in trust in government are not reflected in variations in support for the EU. The same lack of association can be observed for Kosovo, where trust in government ranges from 26% in 2021 to 68% in 2022, and Albania where trust in government varies from 27% in 2017 to 43% in 2018. These findings are in line with other studies, such as the one by Ivan Damjanovski et al. (2020, 338), who find that trust in state institutions is a rather imperfect predictor of individual-level attitudes towards the EU.

Another factor that is occasionally mentioned in the literature emphasizes the role of religious affiliation on attitudes towards the EU in the Western Balkans. On the one hand, scholars have highlighted how Orthodox Christian citizens in Serbia, Montenegro, Bosnia and Herzegovina, and North Macedonia tend to be more suspicious of the West, either because Western Europe is seen as "the source of existential threats to the Orthodox world" or because Orthodox churches "are associated with the political camp of EU skeptics" (see Belloni 2016, 539). Indeed,

Damjanovski et al. (2020, 338) find that affiliation with Orthodox Christianity is strongly correlated with Euroskepticism. On the other hand, the same studies have noted that Muslim religious affiliation in the Western Balkans tends to be positively associated with support for EU membership (Damjanovski et al. 2020, 339; see also Belloni 2016, 539).

Arguments focusing on religious affiliation, however, tend to be either incomplete or incorrect. While the role of Orthodox churches in countries such as Serbia is obvious (see the discussion below), it is also important to note that Orthodox Christians in Albania are no less likely to support the EU than Albanians of other religious affiliations (Damjanovski et al. 2020, 338). Indeed, in the case of Albania, Kosovo, and ethnic Albanians in general, there is no evidence that religious affiliation is associated with differential attitudes towards the EU. While Damjanovski et al. (2020, 338) find that Muslim religious affiliation is associated with positive attitudes towards the EU in Kosovo, their regression analysis does not control for ethnicity, suggesting that the relationship they find is potentially spurious. An analysis of data from the 2003–2004 South-East European Social Survey Project (SEESSP), for example, shows that among Kosovo Albanians there is no discernable difference in support for the EU between respondents who belong to Muslim and Roman Catholic religious denominations (Simkus 2007). The SEESSP survey data reveal that in 2003–2004 97.5% of Roman Catholic Albanians in Kosovo exhibited support or strong support for EU membership and 96.4% of Muslim Albanians in Kosovo expressed the same. The same is true for those who exhibit strong support for the EU. About 83% of Roman Catholic Albanians in Kosovo were strongly in favor of the EU compared to 78% of respondents with Muslim religious affiliation. Similarly, the SEESSP survey data show that in Albania, 96% of Roman Catholics, 96% of Orthodox Christians, and 87% of Muslims declared support for EU membership.

This strongly suggests that studies investigating the individual-level determinants of support for the EU in the Western Balkans need to include ethnicity in order to attain a more accurate picture of the relationship between identity and support for the EU. One key reason for this is that, whereas the "Serbian Orthodox Church has been an important purveyor of [an] exclusionary Serbian identity" and "has held profoundly anti-Western and anti-European positions" (Subotic 2011), religion has not been a politically salient element of Albanian identity, neither in Kosovo nor in Albania. Indeed, language and ethnicity are the pillars of

Albanian national identity, not religion (Lika 2023, 245; Babuna 2000; Krasniqi 2011). Table 3 shows the percentage of survey respondents who declare that EU membership would be a good thing in each Western Balkan country, according to ethnicity. As can be seen from the table, Albanians are consistently supportive of the EU across Albania, Kosovo, and North Macedonia. Serbs, by contrast, are consistently skeptical, not just in Serbia proper but also in Bosnia and Herzegovina, Kosovo, and Montenegro (Table 3).

This chapter employs a more sophisticated identity-based framework to explain the observed variation in support for the EU in the Western Balkans by focusing on the processes of identity convergence and identity divergence in the context of European integration (Subotic 2011). According to this argument, identity convergence is "a process by which domestic political actors nurture, reinforce, and promote a particular [European] version of state identity that best serves their competitive electoral goals" whereas identity divergence is "a mechanism by which domestic coalitions resist norms and rules of Europeanization and instead define the national community in contrast to those European values or requirements domestically deemed illegitimate" (Subotic 2011, 313–314). Extending this argument to public attitudes, support for the EU

Table 3 Respondents who declare that EU membership would be a good thing (by ethnicity)

Country	*Ethnicity*	*2017*	*2018*	*2019*	*2020*	*2021*	*2022*
Albania	Albanians	80.8	83.1	90.5	86.6	83.9	89.1
BiH	Bosniaks	41.2	53	57.4	62.8	32.9	56.6
BiH	Croats	39.4	59.7	38.5	64.3	NA	38.1
BiH	Serbs	18.3	34.9	31.8	34.4	NA	46.6
Kosovo	Albanians	93.1	89	71.8	76.7	93	71.6
Kosovo	Serbs	27.6	16	10.4	39.6	42.5	2.4
Montenegro	Montenegrins	48.5	53.7	51.5	63.6	62.9	66.7
Montenegro	Serbs	21.9	46.9	37.4	30.5	56.7	48.2
N. Macedonia	Albanians	64.5	73.1	79.3	71.9	79.3	72.5
N. Macedonia	Macedonians	50.2	54.6	41.1	49.8	46.3	48.5
Serbia	Serbs	26.3	28.8	31.3	25.9	40.2	36.3

Source Compilation of data by the authors based on surveys conducted by the Balkan Barometer and their annual reports (RCC 2023)

is more likely to occur in countries where the idea of shared European identity resonates with existing conceptions of national identity and existing values and norms, alternative identity narratives are weak and underdeveloped, and previous relationship with EU is positive. Conversely, identity divergence is more likely to occur in countries where the idea of shared European identity does not resonate with existing conceptions of national identity, alternative identity narratives are strong, and the previous relationship with the EU is negative (Subotic 2011, 313–314).

Societies of the Western Balkans all experience demands, constraints, and political pressures from the EU. Disenchantment with or opposition to the EU may stem from a combination of economic concerns, frustrations with EU's conditionality, its paternalism and the length of the integration process, as well as real or perceived threats to national sovereignty and culture (Belloni 2016). These reasons are also compounded by Russia's resurgent role in the Western Balkans (Panagiotou 2011). What ultimately determines whether societies in the Western Balkans remain pro-EU or not, however, is whether domestic political actors, including the publics, have internalized and are able to perpetuate a European version of state identity or not.

In the sections below, this chapter shows that, unlike the above-mentioned explanations of attitudes towards the EU, the state identity framework is much better suited to explain variation in support for the EU in the Western Balkans.

Kosovo and Albania: High Support for EU Membership

As shown in the tables above, the publics in Albania and Kosovo are clearly the most pro-European in the Western Balkans, by far. In Albania, the share of the population that believes that EU membership would be a good thing has consistently been above 80%, and even as high as 89%. In Kosovo, this number has ranged between 70% and 90%. As can be seen from Tables 1 and 3, support for the EU in Albania and Kosovo has always been higher than in the other neighboring countries. What explains the high support for EU membership in Albania and Kosovo?

The Republic of Albania and the Republic of Kosovo are two small European countries inhabited by an overwhelming majority of ethnic Albanians. Both countries are secular and with a strong sense of European identity. There are also significant ethnic Albanians in North Macedonia, Serbia, and Montenegro, who also are among the strongest supporters of EU integration. Albanians in Kosovo, Albania, and the region share a common origin, language, culture, history, and national consciousness. The Albanian national consciousness is premised upon the idea that Albanians are an autochthonous people and direct descendants of the Illyrians (Stipçeviq, 2002; Castellan 2004, 21; Métais, 2006). Albanians thus view themselves as very different from their neighbors, particularly the South Slavs. In addition, the Albanian national identity emphasizes a strong sense of Europeanness, with Albanian political and intellectual elites connecting distinct elements of Albanian history, from Illyrian heritage to the Albanian national hero Gjergj Kastrioti—Skanderbeg's resistance against the Ottoman Empire, to the wars of independence in early and late twentieth century, as pillars of an identity that is Western and European (Gorani 2011; Sulstarova 2012). Moreover, Albanian nationalism is a deeply secular one, "[u]nlike most of the nationalisms that emerged in the twentieth century in the Balkans" (Krasniqi 2011, 192).

Albania has been a member state of the North Atlantic Treaty Organization (NATO) since 2008 and a candidate for membership in the EU since 2014. In 2022, Albania opened negotiations for EU membership. In 2024, Albania opened its first chapters of accession talks with the EU. Like Albania, Kosovo is also strongly focused on Euro-Atlantic integration, with the primary strategic goals of attaining EU and NATO membership. These two countries see no other alternative than full membership in the Euro-Atlantic structures. Indeed, the key feature of Albania and Kosovo's foreign policies is their pro-Western orientation and alignment with EU and US interests. Since the end of communism in Albania in the early 1990s and Kosovo's independence in 2008, every Albanian and Kosovar government has adopted a pro-Western policy and has identified with their Western allies (see for example Krasniqi 2023; Gashi and Kelmendi 2023; Felsen 2023).

Albania and Kosovo's alignment with Western powers is also rooted in their past relations, present support, and future aspirations. Western countries supported Kosovo's liberation and promoted its independence (Lika 2023; Gashi and Kelmendi 2023). After liberation from Serbia in 1999, Kosovo built close relations with Western countries as well as NATO and the EU, which supported its process of reconstruction, democratization, economic development, state-building, and Europeanization (Kelmendi 2012; Musliu 2021; Greiçevci 2022; Ilazi 2024). Since 2008, moreover, the United States and the EU have provided significant aid to support Kosovo's political and economic development. After Kosovo's independence, its Western partners immediately and formally recognized the new state and established diplomatic relations (Lika 2023). They also lobbied for new recognitions and membership in international organizations to help consolidate Kosovo's sovereignty on the international stage. In other words, through its Western alliances, Kosovo's diplomacy has been able to increase the number of official recognitions, become a member of many international organizations, and exercise its sovereignty on the international stage (Lika 2023).

Kosovo's political leadership has been acutely aware of the need for US and EU support of its independence and state-building, and has greatly invested in cultivating pro-American and pro-EU sentiments in Kosovo (Gashi and Kelmendi 2023, 30). For instance, May 9, namely Europe Day, is a public holiday in Kosovo. Kosovo's pro-European orientation is also manifested in its state flag that has a blue field which symbolizes the colors of the EU (Cosentino 2015, 610). As a result, together with the citizens of Albania, Kosovo citizens are the most pro-US, pro-NATO, and pro-EU in the Western Balkans (CISR 2020, 50, 69, 77, and 79). It is also worth noting that Albania and Kosovo have a large diaspora, mainly concentrated in Western countries, which has also influenced the creation of strong ties between its origin states and these countries (Lika 2023).

Another important factor that explains pro-European public attitudes in Albania and Kosovo is that there are no politically salient alternative identity or strategic orientations. In both Albania and Kosovo, all mainstream parties have embraced the mantra of Europeanization and the pro-Western strategic orientation (Kelmendi 2022; Stojarova and Emerson 2013). Cooperation with Western states provides significant political and economic opportunities, especially security guarantees. As a small state with limited resources, Albania benefits greatly from its alliance with the West in general and NATO in particular (Burden 2016). Likewise, security concerns, among others, explain Kosovo's foreign policy alignment. Whereas Albania is a member of the United Nations (UN), Kosovo is not yet a member due to the threat of a veto against its membership from Russia. Kosovo, moreover, has faced obstruction and threats from Serbia, Russia, and their allies. Such threats have to do with the balance of power between supporters and opponents of Kosovo's statehood. Thus, due to Kosovo's state identity, its majority Albanian population's strong sense of Europeanness, as well as Western support for its independence and Euro-Atlantic integration, Kosovo's political elites have not articulated or entertained alternatives to joining the EU and NATO (Lika 2023).

This does not mean that the relationship of Albania and Kosovo with the EU has been entirely uncontentious. EU administrative conditionality and the reforms in the judiciary and economic sectors in Albania have not always been easy or popular (Elbasani 2008; Panagiotou 2011). In particular, "the lack of clear advancement toward the opening of accession process led to the perception that the process has stagnated, resulting in frustration among political elites and citizens alike" (Bino et al. 2023, 175). However, political elites in Albania never articulated an alternative vision to the European membership strategy. Even Tirana's now defunct Open Balkan initiative, which was seen by some as diverting from the EU-led cooperation initiatives in the region, was presented as a project that would lead to faster integration into the EU (Kalemaj 2023). As a result, the Albanian public has remained staunchly in favor of EU membership throughout this time.

The policies of the EU towards Kosovo have at times been even more problematic, especially from the perspective of its majority Albanian population. To begin with, the EU policy toward the Kosovar state is ambiguous and even ambivalent (Lika and Reka 2021, 242). The EU supports Kosovo's membership, but it has not yet succeeded in convincing the five remaining member states—Cyprus, Greece, Romania, Slovakia, and Spain—to recognize Kosovo's statehood. The lack of recognition by five EU member states has had a significant negative impact on Kosovo's EU membership processes (Armakolas and Ker-Lindsay 2020). The EU thus has difficulty in speaking with one voice regarding Kosovo (Lika and Reka 2021, 243). Moreover, the EU has spearheaded rather unpopular demands, such as the arrest of wartime Kosovo Liberation Army (KLA) veterans, and the EU Rule of Law Mission in Kosovo (EULEX) was often a source of frustration due to corruption, ineffectiveness, and perceptions that it violated the sovereignty of Kosovo (Kelmendi 2024; Kelmendi and Skendaj 2023; Kelmendi and Radin 2018). Some of the demands stemming from Brussels as a result of the EU-facilitated dialogue between Kosovo and Serbia have also been deeply unpopular with Albanians in Kosovo. For the most part, however, Kosovo's political elites have framed these unpopular conditions as necessary to realize the European destiny of the country, and have emphasized the different ways in which Kosovo needs the EU and has been helped by the EU in the past. Even when some EU policies are strongly criticized, Kosovo's political elites often tend to go to great lengths to associate such policies with certain individuals representing the EU or certain EU member states, and not the EU as whole. As a result, the public in Kosovo continues to be overwhelmingly pro-EU.

Bosnia and Herzegovina, Montenegro, and North Macedonia: Moderate Support for EU Membership

Democratic and pro-European circles in Bosnia and Herzegovina, Montenegro, and North Macedonia have tried to make progress towards EU membership. Montenegro is the most advanced in the accession process, with all 33 chapters open and three already closed. The EU liberalized the visa regime with the Western Balkan countries: in 2009 for Montenegro, North Macedonia, and Serbia; in 2010 for Albania and Bosnia and Herzegovina; and in 2024 for Kosovo. Montenegro and North Macedonia are NATO members. Bosnia and Herzegovina is blocked in this process because the Bosnian Serbs do not want NATO membership. With the membership of Montenegro in the Alliance, the entire Adriatic Sea is now under NATO control. However, public support for the EU is more uneven, and an important reason for this is a lack of societal consensus on the European identity of these three states. On the one hand, key domestic political actors in all of three of these states have committed to the EU integration process. On the other hand, however, there are also politically powerful actors who resist Europeanization and continue to entertain alternatives to the EU.

These three countries are multiethnic and have deep inter-ethnic polarizations. For example, Bosnia and Herzegovina, which was heavily affected by the war of the 1990s, has not been able to consolidate itself sufficiently due to the obstacles posed by the Serbian entity within it. The federal state is unable to achieve consensus on important issues such as constitutional and institutional reforms because the positions of the three communities are diametrically opposed. The three main communities are also divided on the EU: Bosniaks and Croats are largely favorable to EU accession, while Serbs are largely unfavorable (Gallup Balkan Monitor 2010, 22).

According to Dominik Tolksdorf, several actors are responsible for the failure of the principle of conditionality and socialization in Bosnia and

Herzegovina: the country's political elites who, through their intransigence, undermined the efforts of constitutional reform; the EU which, as a dominant international actor in this state, has failed in its efforts to support a reform process and has applied conditionality inconsistently (Tolksdorf 2015, 414); as well as Serbia's and Russia's interference and involvement through the Bosnian Serbs in the country (Huskic 2020, 90–94). Furthermore, European initiatives such as institutional unblocking, reforms, and progress on the path to European integration have only had a weak impact on the internal politics of Bosnia and Herzegovina (Fouéré and Blockmans 2017, 2–3). Meanwhile, as Roberto Belloni (2016, 541) has noted "Russia has long been a supporter of Republika Srpska and its President Milorad Dodik, who has systematically opposed the social, economic, political and, above all, judicial reforms demanded by the EU in order to make progress towards accession."

Even Montenegro, which is both a NATO member and the most advanced country in the EU integration process, has experienced a lack of societal consensus when it comes to the country's EU future. In the early 2000s, when Montenegro was still in a union with Serbia, "the pro-independence elites in Montenegro more heavily emphasized integration" and individual support for EU integration in Montenegro was also strongly correlated with support for Montenegro's independence (Kelmendi and Pedraza 2022, 523). According to Balkan Barometer data, survey respondents in Montenegro who identify as Montenegrin are consistently more positive about EU membership than respondents who identify as Serb. Serbian and Russian policy-makers have also expressed support for anti-Western parties in Montenegro; during the November 2016 elections they provided considerable financial support to the Democratic Front (DF), the political party of the Serb minority, which opposed Montenegrin membership in NATO (Bajrovic et al. 2018). In order to consolidate its influence, Russia has intervened in the electoral processes and supported leaders, political parties, and extremist groups who threaten peace in the Western Balkans by distributing financial and military aid to them. One of the most striking illustrations is that of the aborted putsch in Montenegro, in 2016, which aimed to eliminate, politically and physically, the Montenegrin leader, Milo Djukanovic, who led his country to NATO membership and played a key role in shaping its pro-Western orientation (Marovic 2020, 149–152).

Meanwhile, North Macedonia was able to begin the process of European integration quite early, despite Greek opposition to its candidacy. In

North Macedonia, too, however, disagreements over the state's identity have interfered with the Europeanization process and have also shaped public support for European integration. While ethnic Albanians have opposed the attempts of Macedonians to define North Macedonia as a monoethnic state, neighboring states have disputed the cultural and linguistic identity of Macedonians. As Besir Ceka (2018, 148) notes, the "external identity challenges—especially the one from Greece—have profoundly affected [North] Macedonia's postcommunist political trajectory. They have not only thwarted the country's Euro-Atlantic aspirations, but have intensified its internal ethnic tensions as well." And, as Belloni (2016, 534) noted earlier, "Macedonians are frustrated and disappointed by the repeated postponement of accession talks due to a dispute with Greece over the country's name." According to him, the name dispute could upset the delicate balance between the two main ethnic groups in the country, as Albanians believed that the country's chances of joining the EU were being compromised by the Macedonians (Belloni, 2016, 534–535).

North Macedonia experienced recurring inter-ethnic confrontations, notably under the government of nationalist leader Nikola Gruevski who, during his mandates (August 27, 2006–January 18, 2016), failed to make progress in resolving the name dispute and acted as a catalyst for inter-ethnic tensions within the country (ICG 2011, 23). As soon as it took office, Gruevski's government pursued a diplomatic offensive, expressing historical demands and defending ancient origins. This included the 2008 naming of the capital's international airport as "Alexander the Great" and the much criticized nationalist project for the development of the capital called "Skopje 2014". Gruevski's nationalism led to a failure to resolve the name dispute and to join the EU. Therefore, during this period, North Macedonia remained a contested state both internally and externally.

The situation in North Macedonia changed with the wiretapping scandal. "Finding himself increasingly isolated from the West, Gruevski flirted with a pivot toward Russia, which had involved itself in the crisis as a strong supporter of the embattled government" (Ceka 2018, 152). Following the defeat of the nationalist VMRO-DPMNE party (the Internal Macedonian Revolutionary Organization–Democratic Party for Macedonian National Unity) in the parliamentary elections of December 11, 2016, and the rise to power of the pro-solution, pro-West coalition led by the Social Democratic Union of Macedonia (USDM) and the Democratic Union for Integration (UDI) of Albanians, efforts to resolve the name dispute reached an unprecedented scale. The new Prime Minister, Zoran Zaev confirmed his determination to resolve the decades-long dispute with Greece. In the days following his accession to power, efforts by the North Macedonian and Greek governments to engage in constructive dialogue intensified. Among the proposals, that of Republic of North Macedonia was agreed upon by the two countries on June 12, 2018. The fall of Gruevski and the ascension to power of the much more pro-Western Zaev played a significant role in the signing of the Prespa agreement. Western actors paid particular attention to its conclusion, as well as to the advisory referendum on September 30, 2018, in North Macedonia. In contrast, Russia, seeking to foster instability in the Balkans, opposed the Prespa agreement and encouraged the citizens of North Macedonia to boycott the referendum on the country's name change (Nechev and Nikolovski 2020, 127–134).

Serbia: Low Support for EU Membership

Why has public support for the EU been consistently the lowest in Serbia? More than a decade ago, Jelena Subotic (2011, 323) noted that the process of Europeanization in Serbia has been marked by "identity divergence, as influenced by the interplay of three factors: (i) the 'European idea' in Serbia was not universally shared and was underdeveloped; (ii) alternative identity narratives, especially those built around the myths of Kosovo and cultural affinity with Russia, were strong and clearly elaborated; and (iii) Serbia's previous relationship with Europe was perceived as negative, painful, and costly, and so expectations for the policy success of Europeanization were weak." These same factors continue to be relevant to this day and have only been exacerbated by Russia's increasingly assertive policies in the Western Balkan region.

Serbia maintains an ambiguous and antagonistic relationship with the EU. On the one hand, several years ago, Belgrade adopted a policy of accession to the EU but, on the other, it has pursued a diplomacy contrary to European interests. One notable recent example is Serbia's refusal to adopt sanctions against Russia in the Russo-Ukrainian war. Serbia's "Janus-faced policy has deep roots and is reminiscent of Yugoslavia's Cold War nonalignment stance" (Bechev 2023). In order to comply with the EU accession criteria, candidate countries, among others, have an obligation to clearly display a European vision and to align themselves with EU foreign policy. The war in Ukraine showed that Russia posed a threat to the stability of its neighborhood and the European continent. Following these events, the EU described Vladimir Putin's Russia as a destabilizing force in Europe and adopted numerous sanctions against Russia. To that end, the EU invited the Western Balkan countries to do the same. Serbia, traditionally close to Russia and considered a strategic partner by Moscow (Bieri 2015, 1–4), refused to apply sanctions against Moscow. It remains Russia's key ally in the Western Balkans, and the one through which Russia tries to maintain or redevelop its influence in this region.

On October 25, 2019, Serbia even became member of the Russian-promoted Eurasian Economic Union (EAEU), a regional project that competes with the EU. Apart from its traditional relations and cultural ties with Russia, Serbia is dependent on energy supplies from Moscow. Thus, it has officially designated itself as a neutral state: It cooperates with NATO through the Partnership for Peace (PfP) while opening its territory to maneuvers by the Russian army (Marciacq 2020, 62–64). Serbia's President Aleksandar Vucic, a proponent of nationalist myths and narratives, publicly supports European integration, but at the same time shows no desire to distance himself from Russia. The EU has tolerated Vucic's stance for several years, and Brussels' influence in Serbia during the Russo-Ukrainian war has proven ineffective (Radeljic and Ozsahin 2023).

As in the past, Russia has great ambitions for influence in the Balkans (Samokhvalov 2017; Bechev 2017). Moscow continues to promote its own political, economic and traditional ties with certain Western Balkan countries (especially Serbia) and ethnic groups (especially Serbs), presenting itself as a closer ally than the EU (Bechev 2017). Moreover, "[i]n contrast to the EU, Russia has always supported Serbia's position on Kosovo" and Serbia's political class "is divided between its wish to join the EU as quickly as possible and its worry about spoiling relations with Russia" (Belloni 2016, 541). Indeed, Russia has long claimed a privileged relationship with the Orthodox Slavic communities of the Western Balkans and this perception of "Slavic brotherhood" is also rooted in some of the populations of the region, mainly in Serbia, which currently has the status of an EU candidate country. Serbs and Russians share close historical, political, religious, and cultural ties. Serbia is a Russophile country (CISR 2020, 53, 58, 63 and 68), and Vladimir Putin enjoys a solid popularity there. Since 2014, many Serbian nationalists have joined pro-Russian forces in the war in Ukraine (Velebit 2017). However, "opinion polls show that a great majority would rather live, work and study in Western Europe than in Russia. What the EU lacks is Russia's emotional appeal, rooted in a common cultural sense of belonging and a shared sense of victimhood at the hands of the West" (EUISS 2016, 23). At a time when relations between Russia and the West are at an all-time low, Serbia is positioning itself between the two sides (Marciacq 2020), and China. This is then reflected in public opinion in Serbia towards the EU, which remains ambivalent, at best.

The implications of these dynamics of identity divergence and stalled Europeanization in Serbia are profound and serious. As Dimitar Bechev (2023) has recently noted, "Serbia's flirtation with Russia—and with China—goes hand in hand with an authoritarian turn in domestic politics" and "[a]nti-Western nationalism is rampant and dominates the public sphere, as in the 1990s." Russia, meanwhile, has been applying an anti-NATO doctrine towards the countries of the Western Balkans for years. With the exception of Serbia, and partly Bosnia and Herzegovina, all the countries in the region are today either members of NATO (Albania, North Macedonia, Montenegro), or have clearly expressed a request in this direction (Kosovo) (Lika 2020). Serbia thus remains the main country in the Western Balkans, or even the Balkans as a whole, through which Russia attempts to maintain or reinforce its multidimensional influence. As a result, the Russian state maintains strong support for Serbia. Inspired by the Russian expansionist project called "Russian world," which aims to extend its influence beyond the borders of Russia (Suslov 2018), Serbian authorities have also formulated a nationalist and expansionist doctrine named as "Serbian world," which aims to exert influence on territories inhabited by Serb communities in the Western Balkans (Morrison and Garcevic 2023). In turn, "Serbia's continued affair with Russia makes its neighbors fearful" (Bechev 2023), which both engenders instability in the region and complicates the process of European integration for the other countries.

Russian authorities have worked tirelessly to reinforce anti-EU and anti-NATO sentiment in the Western Balkans, notably in Serbia, Bosnia and Herzegovina, Montenegro, and North Macedonia. They have encouraged inter-ethnic divisions through disinformation campaigns, deliberately stoking the tensions that led to the wars of the 1990s. The impact of this Russian strategy is significant because opinion polls have shown that, through the spread of such disinformation, Serbian citizens wrongly perceive Russia as a major donor to Serbia, well before the EU (EUISS 2016, 22).

In fact, Russia has activated a complex communication strategy, served by substantial means in favor of certain digital or traditional Serbian media. Likewise, Russian media are omnipresent, including Sputnik, a multimedia news agency, officially launched by the Russian government in 2014 and broadcast in Serbian. Additionally, a number of media groups, which frequently combine conspiracy theories and Serbian ultranationalism, are funded by the Russian authorities in order to support the Russian state's worldview (EUISS 2016, 13). Moreover, Russian strategic communications are backed by a network of diverse organizations, ranging from government agencies to non-governmental organizations (NGO) supported by the government, and which also include associations, student groups, political parties, and the Orthodox Church (EUISS 2016, 13).

Furthermore, in the city of Nish, in the south of Serbia, Russia has built the "Russian-Serbian Humanitarian Center (RSHC)," which is suspected of being a military center of the Russian intelligence services. Moscow continues to denounce the EU's promises of membership to the Western Balkan states by imposing itself as an alternative, particularly for Serbia and the Serb communities living in several Western Balkan countries. Through these efforts, Russia tries to influence destabilization, militarization, war, disinformation campaigns, and non-accession to the EU and NATO (Bieber and Tzifakis 2020; Rrustemi et al. 2019; Bechev 2017). Therefore, the influence projection of Russia in the Western Balkans, particularly in Serbia, constitutes a security threat to the EU and other Western Balkan countries. This Russian influence also shapes public attitudes in Serbia towards EU membership. For the majority of citizens in Serbia, the Russian alternative, combined with the perceived lack of EU commitment to enlargement, constitute key reasons for the low public support for EU membership.

Conclusion

This chapter has analyzed the public opinion towards the EU in the Western Balkans. Since 2000, the European perspective of the Western Balkans has been confirmed on numerous occasions by the EU. The EU statements and engagement nourished public expectations to join the EU in a near period. However, the EU has experienced a gradual erosion of its enlargement policy. The bilateral political disputes and economic difficulties of the Western Balkans, combined with the EU's economic hindrances and the "fatigue of enlargement" have contributed to the creation of a relative power vacuum in the region. For many years, the EU enlargement process has procrastinated for reasons both internal and external to the Western Balkan countries and to the EU itself, which was weakened by multiple crises (economic, political, migratory). Among others, in this context, new players, often described in the literature as rising powers, such as Russia, China, and Turkey, have projected their influences into the region and nourished alternative narratives. The projection of their influence in the Western Balkans varies across countries, but spans political, economic, commercial, military, cultural, and religious spheres. These circumstances show the limitations of EU actorness and its normative power in the Western Balkans. The EU has not been able to speak with one voice and to keep its promises for a rapid enlargement towards the Western Balkan countries.

This chapter has argued that support for EU membership varies between states and within states, particularly among different ethnic groups, such as in the federal state of Bosnia and Herzegovina. While Serbia's population exhibits the lowest levels of support for EU membership, publics in Bosnia and Herzegovina, Montenegro, and North Macedonia are somewhat more favorable. Public opinion in Albania and Kosovo, meanwhile, is strongly in favor of EU membership.

Albania and Kosovo are the most pro-EU countries in the Western Balkans. These states see the EU as the only alternative. The elites, citizens, and institutions of Albania and Kosovo have a clear EU and Western orientation. These two countries have aligned their foreign policies with the EU, including during the war in Ukraine. Their Western orientation is based on past experiences, current support, and future aspirations. Western European countries supported them in the recent past, especially during Kosovo's war for freedom and independence, as well as for international recognition and membership in international organizations. Albania is already a member of NATO and seeks to join the EU as soon as possible. Kosovo also aspires to become a NATO member and to join the EU. As such, EU membership constitutes a top priority for the institutions of Albania and Kosovo. In this regard, the strong pro-EU public attitude observed in these two countries are simultaneously a result of and an important driver of EU membership efforts.

Opinion poll data show that public attitudes in Bosnia and Herzegovina, Montenegro, and North Macedonia have turned more Euroskeptic over time but remain moderately pro-EU. However, public support for EU membership in Serbia is quite low. This country maintains strong links with Russia, which is perceived by Serbian citizens as a friend and traditional ally.

In sum, with the exception of Albania and Kosovo, which are clearly pro-EU, the EU actorness in the other countries of the Western Balkans has not managed to sustain or strengthen public opinion in its favor. This chapter showed that there is a marked Euroskepticism among a significant portion of Orthodox Slavic citizens in the Western Balkans, which undermines the effectiveness of EU actorness. These negative public attitudes are also encouraged by Russia, an EU rival power. As a result, in the context of the war in Ukraine, and the fragile geopolitical situation in the Western Balkans, the EU is trying to be more present in the region and had begun mentioning 2030 as a possible date for enlargement.

References

Anghel, V., and J. Dzankic. 2023. Wartime EU: Consequences of the Russia-Ukraine War on the Enlargement Process. *Journal of European Integration* 45 (3): 487–501.

Armakolas, I., and J. Ker-Lindsay, eds. 2020. *The Politics of Recognition and Engagement: EU Member State Relations with Kosovo*. Cham: Palgrave Macmillan.

Bajrovic, R., R. Kraemer, and E. Suljagic. 2018. *Bosnia on the Chopping Block: The Potential for Violence and Steps to Prevent It*. Foreign Policy Research Institute, March, 1–12.

Babuna, A. 2000. The Albanians of Kosovo and Macedonia: Ethnic Identity Superseding Religion. *Nationalities Papers* 28 (1): 67–92.

Bayer, L. 2023. Charles Michel: Get Ready by 2030 to Enlarge EU, *Politico*, August 28, available at: https://www.politico.eu/article/european-council-president-charles-michel-eu-enlargement-by-2030/ (accessed 3 October 2023).

Bechev, D. 2017. *Rival Power: Russia's Influence in Southeast Europe*. New Haven and London: Yale University Press.

Bechev, D. 2023. Hedging Its Bets: Serbia Between Russia and the EU. *Carnegie Europe*, available at: https://carnegieeurope.eu/2023/01/19/hedging-its-bets-serbia-between-russia-and-eu-pub-88819 (accessed 20 November 2023).

Belloni, R. 2016. The European Union Blowback? Euroscepticism and Its Consequences in the Western Balkans. *Journal of Intervention and Statebuilding* 10 (4): 530–547.

Bieber, F. 2020. *The Rise of Authoritarianism in the Western Balkans*. Cham: Palgrave Macmillan.

Bieber, F., and N. Tzifakis, eds. 2020. *The Western Balkans in the World: Linkages and Relations with Non-Western Countries*. London and New York: Routledge.

BiEPAG. 2017. The Crisis of Democracy in the Western Balkans. Authoritarianism and EU Stabilitocracy. *Policy Papers*, March 1, available at: https://biepag.eu/publication/policy-paper-the-crisis-of-democracy-in-the-western-balkans-authoritarianism-and-eu-stabilitocracy/ (accessed 3 October 2023).

Bieri, M. 2015. The Western Balkans Between Europe and Russia. *CSS Analyses in Security Policy*, n 170, March, 1–4.

Bino, B., L. Lula, and O. Xhaferaj. 2023. Populism and European Integration: An Analysis of Albania's Political Discourse. In *EU Enlargement and the Western Balkans: Current Challenges and Prospects* Conference Proceedings, 175–188. Tirana: University of Tirana, Institute of European Studies.

Burden, B. 2016. *NATO's Small States: Albania as a Case Study*. Dissertation Monterey, California: Naval Postgraduate School.

Castellan, G. 2004. *Histoire des Balkans (XIVe-XXe siècle)*. Paris: Librairie Arthème Fayard.

Ceka, B. 2018. Macedonia: A New Beginning? *Journal of Democracy* 29 (2): 143–157.

Center for Insights in Survey Research (CISR). 2020. Western Balkans Regional Poll. International Republican Institute, February 2, 2020–March 6, 2020, available at: https://www.iri.org/wp-content/uploads/legacy/iri.org/final_wb_poll_for_publishing_6.9.2020.pdf (accessed 28 September 2023).

Cosentino, D. 2015. Designing the Identity of a New State: Kosovo Flag. *The Design Journal* 18 (4): 607–612.

Damjanovski, I., M. Lavric, and A. Naterer. 2020. Predictors of Euroscepticism in Six Western Balkan Countries. *Southeast European and Black Sea Studies* 20 (2): 327–348.

Dopchie, R., and L. Lika. 2024. The EU Enlargement Strategy in the Western Balkans: Assessing the Implications Amidst the War in Ukraine. *European Foreign Affairs Review* 29 (2): 159–176.

Ehin, P. 2001. Determinants of Public Support for EU Membership: Data from the Baltic Countries. *European Journal of Political Research* 40 (1): 31–56.

Elbasani, A. 2008. EU Enlargement in the Western Balkans: Strategies of Borrowing and Inventing. *Journal of Southern Europe and the Balkans* 10 (3): 293–307.

European Commission. 2003. EU-Western Balkans Summit: Thessaloniki Declaration. Thessaloniki, June 21, available at: https://ec.europa.eu/commission/presscorner/detail/en/PRES_03_163 (accessed 3 October 2023).

European Union Institute for Security Studies (EUISS), with contributions from Missiroli, A. et al. 2016. Strategic Communications East and South. *Report*, Paris, n 30, July 20, 1–55.

Felsen, D. 2023. Albania's Foreign Policy in the Twenty-First Century. In *Geopolitical Turmoil in the Balkans and Eastern Mediterranean*, ed. H. Gardner, 159–183. Cham: Springer International Publishing.

Fouéré, E., and S. Blockmans. 2017. *The 'Berlin Process' for the Western Balkans—Is it delivering?* 13 July, 1–5. Centre for European Policy Studies (CEPS), CEPS Commentary.

Gallup Balkan Monitor. 2010. Insights and Perceptions: Voices of the Balkans, available at: https://reforma.bezbednost.org/wp-content/uploads/downloads/2012/09/2010-Balkan-Monitor-Insights-and-Perceptions-Voices-of-the-Balkans-GALLUP-i-European-Fund-for-the-Balkans.pdf (accessed 19 November 2023).

Gashi, D.S., and P. Kelmendi. 2023. The Dynamics of US–Kosovo Relations: An Investigation of Key Factors. In *Kosovo's Foreign Policy and Bilateral Relations*, ed. L. Lika, 29–54. London and New York: Routledge.

Gorani, D. 2011. *Orientalist Ethnonationalism: From Irredentism to Independentism. Discourse Analysis of the Albanian Ethnonationalist Narrative About the National Rebirth (1870–1930) and Kosovo Independence (1980–2000).* Dissertation Cardiff University.

Greiçevci, L. 2022. *The EU as a State-builder in International Affairs: The Case of Kosovo.* New York: Routledge.

Huskic, A. 2020. Bosnia and Herzegovina: Abandoned by the West, Embraced by the East? In *The Western Balkans in the World Linkages and Relations with Non-Western Countries*, ed. F. Bieber and N. Tzifakis, 83–107. London and New York: Routledge.

Ilazi, R. 2024. *The European Union and Everyday Statebuilding: The Case of Kosovo.* London and New York: Routledge.

International Crisis Group (ICG). 2011. Macedonia: Ten Years After the Conflict. Europe Report n 212, August 11, 1–28.

Kalemaj, I. 2023. Open Balkans: Challenges and Opportunities Emanating from Tirana. *Tirana Observatory*, Winter, 29–39.

Keil, S. 2023. Enlargement Politics Based on Geopolitics? A Proposal for a Geopolitics-Driven Enlargement Policy. In *A Year Later: War in Ukraine and Western Balkan (Geo)Politics*, ed. J. Dzankic, S. Kacarska, and S. Keil, 117–124. Italy: European University Institute.

Kelmendi, P. 2012. Civil Society and Contentious Politics in Post-Conflict Kosovo. In *Civil Society in Kosovo Since 1999*, ed. M. Agani, 33–57. Prishtina: Center for Political Courage.

Kelmendi, P. 2022. Rebel Successor Parties and their Electoral Performance in the Balkans. *Security Studies* 31 (3): 446–482.

Kelmendi, P. 2024. Determinants of Individual Support for International Criminal Tribunals. *Ethnopolitics* 23 (3): 294–316.

Kelmendi, P., and C. Pedraza. 2022. Determinants of Individual Support for Independence: Evidence from Montenegro. *Nationalities Papers* 50 (3): 515–534.

Kelmendi, P., and A. Radin. 2018. UNsatisfied? Public Support for Postconflict International Missions. *Journal of Conflict Resolution* 62 (5): 983–1011.

Kelmendi, P., and S. Skendaj. 2023. Protests in Postwar Societies: Grievances and Contentious Collective Action in Kosovo. *Nationalities Papers* 51 (5): 1143–1163.

Krasniqi, G. 2011. The 'Forbidden Fruit': Islam and Politics of Identity in Kosovo and Macedonia. *Southeast European and Black Sea Studies* 11 (2): 191–207.

Krasniqi, A. 2023. Kosovo and Albania, a Special Relationship: Retrospectives and Challenges Toward the Future. In *Kosovo's Foreign Policy and Bilateral Relations*, ed. L. Lika, 55–75. London and New York: Routledge.

Lika, L. 2020. *Les Balkans occidentaux à la croisée de l'intégration européenne et de la projection des puissances émergentes. Analyse du cadre triangulaire entre les Balkans occidentaux, l'Union européenne et la Turquie*. PhD thesis in Political and Social Sciences, University of Liège.

Lika, L. 2021. The Western Balkans at the Crossroads of European Integration and the Emerging Powers' Projection of Influence. *Journal of Cross-Regional Dialogues* 2: 7–30.

Lika, L., ed. 2023. *Kosovo's Foreign Policy and Bilateral Relations*. London and New York: Routledge.

Lika, L. 2024. The Meaning of the Western Balkans Concept for the EU: Genuine Inclusion or Polite Exclusion? *Southeast European and Black Sea Studies* 24 (1): 63–78.

Lika, L., and B. Reka. 2021. The European Union's Relations with the Republic of Kosovo. In *Forging Kosovo: Between Dependence, Independence, and Interdependence*, ed. A. Hajrullahu and A. Vukpalaj, 229–250. Bern: Peter Lang.

Marciacq, F. 2017. The EU and the Western Balkans After the Berlin Process. Reflecting on the EU Enlargement in Times of Uncertainty. *The Friedrich-Ebert-Stiftung*, Sarajevo, 1–24.

Marciacq, F. 2020. Serbia: Looking East, Going West? In *The Western Balkans in the World Linkages and Relations with Non-Western Countries*, ed. F. Bieber and N. Tzifakis, 61–82. London and New York: Routledge.

Marovic, J. 2020. Montenegro: Always at a Crossroads. In *The Western Balkans in the World. Linkages and Relations with Non-Western Countries*, ed. F. Bieber and N. Tzifakis, 146–163. London and New York: Routledge.

Métais, S. 2006. *Histoire des Albanais: Des Illyriens à l'indépendance du Kosovo.* Paris: Fayard.

Morrison, K., and V. Garcevic. 2023. The Orthodox Church, Montenegro, and the 'Serbian World'. *Atlantic Initiative*, Sarajevo, available at: https://atlanticinitiative.org/wp-content/uploads/2023/02/SPC-WEB.pdf (accessed 28 September 2023).

Musliu, V. 2021. *Europeanization and Statebuilding as Everyday Practices: Performing Europe in the Western Balkans*. London and New York: Routledge.

Nechev, Z., and I. Nikolovski. 2020. North Macedonia: A Fertile Ground for External Influences. In *The Western Balkans in the World. Linkages and Relations with Non-Western Countries*, ed. F. Bieber and N. Tzifakis, 126–145. London and New York: Routledge.

Noutcheva, G. 2009. Fake, Partial and Imposed Compliance: The Limits of the EU's Normative Power in the Western Balkans. *Journal of European Public Policy* 16 (7): 1065–1084.

Panagiotou, R. 2011. Albania and the EU: From Isolation to Integration. *Journal of Balkan and Near Eastern Studies* 13 (3): 357–374.

Radeljic, B., and M.C. Ozsahin. 2023. The Inefficiency of the EU Leverage in Serbia During the Russo-Ukranian War. *Southeast European and Black Sea Studi*es 23 (4): 697–716.

Regional Cooperation Council (RCC). 2019. Balkan Public Barometer: Public Opinion. *Analytical report*, Sarajevo, May, 1–114.

Regional Cooperation Council (RCC). 2023. Balkan Public Barometer: EU Membership, available at: https://www.rcc.int/balkanbarometer/results/2/public (accessed 3 October 2023).

Rrustemi, A. et al. 2019. Geopolitical Influences of External Powers in the Western Balkans. *Report, The Hague Centre for Strategic Studies (HCSS)*, September 30, 1–165.

Samokhvalov, V. 2017. *Russian-European Relations in the Balkans and Black Sea Region: Great Power Identity and the Idea of Europe*. Cham: Palgrave Macmillan.

Sanchez-Cuenca, I. 2000. The Political Basis of support for European Integration. *European Union Politics* 1 (2): 147–171.

Simkus, A. 2007. Guest Editor's Introduction: The SEESSP Project. *International Journal of Sociology* 37 (3): 3–14.

Stipçeviq, A. 2002. *Ilirët: historia, jeta, kultura, simbolet e kultit*. Tiranë: Toena.

Stojarova, V., and P. Emerson, eds. 2013. *Party Politics in the Western Balkans*. London and New York: Routledge.

Subotic, J. 2011. Europe Is a State of Mind: Identity and Europeanization in the Balkans. *International Studies Quarterly* 55 (2): 309–330.

Sulstarova, E. 2012. Rilindja's Place in the Orientalism of Intellectuals in Post-communist Albania. *Annales* 22 (2): 391–397.

Suslov, M. 2018. Russian World Concept: Post-Soviet Geopolitical Ideology and the Logic of Spheres of Influence. *Geopolitics* 23 (2): 330–353.
Tolksdorf, D. 2015. The European Union as a Mediator in Constitutional Reform Negotiations in Bosnia and Herzegovina: The failure of Conditionality in the Context of Intransigent Local Politics. *Nationalism and Ethnic Politics* 21 (4): 401–421.
Velebit, V. 2017. Serb Fighters in Ukraine Continue to Worry the West. *European Western Balkans*, December 29, available at: https://europeanwesternbalkans.com/2017/12/29/serb-fighters-ukraine-continue-worry-west/ (accessed 4 October 2023).
Vetik, R. 2003. Elite vs. People? Eurosceptic Public Opinion in Estonia. *Cambridge Review of International Affairs* 16 (2): 257–271.

The 2022 Russia: Ukraine War—A "Watershed" for the EU's Foreign Policy in the Region?

Elisabeth Johansson-Nogués

Introduction

For the European Union (EU), the Russian 2022 invasion has meant a significant change in terms of its engagement with the Ukraine, as well as with some of the other Eastern European countries.[1] Only days into the conflict the EU began to put forward a comprehensive set of measures

[1] "Eastern Europe" here refers to all non-EU member countries east of the EU territory.

This chapter was written in the frameworks of the "Institutional responses to the changing European security order" (*in*RESPONSE) research project (PID2022-140133NB-I00); Ministerio de Ciencia, Innovación y Universidades, Spain as well as the Jean Monnet Chair in "Global Actor EU: The International Relations of the European Union in a Competitive and Fractured World" (GLOBALEUTY) (ERASMUS-JMO-2024-HEI-TCH-RSCH); European Union (EU). Views and opinions expressed are however those of the author only and do not necessarily reflect those of the EU or the European Commission. Neither the EU nor the granting authority can be held responsible for them. The author wishes to acknowledge the research assistance of Francesca Leso.

E. Johansson-Nogués (✉)
Institut Barcelona d'Estudis Internacionals, Barcelona, Spain
e-mail: ejohanssonnogues@ibei.org

L. Lika and D. Riga (eds.), *EU Geopolitical Actorness in a Changing World*, https://doi.org/10.1007/978-3-031-81160-9_8

to support Ukraine in the face of Russian aggression. On the top of over 30 billion euros in financial and humanitarian assistance allocated in the first year of the conflict, support for refugees, trade and energy, the EU and its member states also unprecedentedly approved the use of intergovernmental funds to provide Ukraine with lethal armaments (European Commission 2023a). Furthermore, four months into the conflict, in a highly symbolic move, the EU also granted Ukraine candidate status for EU membership, a concession which the EU had been unwilling to make in the past despite the Eastern European country's petitions. These combined EU assistance initiatives, for their novelty, speed and/or scope, have been seen by some as testimony to a before and after in the EU's foreign and security policy. The President of the European Commission Ursula von der Leyen has, for example, called it a "watershed moment for our Union" (European Commission 2022a).

This chapter is a case study of the EU's economic, humanitarian and military assistance to Ukraine with the aim to investigate whether the EU's response to the 2022 Russia-Ukraine war actually signals a shift in the EU's foreign and security policy actorness in relation to Ukraine and the broader Eastern Europe. The goal is to explore to what extent does the assistance provided to Ukraine in the first year of the war mark a new stage for the EU foreign and security policy in the region? This chapter is based on various sources, including books, edited volumes, scientific articles, official statements and press articles. In terms of the structure, the chapter will proceed in the following way. The first section will provide a brief outline of the EU's engagement with Ukraine and its Eastern neighbourhood until 2022 and provide a discussion of the analytical framework employed. The empirical data on the EU's support to Ukraine is presented in section two. Finally, the chapter concludes with an analysis of the EU's actorness.

The EU, the Eastern Neighbourhood and Ukraine

While a window of opportunity to engage in Eastern Europe had presented itself to the EU already in the 1990s after the dissolution of the Soviet Union, it would not be until in the 2000s that a more concerted EU policy would come about (Johansson-Nogués 2002 and 2007). As Eastern enlargement came to a close, the EU established the European Neighbourhood Policy (ENP) in 2004 and the Eastern Partnership (EaP) in 2009. Influenced by the successes of the enlargement experience, EU policymakers expected that increased interdependence in the form of trade relations, greater economic cooperation, and financial assistance, as well as the potential for enhanced cross-border contacts through a more favourable visa regime, would together act as incentives for neighbouring states to progressively align with EU's norms, such as, democracy, liberal market and rule of law. In this respect, the EU was driven by the assumption that encouraging domestic reforms in neighbourhood countries would strengthen the stability and the prosperity of the region and, in turn, enhance the EU's own security (e.g. *see* Dragneva and Wolczuk 2015; Johansson-Nogués 2002; 2011 and 2018).

The issue of the EU as a foreign and security actor in Eastern Europe has been focus on scholarly attention since the 1990s, but it experienced an upswing in the mid-2000s as a consequence of the launch of the ENP. As the EU's arsenal of policy tools, budget and overall interest to engage in Eastern Europe has grown over the decades, so has the academic interest to critically scrutinize the EU's action in the region. The focus has in particular been on the EU's levers for change in Ukraine and other Eastern European countries through its economic incentives for political and legal reforms (conditionality) (e.g. Wolczuk 2016; Haukkala 2016; Howorth 2017). For yet other scholars, the EU's policies towards its eastern neighbours have been studied through the lens of norm transfer (Browning 2018), (c)overt modes of empire building (Zielonka 2018), "buffer zones" (Marchetti 2018), or focus of intra-EU discourses designed to enhance the ontological security of the EU as an international actor (Johansson-Nogués 2018).

Notwithstanding the varied reported rationales behind EU policies towards Eastern European countries, most observers appear to concur that the EU has in any case been less than successful in its declared objective of promoting the vaunted stability and prosperity in the region. If in the 2004 and through the ENP, the EU aimed to forge a "ring of friends" composed by well-governed prosperous liberal democracies (European Commission 2003), over time the neighbourhood has increasingly taken the appearance of a "ring of fire" (The Economist 2014), orf an "arc of instability" (Mogherini 2015). Authors have pointed to that the EU action in Eastern Europe has been hampered by a lack of sufficient financial resources for reforms, the absence of (credible) prospect of EU membership, as well as an increasingly assertive Russia seeking to establish exclusive relationships with these same countries (Johansson-Nogués 2011; Juncos and Whitman 2015). As a result, some analysts argue that while the ENP and the EaP have driven substantial foreign policy innovation and intra-EU cohesion in terms of how to engage with Eastern European countries parties to those policies, they have not provided the EU with a clear foreign policy profile in the region and its legitimacy to intervene in the post-Soviet space has been undermined by Russian (dis)information as well as the latter's more traditional (geo)political ambitions in the region (e.g. Härtel 2023; Kuzio 2017).

The EU's engagement in the region is held to have been put to the test in the context of the 2014 Crimean crisis. Then Ukrainian President Victor Yanukovych refusal to sign the EU-Ukrainian Association Agreement (AA) set off the Euromaidan protest and a prolonged political crisis in the country. The crisis culminated in Yanukovych's self-exile to Russia, the annexation of Crimea by Russia, and the outbreak of hostilities in the Moscow-backed separatist regions of Donetsk and Luhansk. The EU responded to the conflict by employing a combination of coercive diplomacy and mediation (Chaban et al. 2019). On one front, the EU imposed a range of diplomatic, economic, and individual sanctions against Russia and key figures within its political and economic elite. These sanctions have been periodically renewed over the years and laid the groundwork for the more comprehensive sanction packages seen in the aftermath of the 2022 Russian invasion of Ukraine. Simultaneously, the EU supported the mediation efforts led by Germany and France through the Normandy format. Alongside these diplomatic actions, the EU deepened its engagement with Kyiv. Initiatives such as the AA, the Deep and Comprehensive Free Trade Agreement (DCFTA), the launch of the EU Advisory Mission Ukraine (EUAM Ukraine) and the establishment of a visa-free regime aimed to foster political reforms and economic development between Ukraine and the EU. Financially, the EU provided an estimated €17 billion in loans and grants between 2014 and 2021 to bolster the country's economy and ambitious reform agenda, alongside €193 million in humanitarian aid (EPRS 2022).

However, even in the aftermath of the Crimean crisis and the EU's strengthened assistance package to Ukraine, many scholars still viewed EU's engagement in the region as overall weak (e.g. Nováky 2015; Dragneva and Wolczuk 2015; Wolczuk 2016; Kuzio 2017; Young 2017; Härtel 2023). Despite the EU's financial and technical support to Ukraine, various observers believe that in the end Kyiv was left rather alone and without specific means by which to end the conflict with Russia (Wolczuk 2016; Haukkala 2015). Scholars argue that the 2014 crisis reveals how reluctant the EU and its member states had been up until that moment in terms of getting too involved in Eastern Europe's crises and conflicts. Several EU member states appeared to accept that Russia's claim to sphere of influence in the region needed to be, at least partially, accommodated, which limited the EU's ability to play a more prominent role in the settlement of the Crimean crisis (Young 2017). The EU thus played no formal part in the various peace negotiations, support for military assistance, whether in the form of an EU mission or as an assistance measure to the Ukrainian Armed Forces (UAF) was quickly ruled out, and the issue of candidate status to Ukraine was never really earnestly discussed among the member states.

In order to assess whether the EU's support provided to Ukraine in response to the 2022 Russian invasion points to a new stage for the EU's foreign and security policy and its engagement with Eastern Europe, this chapter will employ the concept of "actorness". Actorness, as defined by Joseph Jupille and James A. Caporaso (1998), is a conceptual framework used to assess the capacity of an entity to function as an autonomous and influential actor in the international system. The concept has been developed to explain the role of non-traditional actors, such as international organizations or other transnational actors, in a global political landscape traditionally dominated by states. It is particularly relevant for understanding how hybrid—i.e. both intergovernmental and supranational—entities, such as the EU, act beyond its borders to influence global governance and/or to shape international outcomes.

Four key dimensions define actorness: *authority*, *autonomy*, *cohesion* and *recognition* (Jupille and Caporaso 1998). *Authority* refers to the legal or institutional framework that grants an entity the right or competence to act in a given domain. For instance, the EU derives its foreign and security policy authority from treaties that delegate to it certain competencies, allowing it to operate on behalf of its member states in these areas. *Autonomy* reflects the degree of relative independence an entity has in its decision-making. An actor with high autonomy can pursue policies and strategies that are distinct from those of other actors. This dimension is crucial because it determines whether an entity can formulate and implement its own policies, rather than merely reflecting the preferences of more dominant actors in the international system. *Cohesion*, the third dimension, concerns the internal consistency and alignment of an actor's policies. For an entity to demonstrate actorness, it must present a (reasonably) unified position on the international stage. In organizations like the EU, cohesion is often tested when member states have divergent interests, yet the ability to reconcile these differences and act collectively strengthens actorness. Finally, *recognition* refers to the external acknowledgment of an entity's role as a legitimate actor. Without recognition by other international players, an entity's capacity to influence global outcomes is limited, regardless of its authority, autonomy, or cohesion.

Based on a case study method, this chapter thus tries to assess whether the EU's assistance provided to Ukraine during the first year of the war points in the direction of a more salient foreign and security policy "actorness", i.e. a novel institutional authority, autonomy, cohesion and recognition in terms of its actions in Ukraine and Eastern Europe, more in general. The chapter is also interested in ascertaining whether this marks a new stage for the EU as an international actor in the region and/or globally. In doing so, the chapter will rely on an extensive analysis of EU directives and communications, as well as speeches by relevant EU officials, which provide a detailed account of the EU's wartime assistance to Ukraine between February 2022 and February 2023.

The First Twelve Months of EU Wartime Support to Ukraine

Since Russia's invasion of Ukraine in February 2022, the EU has significantly increased its support for Ukraine. In the conflict's first year, the EU mobilized over €30 billion in financial, budgetary and humanitarian aid, while an additional €3.6 billion was allocated to bolster the Eastern European country's military capabilities. These sums stand in contrast with the approximate total of €17 billion economic assistance and grants allocated to Ukraine in the seven-year period following the Crimean crisis. This section will provide an outline of all the major forms of EU assistance to Ukraine between 2022 and 2023.

Economic and Energy Support

The substantial economic effects of the war on the Ukrainian economy have prompted the EU to become the largest financial donor in terms of budgetary grants and other types of financial support. The contraction of the Ukrainian economy, decline in public revenues, and of export impediments, together with the rising military expenditure, were estimated to have caused a financial deficit of almost 40 billion US dollars in 2022 (IMF 2022). To help Ukraine address its most urgent budgetary needs and ensure the continuation of essential government functions, the EU significantly ramped up its efforts, mobilizing as noted nearly €30 billion in grants and loans by February 2023. The largest portion of this assistance consisted of macro-financial aid packages in the form of long-term, favourable loans, totalling €25.2 billion, of which €9.2 billion had already been disbursed by February 2023 (European Commission 2023a). The adoption of these macro-financial assistance packages was subject to some debate among EU capitals. As the scale of support grew, the loans exceeded what could be guaranteed through the EU's budget alone, requiring member states to provide additional backing. Reaching an agreement on the €18 billion packages for 2023 was particularly challenging (see, for instance, von der Burchard 2022). Despite this, the Union managed to maintain a united front, solidifying the EU's position as Ukraine's largest financial supporter during the war's first year (Trebesch et al. 2023).

In addition to financial and budgetary aid, the EU introduced trade liberalization measures described as "unprecedented in their scale" by the European Commission (2022b). To stimulate Ukrainian exports, the EU temporarily suspended all tariffs still in place under the EU-Ukraine AA, including revoking anti-dumping duties and common safeguard measures on steel imports from Ukraine (European Commission 2023a). The war severely disrupted Ukraine's ability to trade due to damage to production capacities and logistical challenges, particularly the blockade of the Black Sea. In response, the European Commission, in coordination with EU member states and Ukraine, established EU-Ukraine Solidarity Lanes to enhance connectivity via road, rail and inland waterways, ensuring a reliable flow of Ukrainian imports and exports. Initiatives like "matchmaking platforms" connected logistics demand with supply, while clearance procedures were simplified, and priority was given to Ukrainian goods (European Commission 2022c). Additionally, the EU and Ukraine signed a road transport agreement in June 2022, removing the need for permits and international driving licenses for hauliers (European Commission 2022d). These measures provided critical support to Ukraine's export sectors, particularly agriculture, with the Solidarity Lanes enabling the export of 23 million tons of agricultural products in the first year, generating €20 billion in revenue for Ukraine (European Commission 2023a).

In the energy sector, Ukraine faced significant challenges, as did several EU member states. Key energy infrastructure linking Russia, Ukraine and the EU was targeted early in the conflict. The EU responded with a comprehensive set of measures to ensure the continuous flow of electricity and gas from the EU to Ukraine. The Ukrainian electricity grid was synchronized with the EU in record time in March 2022. The EU also ensured continued reverse gas flows from member states and invited Ukraine to join the EU Energy Platform for joint procurement of gas, liquefied natural gas and hydrogen. Additionally, at the European Commission's request, the Energy Community established the Ukraine Energy Support Fund to address the urgent needs of Ukrainian energy companies (European Commission 2023b). By February 2023, the Ukrainian Ministry of Energy reported that the fund had raised €144 million from governments, financial institutions and private donors (Ministry of Energy of Ukraine 2023).

Humanitarian Aid, Refugees Assistance and Prosecution of War-Related Crimes

The extent of its humanitarian action has been deemed as yet another unprecedented move by the EU. There are estimates that more than 17 million people have required some form of assistance due to the Russian invasion of Ukraine in 2022, including 4 million internally displaced individuals (UNHCR 2023). Housing and infrastructure, whether roads, water, electricity, or gas, have been damaged in several parts of the country and basic public services like education and healthcare have been interrupted. In response to this major humanitarian crisis, the EU has supported the efforts of international humanitarian organizations on the ground, providing €630 million in financial aid. Through the European Humanitarian Response Capacity, the EU has also provided logistical support by offering storage and transport services via hubs located in Vinnytsia, Dnipro and Kharkiv (European Commission 2023c). Furthermore, as Ukrainian healthcare facilities struggled to cope with the growing demand, the EU coordinated medical evacuations, transferring over 1,900 patients to hospitals in the EU during the first twelve months of the war (European Commission 2023c). The EU also played a key role in coordinating the delivery of vital assistance through the EU Civil Protection Mechanism, overseeing the distribution of materials such as medicines, ambulances, shelter supplies, water pumps and power generators. In total, 85,000 tonnes of in-kind assistance, valued at over €545 million, were delivered in the first year of the conflict, marking the largest civil protection operation ever coordinated by the EU (European Commission 2022e).

In another surprising action, the EU acted swiftly to assist those displaced by the conflict. Just days into the war, the EU activated the Temporary Protection Directive (TPD), granting displaced people immediate rights to live and work in the EU and access to accommodation, healthcare, and education. By early 2023, EU member states had granted temporary protection to more than 4 million Ukrainian refugees (European Commission 2023a). This marked the first time the EU triggered the TPD since its adoption in 2001, and the solidarity shown towards Ukrainian refugees has been notably different from the EU's response to similar crises in the past (Bosse 2022).

Aside direct humanitarian assistance, the EU has also supported investigations into potential war crimes launched by the International Criminal Court (ICC), the Ukrainian General Prosecutor, and fourteen EU member states. It allocated €7.5 million to strengthen the Court's capacity for processing digital evidence and adopted measures to assist Ukrainian authorities, who are expected to handle the bulk of the cases (European Commission 2023a). The Council of the EU amended the mandate of the EUAM Ukraine for Civilian Security Sector Reform (CSSR) to include advisory and training support for Ukrainian authorities in investigating and prosecuting international crimes (Council of the EU 2022a). Furthermore, to aid in the collection of evidence, the EU introduced new rules enabling the Agency for Criminal Justice Cooperation (EUROJUST) to preserve, process and exchange evidence related to international crimes (European Parliament and Council of the EU 2022). EUROJUST has played a crucial role in coordinating investigations and facilitating information sharing, including the establishment of a Joint Investigation Team involving Ukraine, six member states (Poland, Lithuania, Estonia, Latvia, Slovakia and Romania), and the ICC Prosecutor (EUROJUST 2022).

Military Support: Equipment and Training

In a final unprecedented step in the history of its foreign and security policy, the EU has also agreed to provide Kyiv with military assistance. Only days into the war, the EU activated the European Peace Facility

(EPF) to finance, through a partial reimbursement procedure, member states' provision of both non-lethal and lethal military equipment to the UAF (Council of the EU 2022b). The Facility funds EU missions and assistance measures that are not eligible for funding from the EU budget under treaty provisions (Council of the EU 2021). The EU's decision to fund the provision of weapons to Ukraine through the EPF revealed some differences in member states' positions, occasionally leading to tensions. The Council of the EU's decision was adopted with the constructive abstentions of three historically neutral member states—Austria, Ireland and Malta—which opted not to supply arms to Kyiv or participate in their joint financing (Council of the EU 2022c). Among the countries participating in the EPF, Cyprus and Hungary refrained from supplying weapons to Ukraine, with Hungary additionally opposing weapon transfers across its own borders (Cyprus Mail 2022; Hungary Today 2022). Differences also emerged among countries providing military assistance in terms of the volume and type of weapons supplied, leading to tensions among EU capitals on certain occasions (e.g. Trebesch et al. 2023; Blockmans and De Agostini 2022). Such tensions, however, did not hinder the overall effort, as no member state vetoed any of the six Council of the EU decisions that, over the course of the first year of the war, raised the EPF's budget cap to €3.6 billion (European Commission 2023a). In addition to funds provided by EPF, various bilateral and multilateral initiatives have been taken in terms of providing Ukraine with missiles and ammunition, as well as with more air defence systems (European Council 2022a).

In addition to supplying equipment, the EU launched the EU Military Assistance Mission Ukraine (EUMAM Ukraine) in November 2022, aiming to train at least 15,000 Ukrainian soldiers over a two-year period (EEAS 2022). This ambitious target makes it the largest military training mission ever conducted by the EU. Beyond its scale, EUMAM Ukraine is distinct in its mandate. Previous EU training missions focused on helping third countries combat terrorism or armed militia groups, whereas EUMAM Ukraine is the first EU mission focused specifically on territorial defence and deterrence (WMCES 2022). The mission aims to enhance the Ukrainian Armed Forces' capacity to protect Ukraine's "territorial integrity [...] and to deter and respond to possible future military offensives by Russia and other potential aggressors" (EEAS 2022). After resolving disagreements over the command-and-control structure, EUMAM Ukraine was launched in November 2022, marking a shift from the exclusively civilian focus that had previously characterized the EU's hitherto involvement in Ukraine (WMCES 2022).

Sanctions on Russia and EU Accession

The EU issued 9 rounds or packages of sanctions against Russia in the first year of the conflict as punitive measures to deter the military aggression. Von der Leyen has argued that the measures entail the "toughest sanctions the world has ever seen", at least the most stringent measures adopted by the EU against any country so far (European Commission 2022f). The first package of 22 February 2022 came only days before the Russian invasion and in response to Russian President Vladimir Putin's recognition of the two Ukrainian territories Donetsk and Luhansk as independent republics (Håkansson 2024). As the conflict escalated, additional packages of increasingly stringent sanctions were adopted on 25 and 28 February, 2 and 15 March, 8 April, 3 June, 21 June and 22 July. The final round of the sanctions within the first year of the conflict was adopted on 16 December 2022. The cumulative impact of these sanctions is unprecedented in both scale and nature, as they encompass measures against individuals and entities, severe financial and trade restrictions, limitations on Russian media broadcasting and restrictions targeting sensitive sectors such as aviation, energy and high technology (Bosse 2022).

Alongside sanctions, the EU has also symbolically supported Ukraine, and other Eastern European countries, through offering EU accession once the countries have met the Copenhagen criteria and the EU finds itself in a position to include new member states. Ukraine applied for EU accession in February 2022 and Moldova in March 2022, both countries were granted EU candidate status in June 2022 (European Council 2022b). Accession negotiations started in December of the same year. Georgia applied for EU accession in March 2022. Its candidate status was confirmed by the EU on 14 December 2023 but later "frozen" in July 2024 as a consequence of the adoption of a controversial "foreign influence" law by the Georgian Parliament in June 2024. Veronica Anghel and Jelena Dzankic (2023) argue that the EU is using (the promise) of the enlargement as security/stability building mechanism for Ukraine and for other Eastern Europe countries, which is very reminiscent of the use of enlargement as a tool to stabilize the Western Balkans at the end of 1990s.

A "Watershed" for the EU's Foreign Policy Towards Ukraine and Eastern Europe?

As seen from the previous section, the EU since the 2022 Russian invasion has tried to influence the course of the conflict by ways of historically unprecedented levels of symbolic (EU candidacy status and sanctions against Russia), financial, material and technical assistance. The EU's willingness to help Ukraine since 2022 can thus arguably be said to be uncontested, especially when contrasted with the much more cautious and low-profile engagement prior to the date. However, the question is whether this significant increase in help and support testifies to an increased EU actorness in relation to Ukraine and the region. Stated differently, can one conclusively say that the EU's wartime assistance to Ukraine since 2022 marks a decisive before and after for the EU's ability to act in Eastern Europe?

The argument of the chapter, as laid out in continuation, is that notwithstanding the novelties and scope of EU's wartime assistance and the at times surprising high levels of intra-EU cohesion even when traditionally divisive issues have been dealt with, on the balance there is perhaps less evidence for increased EU actorness than meets the eye.

First, in terms of *authority*, the EU's foreign and security policy as well as all other supporting economic, humanitarian, or security measures taken by the EU and its member states in the first twelve months of the conflict are well within the bounds of the existing EU Treaties. Similarly, no new tools or extraordinary arrangements, or major leaps forward in European integration, have been generated as a consequence of the war (Genschel 2022; Anghel and Jones 2022).[2] The instruments used thus all existed prior to the Russia-Ukraine war, albeit some had not been employed prior to date or given that particular usage. For example, it could be argued that there has been a marginal increase in terms of authority and actorness due to the EU member states' willingness to rely more on the existing mechanisms of constructive abstention and/or qualified majority voting on different measures related to the Ukrainian war compared to other previous or current foreign and security policy scenarios. The constructive abstention of the neutral states Austria,

[2] The single exception might be the acceleration of cooperation in the area of the Common Security and Defence Policy (CSDP), although moves in this direction had already started prior to 2022.

Ireland and Malta in the context of military assistance to Ukraine is a case in point.

Second, in terms of *autonomy*, the EU as a hybrid intergovernmental-supranational entity, has acted with considerable autonomy from third actors and/or external powers. It has developed a clear policy on Ukraine which is unique to the EU and appears to have evolved fairly independently of similar initiatives of non-EU actors. The area where the EU's autonomy has been less clear is in relation to the military assistance, as here the main coordination efforts have been managed via the North Atlantic Treaty Organization (NATO) and bilaterally between certain EU member states and the United States. Within the EU, certain institutions have acquired a prominent and, some would argue, a more autonomous role in the context of the Ukraine war and more broadly in the Eastern European region. The figurehead for the EU's assistance to Ukraine and to neighbouring countries, as well as the sanctions regime against Russia, has been the European Commission (Håkansson 2024). The represents a shift-over in institutional undertakings compared to in the aftermath of the 2014 Crimean crisis, when the political/diplomatic management of the conflict was mostly left to the member states, in essence France and Germany, while "the entire top trio of the EU institutions, Commission and Council presidents as well as HR, gave themselves a noticeably restrained profile" (Härtel 2023, 9). The post-2022 situation is thus noticeably different. The European Commission has taken a lead not only in the institution's traditional areas of humanitarian and economic assistance, but even had a strong impact on shaping the EU's reception of millions of Ukraine refugees, EU trade liberalization and export assistance with Ukraine (EU-Ukraine Solidarity Lanes).[3] The European Commission's autonomy of action in the region would only increase with the decision by the EU member states to grant candidacy status to Moldova and Ukraine in 2022 and Georgia in 2023. The European Commission traditionally is the main interlocutor between the EU and the accession states, hence the salience of the European Commission as an actor in the Eastern European region has increased. It is also worth noting that within the European Commission, President von der Leyen has in many ways become the EU's most visible face and voice for the EU foreign

[3] The European Commission has also taken the lead in other areas, such as the different sanction packages toward Russia since 2022 as well as in promoting the military and defence cooperation within the EU.

policy towards the region—speaking with Ukrainian and other regional leaders, visiting the war-torn country, and focusing public attention on the importance of making a firm commitment to Ukraine's survival and even victory in the conflict (Anghel and Jones 2022).

Third, in terms of *cohesion*, the normally fairly plural and not always consistent EU foreign policy appears to have acquired an unusual degree of cohesion over the war in Ukraine. The EU's engagement after 2022 can thus said to be markedly different from the fragmented and weak EU response in the aftermath of the Crimean crisis in 2014. Perhaps it is true as Christian Kaunert and Joana de Deus Pereira (2023, 1145) have argued that "Russia's military invasion of Ukraine in February 2022 was first and foremost a warning that prior EU's policies on Russia were inconsistent and lacked a pre-emptive vision regarding Putin's aspirations" in terms of Ukraine and the broader Eastern European region. To Giselle Bosse (2022, 531) the Ukraine war has managed to forge "rare unity among its member states" as well as within EU institutions. Such cohesion arguably springs from the outrage among EU and member states leaders for the Russian aggression, as well as their collective wish to stand in "solidarity" with Ukraine, and other countries receiving the spill-over effects of the conflict. Hence, even in the areas of sanctions against Russia, of energy policies, and on enlargement—normally highly divisive issues among EU member states—there have been notable cohesion within the EU to support such policies (Schimmelfenning 2023). The ensuing cohesion has facilitated the speed at which the EU has managed to act in different phases of the conflict. However, while overall EU cohesion over Ukraine has been better than in most other areas of past and current EU foreign and security policy, there have been moments when this cohesion has been tested. Most macro-financial assistance package prior to their adoption have produced tension between the member states. Mostly due to one or other EU member state making its agreement on the assistance package conditional on political or economic concessions benefiting said member state. The EU-Ukraine Solidarity Lanes have also generated periodic troubles with between the European Commission and determined EU member states as there is a fear that cheap Ukrainian agrifood might undercut EU agricultural produce. Finally, the EU's decision to fund the provision of weapons to Ukraine through the EPF revealed some differences in member states' willingness to supplying weapons to Ukraine, as noted above.

Fourth, in terms of recognition and legitimacy as an actor. Around the world, the EU has become readily recognizable as one of Ukraine's most prominent supporters since 2022. The EU has spoken up in favour of Ukraine in various international contexts such as, for example, the United Nations (UN), or in region-to-region dialogues with African or Latin American countries. It has also worked hard to establish pro-Ukrainian preference coalitions with individual African, Asian, European, as well as Latin and North American countries. However, such efforts have not always found legitimacy in third countries, especially in the Global South. While the EU sees the Ukraine war as a security threat transcending the continent for its implication on internationally held principles and values, outside of the EU there is a perception that the war is mostly "a European problem which required a European solution" with only limited ramifications for global security (Carbone 2023, 547). The EU's diplomatic outreach to African, Asian and Latin American countries in support of Ukraine is thus interpreted in many as putting undue pressure on such third countries to align with the EU's position in favour of Ukraine. They are also concerned about the effects of EU sanctions on Russia and the EU's diplomatic efforts to contain Russia politically and economically in their countries. Finally, the EU has also been accused by third countries of exacerbating the effects of the conflict by its firm support of Ukraine, e.g. in the area of food security and rising costs of agrifood produce, animal feed, energy and fertilizers, or for double standards in its quick and large-scale supportive action for Ukraine compared to its feeble response to other conflict scenarios around the world (e.g. Gaza or some of the African conflicts).

Conclusion

The EU has undoubtedly been more active and engaged in Ukraine since the war broke out in 2022. The economic and humanitarian assistance in the first year of the conflict was substantial. In addition, the EU has also taken unprecedented steps such as, for example, activating its enlargement policy and TPD as well as launching its first military training mission in the region, which all constitutes a considerable shift from the previous EU's timid engagement in Eastern Europe.

However, still, on the balance, it is difficult to decisively say that the Ukraine war has constituted a "watershed moment" for the EU's foreign and security policy, especially if seen through the prism of actorness. In terms of authority, marginal increased actorness can be attributed to the EU's greater willingness and flexibility in terms of using existing Treaty mechanisms in novel ways, although on the whole the EU's action on Ukraine can be considered as well within its Treaty mandate for foreign and security policy. In terms of autonomy, the EU has shown independence of action and strategy from other partners, as well as not conditioned in its action by external pressures on its policies on Ukraine and other Eastern European countries. However, this independence of action away from conditioning external influence is a feature that has been seen habitually in the EU's external action and foreign and security policy since the 1990s onwards, hence, the Ukraine war does not entail any marked difference. The role and autonomy of the European Commission in the context of the 2022 invasion is significant, but it is less a reflection of overall EU actorness as opposed to what one could call "institutional actorness" within the EU. In terms of cohesion, the EU's solidarity with Ukraine and other countries threatened by Russia, as well as the outrage of the Russian aggression generated within the EU, have fomented clear EU unity on the conflict. This is the one aspect where the EU's foreign and security actorness towards the region can be seen as having grown in the first year of the conflict, albeit not without its moments of tension and contradictions among EU institutions and/or EU member states. However, while a definitive "watershed" on attitudes and level of engagement in Ukraine and Eastern Europe, this chapter ventures to hold that the EU cohesion on Ukraine is a mere temporal and conjectural feature of EU's foreign and security policy actorness which is not likely not sustain itself over time whether in the region or elsewhere in the world, when the conditions of the Ukraine war eventually will change. Finally, while EU unity might have increased, such cohesion must be balanced with a determined loss of recognition and legitimacy for the EU as a foreign and security actorness as a consequence of its actions in Ukraine. African, Asian and Latin American leaders have accused the EU of wanting to globalize an intra-European problem, for putting undue diplomatic pressure to fall in line with the EU position on the conflict, and for applying double standards vis-a-vis other global wars.

References

Anghel, V., and J. Dzankic. 2023. Wartime EU: Consequences of the Russia-Ukraine War on the Enlargement Process. *Journal of European Integration* 45 (3): 487–501.

Anghel, V., and E. Jones. 2022. Is Europe Really Forged Through Crisis? Pandemic EU and the Russia-Ukraine War. *Journal of European Public Policy* 30 (4): 766–786.

Blockmans, S., and L. De Agostini. 2022. *Assessing the EU's Military Assistance to Ukraine*. Centre for European Policy Studies, October 21, available at: https://www.ceps.eu/ceps-publications/assessing-the-eus-military-assistance-to-ukraine/ (accessed 26 September 2023).

Bosse, G. 2022. Values, Rights, and Changing Interests: The EU's Response to the War Against Ukraine and the Responsibility to Protect Europeans. *Contemporary Security Policy* 43 (3): 531–546.

Browning, C.S. 2018. Geostrategies, Geopolitics and Ontological Security in the Eastern Neighbourhood: The European Union and the 'New Cold War.' *Political Geography* 62: 106–115.

Carbone, M. 2023. When Elephants Fight, It Is the Grass That Suffers: The Russo-Ukrainian Conflict and the Decentring-Recentring Conundrum in EU-Africa Relations. *Journal of European Integration* 45 (3): 539–557.

Chaban, N., O. Elgström, and M. Knodt. 2019. Perceptions of EU Mediation and Mediation Effectiveness: Comparing Perspectives from Ukraine and the EU. *Cooperation and Conflict* 54 (4): 506–523.

Council of the EU. 2021. *Council Decisions (CFSP) 2021/509 of 22 March 2021 establishing a European Peace Facility, and repealing Decision (CFSP) 2015/528*, March 24. (Official Journal of the European Union L 102/14).

Council of the EU. 2022a. *EUAM Ukraine: Council Further Amends the Mandate to Also Provide Support in the Investigation and Prosecution of International Crimes*, April 13 (Press release 378/22).

Council of the EU. 2022b. *EU Adopts New Set of Measures to Respond to Russia's Military Aggression Against Ukraine*, February 28 (Press Release 189/22).

Council of the EU. 2022c. *Summary Record. Extraordinary Meetings of the Permanent Representatives Committee 22, 24, 27, 28 February, 1, 3 and 4 March 2022*, March 16 (Summary Record 7282/22).

Cyprus Mail. 2022, October 13. Anastasiades: No Cyprus Weapons for Ukraine… Unless Replaced by Equivalent Deterrent, available at: https://cyprus-mail.com/2022/10/13/anastasiades-no-cyprus-weapons-for-ukraine-unless-theyre-replaced-by-equivalent-deterrent/ (accessed 26 September 2023).

Dragneva, R., and K. Wolczuk. 2015. *Ukraine Between the EU and Russia: The Integration Challenge*. Basingstoke: Palgrave Macmillan.

European Commission. 2003. *Communication from the Commission to the Council and the European Parliament. Wider Europe—Neighbourhood: A New*

Framework for Relations with Our Eastern and Southern Neighbours, March 13 (COM(2003) 104 final).
European Commission. 2022a. *Speech by President von der Leyen at the European Parliament Plenary on the Russian Aggression Against Ukraine*, March 1 (Speech/22/1483).
European Commission. 2022b. *EU Takes Steps to Suspend All Duties on Imports from Ukraine*, April 27 (Press Release IP/22/2671).
European Commission. 2022c. *Communication from the Commission to the European Parliament, the Council, the European Economic and Social Committee and the Committee of the Regions. An Action Plan for EU-Ukraine Solidarity Lanes to Facilitate Ukraine's Agricultural Export and Bilateral Trade with the EU*, May 12 (COM (2022) 217 final).
European Commission. 2022d. *Supporting Ukrainian Exports and Improving Connections to the EU: EU Strengthens Cooperation with Ukraine and Moldova*, July 29, available at: https://transport.ec.europa.eu/news/supporting-ukrainian-exports-and-improving-connections-eu-eu-strengthens-cooperation-ukraine-and-2022-06-29_en (accessed 26 September 2023).
European Commission. 2022e. *War in Ukraine: Coordinating the Largest-Ever EU Civil Protection Operation*, May 30, available at: https://civil-protection-humanitarian-aid.ec.europa.eu/news-stories/stories/war-ukraine-coordinating-largest-ever-eu-civil-protection-operation_en (accessed 26 September 2023).
European Commission. 2022f. *2022 State of the Union Address by President von der Leyen*, August 22, available at: https://neighbourhood-enlargement.ec.europa.eu/news/2022-state-union-address-president-von-der-leyen-2022-09-14_en (accessed 28 September 2024).
European Commission. 2023a. *Factsheet: EU Solidarity with Ukraine*, September 14, available at: https://ec.europa.eu/commission/presscorner/detail/en/FS_22_3862 (accessed 26 September 2023).
European Commission. 2023b. *EU Assistance to Ukraine*, available at: https://eu-solidarity-ukraine.ec.europa.eu/eu-assistance-ukraine_en#support-to-the-energy-sector (accessed 26 September 2023).
European Commission. 2023c. *EU Support to Ukraine. Humanitarian Aid and Civil Protection*, March 1, available at: https://civil-protection-humanitarian-aid.ec.europa.eu/system/files/2023-03/EU%20Support%20to%20Ukraine.pdf (accessed 26 September 2023).
European Council. 2022a. *Conclusions—14 and 15 December 2022*, December 14–15 (EUCO 20/23).
European Council. 2022b. *Conclusions—23 and 24 June 2022*, June 24 (EUCO 24/22).
European Parliament and Council of the EU, 2022. *Regulation (EU) 2022/838 of the European Parliament and of the Council of 30 May 2022 Amending*

Regulation (EU) 2018/1727 as Regards the Preservation, Analysis and Storage at Eurojust of Evidence Relating to Genocide, Crimes Against Humanity, War Crimes and Related Criminal Offences, May 31 (Official Journal of the European Union L148/1).

European Parliamentary Research Service (EPRS). 2022. *Russia's War on Ukraine: EU Budget Response*. PE 729.291-March.

European Union Agency for Criminal Justice Cooperation (EUROJUST). 2022. *Romania Becomes Seventh Member of Joint Investigation Team on Alleged Core International Crimes Committed in Ukraine*, October 13, available at: https://www.eurojust.europa.eu/news/romania-becomes-seventh-member-joint-investigation-team-alleged-core-international-crimes (accessed 26 September 2023).

EEAS. 2022. *European Union Assistance Mission Ukraine (EUMAM)*, December 2, available at: https://www.eeas.europa.eu/sites/default/files/documents/2023-EUMAMUkraine.pdf (accessed 26 September 2023).

Genschel, P. 2022. Bellicist Integration? The War in Ukraine, the European Union and Core State Powers. *Journal of European Public Policy* 29 (12): 1885–1900.

Haukkala, H. 2015. From Cooperative to Contested Europe? The Conflict in Ukraine as a Culmination of a Long-Term Crisis in EU–Russia Relations. *Journal of Contemporary European Studies* 23 (1): 25–40.

Haukkala, H. 2016. A Perfect Storm; or What Went Wrong and What Went Right for the EU in Ukraine. *Europe-Asia Studies* 68 (4): 653–664.

Håkansson, C. 2024. The Ukraine War and the Emergence of the European Commission as a Geopolitical Actor. *Journal of European Integration* 46 (1): 25–45.

Härtel, A. 2023. EU Actorness in the Conflict in Ukraine: Between 'Comprehensive' Ambitions and the Contradictory Realities of an Enlarged 'Technical' Role'. *Ethnopolitics* 22 (3): 271–289.

Howorth, J. 2017. 'Stability on the Borders': The Ukraine Crisis and the EU's. Constrained Policy Towards the Eastern Neighbourhood. *Journal of Common and Market Studies* 55 (1): 121–136.

Hungary Today. 2022. FM Szijjártó: EU Supplying Weapons to Ukraine 'Not Our Business', April 20, available at: https://hungarytoday.hu/fm-szijjarto-eu-epf-supplying-weapons-ukraine-war/ (accessed 26 September 2023).

International Monetary Fund (IMF). 2022. *How Ukraine Is Managing a War Economy*, December 2, available at: https://www.imf.org/en/News/Articles/2022/12/20/cf-how-ukraine-is-managing-a-war-economy (accessed 26 September 2023).

Johansson-Nogués, E. 2002. EU's Foreign Policy and Subregionalization in the Baltic Sea area. In *EU Enlargement and Beyond: The Baltic States and Russia*. ed. H. Hubel, 371–392. Berlin: Berliner Wissenschafts-Verlag.

Johansson-Nogués, E. 2007. The EU and Its Neighbourhood: An Overview. In *Governing Europe's Neighbourhood: Partners or Periphery?*, ed. K. Weber, M. Smith, and M. Baun, 21–35. Manchester: Manchester University Press.

Johansson-Nogués, E. 2011.The Decline of the EU's 'Magnetic Attraction'? The European Union in the eyes of neighbouring Arab countries and Russia. *European Foreign Policy Unit Working Paper*, 1. London School of Economics and Political Science, UK.

Johansson-Nogués, E. 2018. The EU's Ontological (in) Security: Stabilising the ENP Area… and the EU-self? *Cooperation and Conflict* 53 (4): 528–544.

Juncos, A.E., and R.G. Whitman. 2015. Europe as a Regional Actor: Neighbourhood Lost? *Journal of Common and Market Studies* 53: 200–215.

Jupille, J., and J.A. Caporaso. 1998. States, Agency and Rules: The European Union in Global Environmental Politics. In *The European Union in the World Community*, ed. C. Rhodes, 213–229. Boulder, CO: Lynne Rienner.

Kaunert, C., and J. de Deus Pereira. 2023. EU Eastern Partnership, Ontological Security and EU-Ukraine/Russian Warfare. *Journal of Contemporary European Studies* 31 (4): 1135–1146.

Kuzio, T. 2017. Ukraine Between a Constrained EU and Assertive Russia. *Journal of Common and Market Studies* 55 (1): 103–120.

Marchetti, A. 2018. Of Borders and Boundaries: The Neighbourhood as the EU's Buffer Zone. In *The Routledge Handbook on the European Neighbourhood Policy*, ed. T. Schumacher, A. Marchetti, and T. Demmelhuber, 130–140. Oxon and New York: Routledge.

Ministry of Energy of Ukraine. 2023. Ministry of Energy: EUR 144.366 Million Raised by Ukraine Energy Support Fund, February 1, available at: https://www.kmu.gov.ua/en/news/minenerho-144366-mln-ievro-nadiis hlo-do-fondu-pidtrymky-enerhetyky-ukrainy (accessed 26 September 2023).

Mogherini, F. 2015. *The European Union in a Changing Global Environment. A More Connected, Contested and Complex World*, available at: https://eucivcap.files.wordpress.com/2017/03/20150625-european_union_changing_global_environment-more_connected_contested_complex_world.pdf (accessed 26 September 2023).

Nováky, N. 2015. Why so Soft? The European Union in Ukraine. *Contemporary Security Policy* 36 (2): 244–266.

Schimmelfenning, F. 2023. The Advent of Geopolitical Enlargement and Its Credibility Dilemma. In *A Year Later: War in Ukraine and Western Balkan (Geo)Politics*, ed. J. Dzankic, S. Kacarska, and S. Keil, 185–193. European University Institute.

The Economist. 2014. Europe's Ring of Fire', September 20, available at: https://www.economist.com/europe/2014/09/20/europes-ring-of-fire (accessed 26 September 2023).

Trebesch, C., A. Antezza, K. Bushness, A. Frank, P. Frank, L. Franz, I. Kharitonov, B. Kumar, E. Rebinskaya. and S. Schramm. 2023. *The Ukraine Support Tracker: Which Countries Help Ukraine and How?* Kiel Institute for World Economy, 2218/February.

United Nations High Commissioner for Refugees (UNHCR). 2023. *Ukraine Situation*, available at: https://reporting.unhcr.org/ukraine-situation (accessed 26 September 2023).

Von Der Burchard, H. 2022. Hungary Infuriates EU with Block on €18B Ukraine aid. *Politico*, November 10, available at: https://www.politico.eu/article/germany-annalena-baerbock-hungary-europe-play-poker-aid-ukraine/ (accessed 26 September 2023).

Wilfried Martens Centre for European Studies (WMCES). 2022. *With the New Ukraine Mission, EU Military Training Becomes More Geopolitical*, October 21, available at: https://www.martenscentre.eu/blog/with-the-new-ukraine-mission-eu-military-training-becomes-more-geopolitical/ (accessed 26 September 2023).

Wolczuk, K. 2016. Ukraine and Europe: Reshuffling the Boundaries of Order. *Thesis Eleven* 36 (1): 54–73.

Young, R. 2017. *Europe's Eastern Crisis: The Geopolitics of Asymmetry*. Cambridge: Cambridge University Press.

Zielonka, J. 2018. The EU and the European Neighbourhood Policy: The Re-making of Europe's Identity. In *The Routledge Handbook on the European Neighbourhood Policy*, ed. T. Schumacher, A. Marchetti, and T. Demmelhuber, 141–151. Oxon and New York: Routledge.

The EU Toolbox: Critical Review of the Means Used for Promoting Geopolitical Actorness

European Union's Use of the Outermost Regions (ORs) and the Overseas Countries and Territories (OCTs) to Promote Its Geopolitical Interests in the Atlantic, Caribbean, Indian, and Pacific Regions

Alexandru Balas

Introduction

The Outermost Regions (ORs) and the Overseas Countries and Territories (OCTs) of European Union (EU) member states have recently gained importance regarding the EU's Common Foreign and Security Policy (CFSP). These regions, countries, and territories are external borders of the EU or of its member states, in (a) regions that are contested between major geopolitical players (United States, Russia, China in the Pacific Islands and the Arctic), (b) are close to conflict zones (maritime security in the Indo-Pacific and, to a lesser extent, the Caribbean—ongoing conflicts in Venezuela and Colombia), and (c) on drugs and human trafficking/illegal immigration routes (the Caribbean and the Atlantic). An assessment of the geopolitical value of these bits and pieces of EU in

A. Balas (✉)
The State University of New York (SUNY), Cortland, NY, USA
e-mail: alexandru.balas@cortland.edu

L. Lika and D. Riga (eds.), *EU Geopolitical Actorness in a Changing World*, https://doi.org/10.1007/978-3-031-81160-9_9

the Atlantic, the Caribbean, the Indian, and the Pacific Oceans is long overdue.

This chapter aims to shed light on the ways in which the EU can make use of these territories and regions to promote its geopolitical interests on a global level. Within the framework of research on external governance (Lavenex and Schimmelfennig 2009), this chapter explores the question: Does the EU use the ORs and the OCTs to promote its geopolitical influence in the Atlantic, Caribbean, Indian and the Pacific regions? It hypothesizes that the EU uses its influence in the ORs and the OCTs to promote its goals in these regions, when there is alignment with the foreign policy and geopolitical interests of France, Spain, and Portugal for the ORs and Denmark, France, the Netherlands for the OCTs. This chapter expands the very limited research done on the OCTs and the ORs (Kochenov 2011; Adler-Nissen and Gad 2012; Freeman 2019) within EU literature. As Paul Nielsen, a former member of the European Commission points out there is an "information deficit" about the EU-ORs/OCTs subject (Nielsen quoted in Freeman 2019, 10). ORs and OCTs seem to be almost an "afterthought" for EU bureaucrats and scholars alike. If they are discussed at all, these places are most of the time included in discussions about sovereignty (Adler-Nissen and Gad 2012), or judicial aspects (Kochenov 2011). Only Isaac Freeman (2019) analyzes the CFSP of the EU with a focus on ORs (La Reunion) and OCTs (Falkland Islands).[1]

First an explanation of the differences between ORs and OCTs is required. The ORs of the EU are an integral part of EU territory and policymaking, while the OCTs are not. There are 9 ORs of the EU: French Guiana, Guadeloupe, Martinique, Mayotte, Reunion Island and Saint-Martin (France), Azores, Madeira (Portugal), and the Canary Islands (Spain). Within these regions the EU's *acquis communautaire* is fully applied as it is within any other part of the EU territory. Unlike the ORs, the OCTs are the closest to the EU a country or territory can get without being part of the EU. These OCTs are technically outside the Union, but within the EU member states to which they belong (Denmark, France,

[1] Freeman's book was written before Brexit and the withdrawal of the OCT status to the 12 British OCTs of Anguilla, Cayman Islands, Falkland Islands, South Georgia and the South Sandwich Islands, Montserrat, Pitcairn, Saint Helena and Dependencies, British Antarctic Territory, British Indian Ocean Territory, Turks and Caicos Islands, British Virgin Islands, and Bermuda.

and the Netherlands). There are 13 OCTs (Aruba, Bonaire, Curacao, French Polynesia, French Southern and Antarctic Lands, Greenland, New Caledonia, Saba, Saint-Barthelemy, Saint Eustatius, Sint Maarten, Saint Pierre et Miquelon, Wallis and Futuna). These 13 OCTs are not third parties to the EU, but rather have an association agreement with the EU, as they are an integral part of EU member states' territories. Their relations with the EU are governed by yearly summits between the Overseas Countries and Territories Association (OCTA) and the EU.

The methodology used for this research is based on analysis of secondary sources (books, scientific articles and reports, official documents of the EU and of the ORs/OCTs, and press articles quoting EU bureaucrats and politicians). Four treaties of the EU (Treaty of Rome, Treaty of Maastricht, Treaty of Amsterdam, and Treaty of Lisbon) are analyzed to understand the legal framework of the relationship between the EU and the ORs/OCTs. Then, discourse analysis is employed to EU geopolitical strategy documents such as the European Union Maritime Security Strategy (EUMSS), the EU Strategic Compass for Security and Defense, the EU Strategy for Cooperation in the Indo-Pacific, Involvement of the Regions in the European Neighborhood and Partnership Policy, EU Arctic Policy, and the EU Strategy Towards the ORs. These documents were chosen because they focus on EU security and defense, with an emphasis on maritime security, seeing that all ORs and OCTs except one (French Guiana) are islands and thus have a major stake in maritime security. EU documents that make specific reference to ORs and OCTs are also chosen. Finally, the third type of documents analyzed are all the available conclusions of the ministerial meetings of the OCTA from 2004 to 2020, and several other OCTA documents (OCTA Strategy for 2021–2027, EU-OCT Forum Conclusions). These OCTA documents provide a glimpse into the role geopolitical interests play for the OCTs and what they want from the EU regarding geopolitical aspects.

Next, the structure of this chapter will be introduced. First, this chapter discusses the institutional framework which governs the relations between the EU and the ORs and the OCTs in terms of foreign and security policy. Second, this study assesses the importance given to the ORs and the OCTs in EU's geopolitical policy documents. Third, this research delves into the specific areas of geopolitical interest for the EU in respect to these European regions, countries, and territories. Finally, conclusions are shared about the potential added value of OCTs and ORs to

EU's geopolitical interests in the Atlantic, Caribbean, Indian, and Pacific regions.

Institutional Framework Governing the Relations Between EU and ORs/OCTs

The relations between the European Communities and the ORs and OCTs can be traced back to the Treaty of Rome (1957). In that treaty, Article 227 deals specifically with France's overseas departments (ORs in current EU jargon), and also with other associated territories (OCTs in current EU jargon). The article states that all the rules of the European Economic Community (EEC) apply to the ORs, while the OCTs benefit from an association with the EEC (Treaty of Rome 1957, pages 153–154).

It is interesting to point out that in 1957, the OCTs mentioned in Annex IV of the Treaty of Rome included the following:

(a) French West Africa—Senegal, French Sudan (Mali), Guinea, Ivory Coast, Dahomey (Benin), Mauritania, Niger, Upper Volta (Burkina Faso);
(b) French Equatorial Africa—Middle Congo (parts of Republic of Congo, Gabon, and Central African Republic), Ubangi-Shari (Central African Republic), Chad, and Gabon;
(c) Saint Pierre and Miquelon;
(d) the archipelago of Comoros, Madagascar and dependencies, the French coast of Somalia (Djibouti);
(e) New Caledonia and dependencies, the French Territories of Oceania and French Southern and Antarctic Lands;
(f) the Autonomous Republic of Togo; the territory of Cameroon administered by France; the Belgian Congo (Democratic Republic of Congo) and Ruanda-Urundi (Rwanda-Burundi), the Somalia under Italian leadership and;
(g) the Dutch New Guinea (the western half of the island of New Guinea which is nowadays part of Indonesia).

This entire list is shown here to allow for a comparison of how much the composition of which countries and territories are included in the OCTs has changed over time. Out of these territories only Saint

Pierre and Miquelon, New Caledonia and dependencies, the French Territories of Oceania (French Polynesia), and the French Southern and Antarctic Lands are still OCTs to this day. All the other OCTs of the EU member states in 1957 have since gained independence or have become an outermost region (Mayotte, which was one of the dependencies in "Madagascar and dependencies"). It would be interesting to develop a research project comparing the socio-economic development and geopolitical importance for the EU of former OCTs with current OCTs and with OCTs which have become ORs over time (Mayotte became an OR on January 1, 2014, after having been an OCT until then).

The next important mentioning of the ORs is in the Treaty of Maastricht (1992), in a special declaration which mentions that all the provisions of the treaty apply to the ORs (the French overseas departments, the Azores and the Canary Islands), too. The OCTs are also mentioned in the Treaty of Maastricht in article 3 which talks about increasing trade and promoting joint economic and social development, and in a Declaration updating article 227 from the 1957 Treaty of Rome. This Declaration is of importance to the geopolitical use of the OCTs by the EU because it talks about what happens when there is a divergence of interest between the OCTs and the Union. In such situations an attempt will be made to reach a solution in accord with the position of the Union, but if this proves to be impossible, the member states concerned may act separately in the interests of their OCTs. Interesting to point out that these provisions applied in 1992 also to Portugal's Macao and East Timor. The fact that the member states, and not the EU as a whole, should act in the interests of their OCTs, added hurdles to the potential development of an EU CFSP centered on the geopolitical dimensions of the OCTs. The EU needs first to convince Denmark, France, and the Netherlands together with the political administrations of these OCTs, of the value of a European-wide geopolitical approach to the OCTs. This European-wide approach is still missing as of 2024.

The Treaty of Amsterdam (1997) in its Article 299 mentions both the ORs and OCTs, for the first time at the European level, rather than in relation to their member states. The integrity and the coherence of the Community legal order are mentioned as primordial in the relations with the ORs and the OCTs. This chapter interprets this as EU's willingness to impose the Union's will on these territories to the largest extent possible, including on issues of the CFSP if there is agreement from the EU member states' metropolis, while acknowledging their specific circumstances. The OCTs mentioned in Annex II of the Treaty of Amsterdam are the current OCTs (as of 2024) plus the British ones[2] that were removed as OCTs in 2020, following Brexit.

The Treaty on the Functioning of the European Union (TFEU) (also known as the Lisbon Treaty) of 2007 dedicated two specific articles to the EU's relations with the OCTs, Articles 198 and 255. Article 198 clearly identifies that EU's interests regarding the OCTs are related to economic and social development, and not geopolitical in nature: "The purpose of association shall be to promote the economic and social development of the countries and territories and to establish close economic relations between them and the Union as a whole" (European Union 2007). Article 255 made it clear that "The provisions of the Treaties shall apply to the European territories for whose external relations a Member State is responsible" (European Union 2007). For the purposes of this analysis, Article 255 is important because it clarifies that there should not be a difference regarding the CFSP between the TFEU and its application in the member states OCTs. Because ORs are an integral part of the EU, there is no reason for the EU to mention them more often. They are briefly mentioned twice in the treaty to emphasize their special characteristics and constraints while highlighting that they are an integral part of the EU.

The reference to ORs and OCTs is minimal in the EU treaties, and it is only focused on socio-economic development of these regions, countries, and territories. There is no direct reference to the EU's potential use of these lands in any geopolitical way. The only (small) references are to the application of the EU CFSP in the ORs and the OCTs. If there are divergences between the Union's CFSP and the OCTs then all efforts will be made to adopt the Union's position and interests, while acknowledging these lands' special circumstances.

This chapter would expect the ORs and OCTs to feature prominently in the 2014 EUMSS given that these regions, countries, and territories enable the EU to have an influence on the world's largest combined maritime areas (European Environment Agency (EEA) 2020). Freeman (2019, 7) argues that "[l]ocated along international trade routes, ORs and OCTs are considered particularly important on the Union's level as well, for they are keeping the EU as a maritime power and maintaining its

[2] See footnote 1 above for a complete list of the British OCTs.

status as a key player in international politics." However, the reality of the EUMSS shows that the ORs and OCTs are merely an afterthought. The 2014 version of the EUMSS only mentions the ORs once: "This Strategy takes particular regard of each of the European sea and subsea basins, namely the Baltic Sea, the Black Sea, the Mediterranean and the North Sea, as well as of the Arctic waters, the Atlantic Ocean and the outermost regions" (Council of the EU 2014, 4). The 2022 EU Strategic Compass for Security and Defense mentions once, only the ORs: "Maritime security in the Baltic Sea, the Black Sea, the Mediterranean and the North Sea, as well as of the Arctic waters, the Atlantic Ocean and the outermost regions is important for the EU's security, our economic development, free trade, transport and energy security. Maritime zones, critical sea lanes of communication and several maritime chokepoints as well as seabeds, are increasingly contested, from the Gulf of Aden to the Strait of Hormuz and beyond the Strait of Malacca" (European Union 2022a, 22). The OCTs are never mentioned in either document. In 2023, the European Commission Joint Communication on an updated EUMSS mentions the ORs and the OCTs in the context of increased geopolitical competition in the Indian and Pacific Oceans (European Union 2023, 2), but with only one suggestion about how these ORs and OCTs could be useful for EU's interests: increased funding to ORs and OCTs through the European Regional Development Fund (ERDF) and Interreg programs (European Union 2023, 15). Thus, in these documents, too, the ORs and OCTs are barely mentioned.

In other EU policy strategy documents, the ORs and OCTs are rarely mentioned regarding geopolitics. Unfortunately, the "Global Strategy for the European Union's Foreign and Security Policy (EUGS)" does not mention the ORs and the OCTs at all, showing that the EU officials were not thinking of these places as having any potential for EU's CFSP in 2016. In the 2008 EU Communication titled "Outermost Regions – an asset for Europe," the EU Commission named the following opportunities for the ORs: outposts of the EU in the world which "play a role in maritime governance for the monitoring of coastal waters (e.g. the fight against illegal fishing, piracy or drug trafficking) or in improving the security of transport (e.g. the management of oil transport in the Caribbean)" (European Union 2008, 7). The 2009 Involvement of the Regions in the European Neighborhood and Partnership Policy mentioned that ORs should be better integrated in their specific regions, with which they share historic and cultural ties (Conference of Peripheral Maritime Regions of

Europe (CPMR) 2009, 6). This document also highlighted the view of the European Commission about how "the OCTs, as outposts of Europe all over the world, should be seen as assets for the EU rather than as a burden" (Blockmans 2011, 309).

The 2017 EU Communication regarding the relations with the ORs (European Union 2017, 3) only mentions geopolitics once, by saying that the EU should consider the specific geopolitical realities of each OR. The annex to this document (European Union Annex 2017, 11) mentions the need for the EU to "maximize the EU use of funding instruments [...] to help the outermost regions manage migration." The 2021 EU Arctic Policy does mention the interest of the European Commission to establish an office in Greenland, considering the strategic minerals that Greenland has and Arctic security interests, in general (European Union 2021a, 7). The 2021 EU Strategy for Cooperation in the Indo-Pacific mentions that "the EU outermost regions and overseas countries and territories, constitutionally linked to its member states, are an important part of the EU's approach to the Indo-Pacific" (European Union 2021b, 1) without providing any suggestions for how this importance should be put into action. The 2022 EU strategy towards the ORs only mentions security three times (European Union 2022a, b, 15 and 22) but only once in relation to geopolitical security with the recommendation to create synergies between different funds to address the migration and (undefined) security challenges facing the ORs. The EU should be defining what are these other security challenges facing ORs.

The other list of documents which frames the EU-OCTs relations from a geopolitical perspective is the list of ministerial final conclusions of the EU-OCTA Forum meetings, which represent the central institution of the relationship. The "Council Decision on the Association of the Overseas Countries and Territories with the EU, including the relations between the European Union on the one hand and Greenland and the Kingdom of Denmark on the other" which has the unusual acronym DOAG, represents the cornerstone document governing the OCT-EU Association. In 2001 the first summit between the EU and OCTs took place in Brussels. In 2003 the OCTA was founded and yearly summits between the EU and the OCTs took place, alternating between Brussels and an OCT location. The objectives of the OCTA are:

- "To consolidate and reinforce solidarity between OCTs and EU stakeholders;

- To make recommendations and carry out various projects/ programmes to enhance opportunities, comparative advantage and natural assets in order to strengthen the position of OCTs at regional and global levels;
- To promote cooperation and develop a knowledge centre and thematic networks in order to consolidate ownership and provide a point of reference for creating and disseminating valuable information on the relationship between the EU and the OCTs;
- To create a framework to engage the private sector, academia and civil society to enhance the profile, reputation and position of the OCTs" (OCTA 2003).

The OCTA is led by the ministerial conference which gathers representatives of all OCTs. The ministerial conference distills the positions and interests of the OCTs in its political declarations. All such ministerial declarations from 2004 to 2020 were analyzed for the purposes of this chapter, to identify the role played by geopolitical interests, if any. This study searched for specific keywords related to geopolitics, security, migration, drug trafficking, and maritime security. First, all these declarations focus on environmental/climate change and trade in the relations between the OCTs and the EU. Second, the OCTs request help to deal with natural disasters (hurricanes, landslides), and with the impacts of economic globalization, financial crisis aftermaths, and improvement of good governance practices. Finally, some geopolitical aspects appear, too. From 2005 onwards, the desire to better integrate with the regional organizations is mentioned regularly and the fact that the EU should think of the OCTs as its privileged partners in the Caribbean, Indian and Pacific regions.

2012 is the year in which the geopolitical value is expressed directly for the first time in the OCTs ministerial conclusions: "From the Arctic to the Tropics to the South Pole, the [...] OCTs are of global strategic value and importance" to the EU (OCTA 2012, 1). In addition, the OCTs ministers point out that the EU-based companies have much to gain by establishing themselves into OCTs because these are "strategically located in regions with emerging markets and [...] offer [...] safe, reliable and accessible trade hubs" (OCTA 2012, 4). Geopolitical concerns are not mentioned again until 2018 when the ministerial conclusions state that "[t]he OCTs provide the EU a geostrategic presence in their regions" (OCTA 2018, 7). In 2018 connections of OCTs with Australia, New

Zealand, Canada, and Iceland as potential partners are mentioned for the first time. The OCTs asked the EU "[t]o strengthen the commitments of the EU towards the OCTs, **recognizing that OCTs contribute to the global dimension of the EU** [emphasized by the author] and can bring a strong added value in the implementation of the partnerships of the EU with the regions to which they geographically belong" (OCTA 2018, 8). In 2019's ministerial conclusions, the OCTs ask the European Commission to recognize that it can use their territory as EU outposts in the regions in which they find themselves.

In 2021 the new OCTA strategy for 2021–2027 was adopted in the background of what it considers a "new, more geopolitical European Commission with policy priorities such as a 'Stronger Europe in the World'" (OCTA 2021, 2). The strategy acknowledges the need for better communication and visibility, both inside the EU, and also to third parties outside the EU, about the EU-OCTs relationship and opportunities, in order to "unlock the value of the OCTs" (OCTA 2021, 3). Then, this strategy promotes the need for OCTs' regional cooperation in their respective parts of the world. This is suggested to be done either individually by OCTs' involvement with regional organizations, such as the Pacific Islands Forum (PIF), the Nordic Council (NC), or the Caribbean States Association (CSA), or in the framework of EU's (Atlantic, Caribbean, Indian, and Pacific) regional strategies and regional protocols.

The 2022 OCT-EU Forum final conclusions do highlight the geopolitical importance of the OCTs: "Due to their geographical and geopolitical location, the partners recognize that the OCTs are part of the EU's geostrategic agenda, as reflected in the new EU Strategy for Cooperation in the Indo-Pacific and the EU's Arctic Policy, which highlight the potential role of the OCTs in the implementation of these strategies" (OCT-EU Forum 2022, 3). This document also highlights the "importance of regional and intra-regional integration and cooperation, not only between OCTs, but also between OCTs and their neighbors, namely African, Caribbean, and Pacific (ACP) countries, EU Outermost Regions or third countries" (OCT-EU Forum 2022, 3). The same geopolitical asset that the OCTs bring to the EU was emphasized by the New Caledonia president Louis Mapou when, during his opening remarks of the 2022 Forum said: "Despite our small populations of one million, our OCTs are positioned in strategic geographical areas, in the Caribbean, the North Atlantic, the Indian Ocean, but also in the Pacific, and this geographical distribution is our asset, and it is a clear opportunity"

(Mapou quoted in OCTA 2022). These thoughts were echoed by the European Commissioner for International Partnerships, Jutta Jurpilainen: "As the world around us becomes more complex and challenging, the EU-OCT partnership remains an immense asset. We share values, standards and interests, and we can support each other as we seek to build more resilience and autonomy" (Jurpilainen quoted in OCTA 2022).

The OCT ministerial documents analyzed for this chapter also reveal the external governance dimension of the EU in the OCTs. External governance is defined in this chapter as the actions of the EU through which it tries to influence actors outside its borders which are of geopolitical and economic interest to itself. Obviously, external governance does not apply to the ORs, as these fall directly under EU governance (internal governance), but it does apply to the OCTs which are outside the EU. These OCTs have adopted almost in its entirety the EU model, while keeping in mind their specific characteristics. The ministerial conclusions constantly and repeatedly reaffirm the concept of OCTs as "belonging to the same EU family" (from OCTA 2009 onwards) as representing the keystone principle for the OCT-EU partnership. OCTs promote the values of the EU in their respective regions, too, in relations with ACP, and other states. The power of the EU external governance in the OCTs is limited by a couple of factors: the limited importance attributed to the OCTs and knowledge about OCTs of EU decision-makers in faraway Brussels, and the EU member states' desire to be the ones fully controlling their OCTs external relations, and not the "Eurocrats" in Brussels. The EU uses a network mode of external governance, acknowledging its OCTs partners as formal equals, despite the obvious asymmetries.

In conclusion, the analysis of the EU policy documents and of the OCTA documents reveal that the geopolitical role of the ORs and the OCTs for the EU only made it on the radar over the last decade. EU policy documents mention the ORs and the OCTs in passing when it comes to geopolitics. The OCTA documents, as expected, mention more of the role of OCTs in geopolitics, but only since 2012. Before that moment, only the involvement (either as members, associate members, or as observers) of the OCTs in their respective regional organizations can be attributed a geopolitical component. After 2012 this study points out how the OCTs position themselves as European outposts in their regions, able and willing to contribute to the global dimension of the EU. 2012 seems to be the tipping point in the EU-OCT relations because it was around the time when the EU tried to homogenize its relations with other Western European countries and territories (the European micro-states of Andorra, Monaco, San Marino but also these OCTs which belong to EU member states) which shared similar values: democracies, market economies, share the European identity, common values and interests, and internal and external borders with the EU (Maiani 2021, 93). Around the same time, the EU was tackling "tax heavens" among its OCTs (Aruba, Curacao, and some of the British OCTs-Cayman Islands, Anguilla, etc. have been at times either non-cooperative jurisdictions for tax purposes or closely monitored by the EU) and micro-state neighbors (Andorra and Monaco were considered "tax heavens"), too. This evidence points out to the rationale for a change in the way the EU interacted with the OCTs, as part of a larger homogenization and consistent approach to smaller third parties to the EU, be it OCTs or micro-states. The next part of this chapter will discuss the specific areas of geopolitical interests between the EU and ORs/OCTs.

Specific Areas of Geopolitical Interest Between the EU and ORs/OCTs

There are several areas of interest that are worth exploring in this chapter when it comes to the EU's geopolitical interests in its faraway regions, countries, and territories:

1. The South Pacific regarding the EU's Indo-Pacific Security Strategy (IPSS) and the increased China-Australia-United States rivalry in the Pacific Islands region (with specific interests regarding rare earth minerals)

   OCTs impacted: French Polynesia, New Caledonia, Wallis and Futuna—France
2. Indo-Pacific Maritime Shipping Lanes Security

   ORs impacted: Reunion and Mayotte, France
3. Drug trafficking and illegal immigration from Latin America (and Africa, in the case of the Canary Islands) to Europe

   OCTs impacted: Aruba, Bonaire, Curacao, Sint Maarten, Saba, Sint Eustatius—the Netherlands and Saint-Barthelemy—France

   ORs impacted: French Guiana, Guadeloupe, Martinique, and Saint-Martin—France; Canary Islands—Spain; Azores Islands—Portugal

4. New "Scramble for the Arctic"—specific focus on shipping lanes because of usage of Northwest Passage, and rare earth minerals deposits

   OCTs impacted: Greenland—Denmark

   The next section will discuss each of these four geopolitical areas of interest in detail.

The South Pacific

In this region, New Caledonia is the most important geopolitical OCT actor. New Caledonia has a large degree of autonomy in its foreign relations. It can directly negotiate with countries and territories in the Pacific and of the United Nations (UN), become associated member of international organizations, and have diplomatic representatives in the Pacific countries and territories.[3] Thus, New Caledonia is a member of the Secretariat of the Pacific Community (SPC) (with its headquarters in Noumea, New Caledonia's capital), the PIF (since 2016), and of the Melanesian Spearhead Group (MSG). The SPC is an international organization focused on development. Its membership consists of 27 Pacific states and territories. The PIF is the main regional inter-governmental organization in the Pacific, with 18 members which work mostly on issues of trade and peacekeeping. The MSG is an organization aiming to improve the economies of its members.[4]

New Caledonia has an active independence movement, but the three independence referenda held in 2018, 2020, and 2021 have all shown support for remaining an OCT within France. The geopolitical rivalries in the region, between China on one hand, and Australia and United States on the other, have led many locals to say that they prefer to remain part of France. Alcide Ponga, president of the oldest pro-France party in New Caledonia, stressed: "It is not in our interest to be independent. We have dinosaurs fighting above us, China and the United States and we are not safe from a conflict in the region" (Ponga quoted in Douah 2023). Nickel is the much-coveted resource of this tropical territory. New Caledonia is

[3] New Caledonia appointed official representatives to represent it in five Pacific countries: Australia, Fiji, New Zealand, Papua New Guinea, and Vanuatu.

[4] New Caledonia is represented by a political party in this organization, the Kanak and Socialist National Liberation Front (FLNKS) coalition of pro-independence parties.

the fourth largest producer of nickel in the world, at a time when nickel is becoming a geostrategic commodity, used in batteries for electric cars. Both China and the EU want to take the lead regarding the production of electric cars, and thus New Caledonia becomes an important geopolitical asset for the EU. A French defense ministry research institute, the *Institut de Recherche Stratégique de l'École Militaire* (Strategic Research Institute of the Military School), wrote in a 2021 report that "An independent New Caledonia would de facto be under Chinese influence" (Charon and Vilmer 2021, 401). China welcomes 57% of all New Caledonia exports, and has also built an "arc" of friends in the Pacific (Papua-New Guinea, Solomon Islands, Kiribati, Vanuatu, Fiji, Tonga). Thus, for France's Paris-Delhi-Canberra axis that French President Emmanuel Macron envisioned as part of its Indo-Pacific strategy, New Caledonia plays a prime role in this effort to contain China's geopolitical influence because of the French military stationed there and its natural resources (nickel). Could this axis become Brussels-Delhi-Canberra, with an increased strategic role of the EU? Definitely. Just as the EU can promote its interests in the Pacific through New Caledonia's (but also French Polynesia's) memberships to the PIF[5] as a counterweight to the Chinese influence through its Pacific "friends." In addition, France has approximately 2,000 troops stationed in New Caledonia.

According to Paco Milhiet, French Polynesia can also play a role in this geopolitical rivalry, too because of its large maritime territory which "represents a geostrategic asset and great development opportunities with implications for air connectivity, submarine cables, space policy, polymetallic nodules" (Milhiet 2022). There are approximately 900 military personnel deployed in French Polynesia together with air and navy equipment. In the context of the EU discussions about a potential European Defense Union (EDU) and an EU Army (EUA), these European troops in the Pacific, could make the EU a player, albeit a small player, in the South Pacific geopolitical competition. Due to its lack of natural resources, the OCT of Wallis and Futuna does not play a role in the geopolitics of the South Pacific.

[5] New Caledonia and French Polynesia joined the PIF in 2016. Wallis and Futuna is an observer to the PIF.

Indo-Pacific Maritime Shipping Lanes Security

In this case, France's two ORs, those of Reunion and Mayotte, are the ones impacted. Freeman (2019, 46) argued that "[f]or five decades (from 1957 to 2007) the ORs were considered as unimportant to the EU, as tools of foreign affairs or as military strategic locations. In the past years, however, this perspective has changed, and nowadays the ORs are considered as highly valuable to promote the EU's CFSP in South America, the Caribbean region, and the Indian Ocean region." These two ORs have become important for the EU CFSP, in the context of EU's Counter-Piracy operation Atalanta launched in 2008. Reunion is the largest OR in the Indian Ocean, second most populous OR overall, and a forward military presence base of the EU.[6] "EU [French] military presence in Reunion helps naval forces to equip themselves with supplies, and carry on their operations" (Freeman 2019, 45). The French Army presence is small with approximately 750 personnel in Reunion and Mayotte, another 430 navy personnel at the naval station in Reunion, and 290 Air Force personnel in Reunion. This military presence of an EU member state allows the EU to project its power in the Indo-Pacific region through the EU Critical Maritime Routes (CRIMARIO) projects, aimed at safeguarding important shipping lanes for the global economy. This project started as CRIMARIO I in 2015 in the Western Indian Ocean (WIO) (where Reunion and Mayotte are located) and continued with CRIMARIO II which extended to South Asia and Southeast Asia. Could such programs to safeguard critical maritime routes be expanded to the Caribbean and the Atlantic, too, with the help of EU's ORs and OCTs in the region?

In addition to safeguarding the Indo-Pacific maritime shipping lanes, the EU also plays a role through its ORs in the region, because of their membership to the Indian Ocean Commission (IOC). This international organization also comprises Seychelles, the Comoros Islands, Madagascar, and Mauritius in addition to Reunion. Its aims are to deal with the environmental challenges in the region, food security, public health, and economic growth in these small island states. Most of the Small Island Developing States (SIDS) are neighbors of EU's ORs and OCTs in the Indian Ocean, the Caribbean Sea, and the Pacific Ocean. The EU can and does work through its ORs and OCTs to establish stronger cooperation

[6] The other forward presence base of the EU is in France's New Caledonia.

ties with the SIDS around the world. Thus, the European Commission recognized the need to "facilitate cooperation" between the ORs and "their neighbors by a closer alignment of rules of the relevant funding instruments and possible setting-up of joint programmes" (European Union 2017, 16–17).

Drug Trafficking and Illegal Immigration

Drug trafficking and illegal immigration impact both ORs and OCTs in the Caribbean and the Atlantic. In the Caribbean, the OCTs most impacted are the ones closest to South America, Aruba, Bonaire, and Curacao (the ABC Islands of Netherlands in the Caribbean). "Aruba, Bonaire, and Curaçao are located 30 to 40 miles north of Venezuela and continue to serve as northbound transshipment points for cocaine originating from the Guajira Peninsula in Colombia and from the Maracaibo are in Venezuela. Cocaine is primarily transported via fishing boats and inter-coastal freighters for transshipment to the United States, other Caribbean Islands, Africa, and Europe. Sint Maarten, the Dutch half of the island of the same name [...] is located in the Eastern Caribbean and is a transshipment hub for cocaine, heroin, and marijuana destined for Puerto Rico and the United States Virgin Islands as well as Europe" (US Department of State 2016) In 2022 Dutch navy ships seized the largest quantity of drugs in the ABC countries, 45 tons of drugs, showing that South American drug cartels are increasingly using this route. Regarding the French Caribbean ORs, "[i]n 2022, 55 percent of cocaine seizures entering mainland France, or 14 tons, came from the French Antilles and French Guiana" (Hernandez-Roy and Bledsoe 2023, 4). In 2022, a scholar at *Université de Guyane* stated that the airport in Cayenne, the capital, has become a veritable "hub for [drug] mules" (Nicolas 2022). Corruption of airport and port officials regarding drug trafficking is quite high in both the French Caribbean ports, plus in the harbor of Degrad des Cannes in French Guiana, and in the French metropolitan harbors of Marseille, Le Havre, and Dunkirk (Hernandez-Roy and Bledsoe 2023, 4).

Illegal immigration is the other geopolitical threat to these small populations regions, countries, and territories for which even several thousand immigrants can represent a challenge. Aruba hosts more than 17,000 Venezuelan refugees since 2021 when Venezuela's economy collapsed. According to the United Nations High Commissioner for Refugees

(UNHCR) "Aruba now has more refugees and migrants from Venezuela per local population than any country in the world: 159 displaced people per 1,000 inhabitants" (Reliefweb 2021). There are another 17,000 refugees in Curacao, too. "French Guiana in South America has emerged as a key destination and transit point for migrants and asylum seekers trying to reach Europe, attracting thousands in 2020 from as far away as Syria and Yemen, as well as many Haitians, Venezuelans, and now Cubans" (Thebia 2021). More than 20,000 asylum seekers have arrived in French Guiana since 2015, raising the percentage of foreign-born population to 1/3 of the entire outermost region. "According to the interior ministry [of French Guiana], between 30,000 and 35,000 migrants are deemed to be working illegally in French Guiana [in 2021]" (Thebia 2021). French Guiana represents the largest landmass of the EU outside continental Europe and has one of the longest EU external land boundaries. Its porous border with Brazil (over 3,000 canoes crossing daily the Oyapock river, which serves as a border), and the relative easiness of Middle Eastern refugees to get visas for Brazil, make French Guiana a prime target for many of these people.

The same challenges of drug trafficking and illegal immigration impact the ORs in the middle of the Atlantic: the Canary Islands, and the Azores. The proximity of the Canary Islands to the coast of Africa, approximately 100 km west from Morocco, make these challenges more difficult than in the Azores Islands. But, even in the Azores there has been a spike in the number of drugs confiscated on ships traveling from Latin America *en route* to mainland Europe. Andras Lorincz, in his 2011 analysis of the EU's relations with the ORs pointed out that "[k]ey targets of foreign relations of the Canaries based on the International Cooperation Law of Canaria are the geographic areas of the Maghreb: Morocco and Mauritania; Sub Saharan Africa, mainly Senegal and Cape Verde as secondary Mali, Gambia and Guinea Bissau. In Latin America: Cuba, Venezuela, Argentina, Brazil and Uruguay. The issue of Sahrawi people is also a section of that policy, taking into account their refugee status" (Lorincz 2011, 12). The Canary Islands are a hub for drugs coming by ship from Ecuador, Colombia, and Brazil, *en route* to European markets. Every few months there is a new story about large quantities of drugs being confiscated in the Canary Islands: 700 kg of cocaine in August 2023 (Europol 2023), 4.5 tons of cocaine in January 2023 (Suarez 2023), etc. The Canaries have also become a hub for illegal immigration, especially from Africa. Over almost two years, from January 2020 to October 2022, the Global Initiative Against Transnational Organized Crime (GITOC) reported more than 60,000 migrants arriving in the Canary Islands (Ruiz-Benitez de Lugo 2022). These numbers echo those in 2005–2006 when approximately 30,000 migrants yearly were arriving in the Canary Islands. In-between the numbers went down to a couple of thousand. This Atlantic route has become much more popular after the Mediterranean route became much more difficult. All of this despite the Canary Islands being home to three military bases (the General Aleman Ramirez base, the Arsenal of Las Palmas naval base, and the Gando airbase) and a large number of Spanish soldiers.

Drug trafficking and illegal immigration are two geopolitical threats for the EU in the Caribbean and the Atlantic. However, the EU has not addressed these in any coordinated fashion. The countries responsible for the ORs and the OCTs are trying to address these issues individually, and not as a united European front. In his study of EU's success in addressing Latin American drug trafficking and organized crime, Joren Selleslaghs makes no mention of the EU working with its ORs and OCTs (Sellaslaghs 2016). On the contrary, Spain is asking for EU solidarity and unity regarding to migration to the Canary Islands (Baczynska and Inti 2023), signaling that the 2022 New Pact on Migration and Asylum (NMPA) to EU (European Union 2023) is not working as planned. The only coordinated project of the EU is the Interreg Amazonia between French Guiana, Suriname, and Brazil to deal with cross-border and transnational cooperation. This Interreg Amazonia could potentially address drug trafficking and illegal immigration, but in studying the work of Interreg Amazonia, the author of this chapter has seen no evidence of such actions yet.

New "Scramble for the Arctic"

The specific focus on this geopolitical issue is regarding the development of new shipping lanes through the Northwest Passage (NWP) linking faster China and the EU, but polluting the Arctic in the process, and the potential mining of rare earth mineral deposits (Ewing 2021) in Greenland which would be usable for wind turbines, electric cars, and electronics. In an article in Foreign Policy magazine, author Regin Winther Pousen called Greenland the next geopolitical battleground "coveted by China, the United States, and global mining companies"

(Pousen 2022). Interestingly, the EU is not mentioned as a major geopolitical player. However, the EU acknowledges that "the implementation of the EU's Arctic policy will help the Union to deliver the targets defined by the EU Green Deal and meet its geopolitical interests" (European Union 2021c). Thus, we should expect a stronger linkage between EU's Arctic Policy and Green Deal in the coming years.

Greenland was an integral part of the EU, as an OR, from 1974 to 1985 when it changed status to an OCT, which it is nowadays, too. Like New Caledonia and French Polynesia, Greenland has a large amount of autonomy in its foreign affairs. The Greenland Self-Government can conduct independent international negotiations with third parties, but in cooperation with the Danish Foreign Service (DFS). In 1984 Greenland joined the NC, an important regional organization. Greenland's international relations are mainly with its neighbors in North America and the Arctic, and deal with fishing and shipping lanes, and more recently trying to attract Chinese investors for its rare earth mineral deposits. But as a 2014 report from Brookings Institution pointed out "efforts to attract Chinese investment in mining projects in Greenland have so far yielded little interest and no significant investment" (Boersma and Kevin 2014, 7). United States perceive Greenland as important for its own geopolitical interests, and thus blockades China's interests in the largest island in the world, which is also an EU OCT. According to Rasmus Gjedssø Bertelsen, a professor at the Arctic University of Norway, "[t]here are clear limits to what the United States tolerates – which have been made clear to the Kingdom of Denmark – it doesn't accept Chinese investments in Greenland" (Bertelsen quoted in Van Brunnersum 2022). Denmark is also looking at strengthening its foreign affairs cooperation with its autonomous region and regularly discusses "the future of international cooperation in the Arctic [and] the EU's engagement in the region" (Edvardsen 2023). Still China remains an important trade partner for Greenland and one to take into consideration in the future Arctic policies. The EU is also realizing that if it does not act swiftly, it will be left out of the geopolitical battle over Greenland, and as a result it opened an office of the European Commission in Nuuk, the capital of Greenland, in 2024. This office would allow it to promote its environmental policies in the Arctic, lobbying against increased shipping and mining around and in Greenland. But, at the same time the EU needs to provide other opportunities for the economy of Greenland if it promotes its environmentalism in the Arctic. Greenland can bring a lot to the geopolitical weight of the EU in the Arctic, and the EU would do well to listen to its Greenlandic partners and learn from their experiences in navigating between the interests of the other major Arctic players such as Canada, Russia, United States, and China.

The four geopolitical areas of concern in the relations between the EU and ORs/OCTs deal with great power rivalries in the South Pacific and the Arctic, and the role that the EU can play in these dynamics, but also with other geopolitical challenges such as maritime shipping lanes security, drug trafficking, and illegal immigration. This analysis shows that the EU is moderately active in the South Pacific, the maritime shipping lanes security in the Indian Ocean, and the Arctic, but significantly less involved in tackling drug trafficking and illegal immigration in the ORs and OCTs. In the latter, the EU member states take the lead. But there is a lot of potential for the EU to get involved much more in these geopolitical challenges, once it recognizes and operationalizes beyond mere words the added value that the ORs and OCTs could bring.

Conclusion

ORs and OCTs are of global strategic importance for the EU allowing it to project power in regions far beyond its European neighborhood. However, only in recent years, ORs and OCTs started being perceived as part of the EU's geostrategic agenda. This chapter shows how the geopolitical assets that OCTs bring to the EU have started being emphasized since 2012 in the OCT ministerial meetings, but it took a decade for these to be taken more seriously by the EU. Even so, most of the policy and strategy papers dealing with common foreign and security affairs produced in Brussels barely mention these remote overseas regions, countries, and territories.

This chapter shows how ORs and OCTs could play a pivotal role, as forward "bases" for the promotion of EU's geopolitical interests in the Atlantic, Caribbean, Indian, and Pacific regions. The ORs and OCTs would benefit from this increased attention in terms of geopolitics from decision-makers in Brussels. ORs/OCTs could have a seat at the EU's CFSP "policy-making table" with respect to issues related to their regions and educate the Brussels-based EU officials about constructive interactions with countries in their respective cultural regions. Because of these regions, countries, and territories the EU can insert itself into the major powers' geopolitical rivalries in the Pacific and the Arctic regions and contribute to maritime security in the Indian Ocean. The EU should also play a larger, more coordinated, role in addressing drug trafficking and illegal immigration throughout the Caribbean and the Atlantic. This chapter does not advocate for an increased military presence in the ORs or the OCTs, but rather an increased EU "soft power" and use of these potential European "hubs" to promote EU's values in these respective regions. The EU should cooperate closer with the member states in which these ORs and OCTs find themselves, because these are on the front-lines of EU's external borders in increasingly geopolitically important regions of the world. Increased EU attention to the OCTs can only be a win-win situation to promote EU's global strategy.

References

Adler-Nissen, R., and P.G. Ulrik. 2012. *European Integration and Postcolonial Sovereignty Games: The EU Overseas Countries and Territories*. London: Routledge.

Baczynska, G., and L. Inti. 2023. Spain Calls for EU Solidarity on Canary Islands Immigration, *Reuters*, available at: https://www.reuters.com/article/europe-migrants-summit-spain-idAFKBN3151KN (accessed 27 October 2023).

Blockmans, S. 2011. Between the Devil and the Deep Blue Sea? Conflicts in External Action Pursued by OCTS and the EU. In *EU Law of the Overseas: Outermost Regions, Associated Overseas Countries and Territories, Territories Sui Generis*, ed. D. Kochenov, 307–351. Alphen aan den Rijn, Netherlands: Wolters Kluwer.

Boersma, T., and F. Kevin. 2014. *The Greenland Gold Rush: Promise and Pitfalls of Greenland's Energy and Mineral Resources*. Washington, DC: The Brookings Institution, available at: https://www.brookings.edu/wp-content/uploads/2016/06/24-greenland-energy-mineral-resources-boersma-foley-pdf-2.pdf (accessed 27 October 2023).

Charon, P., and J.-B.J. Vilmer. 2021. Les operations D'influence chinoises. Un Moment Machiavelien, *Institut de Recherche Stratégique de l'École Militaire*, available at: https://www.irsem.fr/rapport.html (accessed 27 October 2023).

Conference of Peripheral Maritime Regions of Europe (CPMR). 2009. *Involvement of the Regions in the European Neighborhood and Partnership Policy*, available at: https://www.cpmr.org/pub/docs/250_enpi-bis-en.pdf (accessed 27 October 2023).

Douah, C. 2023. Macron in New Caledonia: Why Is the Territory Divided and Will It Break Away from France? *The Guardian*, available at: https://www.theguardian.com/world/2023/jul/24/emmanuel-macron-new-caledonia-trip-will-it-break-away-independence-referendum (accessed 27 October 2023).

Edvardsen, A. 2023. Denmark Wants to Strengthen Foreign and Security Policy Cooperation with Greenland and the Faroe Islands, *High North News*, available at: https://www.highnorthnews.com/en/denmark-wants-strengthen-foreign-and-security-policy-cooperation-greenland-and-faroe-islands (accessed 27 October 2023).

European Economic Community. 1957. Treaty of Rome, available at: https://eur-lex.europa.eu/legal-content/FR/TXT/PDF/?uri=CELEX:11957E/TXT (accessed 27 October 2023).

European Environment Agency (EEA). 2020. *Europe's Seas and Coasts*, available at: https://www.eea.europa.eu/themes/water/europes-seas-and-coasts/europes-seas-and-coasts#:~:text=Including%20its%20outlying%20regions%20(territories,almost%20twice%20that%20of%20Russia (accessed 27 October 2023).

European External Action Service (EEAS). 2023. Overseas Countries and Territories, available at: https://www.eeas.europa.eu/eeas/overseas-countries-and-territories_en (accessed 27 October 2023).

European Union. 1992a. *Treaty of Maastricht*, available at: https://eur-lex.europa.eu/legal-content/EN/TXT/PDF/?uri=CELEX:11992M/TXT (accessed 27 October 2023).

European Union. 1992b. *Declaration 25 Updating Article 227 of Treaty of Rome*, available at: https://eur-lex.europa.eu/legal-content/EN/TXT/PDF/?uri=CELEX:11992M/TXT (accessed 27 October 2023).

European Union. 1997. *Treaty of Amsterdam*, available at: https://eur-lex.europa.eu/legal-content/EN/TXT/PDF/?uri=CELEX:11997D/TXT (accessed 27 October 2023).

European Union. 2007. *Treaty on the Functioning of the European Union*, available at: https://eur-lex.europa.eu/legal-content/EN/TXT/PDF/?uri=OJ:C:2007:306:FULL (accessed 27 October 2023).

European Union. 2008. *Outermost Regions—An Asset for Europe*, available at: https://eur-lex.europa.eu/LexUriServ/LexUriServ.do?uri=COM:2008:0642:FIN:EN:PDF (accessed 27 October 2023).

European Union. 2016. *Shared Vision, Common Action: A Stronger Europe. Global Strategy for the European Union's Foreign and Security Policy (EUGS)*, available at: https://www.eeas.europa.eu/sites/default/files/eugs_review_web_0.pdf (accessed 27 October 2023).

European Union. 2014. *European Union Maritime Security Strategy*, available at: https://data.consilium.europa.eu/doc/document/ST%2011205%202014%20INIT/EN/pdf (accessed 27 October 2023).

European Union. 2017. *A Stronger and Renewed Strategic Partnership with the EU's Outermost Regions*, available at: https://eur-lex.europa.eu/resource.html?uri=cellar:32f72786-b980-11e7-a7f8-01aa75ed71a1.0018.02/DOC_1&format=PDF (accessed 27 October 2023).

European Union. 2021a. *European Union Arctic Policy*, available at: https://www.thearcticinstitute.org/wp-content/uploads/2021/10/Continuity-with-Greater-Confidence-The-EUs-Arctic-Policy-Update-2021.pdf (accessed 27 October 2023).

European Union. 2021b. The EU Strategy for Cooperation in the Indo-Pacific, available at: https://www.eeas.europa.eu/sites/default/files/jointcommunication_2021_24_1_en.pdf (accessed 27 October 2023).

European Union. 2021c. *The EU in the Arctic*, available at: https://www.eeas.europa.eu/eeas/eu-arctic_en (accessed 27 October 2023).

European Union. 2022a. *A Strategic Compass for Security and Defence*, available at: https://www.eeas.europa.eu/sites/default/files/documents/strategic_compass_en3_web.pdf (accessed 27 October 2023).

European Union. 2022b. *Putting People First, Securing Sustainable and Inclusive Growth, Unlocking the Potential of the EU's Outermost Regions*, available at: https://ec.europa.eu/regional_policy/sources/policy/themes/outermost-regions/rup-2022/comm-rup-2022_en.pdf (accessed 27 October 2023).

European Union. 2023. *What Is the New Pact on Migration and Asylum of the EU?* available at: https://home-affairs.ec.europa.eu/policies/migration-and-asylum/new-pact-migration-and-asylum_en#:~:text=Voluntary%20Solidarity%20Mechanism%3A%2023%20EU,seekers%20and%20through%20financial%20contributions (accessed 27 October 2023).

European Union Annex. 2017. *Annex to a Stronger and Renewed Strategic Partnership with the EU's Outermost Regions*, available at: https://eur-lex.europa.eu/resource.html?uri=cellar:32f72786-b980-11e7-a7f8-01aa75ed71a1.0018.02/DOC_2&format=PDF (accessed 27 October 2023).

Europol. 2023. *700kg of Cocaine Caught En Route to the Canary Islands*, available at: https://www.europol.europa.eu/media-press/newsroom/news/700kg-of-cocaine-caught-en-route-to-canary-islands (accessed 27 October 2023).

Ewing, J. 2021. The World Wants Greenland's Minerals, But Greenlanders Are Wary, *New York Times*, available at: https://www.nytimes.com/2021/10/01/business/greenland-minerals-mining.html (accessed 27 October 2023).

Freeman, I. 2019. *The Common Foreign and Security Policy of the European Union. As Implemented in Its Overseas Regions, Countries and Territories and Its Influence on European Integration*. Tel Aviv: Independently Published.

Hernandez-Roy, C., and R. Bledsoe. 2023. *Building Barriers and Bridges: The Need for International Cooperation to Counter the Caribbean–Europe Drug Trade*, Center for Strategic and International Studies, available at: https://www.csis.org/analysis/building-barriers-and-bridges-need-international-cooperation-counter-caribbean-europe-drug#:~:text=In%202022%2C%2055%20percent%20of,affecting%20broad%20sectors%20of%20society (accessed 27 October 2023).

Kochenov, D. 2011. *EU Law of the Overseas: Outermost Regions, Associated Overseas Countries and Territories, Territories Sui Generis*. Alphen aan den Rijn, Netherlands: Wolters Kluwer.

Lavenex, S., and F. Schimmelfennig. 2009. EU Rules Beyond EU Borders: Theorizing External Governance in European Politics. *Journal of European Public Policy* 16 (6): 791–812.

Lorincz, A. 2011. The Importance of the Outermost Regions for Strengthening EU Foreign and Regional Relations, *Paper Submitted to the International Conference on The EU as a Global Actor—From the Inside Out: The Internal Development of the European Union and Its Future Role in an Interdependent World*, Berlin, July 7th–10th, available at: https://www.cvce.eu/content/publication/2013/11/14/9dc2fa22-e8b6-47f6-a1d7-eeb323148a07/publishable_en.pdf (accessed 27 October 2023).

Maiani, F. 2021. Unique, Yet Archetypal: Relations Between the European Union and Andorra, Monaco and San Marino. In *The Proliferation of Privileged Partnerships Between the European Union and Its Neighbours*, ed. S. Gstöhl and D. Phinnemore, 84–101. London: Routledge.

Milhiet, P. 2022. French Polynesia and France's Indo-Pacific Strategy, *The Diplomat*, available at: https://thediplomat.com/2022/05/french-polynesia-and-frances-indo-pacific-strategy/ (accessed 27 October 2023).

Nicolas, T. 2022. *Trafic de drogue: Un phénomène qui gangrène toute la société guyanaise*, available at: https://la1ere.francetvinfo.fr/guyane/trafic-de-drogue-un-phenomene-qui-gangrene-toute-la-societe-guyanaise-1265084.html (accessed 27 October 2023).

OCTA. 2003. *Overseas Countries and Territories Association*, available at: https://www.overseas-association.eu/about-octa/ (accessed 27 October 2023).

OCTA. 2009. *Political Declaration of OCTA's 2009 Ministerial Conference in Brussels*, available at: https://www.overseas-association.eu/content/uploads/2021/04/2009-MC-political_declaration-Bxl.pdf (accessed 27 October 2023).

OCTA. 2012. *Political Declaration of OCTA's Ministerial Conference in Ilulissat*, available at: https://www.overseas-association.eu/content/uploads/2021/04/2012-MC-political_declaration-Greenland.pdf (accessed 27 October 2023).

OCTA. 2018. *2017 Ministerial Conference Political Declaration*, available at: https://www.overseas-association.eu/content/uploads/2021/04/2017-MC-Political-Declaration-Bxl.pdf (accessed 27 October 2023).

OCTA. 2021. *Summary of the New OCTA Strategy*, available at: https://www.overseas-association.eu/content/uploads/2021/12/Summary-OCTA-Strategy-2021-2027-1.pdf (accessed 27 October 2023).

OCTA. 2022. *19th OCT-EU Forum*, available at: https://www.overseas-association.eu/19th-eu-oct-forum/ (accessed 27 October 2023).

OCT-EU Forum. 2022. *19th Overseas Countries and Territories—European Union Forum Conclusions*, available at: https://www.overseas-association.eu/content/uploads/2022/12/Final-Conclusions-EN-22-Nov.pdf (accessed 27 October 2023).

OR: Conference of Presidents. 2023, available at: https://cp-rup.com/en/home-en/ (accessed 27 October 2023).

Pousen, W. 2022. How Greenland's Mineral Wealth Made It a Geopolitical Battleground, *Foreign Policy*, available at: https://foreignpolicy.com/2022/12/18/how-greenlands-mineral-wealth-made-it-a-geopolitical-battleground/ (accessed 27 October 2023).

Reliefweb. 2021. *Aruba and Curacao Fact Sheet*, available at: https://reliefweb.int/report/aruba-netherlands/aruba-and-cura-ao-fact-sheet-july-august-2021 (accessed 27 October 2023).

Ruiz-Benitez de Lugo, L.B. 2022. North-West Passage. The Resurgence of Maritime Irregular Migration to the Canary Islands, *Global Initiative Against Transnational Organized Crime*, available at: https://globalinitiative.net/analysis/maritime-irregular-migration-canary-islands/#:~:text=Over%20the%20last%20two%20years,January%202009%20and%20December%202019 (accessed 27 October 2023).

Sellaslaghs, J. 2016. The EU's Performance in Latin America's Fight Against Drugs and Related Organized Crime. *Global Affairs* 2 (5): 527–537, available at: https://doi.org/10.1080/23340460.2016.1276403?needAccess=true (accessed 27 October 2023).

Suarez, B. 2023. Spanish Police Seize Cocaine Worth $114 Million From Cattle Ship, *Reuters*, available at: https://www.reuters.com/world/spanish-police-seize-cocaine-worth-114-million-cattle-ship-2023-01-28/ (accessed 27 October 2023).

Thebia, B. 2021. In a French Outpost in South America, No Secret EU Gateway for Fleeing Cubans, *The New Humanitarian*, available at: https://www.thenewhumanitarian.org/photo-feature/2021/2/3/french-guiana-cuba-migrants-EU-asylum-life-in-limbo (accessed 27 October 2023).

US Department of State. 2016. *International Narcotics Control Strategy Report*, available at: https://2009-2017.state.gov/j/inl/rls/nrcrpt/2016/vol1/253258.htm (accessed 27 October 2023).

Van Brunnersum, S.-J. 2022. China Failed Tts Arctic Ambitions in Greenland, *Politico*, available at: https://www.politico.eu/article/china-arctic-greenland-united-states/ (accessed 27 October 2023).

Restrictive Measures as a Tool of Foreign Policy: The Case of European Sanctions in Belarus

Nadège Boels

Introduction

Sanctions have been, and still are, an essential element in the foreign policy strategy of the European Union (EU), as they are established to be "an essential tool of the EU's Common Foreign and Security Policy" (CFSP) (EEAS 2023). The EU explains that the sanctions are written within an approach of political dialogue and complementary efforts, as such, they are not considered the first option used in cases of misconduct by the targeted entity. The goal of the EU sanctions is for these entities to abandon the targeted policies while minimizing the adverse consequences on the individuals not responsible or not influential in the targeted policies, principally the local population (EEAS 2023).

In 2020, Belarus was struck by waves of protests denouncing the authoritarian regime of Alyaksandr Lukashenka. The latter has been at the head of Belarus since 1994 and for 28 years, Lukashenka's regime has been characterized by authoritarianism, economic stagnation, and anti-worker social reforms (Buzgalin and Kolganov 2021). In August 2020,

N. Boels (✉)
Department of Political Science, Vrije Universiteit Brussel, Brussels, Belgium
e-mail: nadege.alexandra.boels@vub.be

L. Lika and D. Riga (eds.), *EU Geopolitical Actorness in a Changing World*, https://doi.org/10.1007/978-3-031-81160-9_10

Lukashenka sought to be re-elected as president of Belarus, but his re-election was met with massive protests across the country under the allegation of rigged elections, and a subsequent crackdown of the protests. After a slow reaction at first, the EU finally imposed several rounds of sanctions on Belarus.

Some months later, in February 2022, Russia launched a full-scale military invasion of Ukraine, with combat support from Belarus. The invasion happened under the pretense to demilitarize and de-Nazify the country. What was supposed to be a *Blitzkrieg* portrayed as a special operation soon turned into a full-scale war, killing and wounding thousands, and displacing millions of people (Mudrov 2022). While Minsk has not officially sent troops to Ukraine to fight alongside Moscow, the territory of Belarus was used for the launch of missiles on Ukraine (Council of the EU 2022c; Mudrov 2022; Polovyi 2022). At the same time, the territory was also opened for the transportation "of Russian military personnel and heavy weapons, tanks, and military transporters, allowing Russian military aircraft to fly over Belarusian airspace into Ukraine, providing refueling points, and storing Russian weapons and military equipment in Belarus" (Slunkin and Wilson 2022). Thus, strategical and technical infrastructure has been offered by Belarus to Russia, for which Belarus was once again sanctioned by the EU, with restrictive measures adding on top of the existing sanctions. Thus, Belarus is currently sanctioned by travel bans, asset freezes, and financial restrictive measures for both its internal repression and for its involvement in the invasion of Ukraine.

This chapter seeks to understand the place of restrictive measures in the foreign policy strategy of the EU by answering the following research question: To what extent can restrictive measures be understood as a tool of foreign policy through the lens of Normative Power Europe (NPE)? To test whether the sanctions established against Belarus fit the NPE narrative, this chapter makes use of text analysis. Text analysis looks for meaningful insights and findings in written or spoken texts. The findings can be related to the context of the text data, the content of the text itself, and the structure of the text (Bernard and Ryan 1998). In this analysis, the content of press releases will be investigated, seen as the press releases are the primary narrative-building tool of the EU. Thus, the conceptual framework related to sanctions and to the NPE rationale detailed throughout the chapter will be compared to the press releases of the EU, to analyze whether the motives for establishing sanctions in Belarus fit within the NPE rationale (Dunn 2015, 2018).

The EU has, in academic literature, been portrayed as a global actor diffusing its norms and institutional model through external action (Parthenay 2019; Manners 2002, 2006; Börzel and Risse 2012). The EU is also presented as a global actor adopting a strategy to export its model of regional integration and governance through the promotion of regionalism and interregionalism (Parthenay 2019; Wintgens 2018, 138). However, questioning the validity of this traditional conception, namely NPE, goes hand in hand with the ongoing questioning of the EU as model of integration and development (Lefkofridi and Schmitter 2015; De Angelis 2017; Murray and Longo 2018; Parthenay 2019).

To answer the research question, the chapter first proposes a definition of "sanctions" and portrays the sanctions as a foreign policy tool in general and in the EU's external relations with Eastern Europe in particular. To continue, the rationale of NPE will be explained thoroughly before testing the NPE rationale on the current sanctions established against Belarus. Throughout the full chapter, the strengths and weaknesses of sanctions as a foreign policy tool will be analyzed.

The conclusions of the chapter will show that the current sanctions against Belarus exceed the normative commitments of the NPE rationale, and rather favor the economic and security interests of the EU in Belarus. Thus, it can be argued that, through its system of sanctions, the EU is demonstrating a shift in its international actorness, from a NPE rationale toward EU geopolitical actorness. Moreover, the chapter will demonstrate that the EU is currently distancing itself from using targeted sanctions and slowly moving toward comprehensive sanctions again.

Sanctions: A General Overview

Sanctions as a Foreign Policy Tool

The Common Foreign and Security Policy

Sanctions have, for decades, been a consistent tool in the EU's diplomatic strategies (Giumelli et al. 2021; Kreutz 2005). To determine the role sanctions uptake within the current toolbox of the European foreign policy strategy, this chapter must understand the role of sanctions inside the EU's CFSP, the primary policy shaping the EU's external relations and foreign policy. The EU explains that:

> The Council defines and implements EU foreign and security policy based on guidelines set by the European Council. This also includes the EU's development and humanitarian aid, defense, and trade. Together with the High Representative of the Union for Foreign Affairs and Security Policy, the Council ensures the unity, consistency, and effectiveness of the EU's external action. (Council of the EU 2023a)

In the *Guidelines on implementation and evaluation of restrictive measures (sanctions) in the framework of the EU Common Foreign and Security Policy* (Council of the EU 2018), the Council of the EU explains that if a third country, entity, or individual does not fit within the objectives established by the EU in article 21 of the Treaty of the European Union (TEU), the Council of the EU will adopt restrictive measures against it, with article 21 stating that the EU will pursue common policies and actions to foster the cooperation in international relations. Moreover, the article explains that the cooperation is needed to, most importantly, safeguard its values, fundamental interests, security, independence, and integrity; and to consolidate and support democracy, the rule of law, human rights, and the principles of international law among other objectives. And to obtain those goals, sanctions may be implemented by the EU.

The EU itself explains that restrictive measures or sanctions play an essential role in their foreign policy strategy, as they are established to be "an essential tool of the EU's Common Foreign and Security Policy" (EEAS 2023). Sanctions are written within an approach of political dialogue and complementary efforts, as such not being the first option that is used in cases of misconduct by the targeted entity. The various targeted entities can be governments of a non-EU country, targeted because of their policies, companies providing means to the governments to conduct such policies, groups, and organizations such as terrorist groups, and individuals supporting the targeted policies or involved in terrorist actions, etc.

Targeted Sanctions

Another important observation concerning restrictive measures is the principle of "targeted sanctions." As Clara Portela (2016) explains, the sanctions within the scope of the CFSP are meant to be targeted sanctions or smart sanctions, seen as they are directed to the leaders and the individuals responsible for the deleterious policies. This term and rationale came forward after the "sanctions decade," the 1990s, where the restrictive measures harmed target populations, bringing forward the negative impacts of the sanctions.

The idea of targeted measures was developed in response to the United Nations Security Council's (UNSC) negative experiences with comprehensive trade embargoes to counter the humanitarian damage of comprehensive sanctions. The new normality is to adopt a combination of asset freezes and travel bans, directed toward the responsible individuals. Indeed, in the 1990s, sanction packages of unprecedented breadth were introduced against third countries, notoriously against Iraq (Rose 2005; Hellquist 2012; Portela 2016), causing the rapid appearance of humanitarian crises, due to the economic isolation of the targeted countries (Hellquist 2012; Portela 2016). Marc Lynch (2008) explains that, thus, "the anti-sanctions network" managed to foster "moral outrage over the sanctions, and at consolidating this outrage into an institutionalized normative and policy change at the United Nations level" (Lynch 2008, 167, 169, 195). Therefore, the consensus that existed around the sanction regimes stopped and the comprehensive sanctions were abandoned (Lynch 2008) to favor targeted sanctions.

Sanctions as a Foreign Policy Tool in the EU's External Relations with Eastern Europe

The EU can impose sanctions, regardless of the geographical position of the target. However, evidence suggests that the closer the target is to the EU, the faster (timewise and content-wise) the EU imposes sanctions (Portela 2005). In the literature, two main reasons for the faster sanctioning in neighboring areas are presented: the geographic vicinity of the target to the EU favors sanctions because of the preoccupation of the Union to the close area and reluctance toward external influence in the neighborhood (Hörbelt 2017; Portela 2005). Considering the Eastern European region, these two reasons resonate. First, it seems plausible that the EU would be preoccupied with the stability of the region bordering the EU, and the EU can be reluctant toward an ever-growing influence of Russia in the region. As Portela (2005, 63) explains: "This sensitivity for the European East is not only visible in the Balkans, but also in the cases of Belarus and Moldova. In both instances, the EU reacted with sanctions after a relatively low level of tension had been reported." Therefore, the probability is higher for neighboring countries to be sanctioned by the EU because the EU wants to keep these countries close and thus, sanctions are a real foreign policy tool in Eastern Europe.

Moreover, the restrictive measures of the EU are not simply and straightforwardly used to change the behavior of certain states and governments. Apart from potentially inducing change, restrictive measures shape the symbolic position Belarus holds in the EU as well. An important consideration is that sanctions not only mark the disagreement of the EU with Belarus but also signal a moral distance. Elin Hellquist (2012, i) correctly states that "regardless of whether sanctions successfully induce target change or not, they signal distance to some actors and proximity to others." Indeed, one of the core principles of sanctions is that they nourish international symbolism. And on top of potentially inducing a change in a target, sanctions convey a message to the rest of the world, ranging from disapproval of the target to protecting the domestic state's (or institution's) prestige (Lindsay 1986).

Weaknesses of Sanctions

Debates within the academic literature exist around the effectiveness and the legitimacy of sanctions. Various causes for the questioning of the effectiveness can be identified. First, it is known to be difficult to assess who needs to be the target of restrictive measures, what measures will successfully target them, and who will be suffering from the sanctions apart from the targeted people. As David Lektzian and Dennis Patterson (2015, 47) explain: "This work faces a major difficulty in developing a non-idiosyncratic model capable of identifying, first, which groups are likely to be in power in a targeted country and, second, what type of economic changes will hurt them."

Second, and strongly related to the first point, it would be naive to think restrictive measures solely impact the targeted individuals and authorities. A strong part of sanctions is that the sender country has resonance of the sanctions in its domestic economy. Maarten Smeets (2018, 7) explains that:

> Another important element to be kept in mind in sanction episodes is the fact the sanctions will generally imply economic costs not only to the target, but also to the countries that initiate the sanctions through the loss of business contracts and a reduction or interruption in trade (depending on the scale of the sanctions). These costs will have to be borne by the

consumer and taxpayer, which will be ready to accept this if they believe in the cause and the achievement of the objectives. The costs for the sender can be considerable and undermine both the economic rationale and the political willingness to engage in the sanctions.

Lastly, restrictive measures often lack well-defined objectives and rather chase "change." These ambiguous objectives prevent the EU to lift sanctions when smaller, clearer, and more attainable goals are reached. As such, now, the EU faces long-lasting sanctions, that it can difficultly lift, otherwise losing face and lifting sanctions when "change" has not yet been attained (Smeets 2018).

Strengths of Sanctions

Nevertheless, positive aspects of sanctions are noteworthy as well. An essential strength of sanctions is the fact they prevent military use in cases of crises. Indeed, sanctions allow to put pressure on a target without the use of military means. Smeets (2018, 9) explains that:

> Despite the weaknesses of sanctions and the lack of their effectiveness, it is definitely a preferable policy tool if it contributes to averting armed conflict, but the two often go hand in hand and sanctions are not always given enough time to be effective. Sanctions can (at least in the first instance) provide an alternative for military warfare.

Furthermore, economic sanctions offer adaptability by being capable of modification to suit the specific circumstances of the party at fault. Indeed, sanctions can be customized to match the gravity of the current issue. They can commence with less severe actions and then be progressively heightened if required, enabling a more intricate and adaptable approach. Third, sanctions can serve diverse policy objectives, including discouraging aggression, curbing the spread of nuclear weapons, advancing human rights, countering terrorism, and more (Smeets 2018). This versatility allows for a flexible approach to tackling a wide range of challenges.

Sanctions and NPE

NPE in Eastern Europe

The EU has, in academic literature, been portrayed as a global actor diffusing its norms and institutional model through external action (Parthenay 2019; Manners 2002, 2006; Börzel and Risse 2012). Normative power is generally thought to be the intermediate path between the traditional conceptions of civilian power and military power, differentiating itself by choosing norms over force while disseminating these norms (Laïdi 2006; Parthenay 2019). According to Ian Manners, the EU embodies this normative power by promoting universal values of human rights, democracy, freedom, and the rule of law (Manners 2002, 2006). Generally, the concept of normative power is understood to refer to the idea that an actor can "shape the conception of what is normal" (Diez 2005, 615). Thus, the debate on normative power discusses the way in which the EU asserts itself on the international stage and presents itself as a reference of norms (Santander 2009; Wintgens 2018).

To understand the extent to which the NPE rationale is applicable to the EU's foreign policy strategy, this section places the frameworks that determine the foreign policy in Eastern Europe within the NPE. The main framework to consider is the European Neighborhood Policy (ENP). The ENP aims to bring the Southern and Eastern neighbors of the EU closer to the EU, since 2004 (EEAS 2021). The European External Action Service (EEAS) explains that "this partnership is based on shared values, the promotion of democracy, rule of law, respect for human rights and social cohesion" (EEAS 2021). Bringing up the shared values and the fundamental norms of the EU clearly shows that the EEAS, the agency established for European diplomacy, presents itself as a normative power toward its neighbors.

Moreover, the ENP is supplemented with the Eastern Partnership (EaP), which is the framework within the ENP dedicated specifically to Eastern Europe. The EaP has been in place between the EU and Armenia, Azerbaijan, Belarus, Georgia, Moldova, and Ukraine, since 2009. And the EEAS here explains that "they entail significant reforms that aim to bring the Partner Countries closer to the EU by aligning their legislation and standards to the EU ones. Most importantly, they have the objective of improving the lives of citizens in a tangible way" (EEAS 2022). Again, this chapter can argue that the presentation of the framework of the EaP aligns with the components of the rationale of NPE. Thus, this chapter can conclude that in the presentation of its foreign policy frameworks toward its direct neighbors, the EU emphasizes the importance of values and norms as founding principles of the cooperation.

NPE and the Use of Sanctions

The use of restrictive measures can be written within various rationales of foreign policy strategies. The debate on normative power discusses the way in which the EU asserts itself on the international stage and presents itself as a reference of norms (Santander 2009; Wintgens 2018). Logically, European norms thus require specific attention, because, from the NPE angle, the international actorness of the EU outside the European borders is based on these specific norms (Parthenay 2019). Additionally, this chapter must then question the use of sanctions and the validity of the restrictive measures when the said sanctions protect the norms constituted by the EU. As such, within the rationale of NPE, the norms are the vector of European influence outside its borders and the sanctions are the tool to protect this vector. The sanctions established within the NPE rationale are defined to protect the norms and values on which the EU is based. As such, the European Council and the Council of the EU, who are responsible for the adoption of sanctions, are the protectors of European norms. And while the conception of sanctions within the EU does not pose a real problem, restrictive measures established outside the European borders are more problematic. Indeed, while the norms "shape the conception of what is normal" (Diez 2005, 615), the sanctions oblige (or else putting themselves at risk) third countries to accept a newly imposed normality.

However, as explained by Portela, in recent years, while the EU discursively says that it gives priority to human rights and democracy, in practice the commitment of the EU to normativity can strongly be questioned (Karacasulu and Karakir 2014; Portela 2005). Nilufem Karacasulu and Irem Askar Karakir (2014, 376–377) explain that:

> In recent years, the use of sanctions by the EU has accelerated, mainly toward Iran, Syria, and Libya, [as well as some East European countries]. There are two principal reasons behind the increase in the use of sanctions. One of them is that the EU's role on the international stage has grown considerably, largely due to its recognition of the impact of acting collectively. Another reason for the greater use of the sanctions' regime is related

> to the global economic crisis. Economic crises have weakened the use of soft power in the EU's foreign policy as budgets have been constrained. Within this context, the use of economic sanctions has become a useful tool as it does not depend on economic resources. Thus, it might be argued that EU considerations on normative commitments were exceeded by its security and economic interests.

To assay whether the EU exceeds its normative commitments, and thus invalidates the NPE rationale, the chapter now analyzes the various rounds of sanctions separately, depending on why they were established, thus testing the NPE hypotheses in the case of the various rounds of sanctions against Belarus.

Testing the NPE Rationale on the Current Sanctions Against Belarus

Belarus has, since 2020, been struck by various rounds of sanctions. Multiple causes for the sanctions of the EU can be identified. The EU itself identifies two causes: the Belarusian Presidential elections of 2020 and the subsequent repression, and the 2022 invasion of Ukraine by Russia and the Belarusian position during this invasion. However, a third cause for sanctioning should be added to this list, namely the forced landing of a Ryanair flight in Minsk, as this forced landing exemplifies the attempted shift of EU foreign policy strategy.

The First Cause of Sanctioning

In 2020, Belarus was struck by waves of protests denouncing the authoritarian regime of Lukashenka, who has been the leader of Belarus for over 27 years. In August 2020, the presidential elections were allegedly rigged in favor of Lukashenka, and these results were met with massive protests (Buzgalin and Kolganov 2021). The protests emerged in an already tense internal climate after Lukashenka defined the COVID pandemic as a "psychosis" (Grez 2020).

In the 2020 presidential elections, Lukashenka found himself opposed to Sviatlana Tsikhanouskaya. Formerly unknown to the Belarusian and European public at large, Tsikhanouskaya quite suddenly became the opposition leader after her husband, Siarhiej Leanidavic Cichanouski, was arrested in May 2020 while being one of the opposition candidates of

Lukashenka. Tsikhanouskaya then decided to run in his place against the standing regime. She quickly became the only candidate to be allowed to run, probably because of the sexist reasoning that a female candidate could never pose a real threat (Way 2020). Lucan Ahmad Way (2020, 23) explains that "coming from a candidate without political experience or visible political ambition, her calm, quiet presentation and simple language conveyed a raw moral energy that likely appealed to many." Tsikhanouskaya's campaign was centered around the promotion of free and fair elections, democratic change, and a return to the pre-Lukashenka constitutional order. Her campaign was met with substantial enthusiasm and the firm support of Belarusian workers and students (Way 2020).

However, this enthusiasm was not translated in the election results of August 9, 2020, as the alleged rigged results announced Lukashenka as the winner with 80% of the votes. That night, Tsikhanouskaya fled to Lithuania after allegedly receiving threats from the authorities (Way 2020). In exile, she established a Coordination Council, and reported that, where the votes were correctly counted, she received 60 to 70% of the votes (BBC 2020). The Coordination Council then asked Lukashenka to resign by October 2020. The proposal of resignation was not accepted by Lukashenka and the response of the police to the protests was a violent crackdown with over 400 incidents of protesters arrested and protest organizers tortured, alongside the reports of people facing administrative and criminal penalties for speaking out against the authorities between May and October 2020 (Amnesty International 2021, 2023). Even though the rigged elections were a trigger for the massive protests, for many, the basis of the protests of 2020 was the rejection of the existing Belarusian economic and political system by most of the so-called middle class in the country (Buzgalin and Kolganov 2021).

Following the unacceptable violence of the Belarusian authorities against the protesters and the rest of the population, the EU, through the EU leaders of each member state, called on the authorities to stop violence, risking being sanctioned if the opposite were to happen. Following the repression, violence, and intimidation against peaceful demonstrators, journalists, and opposition members by the Belarusian authorities, the Council of the EU imposed restrictive measures (sanctions) on Belarusian authority members on October 2, 2020 (Council of the EU 2020a).

In total, five rounds of sanctions related to the civic protests in Belarus have been established against various authority members and other individuals close to the Belarusian authorities. As such, 195 individuals and 38 entities have been sanctioned over the repression in Belarus during the five rounds of restrictive measures (Council of the EU 2020b, 2020c, 2021b, 2021c).

In February 2022, the Council of the EU decided to extend the sanctions for another year, considering the gravity of the situation in Belarus and the continuing repression and violence. Thus, the measures were extended to February 28, 2023 (Council of the EU 2022a), applying in total, to 195 individuals and 38 entities sanctioned by asset freezes and travel bans. These restrictive measures have been extended over time and over breadth, meaning that individuals were added to the list of targets and that the sanctions have stood for longer than initially planned, explained by the stagnation and worsening of the domestic situation of Belarus. Indeed, the Amnesty International Report (2023) states that, while the sanctions were established:

> The rights to freedom of expression, association and assembly remained severely curtailed. At least one man was executed. Torture and other ill-treatment were widespread, and impunity prevailed. The justice system was abused to suppress dissent and trials were routinely unfair. National and religious minorities faced discrimination. Refugees and migrants were subjected to violence and refoulement.

This Amnesty International quote immediately reflects the cause of the sanctions; the Belarusian population as well as the fundamental rights are impeded. From various discourses of the European institutions and European officials, the motive for the imposition of the sanctions in relation to the crackdown of the protests was clear: Sanctions are established for the protection of human rights in Belarus and for the promotion of democracy in the Eastern neighborhood. The Council (Council of the EU 2020c) published various press releases with the same message: "In response to the brutality of the Belarusian authorities and in support of the *democratic rights* of the Belarusian people, the Council today decided to adopt 36 additional designations. These sanctions target high-level officials responsible for the ongoing violent repression and intimidation of peaceful demonstrators, opposition members and journalists, among others." Moreover, the Council (Council of the EU 2021b) explains that "[t]he purpose of these sanctions is to put pressure on the Belarusian political leadership to [...] initiate a genuine and inclusive national dialogue with broader society. The EU stands ready to support a peaceful democratic transition with a variety of instruments, including a comprehensive plan of economic support for a democratic Belarus." From these two quotes, the normative commitments of the EU are immediately clear: The sanctions are imposed to protect the democratic rights of the Belarusian population and support the democratic transition within Belarus. This reasoning fosters the value-based motives for restrictive measures and, thus, the legitimation for the imposition of sanctions is clearly normative. Moreover, the sanctions that have been established are confined to travel bans and asset freezes. These two types of sanctions are the epitome of targeted sanctions, seen as they are confined to the people responsible for the malicious policies. Moreover, the subsequent rounds of sanctions, in which the list of targeted individuals broadens but not the scope of the sanctions reiterates the commitment of the EU to targeted sanctions. This first part of the analysis thus easily concludes that the first rounds of sanctions fuel the narrative of NPE.

The Second Cause of Sanctioning

The subsequent rounds of sanctions, the second motive described by the EU, were established against Belarus in March 2022, as a response to the role of Belarus in combat support with Russia in the invasion of Ukraine, starting in February 2022. On February 24, 2022, Russia launched the invasion of Ukraine through air attacks and ground invasion by Russian forces to allegedly demilitarize and de-Nazify the country. Initially conceived as a *Blitzkrieg*, it swiftly escalated into a full-scale conflict, resulting in the tragic loss of life and injuries to thousands (Mudrov 2022). Since the start of the war, the violations of humanitarian law have multiplied, including "extrajudicial executions, deadly strikes on civilian infrastructure and places of shelter, deportations and forcible transfers of civilians, and unlawful killings committed on a vast scale through shelling of cities" (Amnesty International 2023). As the war is ongoing, the full extent of the horrors is unknown, but as civilians are (possibly) targeted, the casualties are enormous (Kimhi et al. 2023).

To understand Belarus' position during the 2022 invasion of Ukraine by Russia, the events must be contextualized since 2014 and the Euromaidan Revolution. Since then, Lukashenka has advanced a dual position *vis-à-vis* Ukraine and Russia: dismissing Euromaidan and describing the Donbas conflict as a "civil war," thus supporting Russia, while simultaneously never officially recognizing Crimea as a part of the Russian Federation, despite clear will by Russia for Belarus to do so (Mudrov 2020; Kimhi et al. 2023). In the following years, Lukashenka continued this behavior, understanding clearly the economic and political importance of its southern neighbor. Moreover, in 2015, Belarus hosted a summit, popularly referred to as Minsk-II, between France, Germany, Russia, Ukraine, "the Donetsk People's Republic," and "the Luhansk People's Republic," two armed pro-Russian separatist states, to discuss the Donbas problem between Russia and Ukraine and elaborate a conclusive solution; the Minsk-II agreement (Golanski 2016). The Minsk-II agreement agreed to a new package of peacemaking measures, the Package of Measures for the Implementation of the Minsk Agreements, comprising an Organization for Security and Cooperation in Europe (OSCE),which observed unconditional ceasefire from 15 February, withdrawal of heavy weapons from the front line, release of prisoners of war, and constitutional reform in Ukraine.

In the first month after the start of the war in Ukraine, Lukashenka went to all extents to justify Russia's invasion of Ukraine, claiming that Ukraine was preparing an attack on its own, and that since Belarus did not start the war per se, their conscience was clear (Information Analysis Portal of Union State, 2022; Kimhi et al. 2023). These words were accentuated by the support Belarus gave the Russian special military operation (Mudrov 2022; Polovyi 2022). Indeed, even though Belarus has not officially sent troops to Ukraine to fight alongside Moscow, the territory of Belarus became a space for the launch of missiles on Ukraine. In addition, Belarus provided access to its territory for the transit of Russian military personnel, as well as the deployment of heavy weaponry, including tanks and military transport vehicles. This enabled Russian military aircraft to utilize Belarusian airspace for operations in Ukraine, establishing refueling points, and storing Russian armaments and military hardware within Belarus (Mudrov 2022; Polovyi 2022). Thus, strategical and technical infrastructure has been offered by Belarus to Russia.

Considering the perverse role of Belarus in the invasion of Ukraine by Russia and the subtle alignment of the Belarusian authorities with Moscow, the EU imposed sanctions on Belarus on top of the already existing sanctions. The EU, through the Council of the EU, issued a package of individual and economic sanctions against 22 individuals and has furthered its restrictions on trade, starting March 2, 2022. Obviously, these sanctions come as an addition to the already imposed sanctions established because of the internal repression (Council of the EU 2022d). Josep Borrell, High Representative of the European Union for Foreign Affairs and Security Policy/Vice-President of the European Commission (HR/VP), explained, in March 2022, that "Belarus' involvement in the ongoing unprovoked and unjustified military aggression against Ukraine will come at a high price. With these measures, [the EU is] targeting those in Belarus who collaborate with these attacks against Ukraine and restricting trade in a number of key sectors" (Council of the EU 2022d). In 2023, Borrell supplemented his previous quote by adding that the EU "[has] adopted new sanctions in reaction to the Lukashenka's illegitimate regime continued systematic, widespread, and gross human rights violations and brutal repression against all segments of the Belarusian society. Today [the EU is] also taking further measures against the Belarusian regime as an accomplice in Russia's illegal and unprovoked war of aggression against Ukraine. We stand by the Belarusian people in their quest for peace and democracy" (Council of the EU 2023c).

A week later, on March 9, the Council (Council of the EU 2022d, 2022e) adopted additional measures to sanction the financial sector of Belarus this time. These said measures are:

- The restriction of the provision of specialized financial messaging services (Society for Worldwide Interbank Financial Telecommunication, SWIFT) to three Belarusian banks;
- The prohibition of transactions with the National Bank of the Republic of Belarus (NBRB);
- The prohibition of the listing and provision of services in relation to shares of Belarusian state-owned entities on EU trading venues;
- The significant limitation of the financial inflows from Belarus to the EU;
- The prohibition of the provision of euro-denominated banknotes to Belarus.

Furthermore, the EU adopted a new round of sanctions over the repression in Belarus following the invasion of Russia, adding 12 individuals and 8 new entities to the list of targets (Council of the EU 2022f). Indeed, Amnesty International reported that hundreds of arrests took place following peaceful protests to denounce the invasion. Protesters were sentenced to detention, many were fined, at least one was executed, torture and ill-treatment was rampant, and human rights defenders were hindered from working; generally, the repression of the Belarusian population intensified (Amnesty International 2023).

Roughly 8 months later, on February 27, 2023, the EU decided to extend the measures for a year. As such, the sanctions as a response to the repression and the involvement in the Russian aggression against Ukraine now stand until February 28, 2025 (Council of the EU 2023b).

To assay how these sanctions relate to the NPE rationale, several factors need to be taken into account to understand the breadth of these sanctions. First, this study must analyze the motives of the EU to impose these sanctions on Belarus. From most of the press releases issued by the Council of the EU after February 24, 2022, it is clear that the motives for imposing the sanctions on Belarus and Russia are not solely normative. Indeed, the EU, through its institutions, explains that the motives are strongly related to the security in the neighboring region. The Council of the EU published that "[t]he European Union reiterates that it does not recognize and continues to condemn the illegal annexation of Crimea as a violation of international law. It remains a direct challenge to international security, with grave implications for the international legal order that protects the territorial integrity, unity and sovereignty of all States" (Council of the EU 2022c). Here, it is clear that international security plays an important role in the decision to impose sanctions. This reflection is reinforced by the next press release where the Council states that "the increasing militarisation of the peninsula by the Russian Federation, including multiple military exercises and the construction of warships, continues to have a negative impact on the security situation in the Black Sea region" (Council of the EU 2022c). Again, the negative security situation in the region of the Black Sea is a concern for the EU. A third quote to materialize this thought is that "the EU together with transatlantic and like-minded partners have been united in making unprecedented efforts to achieve a diplomatic solution to the security crisis caused by Russia" (Council of the EU 2022b). This chapter thus easily states that the EU has established sanctions on Belarus and Russia, because of the security crisis in their direct neighborhood. Of course, some normative considerations can be added to the motives, but it is clear that the primary goal is to have their security under control. This analysis does not make a judgment on the motives for sanctions, but rather explains that the normative commitments of the EU were, in the case of the Russian invasion of Ukraine, exceeded by the security risks in the neighboring region of the EU. Thus, for this first part of the analysis, the chapter can conclude that the EU has shifted away from solely imposing sanctions to protect the norms of the EU.

Secondly, this study must reflect on the breadth of the sanctions imposed on Belarus. The sanctions imposed following the Belarusian role in the Russian invasion of Ukraine are not confined to asset freezes and travel bans but have broadened to sanctions targeting the whole financial sector. Indeed, the prohibition of transactions with the NBRB, the significant limitation of the financial inflows from Belarus to the EU, the prohibition of the provision of euro-denominated banknotes to Belarus, and the restriction of the provision of specialized financial messaging services (SWIFT) to three Belarusian banks signify that the EU has distanced itself from the practice of targeted sanctions. Indeed, these restrictive measures are expanded to the whole financial sector of Belarus, and thus strongly influence the economy of Belarus. Lev Lvovskyi (2023, 1) states that

> [f]ollowing Russia's invasion of Ukraine in February 2022, the Belarusian economy suffered an unparalleled economic shock and entered a severe downturn. Belarus has lost almost all of its exports to its third largest trading partner, Ukraine, and trade volumes with its second largest trading partner, the European Union, have more than halved. A steady 10-month fall in gross domestic product (GDP) still dominates domestic economic trends at the time of writing. To cope with the crisis, the government has resorted to intensifying economic relations with Russia, hiding data in order to disguise the true state of the economy and increased economic interventionism.

From Lvovskyi's analysis (2023), the chapter concludes that the restrictive measures established against the financial sector of Belarus must no longer be considered as targeted sanctions. Their influence on the broader Belarusian economy and population is directly opposed to the aim of targeted sanctions and rather aligns with the rationale of comprehensive sanctions. As such, the analysis demonstrates that the EU has shifted away from normative commitments when imposing sanctions on Belarus over the past years. Indeed, the EU has established restrictive measures starting from normative considerations when imposing sanctions for the crackdown of the democratic protests but evolved toward sanctions established as a response to a potential security threat to the EU, namely the Russian invasion of Ukraine.

Forced Landing of the Ryanair Flight

Then, a third cause for the European restrictive measures against Belarus can also be added, chronologically happening before the Russian invasion of Ukraine. While the EU identifies two causes for the sanctions it establishes against Belarus on its official website, the forced landing of a Ryanair flight in Minsk, Belarus, on May 23, 2021, must be acknowledged as a cause on its own in this analysis. Indeed, the EU (Council of the EU 2021a) explains that:

> On 23 May, the Belarusian authorities, in an inadmissible step, forced a civilian plane to perform an emergency landing in Minsk. The plane, owned by an EU company, flying between two EU capitals and carrying more than 100 passengers, was forced to land by a Belarusian military aircraft. One of the flight passengers, Mr Raman Pratasevich, an independent journalist from Belarus, was retained by the Belarusian authorities and prevented from boarding the plane at the Minsk airport to its original destination. This is yet another blatant attempt by the Belarusian authorities to silence all opposition voices.

On May 23, 2021, Belarus diverged a Ryanair flight, flying from Athens to Vilnius, to Minsk instead. The pretense, a bomb threat on the airplane, happened to be false to arrest the dissent Protasevich and his girlfriend Sofia Sapega. The diversion sheds light on two major considerations; the diversion of this type is unprecedented, and the extent to which independent media is condemned in Belarus (Hinder and Pooja 2021).

Following the diversion, the EU established sanctions against Belarus. However, interestingly, the EU did not impose the sanctions solely based on the airplane diversion. Indeed, the sanctions established following the forced landing were established during the fourth round of sanctions, to sanction the ongoing repression and the diversion of the Ryanair flight. The sanctions established during this round were confined to asset freezes and travel bans.

This chapter argues that, while the EU presents the forced landing as equal to the repression in the motivation for establishing sanctions, the forced landing is actually a *fundamental* event in the EU's foreign policy strategy, as it marks the start of sanctions established due to security interests against Belarus. Charles Michel, president of the European Council stated that these circumstances pose

> a threat to the security of civil aviation and threaten international security; that is why the 27 Heads of State or Government agreed very swiftly and emphatically not only to condemn what happened and to demand the immediate release of Raman Protasevich and Sofia Sapega but also to consider adopting sanctions, including economic ones, by granting a mandate to the Council Charles Michel. (European Council 2021)

From Charles Michel's discourse, the analysis can clearly state that the EU has, in the fourth round of sanctions against Belarus, established sanctions due to the security threat of the forced landing, and not solely to protect the democratic and fundamental rights in Belarus. However, it is important to acknowledge that, while a security-related motive is used, it is not the only motive to impose the sanctions, because the ongoing repression is still an important cause of sanctioning in this fourth round of sanctions.

Thus, this analysis concludes that, while the EU has established sanctions against Belarus due to its normative commitments from the start of the repression following the presidential elections, these commitments were exceeded over time. The fourth round of sanctions established against Belarus marks the start of the shift in the EU's foreign policy strategy in Belarus, with sanctions established because of normative commitments and because of security interests. This first step away from NPE was simply a step away from solely imposing sanctions because of normative commitments, and the sanctions were still written within the rationale of targeted sanctions. However, the subsequent rounds of sanctions established against Belarus because of their role in the Russian invasion of Ukraine were the start of a definitive rupture with NPE within the EU's foreign policy strategy in Belarus. Indeed, here the reasons for establishing sanctions were purely security related and the sanctions were not targeted anymore.

Conclusion

The chapter has looked at how restrictive measures are integrated within the European foreign policy strategy. Given the traditional position that the EU has acquired as being a normative power, the chapter has verified the status of NPE in relation to the motives to impose sanctions against Belarus since 2020.

This chapter concludes that the EU moves away from the ideas of NPE, by establishing sanctions legitimized by security or economic interests, rather than to promote norms. First, the prohibition of transactions with the NBRB, the significant limitation of financial inflows from Belarus to the EU, the prohibition of the provision of euro-denominated banknotes to Belarus, and the restriction of the provision of specialized financial messaging services (SWIFT) to three Belarusian banks signify that the EU has distanced itself from the practice of targeted sanctions and rather switches back to comprehensive sanctions. Furthermore, the motive for imposing these sanctions is in contradiction to the rationale of NPE. Indeed, these comprehensive sanctions have been established as a response to security threats in the direct neighborhood of the EU, namely in Ukraine. The analysis clearly demonstrated that, starting from normative considerations for imposing sanctions, the EU evolved toward sanctions established because of security threats in the immediate neighborhood of the EU, thus being a direct threat to the EU's security as well. The chapter thus concludes that the EU exceeds its normative commitments by favoring its security interests.

Secondly, the chapter can conclude that the EU is moving away from targeted sanctions when the motive to impose sanctions is related to security matters. As demonstrated, the sanctions established following the Russian invasion of Ukraine are rather comprehensive and detach themselves from the rationale of solely using targeted sanctions.

The EU has been using sanctions for decades now as a tool of foreign policy, especially in the Eastern European neighborhood due to the vicinity of the region. Seen as the EU is moving away from normative commitments and seems to favor a more assertive international actorness, it is probable that comprehensive sanctions will play a preponderant role in the shift of strategy.

References

Amnesty International. 2021. Belarus, available at: https://www.amnesty.org/en/location/europe-and-central-asia/belarus/ (accessed 29 September 2023).

Amnesty International. 2023. Belarus 2022, available at: https://www.amnesty.org/en/location/europe-and-central-asia/belarus/report-belarus/ (accessed 29 September 2023).

Art. 21. 09/05/2008 Title V: General Provisions on the Union's External Action and Specific Provisions on the Common Foreign and Security Policy—Chapter 1: General Provisions on the Union's External Action, *Consolidated Version of the Treaty on European Union*.

BBC News. 2020. Belarus Election: Exiled Leader Calls Weekend of Peaceful Rallies. *BBC News*, available at: https://www.bbc.com/news/world-europe-53780685 (accessed 29 September 2023).

Bernard, H.R., and G. Ryan. 1998. Text Analysis: Qualitative and Quantitative Methods. In *Handbook of Methods in Cultural Anthropology*, ed. H.R. Bernard, 595–645. London: Altamira Press.

Börzel, T.A., and T. Risse. 2012. From Europeanization to Diffusion. In *Domestic Politics and Norm Diffusion in International Relations*, ed. T. Risse, 290–307. London and New York: Routledge.

Buzgalin, A.V., and A.I. Kolganov. 2021. The Protests in Belarus: Context, Causes and Lessons. *Critical Sociology* 47 (3): 441–453.

Council of the EU. 2018. *Guidelines on Implementation and Evaluation of Restrictive Measures (Sanctions) in the Framework of the EU Common Foreign and Security Policy*, available at: https://data.consilium.europa.eu/doc/document/ST-5664-2018-INIT/en/pdf (accessed 29 September 2023).

Council of the EU. 2020a. *Belarus: EU Imposes Sanctions for Repression and Election Falsification*, available at: https://www.consilium.europa.eu/en/press/press-releases/2020/10/02/belarus-eu-imposes-sanctions-for-repression-and-election-falsification/ (accessed 29 September 2023).

Council of the EU. 2020b. *Belarus: Alexandr Lukashenko and 14 Other Officials Sanctioned Over Ongoing Repression*, available at: https://www.consilium.europa.eu/en/press/press-releases/2020/11/06/belarus-alexandr-lukashenko-and-14-other-officials-sanctioned-over-ongoing-repression/ (accessed 29 September 2023).

Council of the EU. 2020c. *Belarus: EU Imposes Third Round of Sanctions Over Ongoing Repression*, available at: https://www.consilium.europa.eu/en/press/press-releases/2020/12/17/belarus-eu-imposes-third-round-of-sanctions-over-ongoing-repression/ (accessed 29 September 2023).

Council of the EU. 2021a. *Belarus: Declaration by the High Representative on Behalf of the EU on the Forced Diversion of Ryanair Flight FR4978 to Minsk on 23 May 2021*, available at: https://www.consilium.europa.eu/en/press/press-releases/2021/05/24/belarus-declaration-by-the-high-representative-on-behalf-of-the-eu-on-the-forced-diversion-of-ryanair-flight-fr4978-to-minsk-on-23-may-2021/ (accessed 29 September 2023).

Council of the EU. 2021b. *Belarus: Fourth Package of EU Sanctions Over Enduring Repression and the Forced Landing of a Ryanair Flight*, available at: https://www.consilium.europa.eu/en/press/press-releases/2021/06/21/belarus-fourth-package-of-eu-sanctions-over-enduring-repression-and-the-forced-landing-of-a-ryanair-flight/ (accessed 29 September 2023).

Council of the EU. 2021c. *Belarus: EU Adopts 5th Package of Sanctions Over Continued Human Rights Abuses and the Instrumentalisation of Migrants*, available at: https://www.consilium.europa.eu/en/press/press-releases/2021/12/02/belarus-eu-adopts-5th-package-of-sanctions-over-continued-human-rights-abuses-and-the-instrumentalisation-of-migrants/ (accessed 29 September 2023).

Council of the EU. 2022a. *Timeline—EU Restrictive Measures Against Belarus*, available at: https://www.consilium.europa.eu/en/policies/sanctions/restrictive-measures-against-belarus/belarus-timeline/ (accessed 29 September 2023).

Council of the EU. 2022b. *Ukraine: Declaration by the High Representative on Behalf of the European Union on the Invasion of Ukraine by Armed Forces of the Russian Federation*, available at: https://www.consilium.europa.eu/en/press/press-releases/2022/02/24/ukraine-declaration-by-the-high-representative-on-behalf-of-the-european-union-on-the-invasion-of-ukraine-by-armed-forces-of-the-russian-federation/ (accessed 29 September 2023).

Council of the EU. 2022c. *Ukraine: Declaration by the High Representative on Behalf of the EU on the Illegal Annexation of Crimea and Sevastopol*, available at: https://www.consilium.europa.eu/en/press/press-releases/2022/02/25/ukraine-declaration-by-the-high-representative-on-behalf-of-the-eu-on-the-illegal-annexation-of-crimea-and-sevastopol/ (accessed 29 September 2023).

Council of the EU. 2022d. *Belarus' Role in the Russian Military Aggression of Ukraine: Council Imposes Sanctions on Additional 22 Individuals and Further Restrictions on Trade*, available at: https://www.consilium.europa.eu/en/press/press-releases/2022/03/02/belarus-role-in-the-russian-military-aggression-of-ukraine-council-imposes-sanctions-on-additional-22-individuals-and-further-restrictions-on-trade/ (accessed 29 September 2023).

Council of the EU. 2022e. *EU Imposes Restrictive Measures on 160 Individuals as a Consequence of Russia's Military Aggression Against Ukraine*, available at: https://www.consilium.europa.eu/en/press/press-releases/2022/03/09/eu-imposes-restrictive-measures-on-160-individuals-as-a-consequence-of-russia-s-military-aggression-against-ukraine/ (accessed 29 September 2023).

Council of the EU. 2022f. *Belarus: EU Adopts New Round of Restrictive Measures Over Internal Repression*, available at: https://www.consilium.europa.eu/en/press/press-releases/2022/06/03/belarus-eu-adopts-new-round-of-restrictive-measures-over-internal-repression/ (accessed 29 September 2023).

Council of the EU. 2023a. *The Council of the European Union*, available at: https://www.consilium.europa.eu/en/council-eu/ (accessed 29 September 2023).

Council of the EU. 2023b. *Belarus: EU Prolongs Restrictive Measures for a Year*, available at: https://www.consilium.europa.eu/en/press/press-releases/2023/02/27/belarus-eu-prolongs-restrictive-measures-for-a-year/ (accessed 29 September 2023).

Council of the EU. 2023c. *Belarus: EU Adopts New Round of Individual Sanctions Over Continued Human Rights Abuses and Imposes Further Targeted Measures in Response to Involvement in Russia's Military Aggression Against Ukraine*, available at: https://www.consilium.europa.eu/en/press/press-releases/2023/08/03/belarus-eu-adopts-new-round-of-individual-sanctions-over-continued-human-rights-abuses-and-imposes-further-targeted-measures-in-response-to-involvement-in-russia-s-military-aggression-against-ukraine/ (accessed 29 September 2023).

De Angelis, G. 2017. Political Legitimacy and the European Crisis: Analysis of a Faltering Project. *European Politics and Society* 18 (3): 291–300.

Diez, T. 2005. Constructing the Self and Changing Others: Reconsidering Normative Power Europe. *Millennium* 33 (3): 613–636.

Dunn, W.N. 2015. *Public Policy Analysis*. New-York: Routledge.

Dunn, W.N. 2018. Stage' Theories of the Policy Process. In *Handbook on Policy, Process and Governing*, ed. H.K. Colebatch, 112–130. Cheltenham: Edward Elgar Publishing.

EEAS. 2021. *European Neighborhood Policy*, available at: https://www.eeas.europa.eu/eeas/european-neighbourhood-policy_en (accessed 29 September 2023).

EEAS. 2022. *Eastern Partnership*, available at: https://www.eeas.europa.eu/eeas/eastern-partnership_en (accessed 29 September 2023).

EEAS. 2023. *European Union Sanctions*, available at: https://www.eeas.europa.eu/eeas/european-union-sanctions_en (accessed 29 September 2023).

European Council. 2021. Remarks by President Charles Michel Following the First Day of the Special Meeting of the European Council, available at: https://www.consilium.europa.eu/en/press/press-releases/2021/05/25/remarks-by-president-charles-michel/ (accessed 29 September 2023).

Giumelli, F., F. Hoffmann, and A. Ksiazczakova. 2021. The When, What, Where and Why of European Union Sanctions. *European Security* 30 (1): 1–23.

Grez, M. 2020. *'Better to Die Standing than to Live on Your Knees', Says Belarus President Alexander Lukashenko at Ice Hockey Match*. CNN, available at: https://edition.cnn.com/2020/03/30/sport/belarus-president-alexander-lukashenko-ice-hockey-coronavirus-spt-intl/index.html (accessed 29 September 2023).

Golanski, R. 2016. One Year After Minsk II: Consequences and Progress. *European View* 15 (1): 67–76.

Hellquist, E. 2012. *Creating 'the Self' by Outlawing 'the Other'? EU Foreign Policy Sanctions and the Quest for Credibility*, Doctoral Dissertation, European University Institute, Italy.

Hinder, T.S., and V. Pooja. 2021. Threatening Aviation Safety: Case of Study from the Ryanair Flight 4978 Incident. *Global Research Review* 1 (3): 1–17.

Hörbelt, C. 2017. A Comparative Study: Where and Why Does the EU Impose Sanctions. *Revista UNISCI* 43: 53–71.

Information Analysis Portal of Union State. 2022. *Lukashenko: Belarus Will Stand Together with Russia in All Situations*, available at: https://soyuz.by/en/politics/lukashenko-belarus-will-stand-together-with-russia-in-all-situations (accessed 29 September 2023).

Karacasulu, N., and I.A. Karakir. 2014. EU Sanctions Regime: The Case of Iran. *The Korean Journal of Defense Analysis* 26 (3): 371–387.

Kimhi, S., A. Kaim, D. Bankauskaite, M. Baran, T. Baran, Y. Eshel, B. Adini, et al. 2023. A Full-Scale Russian Invasion of Ukraine in 2022: Resilience and Coping Within and Beyond Ukraine. *Applied Psychology: Health and Well-Being*, 1–19.

Kreutz, J. 2005. *Hard Measures by a Soft Power? Sanctions Policy of the European Union*. Bonn: Bonn International Centre for Conversion.

Laïdi, Z. 2006. L'Europe parie sur la norme plutôt que sur la force. *Etudes* 404 (1): 71–80.

Lefkofridi, Z., and P.C. Schmitter. 2015. Transcending or Descending? European Integration in Times of Crisis. *European Political Science Review* 7 (1): 3–22.

Lektzian, D., and D. Patterson. 2015. Political Cleavages and Economic Sanctions: The Economic and Political Winners and Losers of Sanctions. *International Studies Quarterly* 59 (1): 46–58.

Lindsay, J.M. 1986. Trade Sanctions as Policy Instruments: A re-examination. *International Studies Quarterly* 30 (2): 153–173.

Lvovskiy, L. 2023. *The Belarusian Economy Under Sanctions Since the Start of Russia's War in Ukraine* (SCEEUS, Guest Report Number 1, 2023), available at: https://www.ui.se/globalassets/ui.se-eng/publications/sceeus/the-belarusian-economy-under-sanctions-since-the-start-of-russias-war-in-ukraine.pdf (accessed 29 September 2023).

Lynch, M. 2008. Lie to Me: Sanctions on Iraq, Moral Argument and the International Politics of Hypocrisy. *Cambridge Studies in International* 107 (1): 165–196.

Manners, I. 2002. Normative Power Europe: A Contradiction in Terms? *Journal of Common Market Studies* 40 (2): 235–258.

Manners, I. 2006. Normative Power Europe Reconsidered: Beyond the Crossroads. *Journal of European Public Policy* 13 (2): 182–199.

Mudrov, S.A. 2020. Belarus, Crimea and the Donbas: Belarusian Attitudes to the Post-maidan Events in Ukraine. *Journal of Contemporary Central and Eastern Europe* 28 (1): 85–91.

Mudrov, S.A. 2022. We Did Not Unleash This War: Our Conscience Is Clear". The Russia–Ukraine Military Conflict and Its Perception in Belarus. *Journal of Contemporary Central and Eastern Europe* 30 (2): 273–284.

Murray, P., and M. Longo. 2018. Europe's Wicked Legitimacy Crisis: The Case of Refugees. *Journal of European Integration* 40 (4): 411–425.

Parthenay, K. 2019. Revisiter le pouvoir normatif européen: Le double visage de l'UE en Amérique centrale. *Politique Européenne* 63 (1): 96–124.

Polovyi, T.Y. 2022. *The Republic of Belarus in Russian-Ukrainian War in 2014–2022.* Riga: Baltija Publishing.

Portela, C. 2005. Where and Why Does the EU Impose Sanctions? *Politique Européenne* 3: 83–111.

Portela, C. 2016. Are European Union Sanctions "Targeted"? *Cambridge Review of International Affairs* 29 (3): 912–929.

President of the Republic of Belarus. 2022. *Оперативное совещание с военными [Operational meeting with the military].* Available at: https://president.gov.by/ru/events/operativnoe-soveshchanie-s-voennymi (accessed 29 September 2023).

Rose, E.A. 2005. From a Punitive to a Bargaining Model of Sanctions: Lessons from Iraq. *International Studies Quarterly* 49: 459–479.

Santander, S. 2009. EU-LAC relations: From Inter-regionalism to Selective Bilateralism? In *The European Union and the Rise of Regionalism: Source of Inspiration and Active Promoter*, ed. C. Franck, J.C. Defraigne, and V. de Monriamé, 263–272. Brussels: Bruylant.

Slunkin, P. and A. Wilson. 2022. How to Train Your Dictator: Putin's Control Over Lukashenka. *European Council on Foreign Relations*, available at: https://ecfr.eu/article/how-to-train-your-dictator-putins-control-over-lukashenka/ (accessed 10 October 2023).

Smeets, M. 2018. Can Economic Sanctions be Effective? *WTO. Staff Working Paper*, No. ERSD-2018–03.

Way, L.A. 2020. Belarus Uprising: How a Dictator Became Vulnerable. *Journal of Democracy* 31 (4): 17–27.

Wintgens, S. 2018. Chine-Amérique latine et Caraïbes: Un défi normatif pour l'Union européenne? *Politique Européenne* 2: 134–173.

Bosnia and Herzegovina on the Western Balkan Chessboard: The EU's Soft Power Strategy

Robert Dopchie

Introduction

The process of European Union (EU) enlargement has been widely regarded as a potent conduit for projecting its foundational values beyond its borders, thus constituting a pivotal instrument in the EU's foreign policy toolbox. Anchored in the preamble of the Treaty on European Union (TEU), these core values encompass human rights, freedom, democracy, equality, and the rule of law. Over time, the mechanisms employed for this purpose have undergone refinements since their inception during the late 1990s, notably in preparation for the substantial "big bang" enlargement in 2004. This endeavour necessitated a more nuanced approach, embracing an "acquis-driven" methodology characterized by strategic documents from the European Commission and the imposition of stringent conditionalities. Nevertheless, subsequent to the Thessaloniki Summit in 2003, the scope of EU enlargement expanded to encompass Western Balkan states. Tailored instruments such as the programmes of Community Assistance for Reconstruction, Development

R. Dopchie (✉)
Department of Political Science, University of Liège, Liège, Belgium
e-mail: robert.dopchie@uliege.be

L. Lika and D. Riga (eds.), *EU Geopolitical Actorness in a Changing World*, https://doi.org/10.1007/978-3-031-81160-9_11

and Stabilisation (CARDS), the Special Accession Programme for Agricultural and Rural Development (SAPARD), the Instrument for Structural Policies for Pre-Accession (ISPA), and the Poland and Hungary Assistance for Restructuring their Economies (PHARE) were devised to aid these countries—including Albania, Bosnia and Herzegovina, Croatia, Kosovo, Montenegro, North Macedonia, and Serbia—on their path to fulfilling necessary political and economic reforms. Yet, the consolidation of these varied instruments, each marked by their unique technical, financial, and geographical dimensions, ultimately culminated in the synthesis of these frameworks into a more cohesive structure: the Instrument of Pre-Accession Assistance (IPA) (Directorate for European Integration 2023).

The case of Bosnia and Herzegovina, engaged in the accession process, underscores the confluence of EU financial assistance and conditionality in driving domestic reforms. This chapter endeavours to meticulously assess the effectiveness of IPA I, II, and III in Bosnia and Herzegovina, guided by the central research question: To what extent does the EU effectively harness its soft power to reinforce the dissemination of its foundational values through the apparatus of IPA? The present study is based on books, scientific articles, official websites, as well as on data sourced from the author's personal communications with the Directorate General for European Neighbourhood Policy and Enlargement Negotiations (DG NEAR). The structure of this chapter unfolds as follows: firstly, it revisits Joseph Nye's seminal concept of soft power, albeit intricately contextualized within the contours of the European context; secondly, it conducts a detailed scrutiny of the EU's strategies to concretely translate its overarching goal of value propagation into tangible actions; thirdly, the chapter narrows its focus to Bosnia and Herzegovina, dissecting the multifaceted dimensions of the EU's soft power efficacy through the lens of IPA. By meticulously unravelling these layers, the chapter delves into the intricate interplay characterizing the EU's enlargement paradigm and its efforts to disseminate its foundational values beyond its borders.

Methodology

Soft power is everywhere and has been mobilized, though under other denominations,[1] for years until Joseph Nye first theorized it in his book *Bound to Lead: The Changing Nature of American Power* in 1991. It encompasses "the ability to achieve objectives through attraction rather than coercion or payments," deriving from a country's cultural magnetism, political ideals, and policy (Nye 2004, 11). This conceptualization foregrounds the propensity to attain desired outcomes devoid of coercive means, privileging attraction and endearment (Gallatori 2010, 20), signifying a shift away from the traditional fulcrums of force and wealth, towards symbolizing immaterial essence.

The EU has consistently demonstrated a penchant for employing non-coercive methods, placing its core values at the centre of the enlargement process. Over time, the Union has embraced a soft power approach that has evolved to align more closely with its normative principles, a shift that differs somewhat from Nye's initial intentions (Smith 2005, 105). Indeed, in contrast to Nye's (2004) original conceptualization, the application of the concept within the EU context leans towards the "EU reliance on what are seen as soft aid instruments and trade, rather than military might" (Smith 2005, 105). Highlighting the utilization of economic aspects within the EU's application of soft power is pivotal in this chapter, as it legitimizes the EU's deployment of IPA to incentivize (potential) candidate countries, including Bosnia and Herzegovina, to engage in substantial domestic reforms. Indeed, the examination of three types of EU legislation, encompassing Council Regulations (Council of the EU 2006), Regulations of the European Parliament and the Council (EU Parliament and Council of the EU 2014), and Commission Implementing Decisions (EU Commission 2021), which respectively pertain to the three successive IPA periods (2007–2013, 2014–2020, and 2021–2027), reveals that the EU's projection of its core values is most notably accomplished through prioritized policy-driven assistance, centring around the pivotal prerequisites for membership. The cogent correlation between IPA funding and the embodiment of EU values is particularly reinforced

[1] For instance, Edward H. Carr (1964) spoke about "power over opinion" in the book *The Twenty Years' Crisis*. London: Palgrave Macmillan.

through the lens of negotiating chapters 23 and 24 for EU accession, which notably address judiciary independence, the protection of fundamental rights, and the guarantee of justice.

In the context of the present study, the analysis of IPA programmes proves particularly relevant, as it offers a unique avenue to address a challenge that the existing body of literature on soft power has grappled with: the quantification of the translation of core values into concrete actions and the extent to which these values have been deeply integrated within the recipient countries. The data for this analysis is sourced from multiple channels. Firstly, information pertaining to the pledged and allocated amounts of IPA originates from personal communications with the DG NEAR. Secondly, to gauge the evolving embrace of EU foundational values in Bosnia and Herzegovina, this study relies on secondary data sources, notably Freedom House (Freedom House, n.d.) and Our World in Data (Our World in Data, n.d.). As previously outlined, the examination primarily focuses on the five key core values central to the EU's ethos, even explicitly mentioned in the preamble of the TEU. Lastly, concerning the temporal scope of this analysis, it encompasses the period commencing in 2007 and extending forward. This specific outset bears noteworthy significance, as it aligns with the commencement of IPA I—a pivotal juncture denoting the amalgamation of diverse support mechanisms, including CARDS, SAPARD, ISPA, PHARE, and the instrument for Turkey, into a singular and comprehensive IPA (Directorate for European Integration 2023), as previously highlighted.

IPA funds are characterized by their defined temporal spans and targeted emphases. For instance, IPA I (2007–2013) distinguished between—by then—candidate (Montenegro, North Macedonia, Serbia) and potential candidate (Albania, Bosnia and Herzegovina, Kosovo) countries through disparate conditions. IPA II (2014–2020) introduced a convergence of accession benchmarks, concurrently incentivizing political endeavours, exemplified by Serbia's negotiations on normalizing relations with Kosovo. Finally, IPA III (2021–2027) showcases a multi-year programming approach delineated into five discerning thematic spheres, encompassing transitional facilitation, cross-border collaboration, regional growth, human capital development, and agricultural and rural advancement (Directorate for European Integration 2023). Of course, it is unmistakable that any erosion of these values would act as a deterrent to the advancement within the accession process, imperiling the rights of citizens, deterring investments, and impeding holistic and sustainable economic growth. This becomes particularly significant in the context of beneficiaries under IPA III, where potential repercussions might extend to the privilege of visa-free travel.

Results

Building upon the aforementioned approach, an extensive dataset (refer to Fig. 1) has been gathered. This dataset highlights the amount of IPA funds allocated by the EU to Bosnia and Herzegovina between 2007 and 2022. This information is then juxtaposed against the annual evaluations furnished by both Freedom House and Our World in Data, appraising the adherence to the EU's five fundamental core values: human rights,[2] freedom,[3] democracy,[4] equality,[5] and rule of law.[6] Though an inherent degree of overlap exists among these dimensions of the EU's soft power, their collective elucidation provides a comprehensive grasp of each core value's manifestation.

Before embarking on the analysis of potential correlations between the allocation of IPA funds and the EU core values index, it may be of interest to underscore the importance of providing supplementary insights into the disbursement of EU funds to Bosnia and Herzegovina. As detailed in the section devoted to methodology, the data exclusively originates from the author's personal communications with representatives of the DG NEAR. During the National Program of Bosnia and Herzegovina

[2] Human rights encompass an array of indicators, including safeguards against governmental torture, political violence, and forced labour, in addition to the guarantee of property rights and the unfettered exercise of fundamental freedoms such as movement, religion, expression, and association.

[3] Freedom is dissected into political rights, entailing the participatory agency of individuals and groups within democratic processes, and civil liberties, encapsulating the array of rights enabling unencumbered personal expression and activity. The freedom dimension, during the years 2007 to 2013, was evaluated qualitatively due to the absence of quantitative analysis; thereby, trends have been visually represented to augment interpretability.

[4] Democracy amalgamates elements such as electoral participation, civil liberties, democratic preference, political engagement, and the efficacy of government representation.

[5] Equality is a study in the equal protection of rights and freedoms across the societal spectrum.

[6] Rule of law scrutinizes the separation of powers, the autonomy of the judiciary, the accountability of public officials, and the effective enforcement of civil rights.

Years	2007	2008	2009	2010	2011	2012	2013	2014	2015	2016	2017	2018	2019	2020	2021	2022	2023
IPA Funds (million EUR)	46.631.229	59.936.950	77.389.465	92.639.524	75.348.132	77.031.045	8.985.430	22.581.834	37.200.000	47.000.000	60.300.000	71.282.832	81.898.200	64.520.000	73.000.000	45.500.000	70.000.000
Human Rights (%)	85	86	86	87	87	87	86	86	86	86	81	81	83	82	82	81	Unknown
Freedom (%)	↗	↘	↗	↘	≈	↘	↘	61	60	57	55	55	53	53	53	53	Unknown
Democracy (%)	57,4	57	55,1	53,2	52,4	51,1	50,2	47,8	48,3	48,7	48,7	49,8	48,6	48,4	50,4	50	Unknown
Equality (%)	61	63	63	63	63	63	63	60	60	61	61	59	58	60	57	Unknown	Unknown
Rule of Law (%)	67,5	67,5	67,5	67,5	67,5	66	65	65	65	65	65	62,5	60	60	60	Unknown	Unknown

Fig. 1 Yearly IPA funding vs. Bosnia and Herzegovina's EU core values embrace (*Source* Author's personal communications with the DG NEAR [2022])

spanning the period of 2007–2013, a substantial EU financial commitment of EUR 467 million was designated, and it is notable that the entire allocation was effectively disbursed (DG NEAR). In the subsequent phase, under IPA II, an allocation of EUR 459 million was pledged, with a disbursement realization of approximately 50%, specifically EUR 227 million (DG NEAR). Within this comprehensive framework, a Cross-Border Cooperation (CBC) component was allocated of EUR 15 million an amount that demonstrated an exceptional disbursement efficiency of 99% (DG NEAR). Furthermore, an ancillary component, the Civil Society Facility (CSF), was introduced for the temporal span of 2011–2013, with a reserved allocation of EUR 8 million (DG NEAR). Notably, in 2014, a "Special measure for flood recovery and prevention in Bosnia and Herzegovina" was launched, with a substantial allocation of EUR 46 million, which was fully disbursed (DG NEAR). Concurrently, as the financing period drew to a close, a "Special measure on COVID-19 impact mitigation in Bosnia and Herzegovina" was enacted, endowed with EUR 23 million (DG NEAR). However, it merits acknowledgment that the disbursement for this measure reached a level of EUR 13 million, representing 59% of the designated allocation (DG NEAR).

Figure 2 elucidates a temporal trajectory characterized by conspicuous undulations, underscored by a pronounced upswing subsequent to the advent of the IPA. However, a discernible nadir manifests from 2013 onwards, a phenomenon explicable by Bosnia and Herzegovina's reluctance to apply the European Court of Human Rights (ECtHR) Sejdic and Finci ruling. The said ruling addresses the constitutional and electoral parameters within Bosnia and Herzegovina, which prescribe that aspirants seeking the presidency or vice presidency must affiliate with one of the three principal ethnic groups (Bosniaks, Serbs, and Croats). This regulatory framework effectively marginalizes contenders hailing from minority ethnic groups, notably exemplified by Jakob Finci (Jewish ethnicity) and Dervo Sejdic (Roma ethnicity), precluding their eligibility for these positions (European Court of Human Rights 2009).

The 2009 verdict by the ECtHR in favour of Sejdic and Finci resoundingly asserted that conditions tethered to ethnic identity as prerequisites for candidacy contravene the foundational principles of equality and non-discrimination (European Court of Human Rights 2009). Consequently, following a series of admonitions to Bosnia and Herzegovina, the EU concretized its warnings by significantly reducing funding levels over two

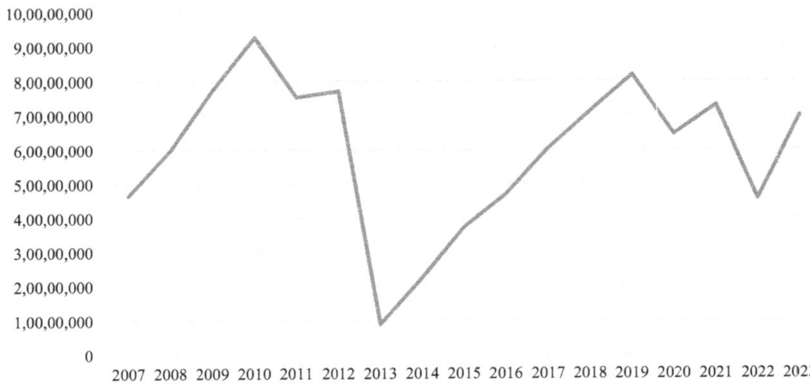

Fig. 2 IPA Funds (million EUR) (*Source* Author)

consecutive years. Furthermore, the keystone Stabilization and Association Agreement (SAA), pivotal for candidate countries on their path to EU accession, hinged upon the unequivocal adherence to the ECtHR's ruling within Bosnia and Herzegovina. Given the non-adherence, the SAA underwent a three-year suspension due to the failure of involved stakeholders to forge consensus on constitutional reforms in the wake of this judicial milestone (Perry 2015, 496). This intermission persisted until the EU changed its approach, enabling Bosnia and Herzegovina to reapply to the SAA without immediate exigencies to implement the Sejdic and Finci provisions. Rather, the Western Balkan state committed to executing requisite reforms in the future, culminating in the restoration of the SAA's operational efficacy in 2015 (Perry 2015). This shift in the EU's stance triggered academics such as Daviddi (2023), who requestioned the EU's (in)consistency in its engagement with Bosnia and Herzegovina.

The analysis of Figs. 2 and 3 yields valuable insights of academic significance. Figure 2 highlights substantial disparities in the allocation of funds across the three successive IPA periods dedicated to Bosnia and Herzegovina. Nevertheless, it is apparent that these funding discrepancies have not engendered an appreciable enhancement in Bosnian society's embrace of the EU's core values. In fact, the country's performance in terms of upholding and actualizing these values has exhibited a discernible decline over time. Neither substantial reductions in funding allocation (2013) nor more generous disbursements (2010 and 2019), have yielded an amelioration of the prevailing situation. These findings bear particular significance as they call into question the efficacy of the EU's well-established "carrot and stick" methodology, which has been a central focus of academic discourse over an extended period (Vandenberghe 2008; Gugiu 2012; Toneva-Metodieva 2014; Vajzovic 2016).

Hypotheses

Given the aforementioned findings, it is now imperative to delve deeper into the inquiry of why neither the carrot nor the stick has proven to be an efficacious instrument wielded by the EU. Accordingly, the ensuing section endeavours to elucidate the reasons behind the EU's ineffectiveness in exporting and disseminating its core values, delineating three pertinent hypotheses for examination: (a) the intricate political structure in Bosnia and Herzegovina, (b) the reluctance of certain ethnic groups to participate in the process, and (c) the external actors' illiberal interference.

(a) **Bosnia and Herzegovina's Complex Political Structure**

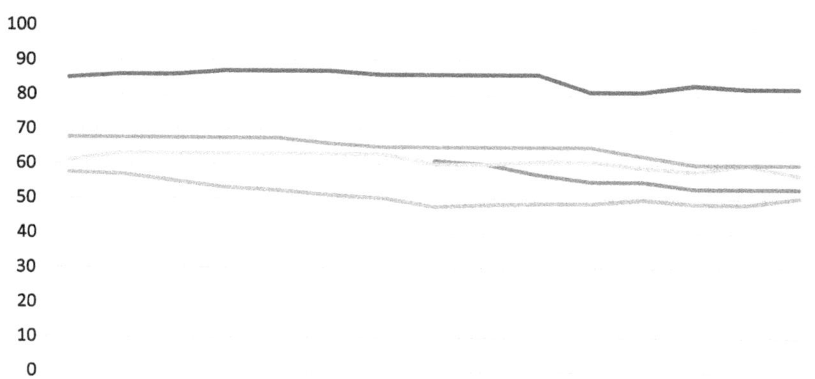

Fig. 3 Bosnia and Herzegovina index trends (2007–2021) (*Source* Author)

The Constitution of Bosnia and Herzegovina establishes a complex and asymmetrical multi-ethnic governance structure, overseen by the Office of the High Representative (OHR). This office was established in 1998 as part of the Dayton Peace Agreement (DPA) (1995) to supervise its implementation and promote the country's integration into Euro-Atlantic institutions. The OHR wields significant powers, including the authority to enact laws, remove elected officials, and dismiss civil servants, all aimed at ensuring compliance with the DPA and preventing a return to conflict. Moreover, with the purpose of ensuring peace between the constituent communities, the country's leadership is comprised of a Presidency with representatives from the constituent nations—Bosniak (50.1%), Croat (15.4%), and Serb (30.8%).

Bosnia and Herzegovina's territorial division corresponds with its ethnic partitioning and consists of four levels of government: state, entity, canton, and municipal (Official Gazette 1995). The country has two entities: the Republic of Srpska and the Federation of Bosnia and Herzegovina, along with the Brcko District, a unique territorial unit under international supervision since the end of the 1992–1995 war. The Republic of Srpska has 57 municipalities, while the Federation of Bosnia and Herzegovina comprises ten federal units, the cantons, each with its own Constitution, Parliament, Government, and judicial powers. The jurisdiction of the central government is delimited, affording both the Federation of Bosnia and Herzegovina and the Republic of Srpska the right to forge special relations ties with neighbouring countries, respectively with Croatia and Serbia. Moreover, alongside their respective state functions and prerogatives encompassing economic policy, territorial integrity, security, and governance at the local level, these entities are vested with a measure of autonomous discretion.

The intricate political landscape of Bosnia and Herzegovina presents a considerable challenge to the seamless integration of the country within the EU. At the national level, this task is primarily entrusted to the Directorate for European Integration (DEI), an autonomous entity operating within the Council of Ministers. The DEI assumes a pivotal role by coordinating legislative alignment, overseeing EU integration decisions, managing EU financial aid, facilitating the translation of EU documents, and providing vital communication and training support to advance the integration process. As such, it stands as the principal operational counterpart to the European Commission in Bosnia and Herzegovina's path towards EU integration.

However, it is at the subnational levels that the European integration process faces even greater complexity. Different regional institutions take charge of coordination within their respective regions, with the Office of the Government of the Federation of Bosnia and Herzegovina overseeing matters in the Federation, the Republic of Srpska Ministry of Economic Relations and Regional Cooperation managing affairs in the Republic of Srpska, and the Brcko District Department for European Integration and International Cooperation handling responsibilities in the Brcko District. Regrettably, there exist limited channels of communication and collaboration among these institutions, despite their crucial roles as the primary stakeholders in Bosnia and Herzegovina's access to IPA funds.

Furthermore, despite the adoption of a coordination system in 2016 by the Council of Ministers of Bosnia and Herzegovina, outlining an institutional and operational framework for collaboration among these institutions, effective vertical and horizontal cooperation remains elusive. The administrative structure of the country and the division of competencies among the different levels of government create additional hurdles to meaningful progress in the European integration process. Achieving successful integration necessitates not only overcoming the inherent complexity of the EU accession process but also fostering efficient collaboration and coordination across the diverse administrative entities of Bosnia and Herzegovina.

Lastly, it is worth examining the linkage between the division of target groups within Bosnia and Herzegovina and the EU's dissemination of its values through the lens of the soft power concept. While it is evident that the EU's soft power is crucial in pursuing its normative objectives, it is also essential to recognize that values cannot be simply imposed on a third country; it necessitates fertile domestic soil in which to take roots (Smith 2005, 105). Effective communication of a message or policy requires careful consideration of not only the messenger (the EU) but also the audience (the third country), as emphasized by Andrew P. Cortell and James W. Davis (2000). In Bosnia and Herzegovina, however, there is not a single, homogeneous audience. Rather, it comprises at least two distinct groups (the residents of the Republic of Srpska and the Federation), or even three (Bosniaks, Croats, and Serbs). The effectiveness of a policy ultimately hinges on how different groups interpret it, each with their distinct interests and concerns. Consequently, as the same message may be received differently by different groups within the same state, giving rise to issues of subjectivity, a nuanced understanding of the audience's nature becomes crucial (Mattern 2007, 98). Moreover, especially when complexity entails the generation of both positive and negative feedback from a particular policy choice or action, the reception within the target state will largely determine the ultimate outcome (Jervis 1997, 96–97). Conversely, when there are no well-established ties between the messenger and the audience, as seen when imposing conditionalities on (potential) candidate countries to undergo substantial economic and political transformations to meet the Union's membership criteria, there is a risk of the EU perceiving others not as partners but rather as objects requiring reforms (Smith 2005, 105).

(b) **Ethnic Group Reluctance in Participation**

In addition to its three presidents, 13 parliaments, and as many prime ministers, and approximately 150 ministries and 700 lawmakers for a population of just over 3 million people (Galdini 2015), another significant challenge has emerged as a hindrance to the implementation of EU values in Bosnia and Herzegovina. This challenge pertains to the reluctance of the Serb community to actively participate in the process of EU integration and, consequently, to fully embrace European values. Bosnia and Herzegovina, being a politically divided and post-war state, remains victim of ongoing nationalist rhetoric perpetuated by its political leaders.

The 2022 presidential and legislative elections in Bosnia and Herzegovina serve to underscore a discernible pattern. Notably, these elections reveal a marked disparity in the voting patterns among the various ethnic communities in the country. While the Bosniak and Croat communities elected representatives from social-democratic and pro-European parties, specifically Denis Becirovic and Dragan Covic, respectively, the Serb community, led by Milorad Dodik in the Republic of Srpska, demonstrated a preference for a divergent political ideology. This choice reflects an endorsement of values that deviate from democratic principles and encompass ethnic intolerance, as well as a denial of the Srebrenica genocide (Balkan Service 2023). These actions by the Republic of Srpska's leaders are in direct contradiction to the fundamental values that constitute the core of the EU's principles. Furthermore, Dodik's recurring threat of secessionism has drawn censure from the EU. Nevertheless, it has also compelled the EU to repeatedly make concessions since 2011, contingent upon Dodik's commitment to refrain from initiating a referendum on independence for the Serb entity, and in contrast to the United States, the EU has never been able to directly implement judicial measures against Dodik himself (Rettman 2023). Instead, the EU focuses its efforts on sanctioning the entity that he leads. For instance, within the framework of the Western Balkans Investment Framework (WBIF), launched in 2009 and operational for the period 2021–2027, with its objectives centred on fostering long-term economic recovery, facilitating the green and digital transition, expediting regional integration, and promoting alignment with EU standards, a deliberate exclusion of financial allocations to the Republic of Srpska has been instituted. In practical terms, while the Federation of Bosnia and Herzegovina has thus received a substantial allocation of 303 million out of a larger 2.1 billion dollar investment package earmarked for infrastructure projects throughout the Western Balkan region, the Republic of Srpska has conspicuously been denied such economic support (Euronews Albania 2023). These economic sanctions are the culmination of a series of warnings issued by the EU to Dodik regarding his secessionist activities, which have been identified as a serious threat to the territorial integrity and unity of Bosnia and Herzegovina. Furthermore, it is noteworthy that Dodik has faced indictment for actions that have jeopardized the DPA and his refusal to acknowledge the authority of the OHR in Bosnia and Herzegovina, currently represented by Christian Schimdt. The situation escalated further when Dodik, as the leader of the Republic of Srpska, issued threats towards Schmidt. He stated that he had given orders to the police to apprehend and forcibly remove the High Representative (HR) for Bosnia-Herzegovina if Schmidt entered the territory of the entity (Dodik quoted in Agence Europe 2023).

Interestingly, polls shed light on the fact that Bosnian political leaders are perceived as the second most pressing issue in the evaluation of internal problems facing the state, ranking just behind unemployment. This sentiment is exemplified by striking statistics: approximately 90% of the local population believes that Bosnia and Herzegovina is headed in the wrong political direction (NDI 2021). However, the reasons behind this widespread disillusionment vary significantly. While it is noteworthy that nearly 95% of the population in the Bosniak and Croat communities express support for EU integration and, consequently, the adoption of EU core values, even prior to the *acquis communautaire*, the same level of enthusiasm is not mirrored in the Republic of Srpska, where only about

60% of its residents favour EU integration (NDI 2021, 8). Instead, a majority of Serbs endorse Dodik's proposition that the Republic of Srpska should disengage from state institutions and delegate some competencies (tax administration, judiciary, intelligence agency, and national army) to regional government bodies (Boffey 2021). They perceive this as an internal matter, one in which the EU has no justifiable reason to intervene. Finally, the perception among Serbs that denying the Srebrenica genocide, a stance contrary to all five values defended by the EU, serves as a convenient means to evade accountability for poor governance and corruption is indicative of the limits of the EU's soft power in this federated entity.

(c) **External Actors' Illiberal Interference**

The final hypothesis, albeit equally plausible, posits that the inefficiency of the EU's soft power in Bosnia and Herzegovina is contingent upon the substantial presence of illiberal powers, notably Russia, and to a lesser extent, China and Turkey, within the state (Bieber and Tzifakis 2020).

Russia's interest in Bosnia and Herzegovina, as well as the broader Western Balkan region, is rooted deeply in history, spanning several centuries. The Russian Empire forged strong cultural, political, and religious connections with some Balkan countries. Amidst competition for control between Catholic Western powers and the Islamic Ottoman Empire, Russia emerged as a staunch ally of the Orthodox Greece, along with the Orthodox Christian Slavic nations of Bulgaria and Serbia (McBride 2022). In the modern era, following the war in Bosnia and Herzegovina, Russia sought to assert its influence through various means. This included sending a delegation to the Dayton peace conference, contributing troops to the North Atlantic Treaty Organization (NATO) led peacekeeping operation in Bosnia and Herzegovina, and securing a seat on the Peace Implementation Council (PIC), a multilateral forum responsible for overseeing the implementation of the DPA (Ruge 2022). This divergence was discernible in various actions, including the contentious threat to obstruct the annual renewal of the European Union Force in Bosnia and Herzegovina (EUFOR Althea), opposition to the PIC's assertion that the Republic of Srpska possessed no legitimate right to secession, scepticism regarding the legitimacy of the International Criminal Tribunal for the former Yugoslavia (ICTY), and a deliberate boycott of the PIC in protest against its endorsement of Christian Schmidt's appointment. Finally, concerning the Federation of Bosnia and Herzegovina's aspirations to accede to NATO, Russian diplomats conveyed a stern caution to the Bosnian tripartite entity, intimating that any such overture would be construed as a "hostile act" towards Russia (McBride 2022).

Moreover, as the Republic of Srpska and its stronger ally, Serbia, face heightened criticism from the EU due to their refusal to denounce the Russian invasion of Ukraine, a stance at odds with Bosniak and Croat members of the tripartite, Sefik Dzaferovic and Zeljko Komsic, Dodik contends that increased Western sanctions against his entity are likely to drive the Republic of Srpska to seek greater support from China (Katic and Milojevic 2023). Notably, it warrants emphasis that symbolically, China has already reaped tangible advantages from its engagement with the Republic of Srpska. This contention is substantiated by the conspicuous presence of Chinese representatives at the commemoration of Republic of Srpska's banned Independence Day on January 9, 2023, a development that was construed as provocative by the Bosniak and Croat communities within the Federation of Bosnia and Herzegovina (Radosavljevic 2023). The provocative character of this event is further accentuated by the historical backdrop wherein the observance of the Republic of Srpska Day was judicially deemed as unconstitutional by the Constitutional Court of Bosnia and Herzegovina in 2015 (Constitutional Court of Bosnia and Herzegovina 2015). Furthermore, resembling Russia's posture, China also currently refrains from extending recognition to the legitimacy of Schmidt as the international HR for Bosnia and Herzegovina (Tijana 2022). Additionally, China has opted to abstain from endorsing United Nations Security Council (UNSC) resolutions that aim to reassess the atrocities perpetrated against the Bosniaks in Srebrenica, a categorization that these resolutions have ascribed as acts of genocide since 2015 (Tijana 2022). These diplomatic actions undoubtedly pose substantial challenges to the EU's concerted efforts to disseminate and fortify its foundational principles via the mechanism of soft power projection within Bosnia and Herzegovina.

Discussion: Shifting Perspectives in the EU's Use of Soft Power Instruments Towards Bosnia and Herzegovina?

The efficiency of the EU's soft power approach in Bosnia and Herzegovina has demonstrated inherent limitations intricately interconnected. The argument posited in this section asserts that the DPA, which ended the Bosnian War of 1992–1995, established a political structure that imposed significant constraints on the country's development for decades to follow. As Fig. 4 illustrates, this political structure permitted two communities, the Croat and the Serb, to form what are termed "special relations" with the country that they felt closely tied to (Croatia and Serbia). While Croatia, having joined the EU in 2013, embraced the EU's core values, Serbia's close ties with China and Russia facilitated increased illiberal influence in the Republic of Srpska. Notably, Dodik's alignment with the regimes of Vladimir Putin and Xi Jinping, despite once being considered a moderate partner by European leaders (Latal and Toè 2016), legitimizes separatist rhetoric among the Serb population within the Republic of Srpska. This dynamic amplifies the strains on Bosnia and Herzegovina's political structure, a situation staunchly opposed by the EU. Indeed, Dodik intermittently raises the spectre of a secession referendum, thereby exacerbating the fragility of Bosnia and Herzegovina's political landscape.

In light of the limited effectiveness of the EU's efforts to promote its core values in Bosnia and Herzegovina through soft power such as the IPA, due to the persistent challenges outlined in Fig. 4, it has become imperative for the EU to break free from the vicious cycle. Yet, given the EU's concerns about the potential for fostering separatism and destabilization by attempting to reshape Bosnia and Herzegovina's post-war political structure, it has opted to prioritize the mitigation of external illiberal influences, which strengthen nationalist rhetoric. To address these persistent challenges, the EU has recently embraced a more assertive foreign policy approach towards Bosnia and Herzegovina. A clear demonstration of this shift is the recent decision to grant EU candidate status to the Western Balkan state.

Indeed, the European Council's decision to confer candidate status upon Bosnia and Herzegovina during the Brussels Summit of December 15, 2022, marked a significant juncture in the country's European path towards potential EU membership. This achievement came after a long

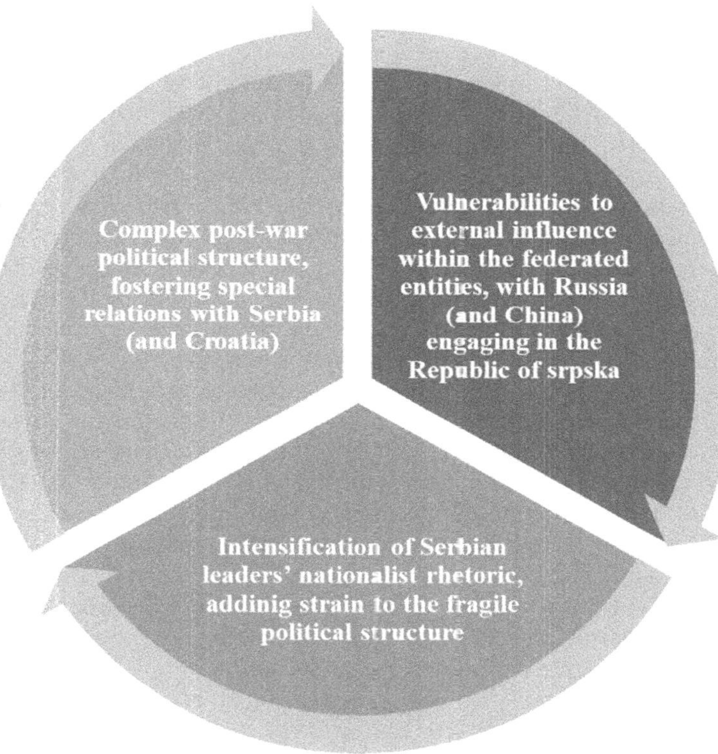

Fig. 4 Challenges to the EU's soft power in Bosnia and Herzegovina (*Source* Author)

wait, spanning over 19 years since Bosnia and Herzegovina, along with other Western Balkan states, was first identified as a potential candidate for EU membership at the Thessaloniki European Council summit in June 2003 (European Council 2003).

However, notwithstanding this major decision, the 2022 annual progress report on Bosnia and Herzegovina revealed only marginal advancements, particularly in the realm of upholding EU values (DG NEAR 2022). Therefore, the European Council's determination to grant candidate status to Bosnia and Herzegovina must be dissected through alternative lenses. As posited by certain scholars such as Veronica Anghel and Jelena Dzankic (2023, 488), the most notable pivotal element influencing the EU's foreign policy in the past year and a half has been the Russian invasion of Ukraine. Hence, if the EU chooses to confer candidate status upon a country in response to geopolitical factors, it signifies the adoption of a geopolitical stance by the Union. In this context, the EU is advocating for a more pragmatic approach, even if it entails a compromise on its core values as an unavoidable consequence.

Shifting towards a more geopolitically oriented foreign policy stance regarding Bosnia and Herzegovina appears as a strategic move by the EU to pursue its three primary objectives within the Western Balkan state: preserving the post-war political structure, mitigating the influence of illiberal external powers, and diminishing the nationalist rhetoric perpetuated by domestic leaders, often fuelled by external interference. However, as depicted in Fig. 4, it becomes evident that the underlying causes of the second and third issues are deeply rooted in the intricate and fragile post-war political structure of the country. Therefore, while the EU may aspire to limit the extent of interference from illiberal powers and curb nationalist rhetoric, the root causes persist. While the symptoms may be somewhat alleviated, the underlying causes of the issue remain resilient.

The EU's failure to effectively influence the development of post-war societies is evident in its approach to Bosnia and Herzegovina. On the one hand, it grants candidate country status to the state, but on the other hand, it maintains that a state under indefinite international supervision of the OHR—which the EU officially continues to support—will not gain EU membership unless its state structure undergoes significant changes. However, as this structure continues to provide a platform for the growing influence of illiberal powers, thus indirectly legitimizing nationalist rhetoric, the EU remains steadfast in its commitment to maintaining the status quo. This persistence in preserving the existing structure inadvertently underscores the EU's enduring foreign policy inconsistencies, as the root causes of the issue do not evolve. These inconsistencies in the EU's foreign policy towards Bosnia and Herzegovina not only hinder the transition to a more geopolitically oriented stance but also diminish the embrace of its foundational values, while it is precisely its values that have historically underpinned the Union's reputation as a soft power force in global politics.

Conclusion

This chapter has scrutinized the efficiency of the EU's soft power dynamics concerning its relations with Bosnia and Herzegovina, a candidate country. The central inquiry revolves around the following research question: To what extent does the EU effectively harness its soft power to reinforce the dissemination of its foundational values through the apparatus of IPA? It initially establishes the link between soft power and IPA, identifying these as the most potent tools for disseminating the Union's fundamental principles (human rights, freedom, democracy, equality, and the rule of law). Subsequently, this study highlights the limited progress in the adoption of these values in Bosnia and Herzegovina and questions the effectiveness of the carrot-and-stick approach employed by the EU in pursuit of this objective. To elucidate the reasons for this lack of progress, three hypotheses are presented: the post-war political structure of the Western Balkan state, persistent interference from illiberal powers, and the escalating nationalist rhetoric of the Republic of Srpska's leaders. These three significant challenges place the EU's foreign policy in a precarious and contradictory position. While the post-DPA political structure in Bosnia and Herzegovina remains vulnerable to external interference and nationalist sentiments, the EU struggles to provide a coherent solution to this dilemma. Furthermore, the EU's attempt to counter both external interference and Bosnian Serb nationalism takes a more assertive stance, which, as a result, reinforces the status quo by emphasizing that any alteration to the political structure is unacceptable and would distance Bosnia and Herzegovina further from EU membership. Thus, the recent designation of candidate country status for Bosnia and Herzegovina does not signify substantial progress in aligning the country with EU values. Rather, it appears to mirror a geopolitical shift in the EU's foreign policy that has emerged since the onset of the 2022 Russian invasion of Ukraine.

Nevertheless, it is also imperative to temper the assumption that the EU's recent geopolitical turn implies a strong diminishment in its commitment to upholding its core values. The temporal framework delineated by IPA III (2021–2027) underscores the EU's sustained engagement in a long-term process. While the decision to grant candidate country status may have been influenced by clear geopolitical considerations, it does not inherently signify a departure from the EU's commitment to regulating the remainder of Bosnia and Herzegovina's path towards EU accession, particularly with regard to the adoption of the EU's central values. Moreover, the IPA remain at the heart of Bosnia and Herzegovina's EU accession process. These mechanisms are deeply rooted in the application of soft power, strategically employed to ensure that the EU's core values are comprehensively embraced and respected within (potential) candidate countries. Therefore, despite the geopolitical dimensions that may have influenced the candidate status decision, the EU's commitment to fostering adherence to its values persists as an integral component of its engagement with Bosnia and Herzegovina.

References

Agence Europe. 2023. Milorad Dodik Orders Police to Arrest and Expel High Representative Christian Schmidt If He Tries to Return to Republika Srspka. *Europe Daily Bulletin No. 13246*, September 9, available at: https://agenceurope.eu/en/bulletin/article/13246/20 (accessed 3 October 2023).

Anghel, V., and J. Dzankic. 2023. Wartime EU: Consequences of the Russia-Ukraine War on the Enlargement Process. *Journal of European Integration* 45 (3): 487–501.

Balkan Service. 2023. Prosecutor Files Case Against Bosnian Serb Leader Dodik for Genocide Denial. Radio Free Europe/Radio Liberty, March 6, available at: https://www.rferl.org/a/bosnia-dodik-genocide-denial/32305177.html (accessed 21 September 2023).

Bieber, F., and N. Tzifakis. 2020. *The Western Balkans in the World: Linkage and Relations with Non-Western Countries*. London: Routledge.

Boffey, D. 2021. Bosnian Serb Leader: Putin and China Will Help If West Imposes Sanctions. *The Guardian*, November 29, available at https://www.theguardian.com/world/2021/nov/29/bosnian-serb-leader-putin-and-china-will-help-if-west-imposes-sanctions (accessed 21 September 2023).

Constitutional Court of Bosnia and Herzegovina. 2015. Bakir Izetbegovic, Clan Predsjednictva Bosne i Hercegovine, November 26. *Official Gazette BiH 100/15*. No. U-3/13.

Cortell, A.P., and J.W. Davis. 2000. Understanding the Domestic Impact of International Norms: A Research Agenda. *International Studies Review* 2 (1): 65–87.

Council of the EU. 2006. Council Regulation (EU) No 1085/2006 of 17 July 2006 Establishing an Instrument for Pre-Accession Assistance (IPA), *L. 210/82*.

Daviddi, R. 2023. Moving the Western Balkans Towards the European Union: The Daunting Case of Bosnia and Herzegovina. In *Integrating the Western Balkans into the EU: Overcoming Mutual Misperceptions*, ed. M. Uvalic, 55–80. Basel: Springer Nature Switzerland.

Directorate for European Integration (DEI). 2023. *Instrument for Pre-Accession Assistance*, available at: https://www.dei.gov.ba/en/instrument-for-pre-accession-assistance (accessed 27 September 2023).

Directorate-General for Neighbourhood and Enlargement Negotiations (DG NEAR). 2022. *Bosnia and Herzegovina Report 2022*, Brussels, available at: https://neighbourhood-enlargement.ec.europa.eu/bosnia-and-herzegovina-report-2022_en (accessed 30 September 2023).

EU Commission. 2021. Commission Implementing Decision of 10.12.2021 adopting the Instrument for Pre-Accession Assistance (IPA III) Programming Framework for the period 2021–2027. *C(2021) 8914 final*, available at: https://neighbourhood-enlargement.ec.europa.eu/system/files/2022-01/C_2021_8914_COMMISSION_IMPLEMENTING_DECISION_EN.pdf (accessed 1 September 2023).

EU Parliament and Council of the EU. 2014. Regulation (EU) No 231/2014 of the European Parliament and of the Council of 11 March 2014 Establishing an Instrument for Pre-Accession Assistance (IPA II). *L. 77/11*, available at: https://eur-lex.europa.eu/LexUriServ/LexUriServ.do?uri=OJ:L:2014:077:0011:0026:EN:PDF#:~:text=The%20Instrument%20for%20Pre%E2%80%93accession,to%20comply%20with%20the%20Union's (accessed 1 September 2023).

Euronews Albania. 2023. EU Excludes Kosovo, Montenegro and Republika Srpska Entity from grants, July 4, available at: https://euronews.al/en/eu-excludes-kosovo-montenegro-and-republika-srpska-entity-from-grants/ (accessed 22 September 2023).

European Council. 2003. EU-Western Balkans Summit: Thessaloniki Declaration, June 21, available at: https://ec.europa.eu/commission/presscorner/detail/en/PRES_03_163 (accessed 3 July 2023).

European Court of Human Rights. 2009. Sejdic and Finci v. Bosnia and Herzegovina [GC]—27996/06 and 34836/06, *No. 125*, available at: https://eur-lex.europa.eu/legal-content/EN/TXT/PDF/?uri=CELEX:32006R1085&qid=1693313968512 (accessed 6 September 2023).

Freedom House. (no date). Expanding Freedom and Democracy, available at: https://freedomhouse.org/ (accessed 23 August 2023).

Galdini, F. 2015. The Country with Three Presidents, 13 Prime Ministers, 700 Lawmakers, and No Decent Government, *Quartz*, November 6, available at: https://qz.com/541301/the-country-with-three-presidents-13-prime-ministers-700-lawmakers-and-no-decent-government (accessed 21 September 2023).

Gallatori, G. 2010. *Cosmopolitan Power in International Relations: A Synthesis of Realism, Neoliberalism, and Constructivism*. Cambridge: Cambridge University Press.

Gugiu, M.R. 2012. EU Enlargement and Anticorruption: Lessons Learned from Romania. *Journal of European Integration* 34 (5): 429–446.

Jervis, R. 1997. *System Effects: Complexity in Political and Social Life*. Princeton: Princeton University Press.

Katic, G., and M. Milojevic. 2023. Bosnian Serbs Chase Closer Ties with Beijing Amid Western Pressure, Looming Debt. Radio Free Europe/Radio Liberty, May 14, available at: https://www.rferl.org/China-In-Eurasia/2023/5/14 (accessed 29 September 2023).

Latal, S., and R. Toè. 2016. Milorad Dodik: From Pro-US Moderate to Bosnian-Serb Separatist. *BalkanInsight*, November 14, available at: https://balkaninsight.com/2016/09/14/milorad-dodik-from-pro-us-moderate-to-bosnian-serb-separatist-09-13-2016/ (accessed 4 October 2023).

Mattern, J.B. 2007. Why "Soft Power" Isn't so Soft: Representational Force and Attraction in World Politics. In *Power in World Politics*, ed. F.S. Berenkötter and M.J. Williams, 98–119. London: Routledge.

McBride, J. 2022. Russia's Influence in the Balkans, Council on Foreign Relations, December 2, available at: https://www.cfr.org/backgrounder/russias-influence-balkans (accessed 21 September 2023).

Nye, J. 1991. *Bound to Lead: The Changing Nature of American Power*. New York: Basic Books.

Nye, J. 2004. *Soft Power: The Means to Success in World Politics*. New York: Public Affairs.

Nye, J. 2011. *The Future of Power*. New York: Public Affairs.

Official Gazette. 1995. Constitution of the Federation of Bosnia and Herzegovina.

Our World in Data. n.d. Research and Data to Make Progress Against the World's Largest Problems, available at: https://ourworldindata.org (accessed 21 September 2023).

Perry, V. 2015. Constitutional Reform in Bosnia and Herzegovina: Does the Road to Confederation Go Through the EU? *International Peacekeeping* 22 (5): 490–510.

Radosavljevic, Z. 2023. Bosnia Braces for Secessionist Serb Parade, *Euractiv*, January 9, available at: https://www.euractiv.com/section/politics/news/bosnia-braces-for-secessionist-serb-parade/ (accessed 3 October 2023).

Rettman, A. 2023. Bosnian Serb President on Collision Course with EU, *EUobserver*, Brussels, July 3, available at: https://euobserver.com/world/157223 (accessed 3 October 2023).

Ruge, M. 2022. The Past and the Furious: How Russia's Revisionism Threatens Bosnia', *European Council on Foreign Relations*, September 13, available at: https://ecfr.eu/publication/the-past-and-the-furious-how-russias-revisionism-threatens-bosnia/ (accessed 17 September 2023).

Smith, K.E. 2005. Beyond the Civilian Power EU Debate. *Politique Européenne* 17 (3): 63–82.

Tijana, C. 2022. Chinese Influence in Bosnia and Herzegovina, Center for European Policy Analysis, September 7, available at: https://cepa.org/comprehensive-reports/chinese-influence-in-bosnia-and-herzegovina/#footnote_28_7126 (accessed 5 October 2023).

Toneva-Metodieva, L. 2014. Beyond the Carrots and Sticks Paradigm: Rethinking the Cooperation and Verification Mechanism Experience of Bulgaria and Romania. *Perspectives on European Politics and Society* 15 (4): 534–551.

Vajzovic, E. 2016. Bosnia and Herzegovina in the EU Integration Process: A Carrot-and-Stick Marathon. In *Europe and the Post-Yugoslav Space*, ed. B. Radeljic, 154–182. London: Routledge.

Vandenberghe, J. 2008. On Carrots and Sticks: The Social Dimension of EU Trade Policy. *European Foreign Affairs Review* 13 (4): 561–581.

EU's Geopolitical Approach in the Eastern Neighbourhood and the Strategic Influence of the Euro-Atlantic Alliance Framework

Valentin Naumescu and Oana Poiană

Introduction

Geopolitics is back. After the Russian expansionist ambitions to restore the former Soviet Union's sphere of influence in Eastern Europe led to a full-scale invasion of Ukraine in February 2022, Europe "rediscovered" the face of war and geopolitical tensions. The West learned that the repeated alerts and warning messages from Central and Eastern Europe (CEE) regarding Russia's preparations for aggression were correct. The Russian invasion of Georgia in August 2008 and the annexation of Crimea in March 2014 were just the first two steps of Vladimir Putin's War.

The European Union's (EU) Eastern neighbourhood is caught nowadays in this strategic, geopolitical, hybrid confrontation launched by Moscow in order to prevent the democratic advance of the West and to

---

V. Naumescu (✉) · O. Poiană
Babeş-Bolyai University Cluj, Cluj-Napoca, Romania
e-mail: valentin.naumescu@ubbcluj.ro

O. Poiană
e-mail: poiana.oana@ubbcluj.ro

L. Lika and D. Riga (eds.), *EU Geopolitical Actorness in a Changing World*, https://doi.org/10.1007/978-3-031-81160-9_12

keep captive in the "*Russkyi Mir*" (the "Russian world")[1]—a nationalist and expansionist strategy—the post-Soviet sovereign countries. The "Russian world" thus became Putin's equivalent concept of the third version of the Russian Empire, after the failure of the Tzarist and Soviet first two versions.

Once the "region of the Eastern Partnership (EaP)", as it was defined in 2009, the EU's Eastern neighbourhood needs today new approaches and instruments. The region faces new realities, different challenges, and revised aspirations, but also growing differences between the countries. The study observes a much higher level of pro-European ambitions in Ukraine and the Republic of Moldova, severely deteriorated democratic conditions in Belarus (no longer an "Eastern Partner"), political duplicity in Georgia combined with high pro-EU public support in the Georgian society, and ambiguity in relations with the West in Armenia and Azerbaijan.

Since 2009, the EaP has been the EU's main political initiative for the six post-Soviet European republics who remained outside the 2004, 2007, and 2013 EU enlargements. For several self-evident reasons, the EaP in its initial form became somehow obsolete and ineffective today, while the heterogeneity of the Eastern neighbourhood has increased. The war changed the whole landscape of the region. Most probably, the EU will operate in the next years with at least two instruments—the *negotiations for EU integration* with Ukraine and the Republic of Moldova as candidate states, and a *revised and tailored EaP* for the three South Caucasus republics, plus a certain form for supporting the Belarusian civil society. The study does not exclude future changes of regimes or orientations in some countries of the region, which would require a change of attitude from the EU.

In 2019, Ursula von der Leyen promised "her (new) Commission will be a geopolitical one" (European Commission 2023). At that time, the tensions with Russia, fears of China's growing strategic influence in

[1] The "Russian World" is a concept and ideology launched in 2007 by Vladimir Putin and the Russian Orthodox Church in order to define the cultural and political sphere of influence of Russia in Eastern Europe, mainly in the former Soviet Union. This doctrine comes with the pretention of "restoring the political unity" of the Russian-speaking space, including all native Russian-speaking communities. It was frequently used to "justify" the invasion of Ukraine, the annexation of Eastern and Southern provinces of Ukraine as well as Georgia's invasion (2008) or the claim that Belarus and the Republic of Moldova would belong to this so-called "Russian world".

Europe and great-power competition at the global level were already in full steam development. After February 24, 2022, the EU needed to take major decisions to support Ukraine on all possible dimensions, including the first time ever decision of Brussels to provide direct military support for the Ukrainian Armed Forces (UAF).

In the summer of 2022, Ukraine and the Republic of Moldova got the official status of candidate countries for EU integration. From an opposite perspective, the EU did not recognize in 2021 the re-election of President Alexander Lukashenko in Belarus because of the abuses and frauds in the electoral campaign, and it suspended any official form of collaboration with the regime of Minsk. After the 2022 Russian invasion in Ukraine, Belarus offered full support for the Russian troops and accepted in 2023 Russian nuclear arms on its territory.

This is the context in which this chapter explores the EU's current geopolitical approach regarding its Eastern neighbourhood. Amid the Russian war against the West and the illiberal revisionism of the rules-based international order, the EU conducts its actions within a coalition of democracies, institutions, national governments, non-governmental organizations (NGOs), private companies, think tanks, and opinion leaders. The EU-North Atlantic Treaty Organization (NATO) partnership and coordination is the strategic axis of the coalition. The current study names this informal coalition the "Euro-Atlantic Alliance Framework" (EAAF), which obviously includes NATO as the main Euro-Atlantic organization, but it is more than NATO or its member states.

EAAF is a coalition of actors, opinion leaders, and policy subsystems, whose actions are based on the theoretical model of the Advocacy Coalition Framework (ACF). Its purposes and outcomes are to produce certain changes in public policies, extend and develop Europeanization, reforms and integration in the neighbourhood, provide support for Ukraine and the Republic of Moldova, as well as combat Russian disinformation and propaganda. EAAF promotes its core beliefs at international level but also at domestic level, in different national societies.

In real terms, it is self-evident that Ukraine cannot succeed alone. The EU in its turn cannot succeed alone in projecting its geopolitical influence in the Eastern neighbourhood. Within EAAF, the entire action is magnified and amplified, with effective, consistent, and substantial results. The aim of the chapter is to analyse the capacity and potential of the EU to form a large coalition in support of its geopolitical vision in its vicinity. For the purpose of the current study, this chapter focuses on the interests and objectives of the main actors involved in the Euro-Atlantic advocacy coalition (states, international organizations, NGOs, private sector), identifies their core beliefs, and explains the changing geopolitical processes that impact EU's policies towards its Eastern neighbourhood. Special attention would be given to the development of the Euro-Atlantic partnership in the wake of the war in Ukraine and the EU-US strategic recalibration of Eastern neighbourhood agendas.

Although there are many studies that analyse separately EU's policies targeting the Eastern neighbourhood or the strategic influence of the Euro-Atlantic framework on the securitization and democratization of this vulnerable area, very little attention has been devoted to the way this influence has shaped EU's politics towards Eastern neighbourhood. Moreover, the current research can be considered a pioneer study since it is one of the very few research endeavours to utilize the ACF for explaining the dynamics of EU policy-making in this area. Thus, the study uses an inductive and interpretative approach, which enables an interpretation of the data collected through qualitative methods such as content and discourse analysis (policy documents and official statements). This chapter attempts to answer the following research questions: How does the Euro-Atlantic alliance framework impact EU's policies towards the Eastern neighbourhood? What were the main strategy changes brought about by the war in Ukraine?

The first section of the study introduces the current geopolitical environment in the Eastern neighbourhood and stresses the importance of the Euro-Atlantic partnership for its securitization and democratization. The second section focuses on the theoretical and methodological frameworks of analysis explaining the utility of the ACF model for the chapter's case study. The third section of the study analyses EU's (global and regional) actorness and the complexity of its policy-making. The fourth section of the study analyses the development of the Euro-Atlantic advocacy coalition in the wake of the war in Ukraine and its potential impact on the strategies and policies targeting the Eastern neighbourhood. The last section of the study presents the main findings and stresses the importance of some stable, long-term strategic objectives related to the EU's Eastern neighbourhood. The political context is dynamic and volatile, with many new issues and questions (e.g., the Hamas-Israel war, which is actually taking place in the EU's geopolitical Southern neighbourhood, the consequences of the European elections of June 2024, the unpredictable US-EU relations after the US presidential elections, etc.) that make any strategy, plan of actions or decision subject of possible future revision.

Theoretical and Methodological Frameworks: Defining EEAF Based on the ACF Model

As it was already pointed out, this chapter aims to explain the geopolitical approach of the EU in the Eastern neighbourhood in relation to the strategic influence of a large coalition of actors, opinion leaders, and policy subsystems, named the EEAF.

Developed in the early 1980s, ACF is a policy-oriented model designed to explain the processes related to policy changes in different areas. Although initially it was used in domestic policy fields (economy, education, healthcare, environment, taxation policy, etc.), more recently ACF entered as a method of research in foreign policy analysis and the International Relations (IR) domain. Providing coherent explanations for policy developments represents one of the key contributions of ACF at international politics' level, as different studies revealed on certain topics (Pierce 2011). Part of ACF, advocacy coalitions are groups of actors who share common values, beliefs and interests, and conduct actions according to these unifying elements. State and non-state actors use to build formal or informal coalitions to promote their interests, values, and beliefs.

The ACF method is used because the EU is traditionally set up, prepared, and ready to work in alliances, coalitions, and multilateral formats. The EU is not a distinct military power but during the past decades it successfully exercised its influence as a "normative power". As Ian Manner has stressed, the EU can be conceptualized as a changer of norms in the international system which by its own nature of being unique in comparison with other pre-existing political forms, is pre-disposed to act in a normative way (Manners 2002). The impact of the EU vision and strategies was always amplified by the collaboration with other liberal democracies, mainly the United States (US), or by its strategic partnership with NATO. The civil society, free mass-media, cultural institutions, NGOs, and sometimes the private sector are also important contributors to the augmentation of the EU values and beliefs.

The fundamental values of the EU, stipulated in the Treaty of Lisbon (2009), are freedom, democracy, rule of law, equality, human rights, and human dignity. This set of values is reflected in all core beliefs and policies conducted by the EU institutions, at different levels—the European Commission, the European Parliament, the Council, and the whole list of agencies and services. The EU values are compatible with those of other state and non-state actors such as the United States, NATO, NGOs, think tanks, and mass-media, so that the advocacy coalition is feasible. In this case, the policy subsystem is the European Neighbourhood Policy (ENP), with its instruments such as the EaP or the EU enlargement policy and the studied advocacy coalition refers to the Euro-Atlantic alliance. According to ACF, a coalition involves coordination and a set of shared policy core beliefs (Osei-Kojo et al. 2022, 1–21). As it has been previously mentioned, the Euro-Atlantic alliance is based on shared values such as the respect for individual rights, democratic principles, and human dignity. Although a stronger coalition necessitates more diplomatic capital, more complementarity, and synergies between EU and NATO activities, the enduring cooperation between the Euro-Atlantic community was possible due to the coordinated efforts of the nations that had a common vision and the motivation to implement it. Moreover, both the EU and the United States share similar beliefs related to regional stability and conflict resolution in the Eastern neighbourhood. Similarly, both actors have the capacity to mobilize significant resources that can shape policy agendas and produce major policy changes at a global level.

The changing geopolitical environment in Eastern Europe has brought similar threats and challenges and created the momentum for increasing the number of EU-NATO political consultations and strengthened their ties. In this sense, the ACF represents a very helpful tool for explaining the impact of the Russo-Ukrainian war on the evolution of the Euro-Atlantic coalition. It also allows to investigate the distribution of power and influence among the coalition members and how a certain disruptive event can represent a driver of coalition success or failure.

EU's Return to Geopolitics in Its Policies Towards the Eastern Neighbourhood

Russia's February 2022 invasion of Ukraine has drastically changed the European strategic environment. It had revealed significant vulnerabilities and sent shock waves globally. EU is confronted now with a landscape dominated by the politics of power and global competition. The Eastern neighbourhood region has evolved into the most neuralgic point on

Europe's geopolitical map, a space where EU's normative goals collide with Russia's pursuit of great-power politics and China's geoeconomic aims.

The war in Ukraine has changed the requirements for EU's actorness, shifted its foreign policy agenda and created the momentum for policy change. If after the illegal annexation of Crimea in 2014, the EU reviewed the ENP and started to implement minor policy changes in its approach towards the Eastern neighbourhood, after February 2022, the change went beyond the discursive level and brought a more geopolitical approach.

According to Cristian Nitoiu and Monika Sus, there are three main ways in which the Eastern neighbourhood has been framed in the literature concerning EU's foreign policy and geopolitics (Nitoiu and Sus 2019, 3–4). The first strand of literature emphasizes EU's enlargement process and its impact on EU's management of borders and territory (Nitoiu and Sus 2019, 3–4). The second focuses on regionalization and regional integration asserting EU's intention to reshape the geographical space according to best practices in regionalism (Nitoiu and Sus 2019, 3–4). The last strand of literature looks at the Eastern neighbourhood through the lenses of EU's global actorness (Nitoiu and Sus 2019, 3–4). These three frames correspond with the evolution of EU's goals in the Eastern neighbourhood. If at the beginning of its existence, the EaP was meant to be a policy tool for expanding EU's governance to its Eastern partners without having a clear geopolitical aim, after the 2014 Ukrainian crisis, the EU has moved away from the transformative and enlargement rhetoric and started to prioritize the resilience of its members and partners. It was during this time that the EU member states began to perceive EaP as a potential geopolitical project (Crombois 2023, 105–106). Moreover, the shift to geopolitics and global actorness is supported by the 2016 EU Global Strategy (EUGS) and the 2022 EU Strategic Compass (EUSC) which have outlined new objectives for strengthening the EU's security and defence policy (Crombois 2023, 105–106).

In 2021, the EU High Representative for Foreign Affairs and Security Policy/Vice-President of the European Commission, Josep Borrell, mentioned that the discussion of 2021 EaP Summit "*confirmed that our Eastern partners have a strong demand for more cooperation and integration with the EU, and the EU is prepared to respond to this demand in a way that reaffirms its role as a significant geopolitical actor in the region*" (Borrell 2021). However, it was not until the outbreak of the

2022 war in Ukraine that the EU fully entered the game of geopolitics. As Bidzina Lebanidze argues, "Ukraine's somewhat unexpected resilience against Russia and U.S. leadership in coordinating the Western response to Russia's war of attrition helped the EU find its geopolitical identity" (Lebanidze quoted in Dempsey 2003).

This historical turning point in EU's foreign policy approach is confirmed by the recent State of the Union Address of von der Leyen, President of the European Commission, who stated: "When I stood in front of you in 2019 with my program for a green, a digital and geopolitical Europe, I know that some had doubts [...]. We've seen the birth of a geopolitical Union, supporting Ukraine, standing up to Russia's aggression, responding to an assertive China and investing in partnerships" (European Commission 2023). Evidently, the Union does not become geopolitical by simply stating it and often EU has been accused that its geopolitical discourse has run ahead of its actions (Youngs 2022) but considering its recent endeavours, the words are finally being matched with actions.

The newly declared geopolitical Union has shown unity on sanctions imposed on Russia (hard power measures),[2] a solid support for Ukraine (including the delivery of arms) and granted EU membership candidacy status for Republic of Moldova and Ukraine with a conditional offer for Georgia. Additionally, the EU is playing a mediator role in the new Armenia-Azerbaijan peace process (increasing the humanitarian aid with 5€ million) and deploys a two-year monitoring mission in Armenia (Sammut 2023).

Although for the moment, the accelerated process of granting EU membership candidacy for the Republic of Moldova and Ukraine and starting accession negotiations is perceived as a mere symbolic act, it has wider geopolitical ramifications. As Ana Andguladze has stated, "the enlargement framework has the potential to provide more empowerment for local actors from civil society and political parties than the Eastern Partnership initiative has ever offered" (Andguladze quoted in Khotenashvili 2022). Furthermore, as Sven Biscop pinpoints, by granting the status of EU member candidate to Ukraine, EU has changed Ukraine's

[2] According to Collin Gray, hard power can be described as the deliberate capability to either impose negative consequences or offer rewards as a means of exerting influence. It is both practical and feasible to associate it with the military and economic tools of policy (Gray 2011, 28).

role from a buffer state to a border state being currently perceived as a member of the Western security architecture (Biscop 2023). Consequently, it is crucial for Ukraine to receive all the support from its Western allies in order to survive and consolidate itself as a border state (Biscop 2023).

The mobilization of the enlargement process coupled with the strategic response to Russia's attack on Ukraine, represent two major political decisions that prove EU's capacity to respond strategically to the new geopolitical environment. Despite its long period of hesitancy, the EU seems to be now more than ever aware that its foreign policy in the Eastern neighbourhood cannot be centred anymore around soft power geopolitics[3] and civilian power[4] discourses and takes the first steps towards adopting a more pragmatic approach adapted to the new geopolitical realities. Under the coordination of Kaja Kallas, the EU foreign and security policy is expected to become more vigorous and coherent.

However, as the last year has shown, its power projecting capacity is rather limited in the military and energy sectors. The war in Ukraine and the subsequent surge in energy prices have intensified the EU's energy ties with the United States. As Soeren Keil (2023) stresses, "in this struggle over hegemony, energy supply, access to ports and infrastructure projects are even more important than the presence of military troops and alliances".

Similarly, the war in Ukraine seems to have confirmed NATO, as a real framework for guaranteeing the territorial defence of Europe (Borrell 2020). According to the newly published Transatlantic Trends, NATO and the EU are perceived as equally important pillars of national security and the support for US involvement in European security and defence remains high (de Hoop Scheffer et al. 2023). However, the majority of respondents from EU member states are in favour of more EU action in security and defence (de Hoop Scheffer et al. 2023).

[3] According to Joseph S. Nye, soft power is "the ability to get what you want through attraction rather than coercion or payments. It arises from the attractiveness of a country's culture, political ideals, and policies" (Nye 2024).

[4] According to Hanns Maull, being a civilian power implies: "a) the acceptance of the necessity of cooperation with others in the pursuit of international objectives; b) the concentration on non-military, primarily economic, means to secure national goals, with military power left as a residual instrument serving essentially to safeguard other means of international interaction; and c) a willingness to develop supranational structures to address critical issues of international management" (Maull 1990, 91–93).

The next section of the study will analyse the development of the Euro-Atlantic advocacy coalition in the wake of the war in Ukraine and its impact on the strategies and policies targeting the Eastern neighbourhood.

The Evolution of the Euro-Atlantic Coalition and the Potential for Policy Change in the Eastern Neighbourhood

The war in Ukraine is not just a war against one state, it is a war against democracy, the liberal order and the entire transatlantic security community. Its ramifications extend far beyond the Ukrainian borders creating a pressing need to address the future of the Eastern European countries in relation to Euro-Atlantic matters (Naumescu 2023, 1). The current study argues that the war in Ukraine revitalized the Euro-Atlantic partnership transforming it into a veritable advocacy coalition that shares very similar geopolitical goals in the Eastern neighbourhood.

Both the EU and the United States have reaffirmed their willingness to strengthen their partnership and asserted their commitment to support Ukraine's fight for freedom and territorial integrity. In January 2023, leaders of NATO and EU signed a Joint declaration stating that "the NATO-EU strategic partnership is founded on our shared values, our determination to tackle common challenges and our unequivocal commitment to promote and safeguard peace, freedom and prosperity in the Euro-Atlantic area" (Joint Declaration on EU-NATO Cooperation 2023). At the NATO Summit in Vilnius, US President Joe Biden reconfirmed that "We will not waver. We will not waver. I mean that. Our commitment to Ukraine will not weaken. We will stand for liberty and freedom today, tomorrow, and for as long as it takes" (The White House 2023).

According to ACF, at the foundational level both the EU and US share the same deep core beliefs (Joint Declaration on EU-NATO Cooperation 2023). The principles, normative values, and the assumptions about the world are more or less the same. Their policy core beliefs that capture their causal perceptions about the ENP, EaP and enlargement issues (the policy subsystem in this case) are similar as well as their perceptions about the principal causes (Russia's attack on Ukraine) and the envisioned solution (working together for maintaining the democratic stability and security of the Euro-Atlantic community). Lastly, their secondary core beliefs refer to the instrumental means that can translate their policy core into concrete solutions/strategies for the policy subsystem.

In this regard, each part of the Euro-Atlantic advocacy coalition already came up with several policy revisions meant to improve the current geopolitical issues within the Eastern neighbourhood. As it has been mentioned before, EU's main actions refer to the new assumed role of a geopolitical actor who granted EU member candidacy status to the Republic of Moldova and Ukraine and supported Ukraine's resilience by providing military support through the European Peace Facility (EPF).[5] NATO decided to create a NATO-Ukraine Council meant to offer a space for political dialogue and cooperation between the Allies and Ukraine with the goal of advancing Ukraine's aspiration for NATO membership. In this sense, it decided to remove Ukraine's requirement for Membership Action Plan (MAP). It offered significant support in the security and defence sector (capability development, training and provision of equipment).

As likeminded actors of the coalition, EU and NATO are expected to increase their degree of coordination by putting together their resources in order to implement a common strategy or at least two separate complementary strategies for the Eastern neighbourhood. To this date, probably the most significant joint action of the Euro-Atlantic community meant to deter Russia was the sanctions imposed on Moscow. However, the coalition could use their specific resources to better coordinate and improve the sanctioning process.

As Jack Crawford pointed out, the political-military alliance structure of NATO serves as a valuable diplomatic instrument for encouraging allies to coordinate sanctions and exchange intelligence on the key elements crucial to Russia's war effort. Nevertheless, NATO lacks the authority to enforce economic policies across the entire Alliance. In contrast, the EU is less skilful at handling defence matters but possesses influential mechanisms for shaping regional trade and commercial policy, as outlined in article 207 of the Treaty on the Functioning of the EU (TFEU). This

[5] The EPF is an off-budget instrument aimed at enhancing the EU's ability to prevent conflicts, build peace, and strengthen international security. It also enables the financing of operational actions that have military or defence implications under the CFSP (European Council 2023).

improvement of sanctions could offer Ukraine a significant advantage for the next period (Crawford 2023).

Similarly, adopting a new Euro-Atlantic strategy for the Black Sea would respond to the long-term strategic objectives of both parties and would represent a lasting security guarantee not just for the EU and NATO member states but also for the aspiring ones in the East. However, on the 27th of July 2023, the US Senate announced the adoption of the National Defence Authorization Act (NDAA) that includes the Black Sea Security Act (Ministry of Foreign Affairs of Romania 2023). The US strategy for the Black Sea could greatly benefit from EU's expertise and experience within the region as it has already implemented so far two policies for this highly *geopoliticized* space (Black Sea Synergy (BSS) and EaP). Another US backed regional initiative that has the potential to bring the Republic of Moldova, Georgia, and Ukraine closer to the Euro-Atlantic structures is the Three Seas Initiative (TSI) that aims to develop the regional infrastructure (transport, energy, and digital). Considering the current political incertitude in the South-Eastern Europe and the difficult relationship with Turkey, NATO should rely more on its regional strategic partners (Romania and Poland) and should explore the potential of these regional cooperation initiatives.

As ACF highlights, the power of a coalition stands in its capacity to mobilize special resources to achieve the desired policy objectives. Thus, the success of the Euro-Atlantic advocacy coalition will depend on the EU and NATO's ability to make use of their resources and complementarities. Both the EU and NATO share a common goal in Eastern Europe, that of securitization. This goal can be achieved by taking a more geopolitical stance on their enlargement processes and a more regional approach to their policies.

The eventuality of the failure of the coalition might be triggered by the undesirability to get involved in common strategies of certain individual actors. Not all Western European NATO members are fully committed to support the costs of securitizing the Eastern European NATO allies and not all EU members are willing to rely solely on NATO for their security and defence.

Conclusion

It seems difficult and risky to shape firm conclusions for such a dynamic, fluid, and non-predictable topic. The war in Ukraine is far from an end and the EU is just entering a period of tentative structural transformations, after the European elections. The founding principle of decisional unanimity in the EU will be hardly challenged in the coming years but it is also difficult to predict whether it can be avoided and with what risks. The return of the pro-Russia Slovakian Prime Minister Robert Fico in the European Council will add a new voice to the already well-known Eurosceptic, pro-Russia, and pro-China option represented by Viktor Orbán. Providing military support for Ukraine at EU level will become even more a matter of hard negotiations in Brussels.

The way the war will end (even not soon) will substantially influence the debates regarding the future of the EU and its geopolitical actorness. The changing relations of the EU with the United States, China, and Russia will reflect but also further influence the outcome of the war and the regional political arrangements.

However, a few ideas emerge from the current context. A revised, updated EaP (as an "EaP 2.0") will most probably continue to serve as an important component of the EU's engagement with the region, as other countries in the EU's Eastern neighbourhood could face political transformations in the coming years and become pro-European, such as Belarus or Armenia. Even for the two candidate states, Ukraine and the Republic of Moldova, the EaP still represents a useful tool.

Safeguarding Europe and preserving transatlantic unity are pivotal responsibilities for Washington, necessitating a probable need for a more enduring troop presence in the Eastern neighbourhood. Does this automatically mean a deprioritization of the Indo-Pacific front or an integration of the two strategic and geopolitical approaches? Will NATO start a process of globalization? The outcome of the US crucial presidential elections of November 2024 will offer part of the answer regarding the future of the transatlantic relations as well as the chances of a new, "reinvented" West.

The Black Sea area emerges as a new centre of gravity in NATO and EU geopolitical strategies. There is now a Black Sea Strategy Act (BSSA) adopted by the US Congress. How can the Eastern neighbourhood benefit/be affected by the war? Again, at the moment, there are rather questions than answers as long as the war in Ukraine continues with all possible scenarios ahead.

During the latter half of the twentieth century, the EU's economic and political project evolved in tandem with NATO's security project. The enlargement of NATO's boundaries facilitated the EU's ability to perceive itself as a peace-focused initiative (Scicluna and Auer 2023, 10). Currently, the Euro-Atlantic advocacy coalition has the capacity to completely transform the Eastern neighbourhood but is there sufficient political will to improve the coordination between EU and NATO? For example, some EU member states are complaining that US Liquefied Natural Gas (LNG) is very expensive, and that the United States could charge less.

The moment for this volume and chapter is opportunistic and risky at the same time. In the EU's Eastern and Southern geopolitical neighbourhoods is no longer one war but two. On one hand, it could be tricky because there is still no clear evidence for any theory, assumptions, scenario or thesis regarding the military, political, and moral conclusions of the war started by Russia and its consequences. The new war in the Middle East, after October 7, 2023, adds new possible challenges for the European (Western) support for Ukraine, dividing the public opinion and introducing new fault lines in European politics. On the other hand, it is a good moment because all issues approached here are hot and relevant for the future of the EU and the global order. Reflecting on them and debating them are initial gains for future final answers.

Acknowledgements This research has been funded by the **Re**ignite **M**ult**i**lateralism via **T**echnology (REMIT) project, funded by the European Union's Horizon Europe research and innovation programme under grant agreement No 101094228.

References

Biscop, S. 2023. War for Ukraine and the Rediscovery of Geopolitics Must the EU Draw New Battlelines or Keep an Open Door? *Egmont Paper*, available at: https://www.egmontinstitute.be/war-for-ukraine-and-the-rediscovery-of-geopolitics/ (accessed 10 September 2023).

Borrell, J. 2020. Why European Strategic Autonomy Matters. *EEAS*, available at: https://www.eeas.europa.eu/eeas/why-european-strategic-autonomy-matters_en (accessed 12 October 2023).

Borrell, J. 2021. We Have to Remain Clear-Eyed and Firm in Our Response—Blog by Josep Borrell on Countering Power Politics in the East, December 21, available at: https://euneighbourseast.eu/news/latest-news/we-have-to-remain-clear-eyed-and-firm-in-our-response-blog-by-josep-borrell-on-countering-power-politics-in-the-east/ (accessed 21 September 2023).

Crawford, J. 2023. Further Together: An Opening for NATO–EU Sanctions Cooperation. *The Royal United Services Institute (RUSI)*, available at: https://rusi.org/explore-our-research/publications/commentary/further-together-opening-nato-eu-sanctions-cooperation (accesssed 10 September 2023).

Crombois, J.F. 2023. The Ukraine War and the Future of the Eastern Partnership. *European View* 22 (1): 103–110.

De Hoop Scheffer, A., M. Quencez, and G. Weber. 2023. Transatlantic Trends 2023. Public Opinion in a Shifting Global Order. *GMF*, September 12, available at: https://www.gmfus.org/news/transatlantic-trends-2023 (accessed 15 September 2023).

Dempsey, J. 2003. Judy Asks: Is the EU Doing Enough for Eastern Europe? *Carnegie Europe*, available at: https://carnegieeurope.eu/strategiceurope/89278 (accessed 21 September 2023).

European Commission. 2023. State of the Union Address by President von der Leyen (2023), available at: https://ec.europa.eu/commission/presscorner/detail/en/speech_23_4426 (accessed 21 September 2023).

European Council. 2023. European Peace Facility, available at: https://www.consilium.europa.eu/en/policies/european-peace-facility/ (accessed 19 October 2023).

Gray, C. 2011. Hard Power and Soft Power: The Utility of Military Force as an Instrument of Policy in the 21st Century. *Strategic Studies Institute*, 1–59.

Joint Declaration on EU-NATO Cooperation. 2023, January 9, available at: https://www.nato.int/cps/en/natohq/official_texts_210549.htm (accessed 10 September 2023).

Keil, S. 2023. Enlargement Politics Based on Geopolitics? A Proposal for a Geopolitics-Driven Enlargement Policy. In *A Year Later: War in Ukraine and Western Balkan (Geo)Politics*, ed. J. Dzankic, S. Kacarska, and S. Keil, 117–124. Italy: European University Institute.

Khotenashvili, M. 2022. Experts' Debrief: Harnessing the EU Accession Perspective for Consolidating Democracy in Accession Trio Countries, *Tepsa*, available at: http://www.tepsa.eu/wp-content/uploads/2022/06/Special-Issue-Democracy-in-the-Association-Trio.pdf (accessed 10 September 2023).

Manners, I. 2002. Normative Power Europe: A Contradiction in Terms? *Journal of Common and Market Studies* 40 (2): 235–258.

Maull, H. 1990. Germany and Japan: The New Civilian Powers. *Foreign Affairs* 69 (5): 91–106.

Ministry of Foreign Affairs of Romania. 2023. Press release, US Senate passes Black Sea Security Act, July 28, available at: https://www.mae.ro/en/node/62500 (accessed 15 October 2023).

Naumescu, V. 2023. *Great Powers' Foreign Policy. Approaching the Global Competition and the Russian War Against the West*. Leiden, Boston: Brill.

Nitoiu, C., and M. Sus. 2019. Introduction: The Rise of Geopolitics in the EU's Approach in its Eastern Neighbourhood. *Geopolitics* 24 (1): 3–4.

Nye, S.J. 2024. *Soft Power: The Means to Success in World Politics*. New York: Public Affairs.

Osei-Kojo, A., K. Ingold, and C.M. Weible. 2022. The Advocacy Coalition Framework: Lessons from Applications in African Countries. *Politische Vierteljahresschrift* 63 (2): 181–201.

Pierce, J.J. 2011. Coalition Stability and Belief Change: Advocacy Coalitions in U.S. Foreign Policy and the Creation of Israel, 1922–44. *Policy Studies Journal* 39 (3): 411–434.

Sammut, D. 2023. Is This the EU's Last Chance to Bring Peace and Reconciliation to Armenia and Azerbaijan? *European Policy Center*, available at: https://www.epc.eu/en/publications/Is-this-the-EUs-last-chance-to-bring-peace-and-reconciliation-to-Arme~543a80 (accessed 3 October 2023).

Scicluna, N., and S. Auer. 2023. Pushing the EU's Boundaries: Enlargement and Foreign Policy Actorness After the Russian Invasion of Ukraine. *Journal of Common Market Studies*, 1–12, available at: https://doi.org/10.1111/jcms.13540 (accessed 27 October 2023).

The White House. 2023. Remarks by President Biden on Supporting Ukraine, Defending Democratic Values, and Taking Action to Address Global Challenges, Vilnius, Lithuania, July 12, available at: https://www.whitehouse.gov/briefing-room/speeches-remarks/2023/07/12/remarks-by-president-biden-on-supporting-ukraine-defending-democratic-values-and-taking-action-to-address-global-challenges-vilnius-lithuania/ (accessed 10 September 2023).

Youngs, R. 2022. The Awakening of Geopolitical Europe? *Carnegie Europe*, available at: https://carnegieeurope.eu/2022/07/28/awakening-of-geopolitical-europe-pub-87580 (accessed 10 September 2023).

EU Strategic Autonomy and Defense Capabilities After the Russian Invasion in Ukraine

Arlind Puka

Introduction

Russia's invasion of Ukraine in February 2022 prompted a significant reappraisal of defense and security in Europe and a review of long-standing assumptions that large scale conflict on the continent was unlikely in the twenty-first century. Following humanitarian, economic, and military aid responses, multiple North Atlantic Treaty Organization (NATO) and European countries announced plans to increase their defense budgets. While the war in Ukraine has increased the continent's focus on defense, European Union (EU) has not fundamentally addressed its deeper structural issues, namely the deeply fragmented and disorganized manner in which Europeans generate their forces (Bergmann and Svendsen 2023). As such, EU, despite having a robust political and economic union, an economy equivalent in size to the United States (US) or China, a population of 450 million inhabitants, and collectively spending more than $345 billion (Tian et al. 2023) annually on defense, is almost wholly reliant on the United States for deterrence and

A. Puka (✉)
CEELI Institute, Prague, Czech Republic
e-mail: arlind.puka@ceeli.eu

L. Lika and D. Riga (eds.), *EU Geopolitical Actorness in a Changing World*, https://doi.org/10.1007/978-3-031-81160-9_13

collective defense. The fundamental question for EU defense over the next decade is whether EU's NATO members can rebuild their military capacity. Europeans are pledging to spend significantly more on defense and it is crucial that these investments have a transformative impact on EU defense. That requires deep cooperation and integration of EU's efforts. Yet defense spending is dictated at the national level. This has created vast discrepancies across the alliance in terms of focus and funding allocated to national defense and created gaps in capabilities needed for collective European defense. NATO, a multilateral, state-based organization, has fundamentally failed at overcoming this dilemma and the result is that the United States remains indispensable to European security (Duke and Vanhoonacker 2016).

The war in Ukraine has changed Europe. The EU has transformed into an important defense actor, providing security assistance to Ukraine, training Ukrainian forces, and providing funding to ramp up ammunition production. Thus, the continent could be entering a transformational period where European countries are at the beginning stages of a massive period of investment in defense. Yet, on the other hand, the war has exposed the dire state of EU defense. The need to support Kiev has further depleted EU forces, with huge quantities of equipment being sent to Ukraine. The Ukraine support effort has also revealed that EU member states militaries are in even worse shape than previously believed, as much of the equipment that existed on paper is in such disrepair it cannot even be donated to a desperate Kyiv. Now, as EU member states turn to replace their equipment, it is finding that their defense industrial capacity is not able to ramp up to meet demand, leaving EU member states torn between buying outside of EU or accepting long delays to boost their own defense industrial capacity. This chapter aims to answer the following question: To what extent will the proposed measures really increase the EU's ability and willingness to act and what should the EU be able to do autonomously when and if partners (above all the United States) choose not to engage?

Regarding the methodology, this chapter is based on various sources such as books, academic journals, official documents, and newspapers. The first section focuses on the capacity of the EU to act autonomously, and on means and tools to reduce external dependency in the defense area, while continuing to cooperate with partners in a multilateral setting. The second section analyzes the EU Strategic Compass (EUSC) and whether or under which circumstances the EU would be willing to engage on its own in more robust military operations. The third section examines the defense investment of the EU member states, recent NATO members, and aspiring ones. The last section pays particular attention to the EU defense capabilities by devising a new strategic approach to defense and security; obtaining the military capabilities necessary to pursue that strategic approach; and staying ahead in the technology stakes.

EU Strategic Autonomy: Its Self-Reliance

EU strategic autonomy (EU-SA) refers to the capacity of the EU to act autonomously—that is, without being dependent on other countries—in strategically important policy areas. These can range from defense policy to the economy, and the capacity to uphold democratic values (EU strategic autonomy 2013-2023 From concept to capacity, European Parliament 2022). "We Europeans should take our fate into our own hands"—alluding to difficulties with former US President Donald Trump, Brexit, and the confluence of security crisis on and around the continent affecting the EU–German Chancellor Angela Merkel captured the collective mood in European capitals back then in 2017 (Blockmans et al. 2022). The events in Afghanistan in 2021 left the allies to face the harsh reality of the US departure from the world stage. America's allies—most notably in EU—saw the United States walking away, washing its hands of a crisis it played a large part in creating, and with scant regard for the problems that doing so creates elsewhere (McGee 2021). The reason this is so hard for allies to swallow is because so much of the world's foreign policy, especially in EU is based on the assumption that the US' commitments to the values-based Western order, through the United Nations (UN) and NATO, are iron-clad (McGee 2021). Trump's presidency presented Europe with a single problem *vis-à-vis* the alliance: the man in the White House (McGee 2020). The fact that the former US President was genuinely willing to question the transatlantic alliance forced EU to consider several uncomfortable realities (McGee 2021; Aggestam and Hyde-Price 2019). Tensions over the war in Ukraine have relaxed, but could ramp up again if EU continues to fall behind the United States when it comes to providing financial and military support for Kyiv (Fix and Mankoff 2022). EU cannot afford a rift on this issue while Ukraine's—and its own—security is on the line (Costa and Barbé 2023). As the United States prepares for the 2024 presidential race to begin, EU should not take US support in this war for granted (Dijkstra and Schuette 2021). What happens if the next US administration decides to follow its own vision for conflict transformation—for example, by advocating to "*freeze*" the war and thus ending the assistance? (Balbon 2022).

While EU has considerable humanitarian and economic capabilities, compensating for the loss of US military and intelligence support seems unrealistic, because the EU firms don't have the supply, coordination, or speed to match the war-time demand (Gridneff 2022). More importantly, however, a transatlantic divide would massively weaken Ukraine's negotiating position with regard to Russia. However, since the Russian full-scale invasion in Ukraine, the United States has been able to deliver and has given more to Ukraine than any other country in the world. So far, the US Congress has approved about $113 billion in aid to Ukraine, according to calculations by the US State Department Office of Inspector General (Zachary 2023). Despite that fact, the recent data shows that the EU has clearly overtaken the United States in promised aid to Ukraine, with total EU commitments now being twice as large. The main reason is the EU's new €50 billion "Ukraine Facility," but also other European countries outside the EU such as Moldova have upped their support by increasing the military budgets (Trebesch 2023). The EU's "Ukraine Facility" is part of the EU's budget plans until 2027, showing a lasting commitment to support Ukraine.

EU's strategic autonomy has been defined as the ability to act autonomously as well as to choose when, in which area, and if, to act with like-minded partners (Lazarou and Wilson 2020). The capacity to act autonomously implies both the ability to decide and to implement decisions in an autonomous manner. "Strategic autonomy" is not about self-sufficiency, but about means and tools to reduce external dependencies in areas deemed strategic and where dependencies could compromise autonomy, while continuing to cooperate with partners in a multilateral setting. A key moment in common EU action was the European Council meeting of 10–11 March 2022, which adopted the Versailles Declaration (Council of European Union 2022). Although the Versailles Declaration mentions "European sovereignty" only once, in point 7, it is a remarkably robust expression of political will to achieve greater EU-SA. As regards defense, point 8 states that increased investment in defense capabilities should happen "in a collaborative way within the EU" and "stimulate Member States" collaborative investments in joint projects and joint procurement of defense capabilities (Calcara 2021).

European strategic autonomy has always been an amorphous and rhetorical concept (Cottey 2023). When then EU High Representative for Foreign Affairs and Security Policy and Vice President of the European Commission (HR/VP), Federica Mogherini, made strategic autonomy a centerpiece of the 2016 EU Global Strategy (EUGS) (European External Action Service (EEAS) 2016), some member states were wary. They were willing to live with the language because it did not involve very specific commitments. There has also long been a gap between rhetoric and delivery of strategic autonomy (Pieper and Lak 2019). Real autonomy from the United States on defense would require significantly increasing defense spending and/or much deeper integration—a Euro moment—in defense. EU member states have not been willing to take these steps. However, many things have changed with Russia's war on Ukraine. First, the war has reinforced the centrality of US political leadership and military power in European security, weakening the position of those who argue that EU should aim to do it alone (Koenig 2022). Second, EU member states are now significantly increasing defense spending (Koenig 2022). They are doing so, however, in a context where Russia is the primary threat and NATO is the primary framework for collective military planning—pointing away from European strategic autonomy. Third, from European reliance on critical supply chains, dwindling defense investments, and lagging technological innovation and full-spectrum capability development, to inefficiencies in arms procurement, the war has consolidated the primacy of NATO, which remains the foundation of collective defense (Koenig 2022). It has also highlighted the central role of the United States in European security and defense, in terms of both (geo)political leadership and operational support.

NATO inevitably remains the key pillar of European security and defense. The EU has not necessarily been damaged by this recognition, however, provided it can now commit to rethinking its priorities. The war has caused NATO's stock to rise, primarily because those European countries threatened most by Russia place more trust in the United States than they do in the principal champion of strategic autonomy, France (Dempsey 2023). It still makes sense to have a developed EU pillar within the Euro-Atlantic alliance framework, with complementarity, avoiding duplication. Strategic autonomy is desirable in terms of EU developing the defense capabilities to reduce dependence on the United States, something US administrations have also been keen to promote.

Strategic Compass

On 21 March 2022, the EU's Foreign Affairs Council approved the EUSC for Security and Defense (European Council 2022). The document sets out priority actions in 4 work strands: crisis management (ACT), resilience (SECURE), capabilities (INVEST), and partnerships (PARTNER) (European Council 2022). It represents the most concrete and realistic roadmap for the EU as security provider in the block's history.

Under ACT, the Compass proposes to adapt the way in which the EU conducts Common Security Defense Policy (CSDP) missions and operations to the current environment. By creating more robust, flexible, and comprehensive CSDP missions (Kmec 2023), the EU is able to adapt to changing regional and international circumstances and increase operational effectiveness (Hyde-Price 2018). To complement the EU's crisis management objectives, the newly proposed EU Rapid Deployment Capacity (EU RDC), allows the EU to quickly deploy troops into different crisis areas. This also includes the possibility of increased cooperation with partners' security and defense forces, facilitated by the European Peace Facility (EPF) which allows the EU to provide training and military assistance to partners. Under the resilience objective, the EU Cyber Defense Policy Framework (CDPF) allows the EU to protect its citizens and institutions from cyberattacks and a new EU Hybrid Toolbox (EUHT) should fortify the EU's capabilities to counter foreign manipulation and interference. The SC also proposes measures to increase resilience against climate change and promote a carbon climate-neutral EU presence on the ground. With respect to INVEST, member states agree on a substantial increase in defense spending. To alleviate this commitment, the EUSC refers to some of the European Commission's initiatives which include incentives for EU countries to expand their collaborative investments. This could include a value-added tax (VAT) waiver and a reinforced European Defense Fund (EDF) bonus system. The last key component of the EUSC is to strengthen "partnerships." Indeed, the EU places great emphasis on the importance of partners for the EU as a global strategic player. Among this commitment, improving engagement with organizations such as NATO, the UN, the Organization for Security and Co-operation in Europe (OSCE), the African Union (AU), and the Association of Southeast Asian Nations (ASEAN) is crucial.

The war in Ukraine changed the EUSC in three ways: it sharpened the focus, it triggered a leap in European defense spending, and it enhanced the sense of urgency regarding the implementation. The EU's capacity to act militarily will continue to depend on the political willingness of all member states. One could argue that the Ukrainian case shows that they can rapidly agree on military measures. However, this case is more like a one-off: It is a situation with clear aggression inflicted on an EU partner, direct threats to EU member states, immediate consequences for them (e.g., massive refugee flows, high inflation, economic crisis), and a united West led by a pro-European US President, Joe Biden. It is hard to imagine that a more distant crisis, in Africa say, with more disparate member state interests and threat perceptions and a disengaged US would trigger a comparable degree of EU unity. At the very least, this has rarely been on display in the past and negative experiences with Libya, Afghanistan, and, more recently, Niger are no help here. The war in Ukraine could, in fact, further reduce the willingness of war-weary public opinion to back military EU operations in the broader neighborhood.

Spending more on defense does not automatically mean spending better. There is a risk of a "reverse post-2008 scenario" when the member states engage in uncoordinated defense budget cuts. A look at the member states' compliance with EU spending objectives in the past eight years is troubling in this regard. While defense spending has been on the rise and despite the clear focus of the EU's defense initiatives on increasing collaboration, the share of joint investment dropped. The share of collaborative defense procurement dropped from 21% in 2016 to a low of 11% in 2020 and the share of collaborative investment in research and technology decreased from 13% in 2015 to 6% in 2020.

The Compass carefully avoids the notion of strategic autonomy, which figures just once in the entire text (Cesnakas and Juozaitis 2022). Considering the controversy attached to the very concept, this was a wise choice. The Compass does not provide a clear-cut answer. While it underlines NATO's primacy in the field of collective defense, it is vague on the EU's role in crisis management and in protecting its citizens. It provides a roadmap for the development of the EU's crisis management toolbox but is agnostic on its political aims. It thus proposes a new EU Rapid Deployment Capacity (EU RDC) that should "initially focus on rescue and evacuation operations, as well as the initial phase of stabilization operations" (European Council 2022). However, it does not say what comes later and whether or under which circumstances the EU would be willing to engage on its own in more robust military operations.

Against the backdrop of the war in Ukraine and repeated Russian threats directed toward member states, it is noteworthy that the Compass does not include any substantive appreciation or concretization of the EU's mutual assistance clause (Article 42.7 Treaty of the European Union (TEU)). It is ambiguous about how Article 42.7 TEU might fit or not with NATO Article 5 in case of a massive cyber-attack. Article 5 is the cornerstone of the NATO and states that an attack on one member of NATO is an attack on all of its members. Despite its importance, NATO has only invoked Article 5 once in its history—in response to the terrorist attacks of September 11, 2001. More broadly, it is unclear how EU-NATO cooperation should be deepened. The Compass promises to "further strengthen, deepen and expand our strategic partnership, political dialogue and cooperation with NATO across all agreed areas of interaction, including new key work strands such as resilience, emerging disruptive technologies, climate and defense and outer space" (European Council 2022).

Meanwhile, in the background looms China, which poses increasing problems for both the EU and NATO (Biba and Wolf 2023). In 2019, the EU's strategic outlook for relations with China distinguished between areas of cooperation, competition, and "systemic rivalry" (European Commission 2019). In the years since, the balance has tilted away from cooperation and toward systemic rivalry. Though China does not (yet) pose a direct military threat to Europe, it is increasing its military footprint in parts of Africa and the Middle East, supporting non-democratic regimes and strengthening its global influence (Bond and Scazzieri 2022). It has not given direct defense or defense industrial assistance to Russia so far, but in its rhetoric, it has placed the blame for the war on NATO and the West, rather than Moscow (Bond and Scazzieri 2022). Europe's greatest security concern about the rise of China, however, is that it will drag American resources and political attention away from the Euro-Atlantic area and the continuing problem of Russian aggression, and that EU on its own will lack the capacity to deal with the security challenges it faces. Despite acknowledging China as a systemic rival, European allies do not see Beijing as a threat to the same degree that the United States does, and lack the appetite for a more confrontational stance toward Beijing, including in the military sphere (Bond and Scazzieri 2022). It is also possible that a consensus between allies over how to approach China will remain elusive, with EU having more limited appetite to put economic ties with China at risk at a time when the cost of living is a major concern for voters.

Greater Defense Spending and an Enlarging NATO

While many European countries have announced increases in defense spending, a lot of them will find it politically challenging to spend more on defense when faced with an economic downturn. Allies need to invest significant sums to increase their military deployments and pre-positioned stocks on NATO's eastern flank, and to improve the readiness of their forces and their ability to operate together.

Western defense spending fell dramatically in real terms after the Cold War. America's expenditure went from 6% of Gross Domestic Product (GDP) in 1989 to around 3% a decade later; that of European countries went even lower (The Economist 2023). The planned increase in European defense spending does not represent a reversal in long-term trends. Defense funding has been rising in recent years in many European countries, in part because of NATO calls for increased spending and NATO members' commitment to that end, resulting in a compound annual growth rate of 6% between 2015 and 2021 (The Economist 2023). Even with this growth, many countries did not follow NATO's guideline that each nation should spend 2% of its GDP on defense—a target set back in 2006 (NATO 2022). According to the NATO Secretary General's, Jens Stoltenberg, Annual Report 2022, only five countries that are members of both the EU and NATO met the goal of spending 2% of GDP on defense in 2022: Greece, Lithuania, Poland, Estonia, and Latvia (Stoltenberg 2023).

EU countries were quick to tear down taboos. Germany decided to spend more on defense and provided military assistance to Ukraine (Deutsche Welle 2002), as it committed to €100 billion defense spending bills to reach the 2% NATO spending target (Hille 2022), but this will only be achieved by 2027. This was a major shift, considering that the country's military spending, as a percentage of GDP averaged only 1.3% between 2008 and 2021 (Stoltenberg 2023). In January 2023, French President Emmanuel Macron declared his country would reach NATO's 2% goal by 2025 and that its military spending would increase by a third by 2030 (Le Monde 2023). Poland set a defense budget of 2.4% of its GDP for 2022, increased it to 3% in 2023 (Cavendish et al. 2022), and the government will spend over 4% of GDP on defense in 2024 (Charlish and Florkiewicz 2023). In terms of the share of GDP spent on defense, Warsaw would then even be ahead of Washington. Denmark reversed its 30-year opt-out of EU's CSDP (Murray 2022). On 4 April 2023, Finland became NATO's newest member as 31st ally (NATO 2023). On 16 May 2022, the Swedish Government decided that Sweden will apply for NATO membership. In July 2022, all NATO member states signed the Accession Protocols for Sweden paving the way for Sweden's accession to NATO (Swedish Government 2022). However, Turkish and Hungarian parliament will have the final say on Sweden's NATO membership as the countries have not yet ratified Sweden's NATO bid. Turkey will keep its promise to ratify Sweden's NATO bid if US President Biden's administration paves the way for F-16 jet sales to Ankara (Hayatsever and Gumrukcu 2023). Sweden now plans to spend 2% of GDP on defense (Ahlander 2022).

Other countries outside the NATO fold have also reevaluated their security postures and relationship with the alliance. Austria is considering establishing a near-term, fixed GDP spending target for defense that would be higher than previous levels. This might entail a significant funding increase, as the country has had one of the lowest European defense budgets in terms of GDP percentage since the Cold War ended. Currently, Austrian military spending amounts to only about 0.7% of GDP (Wozniak 2022). A comparison between EU and United States forecasts shows that the transatlantic spending gap could shrink from 2.4% points in 2020 to 1.3% points by 2028. This may partly defuse bipartisan criticism in the United States that EU does not pull its weight in providing for its own security. Greater burden-sharing would also better prepare EU for a scenario in which the US limits its engagement in Europe's security.

However, some states are already struggling to live up to their promises. According to Eva Högl, German Parliamentary Commissioner for the Armed Forces, Germany had not yet spent "a single euro" from its 100 billion euros special fund (Högl quoted in Koenig et al. 2023). The country will only reach the 2% goal in 2024—and only with the help of the special fund (The Economist 2023). Once the fund is exhausted, however, it is unclear whether Germany will be able to meet NATO's 2% goal (Martuscelli 2023). In the same vein, Italy is expected to fall short of its announced objective of reaching the 2% in 2028 (Amante 2023). Furthermore, the extent to which EU member states have increased their defense spending varies significantly. While the announced increases in Central and Eastern Europe (CEE) mean that they would soon exceed NATO's 2% goal, others such as Spain are only planning to do so from 2029 onwards (Wilson 2022). Belgium does not intend to meet the target before 2035 (Kockartz 2022).

These variations indicate that, despite the overall convergence of threat perceptions on Russia—as seen inter alia in NATO's new Strategic Concept and the EUSC—the sense of urgency between North-Eastern and South-Western European countries still differs. France and Italy, for instance, still seem to prioritize the EU's Southern neighborhood. And although defense spending of countries in CEE will remain lower in real monetary terms, their influence in the EU and NATO is likely to increase as they have shown strong commitment in keeping their pledges (Helwig 2023). This may ultimately contribute to the power balance in both organizations shifting in favor of CEE (Drea 2022). Nearly two decades ago, then-US Defense Secretary Donald Rumsfeld was ridiculed in Paris and Berlin when he said Europe's center of gravity was "shifting to the East" away from the "old Europe" dominated by France and Germany. Rumsfeld may have been a little early in describing the shift, but his words seem to finally be coming true today (Drea 2022).

In addition, economic factors could reduce both the impact of these extra funds and the willingness of EU member states to live up to their promises. Inflation amounted to 5.3% in the Eurozone during three quarters of 2023 and was highest in the Baltic countries, with rates ranging between 15.2 to 17.2% (Eurostat 2023). If unchecked, it will eat up part of the announced defense investments. According to recent estimates, only 50 to 70 billion euros could be left of Germany's special fund to spend on hardware after inflation and additional costs are priced in (Knight 2023). Meanwhile, limited economic growth in the coming years, a consequence of both the pandemic and disruptions caused by Russia's war on Ukraine, are likely to increase domestic distributional conflicts (Fernandez et al. 2023). After a rebound of GDP growth in 2021 to 5.4%, the EU economy is expected to only grow at 0.8% and 1.6% in 2023 and 2024 respectively (Eurostat 2023). Prioritizing defense investment over social spending will thus become more difficult for many policy-makers.

The European Parliament has backed the European Commission's proposal to spend more money on defense in next year's EU budget even though financial resources are scarce. According to the compromise agreement on the 2024 EU budget, the Parliament's negotiators would like to see a €625 million increase for the EDF, and an additional €45 million for military mobility (Pugnet 2023). If the European Council backs the Parliament and European Commission's reviewed position, the EDF would benefit from €1,26 billion and the military mobility program from €286 million in 2024 (European Commission 2022a). The EU has been under-investing in defense compared with its peers: according to the European Commission, EU member states spent 20% more in 2021 than in 1999, whereas Russian spending had increased by almost 300% over the same period (European Commission 2022a). Russia plans to increase budget spending by 26% to $383 billion in 2024; Prime Minister Mikhail Mishustin declared in September 2023, with hefty increases in military and social spending expected ahead of a March 2024 presidential election (Mishustin quoted in Marrow et al. 2023). Defense cuts after the 2008 financial crisis have left EU member states with a current underinvestment gap of around €160 billion (European Commission 2022a). Even if EU member countries fulfilled all their spending promises, it would take years to procure the equipment needed. The value of new spending is likely to be eroded in real terms by inflation, especially if it persists at its current high rate. Much of the new spending is likely to go toward refilling stocks of weapons that have been sent to Ukraine, and to ensuring that European armies are ready to be deployed at short notice, rather than providing wholly new capabilities. This is particularly true in Germany, where successive governments have under-funded the military for many years.

Critical Capabilities

EU member states are required to take tough decisions on what to prioritize. This is no easy task, given an array of security threats and vast capability gaps caused by years of defense underinvestment. When setting priorities, European states have traditionally faced a dilemma between crisis management and territorial defense, and between EU's neighbors to the East and the South. The Russian war on Ukraine has at least temporarily rendered this dilemma less salient. Member states have converged in their threat perceptions of Russia and collectively tilted toward territorial defense and EU's Eastern neighborhood. Meanwhile, the war has brought another dilemma to the fore. It has shown that Europeans have to prepare for old warfare, dominated by mass and attrition, while simultaneously getting ready for new warfare characterized by an increased use of cheap, unmanned systems and a greater reliance on data connectivity. This requires staying on top of developments in warfare, increased innovation spending, as well as concerted action to face a broadening range of dependencies (Koenig et al. 2023). In May 2022, the European Commission presented an analysis of the defense investment gaps, and proposed further measures and actions necessary to strengthen the European defense industrial and technological base (European Commission 2022b). In terms of capability gaps—three urgent priorities have been highlighted: replenishing stockpiles, replacing Soviet-era legacy systems, and reinforcing air and missile defense systems. Beyond these urgent capability gaps, the Joint Communication proposed to work on a number of specific strategic medium- to long-term capabilities in the air, land, maritime, space, and cyber defense domains (European Commission 2022b).

Based on the defense investments gaps analysis, the European Commission presented the European Defense Industry Reinforcement through common Procurement Act (EDIRPA) in July 2022 (European Commission 2022c). EDIRPA is a short-term instrument, subject to ongoing interinstitutional negotiations, intended to boost joint procurement and worth €500 million for the period 2022–2025. EDIRPA's transformative capacity does not rest on its current budgetary allocation, which remains rather modest in comparison to the needs, but on the principle it sets, namely that common procurement of defense equipment can be funded from the EU budget.

In May 2023, the European Commission presented the Act in Support of Ammunition Production (ASAP), an instrument intended to facilitate "the timely availability and supply of relevant defense products in the Union" (European Commission 2023a). ASAP aims to help the European defense industry ramp up its research and manufacturing capacity to meet the needs of the EU member states as they replenish their stocks and continue to support Ukraine, and will receive funding of up to €500 million from the EU budget (European Commission 2023a). Prior to the outbreak of Russia's war on Ukraine, the EU was already exploring ways to bolster defense capabilities and strengthen the European defense industry, with the EDF, preceded by a preparatory action on defense research, as a dedicated instrument. In addition to the EDF, two other interlinked mechanisms were either created, the Coordinated Annual Reviews on Defense (CARD), or activated, Permanent Structured Cooperation (PESCO) (Articles 42.6 and 46 TEU and Protocol 10), at the time. PESCO is a treaty-based mechanism allowing for differentiated integration in defense. With Denmark giving up its long-standing opt-out in defense, the number of EU member states participating in PESCO rose to 26, Malta being the only EU member state outside of PESCO. There are currently 68 PESCO projects, with military mobility—a project allowing the transfer of personnel and equipment from one end of the European continent to the other—as a flagship. In parallel, the European Commission presented a joint communication on improving military mobility and an action plan, a dual-use initiative funded under the Connecting Europe Facility (CEF) for €1.5 billion in the period 2021–2027. The concept of military mobility originates in NATO and the EU's complementary efforts can only boost the Union's cooperation with the Alliance.

Many observers have been taken aback by how similar warfare in the twenty-first century is to that of the twentieth century: Attrition warfare has returned; questions of ammunition production and getting tanks to the frontline are central; and the old adage that "mass has a quality of its own" rings true again. Traditional warfighting capabilities, such as large quantities of armored fighting vehicles and artillery, are essential for territorial defense and reclaiming territory, and show the continued importance of kinetic force (Lange 2023). Despite the important role new technologies have played in Ukraine, they merely enhance the effectiveness of traditional core territorial defense capabilities. Among the new technologies, unmanned aerial systems have been the most visible ones in the war. These have appeared in many forms: small, commercial drones used for Intelligent Reflecting Surfaces (ISR) purposes, larger military-grade armed drones, and loitering munitions ("kamikaze drones") used for devastating one-time strikes. Although the role of armed drones has decreased as the conflict has progressed, small ISR drones and loitering munitions have remained highly relevant. Drones and loitering munitions have existed for years. The revolutionary element is the extremely low production cost, enabling their use in great quantities and rendering them expendable. An Iranian-made Shahed-136 loitering munition, used extensively by Russia to attack Ukrainian cities, costs between 20.000 to 50.000 US dollars (Misilyuk 2022). Commercial ISR drones can cost as little as 2.000 US dollars (Myre 2023). This allows drone usage in large quantities in this war. For example, Ukraine alone loses approximately 10.000 drones per month while reliable numbers for Russian losses are hard to come by (Watling and Reynolds 2023).

Based on the defense investment gaps analysis, released by the European Commission, there are three priorities for capability development and procurement stand out. First, EU member states should keep investing in classical core capabilities for territorial defense, such as armored fighting vehicles and artillery. Without these systems, territorial defense is hardly possible. At the very least, EU member states should replenish them enough to make up for the systems donated to Ukraine. Second, EU member states should take note of the innovations brought about by Russia's war against Ukraine. The increased relevance of drones and loitering munitions has consequences for air defense which they must take into account. Russia will likely continue to use cheap, expendable loitering munitions to attack Ukraine (Genschel et al. 2023). EU member states should prepare for this, either by investing in drone capabilities themselves, investing in air-defense capabilities that can efficiently neutralize (autonomous) drones and loitering munitions, or by regulating the proliferation of these systems (Koenig et al. 2023). The defense investment gaps analysis partly recognizes this, by emphasizing the importance of investing in drone capabilities and mentioning the Eurodrone as a promising project (European Commission 2022a). This drone will, however, not be delivered until 2029 and the French Senate already criticized it for being too heavy and expensive (Buzzonni et al. 2022). It does not seem to be a great example of the cheap and expandable aerial systems that play such a large role in the current war in Ukraine. This raises the question whether EU member states should prioritize investments in much cheaper systems, such as smaller ISR drones, when it comes to drone capabilities. Some EU member states have already come to this conclusion—in May 2023, the Czech Republic canceled the procurement of three larger Israeli Heron 1 drones and announced it would acquire two hundred smaller ISR drones instead (Defence Industry Europe 2023). Third, EU member states should invest in better data connectivity of their armed forces. In Ukraine, it is the factor that allows other innovations to reach their full potential. The defense investment gaps analysis therefore recommends investing in an "ultra-secured" European connectivity program.

A precondition for strengthening European armies is that EU can source the necessary raw materials—EU is dangerously dependent on others. For almost all military assets, including tanks, fighter aircraft, ammunition, and submarines, the EU faces a very high supply risk with regard to certain components needed to build a military force, such as aluminum, natural graphite, and a high-risk regarding beryllium, chromium, and copper (Girardi 2023). This becomes especially apparent when looking at supply chains of drones. Drones require a wide range of critical and strategic raw materials. EU is particularly dependent on China, which enjoys a strong industrial position in every step of the drone-making process. While China is by far the largest supplier of raw materials, African and Latin American countries have notable capacities, with each continent supplying 11% of all needed materials (Girardi 2023, 63). In later steps of the drone production process, including the manufacturing of components and subsystems, the situation looks somewhat better, as either European countries themselves or their partner nations such as the United States and Japan have relevant capacities.

The EU does recognize this vulnerability and has identified 34 raw materials as critical, some of which have additionally been designated as strategic raw materials (European Commission 2023b). The main supplier of these materials is often China. To address these dependencies, the EU proposed the Critical Raw Materials Act (CRM Act) in 2023. It sets out a range of goals to re-shore some extraction and processing capacities back to the EU to reduce dependencies and enhance diversification (European Commission 2023b). These are ambitious goals that will take time to implement. Until then, the production of military capabilities in EU remains vulnerable to supply chain shocks. In addition to raw materials, the EU faces a huge vulnerability in the field of semiconductors. Microchips are necessary for almost all technological devices, including weapons systems and drones. Yet, the semiconductor market is one of a kind: it is fundamentally dependent on only a few companies with unique capabilities. Great power competition between the United States and China as well as concerns about a potential escalation of the conflict in Taiwan heighten the issue of reliable supply chains in this field. The EU has reacted to these developments by introducing the European Chips Act (ECA) to advance European competitiveness. It seeks to mobilize 43 billion euros in public and private investment by 2030 to boost EU's technological capabilities and increase supply chain security (European Commission 2023b). While the EU is right to take urgent action in bolstering its competitiveness in the chip field, critics have warned that this type of industrial action could lead to inefficiencies, such as overcapacity (European Commission 2023b).

Conclusion

Since the end of the Cold War, EU has had the luxury of not having to take its own defense very seriously and has relied on the United States to deter any major threat. The European defense industry is quite fragmented and underinvested and, new investments take years to materialize even if the EU will overwhelm them with funds, as in the case of artillery ammunition production (Orenstein 2023). While many European countries have announced extra defense spending, many of them find it politically challenging to spend more on defense when faced with an economic downturn and competing priorities. At the moment, they are still missing NATO's overall defense spending commitment as well as the European Defense Agency (EDA) targets on defense innovation and collaborative equipment spending. Even if Europeans were to realize the announced defense spending increases, they would still collectively fail to meet NATO's 2% goal by 2028 (not to mention the actual target date of 2024) (European Commission 2023c).

Spending better together requires identifying a limited number of cooperation priorities which have the potential to generate significant economies of scale, provide important European public goods, and enhance the EU's role as a strategic enabler of NATO (Ewers-Peeters 2023). In an ideal world, cooperation priorities would be agreed top-down, based on fully harmonized EU and NATO planning processes (Schuette 2023). Another requirement for strengthening European defense industries is to reduce critical dependencies. The European Commission suggested drawing up a list of defense-relevant products, including raw materials and components, which are or could in the future be affected by disruptions to the single market. It proposes continuous monitoring, based on information from the industry, which would enable it to draw up emergency responses to current or future shortages.

As during the sovereign debt crisis with the creation of the European Stability Mechanism (ESM), a rapid initiative for a limited treaty review is required to abolish defense's exemption in public procurement (as contained in Article 346 (1b) Treaty on the Functioning of the European Union (TFEU)). It should allow for an EU-wide defense equipment market to emerge through co-decision, thus being faster than ongoing initiatives (Perotto 2023). It would also give an important signal that the EU wants to integrate member states' policies from the bottom up. It might also be the basis for a more autonomous EU within NATO, further to both organizations' declaration for "stronger and more capable European defense."

It would be a mistake for Europeans to think that the United States will willingly continue to bear the largest share of the burden. They will have to do more, acting nationally, in small groups and through the EU and NATO. EU can no longer afford to treat its own security as a matter of little consequence—it has to be taken seriously this time.

References

Aggestam, L., and A. Hyde-Price. 2019. Double Trouble: Trump, Transatlantic Relations and European Strategic Autonomy. *Journal of Common Market Studies* 57: 114–127.

Ahlander, J. 2022. Sweden Plans to Up Defence Budget to 2% of GDP as Russia Threat Looms, *Reuters*, available at: https://www.reuters.com/world/europe/sweden-finland-further-strengthen-security-cooperation-2022-03-05/ (accessed 2 October 2023).

Amante, A. 2023. NATO Wants Italy to Hit Spending Target as Soon as Next Year, *Reuters*, available at: https://www.reuters.com/article/italy-defence-idINL8N34W3PY (accessed 2 October 2023).

Balbon, N. 2022. Is European Support for Ukraine Dependent on the United States. *Carnegie Europe*, available at: https://www.cfr.org/article/europe-has-step-ukraine-keep-us-stepping-back (accessed 2 October 2023).

Bergmann, M., and O. Svendsen. 2023. Transforming European Defense: A New Focus on Integration. *CSIS—Centre for Strategic and International Studies*, 6, available at: https://csis-website-prod.s3.amazonaws.com/s3fs-public/2023-06/230616_Bergmann_Transforming_Defense.pdf?VersionId=47opF2RS0DhfOOAFyyjutYkWto_vbcRg (accessed 2 October 2023).

Biba, S., and R. Wolf, eds. 2023. *Europe in an Era of Growing Sino-American Competition: Coping with an Unstable Triangle*. Oxon and New York: Routledge.

Blockmans, S., D. Macchiarini Crosson, and Z. Paikin. 2022. The EU's Strategic Compass: A Guide to Reverse Strategic Shrinkage? *Centre for European Policy Studies (CEPS)*, No. 2022–14.

Bond, I., and L. Scazzieri. 2022. The EU, NATO and European Security in a Time of War, *Centre for European Reform*, available at: https://www.cer.eu/publications/archive/policy-brief/2022/eu-nato-and-european-security-time-war (accessed 2 October 2023).

Buzzonni, L., L. Brillaud, and N. Schmidt. 2022. The Eurodrone: An Industrial Project Fuelled by Politics, *Investigate Europe*, available at: https://www.investigate-europe.eu/posts/eurodrone (accessed 2 October 2023).

Calcara, A. 2021. *European Defence Decision-Making: Dilemmas of Collaborative Arms Procurement*. Oxon and New York: Routledge.

Cavendish, G., D. Chinn, N. Griesmann, H. Lavandier, and T. Otto. 2022. Invasion of Ukraine: Implications for European Defense Spending, McKinsey and Company, available at: https://www.mckinsey.com/industries/aerospace-and-defense/our-insights/invasion-of-ukraine-implications-for-european-defense-spending (accessed 2 October 2023)

Cesnakas, G., and J. Juozaitis, eds. 2022. *European Strategic Autonomy and Small States' Security: In the Shadow of Power*. Oxon and New York: Routledge.

Charlish, A., and P. Florkiewicz. 2023. Poland's 2024 Budget to See Big Spending on Defense, Social Benefits, *Reuters*, available at: https://www.reuters.com/world/europe/polands-2024-budget-see-big-spending-defence-social-benefits-2023-08-24/ (accessed 2 October 2023).

Costa, O., and E. Barbé. 2023. Transformation of Europe After Russia's Attack on Ukraine. *Journal of European Integration* 45 (3): 431–466.

Cottey, A. 2023. Is European Strategic Autonomy Over? *Carnegie Europe—Carnegie Endowment for International Peace*, available at: https://carnegieeurope.eu/strategiceurope/88838 (accessed 2 October 2023).

Council of European Union. 2022. Informal Meeting of the Heads of State or Government, Versailles Declaration, March, 10–11, available at: https://www.consilium.europa.eu/media/54773/20220311-versailles-declaration-en.pdf (accessed 2 October 2023).

Defence Industry Europe. 2023. Czech Republic: 200 Smaller Drones Instead of Three Herons, available at: https://defence-industry.eu/czech-republic-200-smaller-drones-instead-of-three-herons/ (accessed 2 October 2023).

Dempsey, J. 2023. Is European Strategic Autonomy Over? *Carnegie Europe*, available at: https://carnegieeurope.eu/strategiceurope/88838 (accessed 2 October 2023).

Dijkstra, H, L. von Allwoerden, L. Schuette, et al. 2021. Donald Trump and the Survival Strategies of International Organizations: When Can Institutional Actors Counter Existential Challenges? NestIOr Working Paper, available at: https://www.researchgate.net/publication/351480855_Donald_Trump_and_the_survival_strategies_of_international_organizations_When_can_institutional_actors_counter_existential_challenges (accessed 2 October 2023).

Drea, E. 2022. With Ukraine War, EU Balance of Power Shifts East: Russia's War Has Opened up a Vast Strategic Chasm Within the European Union, *Foreign Policy*, available at: https://foreignpolicy.com/2022/06/21/eu-russia-ukraine-war-european-union-france-germany-poland-eastern-europe-baltics/ (accessed 2 October 2023).

Duke, S., and S. Vanhoonacker. 2016. EU-NATO Relations: Top-Down Strategic Paralysis, Bottom-Up Cooperation. In *The EU, Strategy and Security Policy: Regional and Strategic Challenges*, ed. L. Chappell, J. Mawdsley, and P. Petrov, 153–168. Oxon and New York: Routledge.

European Commission. 2019. EU-China—A Strategic Outlook, *Joint Communication to the European Parliament, European Council and the Council*, available at: https://eur-lex.europa.eu/legal-content/EN/TXT/PDF/?uri=CELEX:52019JC0005 (accessed 2 October 2023).

European Commission. 2022a. Joint Communication to the European Parliament, the European Council, the Council, the European Economic and Social Committee and the Committee of the Regions on the Defense Investment Gaps Analysis and Way Forward, available at: https://eur-lex.europa.eu/legal-content/EN/TXT/PDF/?uri=CELEX:52023JC0020 (accessed 2 October 2023).

European Commission. 2022b. European Defence Industry Reinforcement Through Common Procurement Act (EDIRPA), available at: https://www.europarl.europa.eu/RegData/etudes/BRIE/2023/739294/EPRS_BRI(2023)739294_EN.pdf (accessed 2 October 2023).

European Commission. 2022c. EU Steps Up Action to Strengthen EU Defense Capabilities, Industrial and Technological Base: Towards an EU Framework for Joint defense Procurement, available at: https://ec.europa.eu/commission/presscorner/detail/en/ip_22_3143 (accessed 2 October 2023)

European Commission. 2023a. Act in Support of Ammunition Production (ASAP), available at: https://defence-industry-space.ec.europa.eu/eu-defence-industry/act-support-ammunition-production-asap_en (accessed 2 October 2023).

European Commission. 2023b. Critical Raw Materials, available at: https://commission.europa.eu/strategy-and-policy/priorities-2019-2024/european-green-deal/green-deal-industrial-plan/european-critical-raw-materials-act_en#:~:text=The%20European%20Critical%20Raw%20Materials%20Act%20is%20an,supply%20of%20critical%20raw%20materials%20in%20the%20EU. (accessed 2 October 2023).

European Commission. 2023c. European Economic Forecast: Winter 2023, Luxembourg, *European Economy Institutional*, Paper 194.

European Council. 2022. A Strategic Compass for Security and Defense—For a European Union that Protects Its Citizens, Values and Interests and Contributes to International Peace and Security, available at: https://www.consilium.europa.eu/en/press/press-releases/2022/03/21/a-strategic-compass-for-a-stronger-eu-security-and-defence-in-the-next-decade/ (accessed 2 October 2023).

European External Action Service (EEAS). 2016. EU Global Strategy 2016—A Global Strategy for the European Union's Foreign and Security Policy, available at: https://www.eeas.europa.eu/eeas/global-strategy-european-unions-foreign-and-security-policy_en (accessed 2 October 2023).

European Parliament. 2022. EU strategic autonomy 2013—2023: From concept to capacity. Available at: https://www.europarl.europa.eu/RegData/etudes/BRIE/2022/733589/EPRS_BRI(2022)733589_EN.pdf (accessed 2 October 2023).

Eurostat. 2023. Euro Area Annual Inflation Stable at 5.3%, Luxembourg, available at: https://ec.europa.eu/eurostat/documents/2995521/17396139/2-31082023-AP-EN.pdf/06f6eed0-f52a-81cc-16e3-30aaf64d81b8 (accessed 2 October 2023).

Ewers-Peeters, N. 2023. *Understanding EU-NATO Cooperation: How Member-States Matter*. Oxon and New York: Routledge.

Fernandez, O., M. Vandendriessche, N. Agell, and J. Franco. 2023. The Impact of Russia's 2022 Invasion of Ukraine on Public Perceptions of EU Security and Defence Integration: A Big Data Analysis. *Journal of European Integration* 45 (3): 463–485.

Fix, L., and J. Mankoff. 2022. Europe Has to Step Up on Ukraine to Keep the U.S. From Stepping Back. *Council on Foreign Relations*, available at: https://www.cfr.org/article/europe-has-step-ukraine-keep-us-stepping-back (accessed 2 October 2023).

Genschel, P., Leek, L., and J. Weyns. 2023. War and Integration. The Russian Attack on Ukraine and the Institutional Development of the EU. *Journal of European Integration* 45 (3): 343–360.

Girardi, B. 2023. Strategic Raw Materials for Defense: Mapping European Industry Needs. *Centre for Strategic Studies*, The Hague, available at: https://hcss.nl/wp-content/uploads/2023/01/Strategic-Raw-Materials-for-Defence-HCSS-2023-2.pdf (accessed 2 October 2023).

Gridneff, I. 2022. Why Europe's Defense Industry Can't Keep up, *Politico*, available at: https://www.politico.eu/article/europe-defense-military-industry-keep-up-demands/ (accessed 2 October 2023).

Hayatsever, H., and T. Gumrukcu. 2023. Turkey Will Back Sweden's NATO Bid If U.S. Keeps Promise on F-16 sale-Erdogan, available at: https://www.reuters.com/world/turkey-will-back-swedens-nato-bid-if-us-keeps-promise-f-16-sale-erdogan-2023-09-26/ (accessed 2 October 2023).

Helwig, N. 2023. EU Strategic Autonomy After the Russian Invasion of Ukraine: Europe's Capacity to Act in Times of War. *Journal of Common Market Studies* 61: 57–67.

Hille, P. 2022. Germany Commits €100 Billion to Defense Spending, *Deutsche Welle*, available at: https://www.dw.com/en/germany-commits-100-billion-to-defense-spending/a-60933724#:~:text=German%20Chancellor%20Olaf%20Scholz%20announced%20a%20plan%20to,spending%20on%20defense%20in%20line%20with%20NATO%20demands (accessed 2 October 2023).

Hyde-Price, A. 2018. The Common Security and Defence Policy. In *The Handbook of European Defence Policies and Armed Forces*, ed. H. Meijer and M. Wyss, 392–406. Oxford: Oxford University Press.

Kmec, V. 2023. *EU Missions and Peacebuilding: Building Peace Through the Common Security and Defence Policy*. Oxon and New York: Routledge.

Knight, B. 2023. What Happened to the German Military's €100 Billion Fund? *Deutsche Welle* available at: https://www.dw.com/en/what-happened-to-the-german-militarys-100-billion-fund/a-64846571 (accessed 2 October 2023).

Kockartz, A. 2022. Belgium's Government Increases Defense Budget by 2% of GDP, *VRT NWS*, available at: https://www.vrt.be/vrtnws/de/2022/06/19/belgiens-regierung-erhoeht-den-verteidigungsetat-um-2-des-bip/ (accessed 2 October 2023).

Koenig, N. 2022. Putin's War and the Strategic Compass: A Quantum Leap for the EU's Security and Defence Policy? *Hertie School—Jacques Delors Centre*, available at: https://www.delorscentre.eu/en/publications/detail/publication/putins-war-and-the-strategic-compass-a-quantum-leap-for-the-eus-security-and-defence-policy (accessed 2 October 2023).

Koenig, N., L. Schütte, N. Knapp, P. Köhler, I. Kump, and J. Pauly. 2023. Defense Sitters Transforming European Militaries in Times of War—Special Edition of the Munich Security Report on European Defense, *Munich Security Conference (MSC)*, available at: https://securityconference.org/assets/01_Bilder_Inhalte/03_Medien/02_Publikationen/2023/European_Defense_Report_-_Defense_Sitters/Defense_Sitters_European_Defense_Report_MSC.pdf (accessed 2 October 2023).

Lange, N. 2023. How to Beat Russia: What Armed Forces in NATO Should Learn from Ukraine's Homeland Defense, *GLOBSEC*, available at: https://www.globsec.org/what-we-do/publications/how-beat-russia-what-armed-forces-nato-should-learn-ukraines-homeland (accessed 2 October 2023).

Lazarou, E., and A. Benjamin Wilson. 2020. On the Path to Strategic Autonomy: The EU in an Evolving Geopolitical Environment. *EPRS—European Parliamentary Research Service*, available at: https://www.europarl.europa.eu/RegData/etudes/STUD/2020/652096/EPRS_STU(2020)652096_EN.pdf (accessed 2 October 2023).

Le Monde. 2023. Macron Announces Military Spending to Increase by a Third Until 2030, available at: https://www.lemonde.fr/en/politics/article/2023/01/20/macron-presents-significant-increase-in-military-spending-until-2030_6012339_5.html (accessed 2 October 2023).

Marrow, A., D. Korsunskaya, and V. Soldatkin. 2023. Russia Plans 26% Rise in Budget Spending in 2024 Election Year, *Reuters*, available at: https://www.reuters.com/business/aerospace-defense/russia-plans-26-rise-budget-spending-2024-2023-09-22/ (accessed 2 October 2023).

Martuscelli, C. 2023. Germany Misses Two Percent Target for Defense Spend, *Politico*, available at: https://www.politico.eu/article/germany-to-miss-2-percent-nato-defense-spending-target-think-tank/ (accessed 2 October 2023).

McGee, L. 2020. Joe Biden's Victory Isn't Enough on Its Own to Heal the Wounds Trump Inflicted on Europe. *CNN Politics*, available at: https://edition.cnn.com/2020/11/14/europe/biden-european-union-transatlantic-reset-analysis-intl/index.html (accessed 2 October 2023).

McGee, L. 2021. Afghan Withdrawal Leaves Allies to Face Harsh Reality of US's Departure from World Stage. *CNN Politics*, available at: https://edition.cnn.com/2021/08/24/politics/biden-afghanistan-weakens-the-west-globally-intl-cmd/index.html (accessed 2 October 2023).

Misilyuk, G. 2022. Iranian Drones in the Russian Invasion: Analysis by Molfar Experts, *Molfar*, available at: https://molfar.com/en/blog/shahed (accessed 2 October 2023).

Murray, A. 2022. Denmark Votes to Drop Eu Defence Opt-Out in 'Historic' Referendum, *BBC News*, available at: https://www.bbc.com/news/world-europe-61644663 (accessed 2 October 2023).

Myre, G. 2023. A Chinese Drone for Hobbyists Plays a Crucial Role in the Russia-Ukraine War, *NPR*, available at: https://www.npr.org/2023/03/21/1164977056/a-chinese-drone-for-hobbyists-plays-a-crucial-role-in-the-russia-ukraine-war (accessed 2 October 2023).

NATO. 2022. Defence Expenditure of NATO countries (2014–2022), *Public Diplomacy Division, Press Release*, Communique PR/CP52022)105, June 27, available at: https://www.nato.int/nato_static_fl2014/assets/pdf/2022/6/pdf/220627-def-exp-2022-en.pdf (accessed 2 October 2023).

NATO. 2023. Finland Joins NATO as 31st ally, 4 April, available at: https://www.nato.int/cps/en/natohq/news_213448.htm (accessed 2 October 2023).

Orenstein, M. 2023. The European Union's Transformation After Russia's Attack on Ukraine. *Journal of European Integration* 45 (3): 333–342.

Perotto, G. 2023. The Legal Framework of the EU Defence Industry and the Pursuit of Strategic Autonomy. *European Papers* 8 (2): 475–486.

Pieper, M., and M. Lak. 2019. The End of Transatlanticism? EU Security and Defence Policies and the 'Strategic Autonomy' Debate from a Historical and Contemporary Perspective. *Studia Europejskie-Studies in European Affairs* 4: 23–44.

Pugnet, A. 2023. European Parliament Supports Increase in 2024 Defense Budgets, *Euractiv*, available at: https://www.euractiv.com/section/defence-and-security/news/european-parliament-supports-increase-in-2024-defence-budgets/ (accessed 2 October 2023).

Schuette, L.A. 2023. Shaping Institutional Overlap: NATO's Responses to EU Security and Defence Initiatives Since 2014. *The British Journal of Politics and International Relations* 25 (3): 423–443, available at: https://doi.org/10.1177/13691481221079188 (accessed 2 October 2023).

Stoltenberg, J. 2023. The Secretary General's Annual Report 2022, *NATO*, available at: https://www.nato.int/cps/en/natohq/opinions_212795.htm (accessed 2 October 2023).

Swedish Government. 2022. Sweden Applies for NATO Membership, available at: https://www.reuters.com/world/europe/swedish-government-takes-formal-decision-apply-nato-membership-2022-05-16/ (accessed 2 October 2023).

The Economist. 2023. Europe Is Struggling to Rebuild Its Military Clout, available at: https://www.economist.com/europe/2023/05/07/europe-is-struggling-to-rebuild-its-military-clout (accessed 2 October 2023).

Tian, N., D. Lopes da Silva, X. Liang, L. Scarazzato, L. Béraud-Sudreau, and C. De Oliveira Assis. 2023. Trends in World Military Expenditurin 2022. *SIPRI—Stockholm International Peace Research Institute*, available at: https://www.sipri.org/sites/default/files/2023-04/2304_fs_milex_2022.pdf (accessed 2 October 2023).

Trebesch, K. 2023. Ukraine Support Tracker: Europe Clearly Overtakes US, with Total Commitments Now Twice as Large. *Kiel Institute for the World Economy*, available at: https://www.ifw-kiel.de/publications/news/ukraine-support-tracker-europe-clearly-overtakes-us-with-total-commitments-now-twice-as-large/#:~:text=Europe%20has%20clearly%20overtaken%20the,with%20new%20multi%2Dyear%20packages (accessed 2 October 2023).

Watling, J., and N. Reynolds. 2023. Meatgrinder: Russian Tactics in the Second Year of Its Invasion of Ukraine, *RUSI*, available at: https://www.rusi.org/explore-our-research/publications/special-resources/meatgrinder-russian-tactics-second-year-its-invasion-ukraine (accessed 2 October 2023).

Wilson, J. 2022. Spain Boosts Military Spending to Close Gap with NATO goal, Associated Press, available at: https://apnews.com/article/nato-russia-ukraine-spain-eastern-europe-madrid-61f2e9644404358defb517dcd37a2170 (accessed 2 October 2023).

Wozniak, J. 2022. Austrian Military Spending Amounts for Only About 0.7% of GDP, *Overt Defense News*, available at: https://www.overtdefense.com/2022/10/12/austria-to-increase-defense-budget-by-25-in-2023/ (accessed 2 October 2023).

Zachary, B.W. 2023. $113 billion: Where the US Investment in Ukraine Aid Has Gone. *CNN Politics*, available at: https://edition.cnn.com/2023/09/21/politics/war-funding-ukraine-what-matters/index.html (accessed 2 October 2023).

Conclusion: Assessment of the EU Geopolitical Actorness in a Shifting World Order

Liridon Lika and Dealan Riga

Introduction

This edited book explored the European Union's (EU) renewed engagement with the world, driven by its ambition to assert itself as a geopolitical actor. While the EU has actively strengthened and refreshed its global partnerships, the book highlights the need to grasp the strategic significance of this shift. Addressing the challenges posed by increasing complexity, the volume offers valuable insights into the EU's evolving approach, with a particular focus on its more assertive role in global affairs. It examined the transformation of EU actorness and the demands that geopolitical positioning entails. The book also calls for a re-evaluation of academic literature, urging scholars to reassess conceptual frameworks in light of the EU's pursuit of strategic positioning beyond its traditional

L. Lika (✉) · D. Riga
Department of Political Science, University of Liège, Liège, Belgium
e-mail: liridon.lika@uliege.be

D. Riga
e-mail: Dealan.Riga@uliege.be

L. Lika and D. Riga (eds.), *EU Geopolitical Actorness in a Changing World*, https://doi.org/10.1007/978-3-031-81160-9_14

role. At the core of the EU geopolitical leadership lies a fusion of normative power and strategic interests, a dynamic that reflects its resilience in a post-pandemic world shaped by new geopolitical forces, such as the wars in Ukraine and in the Middle East.

From a conceptual perspective, this book contributes to the ongoing debate in academic literature concerning actorness (Dopchie and Lika 2024; Santander and Vlassis 2020), bridging the gap between its role as a low-politics tool and the EU ambition to take on a leadership role in geopolitics, exemplified by the European Commission and the pursuit of strategic autonomy. It sheds light on the EU's security role within the context of foreign policy, challenging traditional notions that often view geopolitics through a state-centric paradigm. Accordingly, this contribution opens a research agenda challenging the assumption that achieving a unified EU geopolitical positioning is de facto unattainable. It underscored, throughout each chapter, that EU engagement in high politics is achievable, even though geopolitical actorness remains a challenge, as the EU is ill-equipped to efficiently navigate such terrain. Therefore, this edited book aimed to propose and open an academic research agenda, fostering a reflection on the new challenges, requirements, and developments generated by the continuously shifting world order and their impact on the EU actorness.

The concluding chapter encapsulates the essence of the edited volume by synthesizing key insights from the book's contributions. Its principal aim is to provide a comprehensive summary and assessment of the EU geopolitical actorness within the context of a dynamically shifting world order. This involves a thorough examination of research results to address the central question: Is the EU's determination to establish a new geopolitical leadership accompanied by the implementation of the practical requirements entailed by these shifts? Concurrently, the chapter engages in a reflective exploration of the research objectives defined at the very beginning of the present book (see the introductory chapter). It delves into: (a) investigating the extent to which the EU possesses the necessary capabilities to transition effectively from a normative to a strategic and geopolitical focus; (b) examining the roles played by third-party states in fortifying the EU's capacity to establish itself as a geopolitical actor; and (c) assessing the EU's ability to execute this transformative process within the framework of its foreign affairs toolbox. In essence, this concluding chapter aims to distill crucial lessons and insights from the collective body of work presented in the book. It begins by assessing the EU's effectiveness in renewing its actorness, building on classical challenges such as disunity and inconsistency. It then provides an overview of the research results, framing them as responses to the three research objectives of the book (see the introductory chapter). Subsequently, the chapter elaborates on transversal findings related to the main research question, highlighting key themes and insights that have emerged from the collective content. Finally, it reflects on the research's limitations and outlines a new research agenda to build on its findings.

EU's Response to Actorness Weaknesses: Assessing How Geopolitical Actorness Aligns with Unity and Consistency

This section examines the weaknesses in the EU actorness (see the introductory chapter) and questions how these have been addressed in the shift from normative to strategic and geopolitical concerns. The chapter critically analyzes the evolution of the European Enlargement Policy (EEP) and the European Neighbourhood Policy (ENP), often cited as examples of the EU's limitations in both consistency and unity. Scholars have highlighted a lack of unity in EEP, where member states frequently defend divergent positions (Lika 2021; Meka and Bianchini 2020), as demonstrated by the EU's ambiguous and ambivalent policy toward the Republic of Kosovo (Lika and Reka 2021). The EU has not yet managed to convince its five member states (Cyprus, Greece, Romania, Slovakia, and Spain) to officially recognize this Western Balkan state. This EU's stance significantly impacts Kosovo's European integration process and shows that Brussels has difficulty speaking with one voice. The EU's inability to present a unified stance has also been noticed during the 2019 Moldovan constitutional crisis or regarding Georgia's path toward EU integration. In the Western Balkans, the EU foreign policy has been inconsistent. The EU's lack of consistency was also evident in the Union's response to Ukraine's 2013–2014 Euromaidan crisis, where the EU failed to provide tangible security guarantees, leaving Eastern Europe more vulnerable to Russian assertiveness. Additionally, the EU's multiple crises have influenced its approach towards the Western Balkans and Eastern Europe. For example, the 2015 refugee crisis acted as a pivotal moment for EU–Western Balkans relations, with the Western Balkan countries becoming essential partners in managing migration flows. These developments have introduced new challenges in the Western Balkans, in particular border dynamics, which continue to be affected by territorial disputes and societal divisions. The 2016 EU–Turkey deal has further complicated the EU's involvement in the region, as Turkey has emerged as a significant contender for influence (Lika 2019). Overall, the EU's polycrisis have exacerbated existing disunity and inconsistency. The remaining question is how these dynamics have been affected by the EU's strategic shift following Russia's invasion of Ukraine.

On November 2023, the European Commission adopted the 2023 enlargement package, recommending the opening of negotiations with Ukraine and the Republic of Moldova, and granting candidate status to Georgia (European Commission 2023; DG NEAR 2023), while on March 2024 the European Council decided to open accession negotiations with Bosnia and Herzegovina (European Council 2024). It is now up to the Council of the EU to review these recommendations and decide on the next steps in the enlargement process. On October 15, 2024, Albania opened the first fundamental chapters in the EU accession negotiations (Council of the EU 2024). These examples clearly show that the EU's response to geopolitical turmoil in the context of the war in Ukraine has been marked by a proactive stance on enlargement. In the months following Russia's full-scale invasion of Ukraine, the EU introduced significant changes to its neighborhood and enlargement policies in a more strategic direction (see the chapters of Maria Raquel Freire and Elisabeth Johansson-Nogués). Echoing the findings of this volume, strategic challenges have demanded a response from the EU on these issues. However, the book also highlights that the EU's effectiveness in addressing these challenges is far from straightforward. This section aims to scrutinize how these developments have impacted the EU's longstanding weaknesses in actorness, particularly in terms of unity and consistency in the face of multiple crises.

In terms of unity, Freire et al. (2022) elaborated on how the war in Ukraine created momentum for EU proactivity, as member states showed a clear and unified stance in responding to Russia's aggression. This cohesion provided a window of opportunity to renew the EEP and ENP. As a result, the EU was able to speak with one voice, achieving significant outcomes such as granting candidate status to Ukraine, the Republic of Moldova, Georgia, and Bosnia and Herzegovina. However, this unanimity must be nuanced, as the long and complex accession process is already revealing challenges to European unity. Divisions have emerged regarding how these accession processes should proceed, with France, Germany, and the Netherlands being particularly cautious about immediate membership. For instance, the French President, Emmanuel Macron, has proposed a European Political Community (EPC) as an alternative to full EU membership (AFP 2022). It is too early to determine whether Ukraine, Republic of Moldova, and Georgia will join the EU, but it is clear that political debates among member states will continue to impede these processes. While the integration of strategic elements into EEP has produced tangible short-term results, its long-term effectiveness remains uncertain due to the volatility of EU unity. This observation aligns with broader insights from the book, which suggested that geopolitical actorness requires even stronger unity than classical actorness. Ukraine's candidate status is a clear sign of the EU's strategic positioning, made possible by the temporary unity of its member states. However, the sustainability of this geopolitical actorness in the long term will depend on maintaining this unity, making it an even more critical requirement for the EU's future strategic role.

Regarding consistency, the EU's approach focuses on the security issue in order to avoid a deterioration of the situation especially in the Western Balkans. The Union's decisions are guided by strategic considerations. As argued by Robert Dopchie and Liridon Lika (2024, 175), the EU's normative power in the Western Balkans has faced significant limits and recent EU policies toward the region indicate a strategic shift. The EU's main focus is on crisis management and easing tensions in the Western Balkans. In this sense, the war in Ukraine has shown the importance of regional stability, pushing the EU to dynamically engaging in crisis management and affirming itself as a geopolitical actor (Dopchie and Lika 2024, 176). As a result, the EU's actions toward the Western Balkan countries are characterized by ambiguity and inconsistency, particularly as regards its normative approach. Similar development holds true for other neighborhood countries which observe EU's strategic turn as being inconsistent regarding their own situation. In conclusion, the EU's geopolitical role continues to struggle with longstanding inconsistencies. The book highlights that incorporating strategic elements into EU foreign policy has, paradoxically, exacerbated some of these inconsistencies. As the EU's geopolitical approach fails to fully account for global dynamics, leftover stakeholders increasingly question EU's actions.

Therefore, it can be argued that, for now, the EU's geopolitical actorness is amplifying, rather than resolving, contradictions within its external policies.

EU Geopolitical Actorness as a Tool for Further Consolidation of the EU's Position in the International Stage

This book is structured around three research objectives: (a) the EU's practical efforts to achieve a geostrategic shift, (b) the roles of third parties in advancing the EU's strategic agenda, and (c) the renewal of its foreign policy toolbox. This concluding chapter synthesizes the individual chapters' findings within the framework of these research objectives.

Firstly, the volume challenged the notion that speech acts alone can signify a substantial shift. Instead, it focused on assessing the practical actions undertaken by the EU. Specifically, the first part of the book addressed this objective by exploring whether the EU has the necessary capabilities to transition from a normative to a strategic and geopolitical focus. The contributors critically examined this shift, questioning its feasibility from both analytical and conceptual as well as empirical perspectives.

In her chapter, Maria Raquel Freire argued that the war in Ukraine, as other geopolitical upheavals, acts as catalyst, providing a unique window of opportunity for the EU to rejuvenate its foreign engagements. Accordingly, this chapter added to the existing literature on actorness by examining critical vulnerabilities while closely analyzing the EU's transformative potential amid these challenges. It brought to light the intricate dynamics of a changing global landscape and the evolving roles of various actors in shaping the international order. The war in Ukraine has shattered the assumptions of numerous economic and political actors in Europe regarding the long-term stability of peace on the continent and the relationship between the EU, its member states, and Russia. Beyond disrupting economic and political ties between the EU and Russia, the conflict has prompted broader questions about energy security, supply chains, defense policy, and alliances.

Vincent Bricart further illustrated how the shifting world order and the geopolitical positioning of both allies and rivals of the EU play a crucial role in reshaping how the EU perceives and defines itself. This dynamic process ultimately leads to the renewal of the EU's foreign policy. The evolving landscape of alliances and rivalries influences the EU's self-perception, prompting a re-evaluation of its role and priorities in the realm of international affairs. In his chapter, Bricart offered an insightful overview of how the EU positions itself within the dynamic landscape of international relations. He emphasized the crucial influence of discourses, narratives, and interactions with major global powers such as the United States, China, and Russia, in shaping the EU's identity and delineating its role as a key international actor. Bricart argued that the EU's identity is a socially constructed concept intricately tied to the discourses present in its strategic documents and the narratives surrounding its strategic partnerships. Far from being static, the representation of the EU undergoes a gradual evolution, responsive to changes in the international arena, especially those involving major powers. This dynamic process reflects the adaptability of the EU in navigating and defining its position in the ever-changing global landscape.

Adrian Szumowski, considering the significant challenges posed by illiberal forces to EU decision-making, stated that the fate of the European actor and its influence is presently in a precarious state. In order to provide a comprehensive outlook on the potential trajectory of EU actorness, he has outlined four scenarios: the hyperpower EU (success), the normative power EU 2.0 (partial success), the international organization EU (partial failure), and the European confederation (failure). Accordingly, the chapter argued that the EU hyperpower and confederation alternatives are currently low or improbable in the existing state of affairs. However, it affirmed the notion that the ongoing shifts in the world order may indeed create an opportunity for the renewal not only of EU foreign policy but also of the broader European project.

The first research objective sought to provide valuable insights into the EU's willingness and efforts to ensure this strategic shift. While the trajectory of this shift remains unclear, there is little doubt that Brussels is making a concerted attempt to achieve it. Conceptually, geopolitical actorness can be viewed as a product of multiplexity, where external pressures prompt the EU to take action in the strategic sphere. As member states face these challenges, they often turn to supranational management, creating an opportunity for the EU to assume a greater role in strategic matters, thus enhancing its geopolitical actorness.

The second research objective aimed to reflect on the international reception of EU's attempt to integrate greater strategic capabilities.

The book illustrates that the global geopolitical and geoeconomic shift significantly impacts EU foreign policy in the Western Balkans, Eastern neighborhood, Middle East, and the Indo-Pacific. These processes are structured around four interconnected mechanisms. First, the emergence of alternative models of governance challenges the EU's promotion of democratic rule of law-based governance. This results in a backlash against fundamental values advocated by the EU. Second, the security and stability challenges caused by Russia's war against Ukraine and its repercussions in the studied regions undermine security and stability in these regions, calling for a stronger role for the EU as a provider of security and resilience. Third, the weaponization of transboundary issues, such as trade, energy, and migration, by illiberal powers acts as a tool against the EU, potential and candidate countries, and neighbors. This reveals weaknesses in the EU's foreign affairs toolbox, requiring creative solutions to ensure the resilience of potential and candidate countries, and neighbors. Fourth, geopolitical competition and fundamental values come into play as illiberal powers actively seek projection of influence in studied regions. The EU, in response, aims for a stronger geopolitical role in these parts of the world. This poses a challenge for the EU's foreign policy to maintain consistency between achieving geopolitical objectives and adhering to fundamental values.

Regarding the Western Balkans, in their chapter, Pëllumb Kelmendi and Liridon Lika showed that Albania and Kosovo are entirely pro-Western states and share common interests and values with Western countries, the North Atlantic Treaty Organization (NATO), and the EU. EU membership is the top priority for the governments of Albania and Kosovo, with strong pro-EU support from the citizens of both states. Further, this chapter has also shown that there is evident Euroscepticism among a significant part of Orthodox Slavic citizens in the Western Balkans, which undermines the effectiveness of EU actorness. These negative public attitudes are also encouraged by EU's rival power, Russia. Therefore, in the context of the Russian invasion of Ukraine since 2022, and the tense geopolitical situation, as well as the influence strategies of Russia and China in the Western Balkans, the EU is trying to be more present in the region and has recently mentioned on several occasions 2030 as a possible date for enlargement. Therefore, the international context has influenced the EU strategy toward the Western Balkans.

Moreover, the increased involvement of new powers, such as Russia, significantly impacts the EU regional actorness within the ENP. This impact is particularly evident in the Eastern dimension of the ENP, which vividly reveals the fluid nature of the EU's territory and geographical imagination. Contrary to fixed Eastern limits, as evidenced by waves of enlargement in the 2000s, these borders are subject to conflicting symbolic interpretations and a complex set of regulatory regimes. The applications for EU membership by Ukraine, the Republic of Moldova, and Georgia, following the Russian invasion of Ukraine in late February 2022, highlight the unstable political dynamics these countries have experienced in the post-Soviet era, marked by territorial conflicts with Russia (Transnistria in the Republic of Moldova, South Ossetia and Abkhazia in Georgia, and occupied territories in Ukraine). While external observers in 2014 viewed the turmoil in the Eastern Partnership (EaP) as a potential step toward EU membership, recent developments indicate a stronger inclination of Ukraine, the Republic of Moldova, and Georgia to embrace the EU's integration process. However, according to Elisabeth Johansson-Nogués, through the prism of actorness, it is still difficult to confirm that the war in Ukraine has constituted a "watershed moment" for the EU's foreign and security policy.

Raluca Moldovan's chapter highlighted that despite being acknowledged as a legitimate actor in global politics, the EU has struggled to exert significant influence in the Middle East. Moldovan argued that the carrot-and-stick approach frequently employed by the EU has not resulted in a substantial change in the behavior of countries such as Turkey, Iran, and Saudi Arabia, in line with Brussels' expectations. According to Moldovan, the EU's global credibility as an actor could be enhanced by its continued efforts, especially in the aftermath of the 2022 war in Ukraine. This involves the coherent utilization of international forums to impede further erosion of norms crucial to the international order, such as the inviolability of international borders and the non-use of force. Additionally, Moldovan suggested that the EU's global credibility would benefit from consistent and timely actions in situations where protection is sought.

In a similar vein, Dealan Riga has drawn the attention to the requirements of a consistent foreign policy in faraway regions such as the Indo-Pacific. Embedded in complex power dynamics, the region's specificity in terms of economic integration and security needs is challenging traditional EU's strategic functioning. Indeed, existing regional agreements, including great powers such as the United States and China, undermine EU capabilities to use classical economic assertiveness to promote its norms. Yet, this chapter underscored that the EU has a challenging time in adapting this reality. It has shown EU's difficulties in addressing regional needs in terms of economic inclusiveness by launching bilateral framework to cover its poor multilateral efforts. Furthermore, the trilateral security partnership for the Indo-Pacific region between Australia, the United Kingdom, and the United States (AUKUS) demonstrates its poor record in being perceived as a security provider for the region. While the EU's strategic efforts toward the region are overwhelming, its success remained hardly dependent on its alignment with third partners and local compliance to promote its values.

The second research objective emphasized the way shifting world order has cast doubts on EU actorness both regionally and globally. In response to these challenges, the EU should explore new strategies to bolster its actorness in every region under examination. This involves creating the necessary conditions for a peaceful and prosperous world, thereby contributing to the maintenance of global rules and norms that underpin the multilateral international system. To achieve this, the EU should identify both the barriers and opportunities for a more robust, democratic, and effective global governance, reflecting a commitment to promoting stability and adherence to shared principles worldwide. Yet, all the case studies point in the same direction: Whether in the Western Balkans, the Eastern neighborhood, the Middle East, or the Indo-Pacific, the EU's foreign policy struggles to be seen as effective. As highlighted in this book, the Union often lacks critical foreign policy tools, particularly in the realm of security, to effectively achieve its objectives. Otherwise, while the first research objective emphasized the EU's aspirations and potential to attain geopolitical actorness, the second underscored the many obstacles standing in its way. Consequently, the third research objective, which examined the changes in the EU's foreign policy toolbox, is crucial. It reflected the EU's efforts to navigate and respond to the complex challenges posed by the evolving global landscape.

In her chapter examining the use of restrictive measures as a foreign policy tool on Belarus since 2020, Nadège Boels argued that the EU is moving away from the concept of normative power. Instead, it is establishing sanctions legitimized by security or economic interests rather than solely aiming to promote norms. Over time, the EU has framed and reframed its relations with states in the post-Soviet space to adapt to a new reality marked by increased connectivity, economic exchange, and potential challenges. While opportunities have emerged for the EU's bordering processes, both soft and hard, they have also reacted to Russia's actions, which have consistently alternated between attracting and resisting closer affiliation with former Soviet countries (Toal 2017; Graney 2019). Simultaneously, since their independence, these countries have developed their own identities and aspirations, which have, at times, either accommodated, clashed with, or co-shaped the EU's bordering processes (Laruelle 2016).

In his chapter, Robert Dopchie highlighted that while the EU remains committed to promoting its core values, geopolitical considerations often force the Union to prioritize geopolitical interests over its norms. Despite significant financial support allocated under the Instrument for Pre-Accession Assistance (IPA), and the use of the carrot-and-stick method, few tangible improvements have been noted in the EU's ability to effectively export its values to Bosnia and Herzegovina. Dopchie also reflected on the persistence of past inconsistencies in the EU's foreign policy, suggesting that these challenges continue to hinder its normative influence, even as strategic agendas take precedence. The chapter by Kelmendi and Lika demonstrated that support for EU membership varies significantly across states in the Western Balkans and within countries among different ethnic groups, such as in the federal state of Bosnia and Herzegovina. On the one hand, according to the findings, the level of public support for EU membership is the lowest in Serbia, a traditional ally of Russia and China. On the other hand, countries like Bosnia and Herzegovina, Montenegro, and North Macedonia exhibit a more positive perception of the EU. Albania and Kosovo are the most pro-EU countries in the Western Balkans. These variations highlight the nuanced dynamics and differing sentiments toward EU integration within the Western Balkan region.

In certain instances, the EU relationships with various parts of the world have historical foundations, exemplified by its connections with Outermost Regions (ORs) and Overseas Countries and Territories (OCTs). According to Alexandru Balas, ORs and OCTs hold global strategic significance for the EU, enabling it to extend its power and influence far beyond the borders of the EU itself. These regions, countries, and territories are considered integral to the EU's geostrategic agenda, serving to advance its geopolitical interests in the Atlantic, Caribbean, Indian, and Pacific areas. Balas suggested that due to these regions, countries, and territories, the EU can actively engage in the geopolitical rivalries of major powers in the Pacific and Arctic areas, as well as in the Indian Ocean.

As Valentin Naumescu and Oana Poiană emphasized in their chapter, other regions, such as the Black Sea area, have emerged as new centers of gravity in the geopolitical strategies of both NATO and the EU. Furthermore, in her chapter, Freire stressed that the EU's narrative underscores the importance of blending its role as a normative actor with a more strategic and geopolitical approach. This involves integrating principled pragmatism and resilience to offer a renewed framework for conceptualizing security. The recognition of these evolving regional dynamics and the need for a comprehensive approach reflect a shift in the geopolitical considerations and strategies of both NATO and the EU. Concepts such as strategic autonomy still elude the current conceptual toolboxes. The case studies have examined how the EU geopolitical actorness is crafted to address complex global challenges. Arlind Puka, in his chapter, highlighted the pressing need for a single market for defense equipment, particularly since the onset of the war in Ukraine.

The third research objective revealed the EU's efforts to articulate its existing instruments in a more strategic manner. Consequently, the study of the renewal of the EU's foreign policy toolbox provides a fresh perspective on its attempts to ensure geopolitical actorness. However, all the chapters also highlighted weaknesses—both new and inherited from previous limitations in its actions. While the EU's toolbox is undergoing a strategic transformation, its effectiveness remains to be seen. Ultimately, the three research objectives confirmed that the EU geopolitical Commission is more than just a speech act; they also underscored the challenges the EU faces in managing this shift. Many countries of the world remain hesitant to view the EU as a genuine geopolitical actor, and its renewed foreign policy toolbox continues to suffer from significant weaknesses that contribute to its inconsistency. Thus, the EU geopolitical actorness is still in a nurturing stage, with its relative success difficult to predict in the coming years, as numerous hurdles remain to be addressed to achieve a significant level of efficiency. The next section will explore these hurdles by emphasizing the cross-cutting findings of the book.

A Renew Actorness Facing Unforeseen Hurdles: Assessing the EU's Shift

Despite geopolitical actorness being a work in progress, the book clearly indicates that the EU is seeking a new mobilizing narrative that combines normative and strategic aspects. The emergence of concepts such as strategic autonomy is part of this effort. However, as previously mentioned, several limitations could provoke significant backlash against this dynamic. With this in mind, this section draws on the diverse chapters presented in this edited book to provide cross-cutting insights, specifically focusing on: normative resilience, efficiency backlash, path dependency related to polycrisis, security lag, and the political will required to achieve a strategic turn.

The book underscores the observation that the EU's core foreign policy objectives, despite being strategically articulated, essentially remain normative. Whether defending a rule-based system, democracy, or fostering sustainable development, the EU's foreign policy consistently aligns with the promotion of specific norms. However, Freire underlined that the EU's narrative emphasizes the importance of combining its normative role shaping EU actorness and characterized by the promotion of the rule of law, democracy, and human rights, with a more strategic approach. Here, principled pragmatism and resilience aim to offer a renewed framework for understanding security. Consequently, it can be considered that the EU's normative commitment and resilience do not imply a complete neglect of strategic interests. This perspective found support in Boels' input, emphasizing that sanctions, deeply intertwined with EU's values and norms promotion, may now be established due to security threats in the EU's immediate neighborhood. Thus, one may conclude that EU actorness, even when viewed through the lens of strategic and geopolitical interest, should not abandon its normative power; instead, it remains a crucial factor in EU foreign policy, which, through the incorporation of strategic elements, tends to become more multifaceted.

A second significant finding centers on the persistent challenges the EU faces in managing its foreign policy consistently and efficiently. This book identified major EU inefficiencies, beginning with Kelmendi and Lika, who highlighted the EU's inability to influence the local populations, in particular the Orthodox Slavic ones in the Western Balkans.

The results obtained from public opinion indicate growing Euroscepticism in the Western Balkans, with the exception of Albania and Kosovo. These backlashes against Europeanization are deeply problematic given the EU's longstanding engagement in the region. This trend also extends to ongoing procedures, as Dopchie accurately stressed the inefficiency of IPA in fostering democratic governance. While various local political structures, illiberal powers, or sub-regional divides may explain these weaknesses, insufficient efforts have been made to recalibrate IPA tools. Furthermore, Riga emphasized that the situation might be even more problematic when it comes to new tools. The EU's bilateral proposals for economic integration in the Indo-Pacific hardly meet the region's needs in terms of inclusiveness, leaving the EU ill-equipped to counter China's economic stranglehold on the region. Thus, this book highlights the numerous internal and structural reforms the EU needs to address. The EU needs to adopt a more pragmatic approach and ensure more adaptive policy-making when faced with backlash. However, such a shift requires strong political commitment, leading to the next findings in this book.

The third finding is related to the polycrisis the EU has undergone which still impacted its contemporary efforts, which are further fueled by the EU's high dependence on intergovernmental settings, leaving strong foreign policy engagement reliant on the momentum caused by crisis management. Indeed, persisting crises, including the refugee crisis, geopolitical conflicts around the EU, the rise of populism, Brexit, and the coronavirus pandemic, have underscored a certain lack of solidarity among EU member states, revealing an inability to speak with a unified voice. In essence, these crises have increased a lack of coherence and consistency in terms of foreign policy, and even the absence of a common strategic vision. The literature has long stated that the EU lacks a mobilizing narrative—a collective story about its relevance in the twenty-first century. In other words, several authors emphasized that the EU needs a new contract based on the combination of norms and force (Lamy et al. 2017, 169–227). Similarly, these authors have underscored how the intergovernmental setting of the EU may undermine its efforts to promote geopolitical actorness (Lamy et al. 2017).

Szumowski, while attempting to forecast how EU integration might evolve given the momentum of the war in Ukraine, noted that the EU as a hyperpower scenario is dependent on the concert of powers, namely that the merger of 27 member states will create potential for the strategic autonomy of the EU, and will empower it to seek its national interest. Yet, he also emphasized that given the current state of play, this scenario is unlikely. Riga has highlighted the way the coexistence of the EU, France, Germany, and the Netherlands in the Indo-Pacific underscores strong divergences and might be announcing a lack of unity required for a consistent implementation of EU policy toward the region. Accordingly, Puka, when delving into the EU's quest for strategic autonomy, also mentioned EU unity as a key to ensuring a coherent defense policy. In the same vein, OCTs and ORs strategic use by the EU requires an even stronger cooperation through intergovernmental settings. As demonstrated by Balas, the EU should collaborate more closely with the member states in which these ORs and OCTs find themselves. These regions, countries, and territories are on the frontlines of the EU's external borders in increasingly geopolitically important areas of the world. Yet, many authors elaborate on the way the war in Ukraine has fostered unity across the Union. Nevertheless, to ensure a consistent geopolitical actorness, the EU needs to work on the long-term and on a wider range of issues.

The fourth finding revolved around the complexity for the EU to develop a clear security foreign policy that is essential for its geopolitical positioning. In this regard, Naumescu and Poiană emphasized that during the latter half of the twentieth century, the EU's economic and political project evolved in tandem with NATO's security mission. Throughout the book, security concerns have consistently relied on the EU's strategic alignment with the United States, leaving the EU ill-equipped to ensure its own strategic positioning. Furthermore, the EU tends to perceive itself as a peace-focused initiative, as highlighted by Bricart in his chapter to the co-construction of EU's identity in international relations. However, Bricart also emphasized that the United States views the EU as less relevant in security and military terms compared to NATO or its member states. Regional studies in the second part of this book have also demonstrated how challenging it is for the EU to be perceived as a strong strategic actor worldwide, especially in terms of security concerns. Moldovan, for instance, has underscored that in regions where the EU struggles to apply any kind of soft power, its security record is not negligible. The Middle East, in particular, has been reluctant to endorse any form of EU leadership, casting doubt on the feasibility of EU geopolitical actorness in both security and economy. It is important to note, however, that EU strategic positioning is a nascent effort, and the security capabilities of the organization might be evolving over time.

Last but not least, a common finding across every chapter of this edited book was that the EU is actively striving to shift its actorness to incorporate strategic and geopolitical considerations. Its claims, objectives, and international behavior extend beyond the existing academic literature, prompting scholars to scrutinize this shift, and this book serves as evidence of the ongoing process. The EU's regional engagement has been evolving, particularly catalyzed by the war in Ukraine, which has provided momentum for a renewal of EU foreign policy. The utilization of European instruments has been adapted to include strategic considerations, as evidenced by the re-evaluation of OCTs and ORs, sanctions, and defense policy. While the book highlighted various pitfalls and overall weaknesses in the EU foreign policy actions, it also underscored that a change is underway. Although forecasting its exact direction is challenging, this book makes it clear that the EU's commitment to establishing a new geopolitical leadership is partially aligned with the practical requirements dictated by these ongoing shifts. Thus, the book responds affirmatively to its research question, while acknowledging a nuanced approach to this alignment in every chapter.

From Findings to Framework: Integrating Geopolitical Actorness into Academic Debate

As the EU geopolitical actorness undergoes numerous attempts to be designed, it is imperative for scholars to further explore the research agenda on EU geopolitical actorness. Several avenues for future research can be identified.

Firstly, conducting more in-depth research on strategic autonomy and military aspects would significantly enhance the understanding of EU foreign policy. While concepts such as geopoliticization capture one aspect of this narrative, the emphasis on geoeconomics and trade policy often overshadows the implications these processes may have for EU diplomacy. Although actorness has frequently been framed within the context of trade policy, this book argues that EU foreign policy deserves closer scrutiny. Therefore, a research agenda that explores the strategic evolution of the EU in global affairs beyond trade policy, is essential.

Secondly, there is a pressing need for additional studies examining how the context of the war in Ukraine since 2022 has influenced the EU's enlargement strategy toward the Western Balkans and Eastern Europe. While enlargement policy is discussed in this concluding chapter,

Ukraine's candidate status is a relatively new development, and its long-term evolution should be understood in the context of EU strategic foreign policy. This book highlights the risks posed to the EU's consistency, but further research is necessary to better grasp the long-term implications of this activated EEP. Moreover, the focus on Ukraine, the Republic of Moldova, and Georgia tends to overshadow the fact that the ENP also encompasses other regions of the world. Consequently, the EU's strategic engagement with the Maghreb, the Middle East, and other Caucasian states warrants greater scrutiny. As the EU adapts its foreign policy toolbox, it is likely that these regions will also be targeted by new mechanisms and strategies.

Thirdly, in light of the evolving global order and the increasing demand for security, examining how the EU can position itself as a key security provider without jeopardizing its current transatlantic ties is a critical area for exploration. This book encourages academia to reevaluate the potential of the Permanent Structured Cooperation (PESCO) and the Common Security and Defense Policy (CDSP) in enhancing the EU's image as a security provider. While it emphasizes the key role played by NATO in European security policy, the concept of EU geopolitical actorness underscores the need to strengthen other cooperative frameworks within the EU, such as PESCO. However, Brussels has been ambiguous about the future of these policies. Therefore, a research agenda focused on the coexistence of European security mechanisms alongside transatlantic defense structures should be pursued.

Fourthly, a more detailed study of the EU's role within international organizations would significantly enhance the understanding of its external actions. Indeed, the EU's participation in international forums has been framed as a key element of its actorness. However, issues such as lagging the World Trade Organization (WTO) reforms and multilateralism crises have overshadowed these dynamics. Nonetheless, discussions about reforming the WTO remain a crucial part of the EU's international agenda. The same logic applies to the United Nations (UN), whose inability to provide a coordinated response in the wake of the wars in Ukraine and in the Middle East highlights the urgent need for reform. Studies on international organizations should also consider regional organizations as key stakeholders in facilitating significant reforms, even though nation-states continue to play a central role in these discussions.

Ultimately, this book aims to position EU foreign policy at the center of the discussion regarding its geoeconomic turn. The emphasis on trade policy has often overshadowed major initiatives undertaken by the EU, such as the Global Gateway, which should be understood within the context of the EU's quest for geopolitical actorness. However, this book cannot cover global dynamics comprehensively. It invites scholars to reflect on EU geopolitical actorness in Africa, especially in light of the recently proposed Africa–Europe investment package, and in Latin America, where the EU is renewing its ties with Argentina over raw materials, beyond the EU–Mercosur trade agreement. Additionally, while this book concentrates on the Ukraine war as a key geopolitical turmoil, the current conflicts in the Middle East warrant further scrutiny. The EU's hesitant moves in this region may suggest that its geopolitical actorness faces additional weaknesses that are not addressed in this volume. In the end, this book seeks to foster a broader reflection on the EU as a global actor. While it cannot cover every topic area, it may encourage scholars to consider that the EU's shift from a normative to a strategic and geopolitical focus extends beyond trade policy.

References

AFP. 2022. What Does French President Macron's Proposed 'European Political Community' Entail? *France 24*, June 26, available at: https://www.france24.com/en/europe/20220623-what-does-french-president-macron-s-proposed-european-political-community-entail (accessed 20 November 2023).

Council of the EU. 2024. Second Meeting of the Accession Conference with Albania at Ministerial Level, *Press release*, 15 October 2024, available at: https://www.consilium.europa.eu/en/press/press-releases/2024/10/15/second-meeting-of-the-accession-conference-with-albania-at-ministerial-level/ (accessed 16 October 2024).

Directorate-General for Neighbourhood and Enlargement Negotiations (DG NEAR). 2023. Commission Adopts 2023 Enlargement Package, Recommends to Open Negotiations with Ukraine and Moldova, to Grant Candidate Status to Georgia and to Open Accession Negotiations with BiH, Once the Necessary Degree of Compliance Is Achieved. Brussels, available at: https://neighbourhood-enlargement.ec.europa.eu/news/commission-adopts-2023-enlargement-package-recommends-open-negotiations-ukraine-and-moldova-grant-2023-11-08_en (accessed 20 November 2023).

Dopchie, R., and L. Lika. 2024. The EU Enlargement Strategy in the Western Balkans: Assessing the Implications Amidst the War in Ukraine. *European Foreign Affairs Review* 29 (2): 159–176.

European Commission. 2023. Communication from the Commission to the European Parliament, the Council, the European Economic and Social Committee and the Committee of the Regions, Brussels, 2023 Communication on EU Enlargement Policy, COM(2023) 690 final, available at: https://neighbourhood-enlargement.ec.europa.eu/system/files/2023-11/COM_2023_690%20Communication%20on%20EU%20Enlargement%20Policy_and_Annex.pdf (accessed 20 November 2023).

European Council. 2024. European Council meeting (21 and 22 March 2024)—Conclusions, Brussels, 22 March 2024, EUCO 7/24, available at: https://www.consilium.europa.eu/media/70880/euco-conclusions-2122032024.pdf (accessed 16 October 2024).

Freire, M.R., et al. eds. 2022. *EU Global Actorness in a World of Contested Leadership. Policies, Instruments and Perceptions*. Cham: Palgrave Macmillan.

Graney, K. 2019. *Russia, the Former Soviet Republics, and Europe Since 1989: Transformation and Tragedy*. New York: Oxford University Press.

Lamy, P., N. Gnessoto, and with J-M. Baer. 2017. *Où va le monde? Le marché ou la force?* Paris: Odile Jacob.

Laruelle, M. 2016. *The European Union in a Reconnecting Eurasia: Foreign Economic and Security Interests*, CSIS Report, 1–28. Lahman: Rowman & Littlefield.

Lika, L. 2019. The European Regional Order in the Western Balkans Facing the Disrupting Role of Middle and Great Emerging Powers, *Leuven Centre for Global Governance Studies, EUCROSS Working paper*, 1–23.

Lika, L. 2021. Coordinator and Guest Editor, Special Issue—Western Balkans, European Union and Emerging Powers, *Journal of Cross-Regional Dialogues*, n° 2.

Lika, L., and B. Reka. 2021. The European Union's Relations with the Republic of Kosovo. In *Forging Kosovo: Between Dependence, Independence, and Interdependence*, A. Hajrullahu, and A. Vukpalaj, 229–250. Bern et al.: Peter Lang.

Meka, E., and S. Bianchini, eds. 2020. *The Challenges of Democratization and Reconciliation in the Post-Yugoslav Space*. Baden-Baden: Nomos.

Santander, S., and A. Vlassis. 2020. EU in Global Affairs: Constrained Ambition in an Unpredictable World? *European Foreign Affairs Review* 25 (1): 5–22.

Toal, G. 2017. *Near Abroad: Putin, the West, and the Contest over Ukraine and the Caucasus*. New York: Oxford University Press.

Index

A

B

C

L. Lika and D. Riga (eds.), *EU Geopolitical Actorness in a Changing World*, https://doi.org/10.1007/978-3-031-81160-9

G

H

I

J

L

M

GPSR Compliance
The European Union's (EU) General Product Safety Regulation (GPSR) is a set of rules that requires consumer products to be safe and our obligations to ensure this.

If you have any concerns about our products, you can contact us on

ProductSafety@springernature.com

In case Publisher is established outside the EU, the EU authorized representative is:

Springer Nature Customer Service Center GmbH
Europaplatz 3
69115 Heidelberg, Germany

www.ingramcontent.com/pod-product-compliance
Lightning Source LLC
Chambersburg PA
CBHW071649150925
32623CB00005B/381
9783031811593